The Berg Companion

The Berg Companion
edited by
Douglas Jarman

NORTHEASTERN UNIVERSITY PRESS
BOSTON

First published in Great Britain in 1989 by Macmillan Press Ltd.
First published in the United States of America in 1990 by Northeastern University Press, Boston.

Library of Congress Cataloging-in-Publication Data

The Berg Companion / edited by Douglas Jarman.
    p.   cm.
  includes index.
  ISBN 1-55553-068-0 (alk. paper)
  1. Berg, Alban, 1885–1935—Criticism and interpretation.
I. Jarman, Douglas
ML410.B47B53 1990   89-8581
780'.92—dc20   CIP
                MN

Printed on neutral paper.
Manufactured in Great Britain.
95 94 93 92 91 90 5 4 3 2 1

Contents

Acknowledgements   vi
Preface   vii

The Man and his Environment
Berg's Vienna   *Martin Esslin*   1
Berg's character remembered   *Joan Allen Smith*   13

The Songs
Berg the composer of songs   *Mark DeVoto*   35
A conservative revolution: the music of
   the Four Songs op. 2   *Stephen W. Kett*   67

The Instrumental Music
Berg's development as an instrumental composer   91
  Bruce Archibald
Musical progression in the 'Präludium' of
   the Three Orchestral Pieces op. 6   *Michael Taylor*   123
'Freundschaft, Liebe, und Welt': the secret
   programme of the Chamber Concerto   *Barbara Dalen*   141
Alban Berg, Wilhelm Fliess, and the secret
   programme of the Violin Concerto   *Douglas Jarman*   181

The Operas
Berg and German opera   *Derrick Puffett*   197
Between instinct and reflection: Berg and the
   Viennese dichotomy   *Christopher Hailey*   221
The sketches for *Lulu*   *Patricia Hall*   235
Some further notes on my realization of
   Act III of *Lulu*   *Friedrich Cerha*   261
The first four notes of *Lulu*   *George Perle*   269

List of compositions   291

Contributors   293

Index   295

Acknowledgements

With the exception of excerpts from Opp. 1 and 2 all quotations from Berg's published works are reproduced by friendly permission of Universal Edition, A.G., Vienna.

Quotations from the Piano Sonata Op. 1 and the Four Songs Op. 2 are reprinted by permission of Robert Lienau, Berlin.

The excerpts from Bartók's Fifth String Quartet are reproduced by permission © Copyright 1936 by Universal Editions; Copyright Renewed. Copyright & Renewal assigned to Boosey & Hawkes, Inc. for USA.

Facsimiles of Berg's sketches are reproduced by kind permission of the Music Department of the Austrian National Library, Vienna. The example from the holograph fair copy of the full score of the Chamber Concerto is from the archive of the Arnold Schoenberg Institute, Los Angeles and is reproduced with the permission of the Institute.

The quotation from George Perle's *Windows of Order* is reprinted by permission of Galaxy Music Corporation, Boston, MA, USA.

Preface

The last few years have seen an extraordinary explosion of interest in Alban Berg. Both Berg's life and his music have become the focus of public and scholarly attention in a way that would have been unimaginable 20 or 30 years ago.

That this is so is due to a combination of factors. On one level it is a manifestation of a growing interest in the society and culture of which Berg himself formed a part, the society described by Martin Esslin in the opening essay of the present book. The recent publication of a number of books on the subject, as well as the mounting in the last few years of various important exhibitions and concert series centred on the period (the London Barbican's 1985 'Mahler and the Twentieth Century' series, the Edinburgh Festival's 1983 'Vienna 1900', and above all the great Austrian 'Vienna 1900—Traum und Wirklichkeit' exhibition which has now been seen in Paris and New York as well as in Vienna itself) all bear witness to the fascination which *fin-de-siècle* Vienna continues to exert on our imaginations. Such events have made us increasingly aware of the extent to which our own view of the world has its origins in the extraordinary intellectual ferment of Vienna at the turn, and in the first decades, of the 20th century.

One notable musical feature of this growing interest has been the 'rediscovery' of the music of such major figures as Franz Schreker and Alexander von Zemlinsky, as well as that of a host of other, lesser, and until recently almost forgotten, composers of the period—a salutary reminder that we have until now, perhaps, been too eager to consider the Second Viennese School as an isolated phenomenon, divorced from the larger historical context that the music of these composers provides. Certainly Berg's own declarations of loyalty to his teacher have led us to concentrate on his role as a member of the Schoenberg circle and to ignore his debt to these other contemporaries and immediate forbears. It is an omission that both Derrick Puffett and Christopher Hailey attempt to rectify in their respective essays.

We can also, I think, see the present interest in Berg as one further stage in a process of reassessment that has been taking place over the last 25 years. Until recently it was generally agreed that Berg was the most conservative and backward-looking of the three composers of the Second Viennese School. His music, it was said, represented an attempt to reconcile the demands of the twelve-note system with those of tonality, his handling of the twelve-note method and his compositional techniques in general were said to be 'freer' and 'less systematic' than those of Schoenberg and Webern. Such was the established and conventional view of Berg and it was a view that was accepted by all writers on the composer and upon which most critical assessments were based.

I have remarked elsewhere on how

To those critics writing during or immediately after Berg's own lifetime his relation to traditional music and his supposedly free handling of the twelve-note method were things to be admired and applauded; such things could be represented as a triumph of 'innate musicality' over what many of these writers regarded as a dry, cerebral and inherently unmusical system. In the years after the second world war, on the other hand, the same aspects of Berg's music that these earlier writers had praised became something to be condemned. Berg's supposed freedom and his attachment to tradition had no place in the austere world of total serialism. To Boulez and the young European composers of the early 1950s such things were evidence of a kind of moral backsliding, if not of actual degeneracy; they indicated an unacceptable willingness to compromise and a refusal to recognize the far-reaching implications of the twelve-note system. 'The dodecaphonic language,' declared Boulez in his famous 1948 article on Berg, 'has more imperious necessities than domesticating a Bach chorale.'[1] Both the pre- and post-war commentators accepted the same conventional view of Berg and what both groups put forward as reasoned technical arguments were, in fact, little more than their responses to that traditional view. Since these responses had less to do with the music than with the vagaries of scholarly and compositional fashion Berg's critical standing fluctuated wildly during these years.[2]

It is, however, in the nature of Berg's music that it does not advertise its novelties. Embedded in a language not far removed from that of the late Romantic composers, the intricate technical secrets of Berg's compositions only reveal themselves after long and patient study. The recent publication of a number of detailed analytical books and articles has now made us aware of the forward-looking nature of Berg's infinitely ingenious and sophisticated compositional techniques. The 'free' and 'unsystematic' Berg of the earlier textbooks—the 'conservative' and 'backward-looking' composer with a nostalgic hankering for a vanished tonal past—has been replaced by a Berg who not only seems strikingly relevant to present-day concerns, but whom we can claim, as George Perle does in his book on *Wozzeck*, to have been 'the most forward-looking composer of our century'.[3]

Among the books and articles that have most influenced our present understanding of Berg's music, pride of place must go to those of George Perle, who, with the recent publication of his two-volume study of the operas, has crowned an association with Berg's music that has lasted some 30 years. That our evaluation of Berg's stature has changed radically over the last 20 years and that Berg's music is now the focus of so much analytical attention is largely due to Perle's work. The analytical essays in this book, which include one by Professor Perle himself, give some indication of the vitality, the diversity, and the sophistication of the work being done in this area at present.

But recent developments in Berg studies have their origins, above all else, in the sudden availability of a wealth of previously unknown material following the death of the composer's widow in 1976. During her lifetime Helene Berg was a jealous guardian of her husband's estate, refusing to allow publication of the large number of early songs which Berg composed before and during his period of study with Schoenberg, delaying the publication of the scores of those works that had not been published at the time of the composer's death (so that even as late as the mid-1960s there were no published scores of such major works as the Altenberg Songs and *Der Wein*) and refusing access to many of the manuscripts in her possession. It will be many years, as the material is studied and evaluated, before the full significance of these newly available sources becomes apparent. But three important events—of greater importance, perhaps, than anything that has happened in the field of Berg scholarship and performance in the last 40 years—have already occurred as a result of the lifting of the restrictions that persisted during Helene Berg's lifetime. They are events that have already had, and will continue to have, far-reaching effects on Berg studies.

The first of these events was the world première of the complete three-act *Lulu* in 1979. When Berg died in December 1935 he left a short score of *Lulu* that was complete in almost every respect but of which only the first two acts and a small part of Act III were completed in full score. Berg had already orchestrated two sections of the final act—the Variations which form the orchestral interlude between scenes 1 and 2 and the final Adagio of Act III, scene 2—for inclusion in the *Lulu* Suite before he began to score the main body of the opera but of the rest of Act III there stood in full score only 286 bars of the first scene.

During her lifetime Helene Berg had refused to allow anyone to complete the orchestration of the opera and *Lulu* had, of necessity, been performed as a two-act torso, with opera companies being forced to devise a makeshift version of the missing Act III with whatever they could cobble together from the final movements of the *Lulu* Suite and the text of the original Wedekind play. On 24 February 1979, almost three years after the death of Helene Berg and 44 years after the death of the composer, the world première of the three-act *Lulu*, with the third act realized by Friedrich Cerha, took place at the Paris Opéra. The event generated an unprecedented amount of interest. Performances were broadcast and televized, radio programmes and editions of specialist music journals were devoted to discussions of the opera, and the arts pages (and even, in some cases, the news pages) of daily newspapers covered the background history of the work.

It would be naïve to assume that the enormous amount of publicity that preceded the première sprang entirely from an interest in Berg's music; both the risqué subject and the tortuous posthumous history of the opera had all the elements of a good press story. Nonetheless, among those quality papers that were at least as interested in the music as they were in the sensational background of the piece, the first night was universally acknowledged as an event of historic significance: 'a red-letter day in the annals of opera' according to the London *Observer*; 'the musical event of the decade, if not of the post-war years' according to the *Guardian*. Productions throughout Europe and America followed and were received as warmly, and preceded by almost as much publicity, as the Paris première.

At the centre of these events was Friedrich Cerha, whose brilliant realization of Act III had made the première possible, and who in 1979 published his *Arbeitsbericht zur Herstellung des 3. Akts der Oper 'Lulu'*, in which he provided a detailed critical commentary on the state of the material and the nature of his work on the opera. The vocal score of Act III was published in 1977, followed by the full score in 1986.

During the period between the publication of the vocal and full scores of the work the discovery of new material and the experience of staging the piece had led Cerha to reconsider his solutions to some of the problems presented by Berg's *Particell*. The published orchestral and vocal scores thus differ from one another in a number of small but important respects. The essay published here, in which Friedrich Cerha discusses the nature of, and the reasons for, these second thoughts, forms an important—and to the performer or Berg scholar an essential—supplement to the earlier *Arbeitsbericht*. To the non-specialist music lover it provides a unique view into the musicologist's workshop and into the kind of decisions that have to be faced by anyone preparing such an edition.

The second significant event in the last few years has been the publication of two catalogues, prepared by Dr Rosemary Hilmar, of the Berg material in the possession of the Music Department of the Austrian National Library (the ÖNB). Until recently anyone hoping to see any of this material faced a daunting series of obstacles. During Frau Berg's lifetime the collection of manuscripts in her possession was divided into two groups. One of these was deposited in the Music Department of the ÖNB; the other was retained by Frau Berg and was only transferred to the library after her death. During Frau Berg's lifetime the manuscripts deposited in the ÖNB remained the property of Helene Berg, who instructed the library as to which manuscripts a scholar should be allowed to consult and which were to remain unavailable. Since the material remained uncatalogued, one had no way of knowing which manuscripts were deposited in the library. Nor, having obtained permission to see a manuscript, could one be sure what would finally appear. The uncatalogued and unordered manuscripts were contained in a number of cardboard folders, the supposed contents of which were identified only by the title that Helene Berg had seen fit to write on the cover of each. These titles were frequently incorrect. The publication in 1980 and 1985 respectively of Rosemary Hilmar's two catalogues of the ÖNB Berg holdings was, therefore, an event of major importance in the development of Berg studies. Scholars were, at last, able to appreciate the full extent of the collection (the largest and most significant collection of Berg manuscripts anywhere in the world) and were able to have access to this material and have microfilms made of it. The essays by Patricia Hall (on the sketches for *Lulu*) and Brenda Dalen (on the sketches for the Chamber Concerto) are the first fruits of the intense study of these newly available sources that is under way at the moment.

The last of these important events was the discovery by George Perle of a score of the Lyric Suite which Berg himself had annotated. In this score the composer revealed the secrets of the previously unknown programme upon which the piece was based. Perle's subsequent articles about his discovery not only told us for the first time about Berg's relationship with Hanna Fuchs-Robettin (and demonstrated the way in which every aspect of one of Berg's most important compositions was determined by this relationship with a woman whose name did not even appear in any of the books on Berg) but also, and equally importantly, overturned the picture of Berg's life and character that had been carefully fostered by his widow and that had been accepted and endorsed by everyone who had written about the composer.

We had known, even before Professor Perle's discovery, that a number of Berg's works were based on or included references to autobiographical elements; we also knew of the composer's interest in numerology—Berg's own 'Open Letter' on the Chamber Concerto is primarily concerned with such things. Not until the publication of Perle's Lyric Suite articles, however, were we aware of the full extent to which the objective structure of Berg's music—the formal design, the proportions, the metronome markings, and even the choice of pitches—was determined by subjective extra-musical factors; nor did we have concrete evidence of Berg's consistent association of particular numbers and pitches with specific individuals—evidence that was concrete enough for us to be sure that we were not ourselves reading a significance into any supposed extra-musical 'message' we found elsewhere in his music. Such evidence of Berg's thinking has opened up a new area of research which, although by its very nature fraught with dangers, must be investigated if we are to understand Berg's creative psychology. Brenda Dalen's essay on the Chamber Concerto provides new evidence of Berg's programmatic and biographical obsessions. My own essay on Berg's knowledge of the theories of Wilhelm Fliess and the relation that these theories have to the Violin Concerto gives some indication of the further ramifications of Perle's original discovery.

The *Berg Companion* attempts both to give the reader some idea of the range and excitement of the work being done in the field of Berg studies at the moment and to provide information that will be of use to the Berg scholar, the student, and to the non-specialist music lover alike. To this end the book is divided into four sections. The first section, in which Martin Esslin writes about the social, political, and artistic life of *fin-de-siècle* Vienna, and in which Joan Smith brings together the reminiscences of those friends and acquaintances of Berg's whom she interviewed, is designed to place the composer in a personal and cultural context. Each of the other three sections deals with a different area of Berg's compositional output: the vocal music (that is, the music for solo voice with either a piano or orchestral accompaniment), the instrumental music, and the operas. Each of these sections consists of an introductory article followed by a number of more detailed studies. In the case of the vocal and the instrumental music the introductory essays, by Mark DeVoto and Bruce Archibald respectively, provide a survey of Berg's output and discuss his development as a composer in those areas. In the case of the operas, where no such survey of

Berg's development is possible (there are, after all, no 'trial runs' for *Wozzeck* in Berg's output), the two introductory essays by Derrick Puffett and Christopher Hailey place *Wozzeck* and *Lulu* in the context of Berg's immediate operatic forerunners and his contemporaries.

With the exception of my own essay, which first appeared in the *Newsletter of the International Alban Berg Society*, and Brenda Dalen's essay, which derives from a paper read on 6 November 1986 to the annual conference of the American Musicological Society in Cleveland, Ohio, all of the essays have been written specially for the present book.

I am grateful to Jannet King of Macmillan for her advice and encouragement during the early stages of preparing this book and to Dr David Roberts for his expert and meticulous work during the final stages. Above all, however, I am deeply grateful to the contributors for their constant help and co-operation.

Douglas Jarman
Hebden Bridge
23 September 1987

Notes

1. Pierre Boulez, *Notes of an Apprenticeship*, trans. Herbert Weinstock, (New York: Alfred A. Knopf, 1968), p. 240.

2. See my article ' "Man hat auch nur Fleisch und Blut": Towards a Berg Biography' in the forthcoming volume of essays on Berg, edited by Robert Morgan and David Gable, to be published by Oxford University Press.

3. George Perle, *The Operas of Alban Berg*, vol 1: *Wozzeck* (Berkeley and Los Angeles: University of California Press, 1980), p. xv.

The Man and his Environment

BERG'S VIENNA

MARTIN ESSLIN

Like so many of his contemporaries among Viennese artists and intellectuals, Berg harboured an intense love–hate for his native city. He detested the philistinism and obtuseness of its public and its authorities, their indifference and hostility towards the most talented and innovative of its citizens, the complacency of their pride in a great tradition of composers of genius—Mozart, Beethoven, Schubert—who, in their time, had been equally neglected and victimized. But, at the same time, he could not tear himself away from its beauty, its atmosphere, its unique melancholy charm. Indeed, like so many of the embattled intellectual and artistic leaders of the city, he seemed to need the stimulus of having to fight against the boneheaded tastes and antediluvian opinions of the large majority of its pusillanimous petty bourgeois citizens.

The Vienna into which Berg was born and where he spent the first 30 years of his life was the capital of a great empire and an industrial centre. Yet, more than the other major capitals of Europe at that time, Vienna still retained its character as a city of small artisans and shopkeepers, narrow in their outlook, as sentimental as they were pleasure-loving, fond of their wine, their songs and their *Gemütlichkeit* (cosiness). It was a city where the shopkeepers all knew their customers and gossiped with them. Although Berg's father ran a thriving export business, his mother still kept a shop, a *Devotionalienhandlung*, where devotional articles such as religious pictures, prayer-books, rosaries, and crucifixes were sold. (According to a family tradition, recalled by Berg's nephew, Anton Bruckner came into this shop one day to have a crucifix repaired. It was a very special object: mounted on an articulated handle at Bruckner's bedside, so that he could draw it towards him 'to kiss the Lord'. When the faulty joint had been restored, Bruckner insisted that the crucifix had been shortened in the process and it took a long time to persuade him that it remained its original size.)

Although Vienna had some two million inhabitants at this period, the city had retained the compactness of a much smaller town, simply because the old

1

central part, around which the outlying districts were arranged in concentric rings, remained, in the mind of the Viennese, the actual 'city' where everything that mattered could be found. Lying in the true centre of the conurbation, this inner city (*die Innere Stadt*) was equally quickly and easily accessible from all the suburbs. In 20 minutes, at most half an hour, one could walk from the districts beyond the inner ring road (the famous *Ringstrasse*) and even from beyond the outer ringroad (the *Gürtel*) into the central area where the principal coffee houses were located.

These coffee houses played an important part in the city's intellectual life and shaped its character. They were spacious and comfortable. They provided local and international newspapers and magazines (mounted on characteristic wooden frames) to read; notepaper, pen and ink, even reference books if one wanted to write; chess sets, playing cards, and billiard tables. They served dozens of different varieties of coffee, always accompanied, on a silver platter, by a glass of water which was renewed at half-hourly intervals, even if the guest had not placed another order, to show that he was still welcome. One could spend a whole afternoon and evening in these pleasant surroundings at the cost of a single cup of coffee. The waiters were polite and helpful, they took and transmitted messages, and even lent the customers money when necessary. Each coffee house developed its clientele of *Stammgäste*, habitués, for whom it became a second home, like a London club. Groups and cliques of various kinds formed around these coffee houses, so that one knew where literati of a certain type, artists of a specific school, musicians of a given tendency were to be found. There were actors', doctors', architects', and prostitutes' coffee houses.

These specialized worlds, however, overlapped. Members of one circle frequently dropped in on other cliques in their haunts, and so, among the intellectual élite, everybody to some degree knew everybody else. Journalists, poets, composers, painters, philosophers, scientists, and politicians met and debated issues or engaged in heated and acrimonious quarrels, which were often continued in the pages of the newspapers.

High among the topics of debate in Vienna was the theatre and music. Changes in the management of the leading theatres, quarrels among the stars of the opera were headline news. Vienna was proud of being a *Theaterstadt* (theatre city) and one of the great centres of the Western musical tradition, with a rich array of concert halls and a vast, if, on the whole, conservative repertoire of concerts.

The young music lovers of the city tended to meet in the cheaper sections of the *Hofoper* (Imperial Court Opera). To get into the 'fourth gallery' (the gods) or the standing room behind the stalls (*Stehparterre*), one had to queue, often for hours. In the excited discussions that developed among the waiting enthusiasts, who tended to be divided between traditionalists and avant-gardists (*Neutöner* and even, still, *Wagnerianer*), friendships and love-affairs often developed. Berg first saw his future wife, Helene, in the fourth gallery of the opera.

From 1897 to 1907 Gustav Mahler, himself a highly controversial figure, presided over the opera house. But here too the intimate small-town atmosphere of the city made it possible for Berg, on one occasion in 1909, to approach Mahler in a restaurant. Mahler asked Berg whether he wanted to become a conductor. When Berg said he did not, Mahler nodded: 'You are right, if you want to compose you mustn't go into the theatre.'

The Austrian educational system, perhaps because it was still very archaic, reflecting the ideals of medieval and Renaissance classical scholarship, produced an educated élite (*die Gebildeten*) with a fairly homogeneous array of interests: whether you were an engineer, medical man, scientist, or merchant, you went to the theatre and concerts, read the latest poetry, and kept abreast of trends in philosophy and science. Music-making in the home was part of this culture. As one wit once put it: nowhere else in the world are the local dentists such good string quartet players as in Vienna.

The dividing line between the *Gebildeten* and the bulk of the population was the passing of the final examination of the *Gymnasium* (grammar school) to obtain the *Matura* (maturity certificate). This not only entitled its holder to continue his studies at the university, but also (in the case of young men) exempted them from the three-year military service. They entered the army as officer cadets and only had to serve one year as *Einjährig-Freiwillige* (one-year volunteers). The acquisition of the *Matura* thus constituted the entrance into the upper social class. To fail here was a social disaster. Hence strenuous efforts had to be made to pass the examination. Berg himself had to repeat two years at school in order to qualify.

Much has been written about the intellectual ferment of *fin-de-siècle* Vienna which produced so many of the important revolutionary ideas of the 20th century: psychoanalysis, analytical philosophy, functional architecture, and design; *art nouveau* and expressionist painting; and twelve-note music. Why should the most backward of the European states have produced so many of the most advanced ideas of our time? The explanation, it seems to me, may well be that it was in this, the most ramshackle specimen of 19th-century bourgeois social structures, that the break-up of that civilisation first showed itself and produced not only the first flowering of a new artistic and intellectual universe, but also its most disastrous disintegrative force. One must not forget that Adolf Hitler and modern anti-semitism also originated in Vienna at the very same time.

It is no coincidence that it was Vienna that produced the leading prophet of the post-bourgeois age, Karl Kraus (1874–1936), who coined the significant phrase that the Austro-Hungarian monarchy at that time was an 'experimental laboratory for the end of the world' and entitled his vast satirical–documentary–poetic drama about the First World War *Die letzten Tage der Menschheit* (The Last Days of Mankind).

Kraus, an habitué of the famous Café Central, was the most controversial, the most hated, but also the most fanatically adored figure of his time. He was worshipped by a dedicated crowd of followers, the *Krausianer*, who eagerly followed his every move. The young Alban Berg was one of them.

A small, sharp-featured man with a slight hunchback, Kraus had, since 1899, been the editor and almost sole author of the periodical *Die Fackel* (The Torch) in which he pursued a relentless crusade against what he considered the deadly plague of his time—the popular press. He wielded his pen with lethal satirical wit in cascades of linguistic virtuosity. He was thus, paradoxically, while engaged in a fanatical war against journalism, the greatest journalist of his time.

Kraus prophetically diagnosed the nature of the deadliest cultural menace threatening civilisation in the 20th century: the rise of the mass media. He was convinced that, language being the basis of all thought, degeneracy of language would lead to the degeneracy of mankind's ability to think clearly and logically. The introduction of universal free education during the 19th century had, he argued, produced a vast mass of semi-literate individuals, who, while being able to read and write, lacked the skills of speaking and thinking logically. The popular press was not only read but also largely written by these semi-literates. Moreover, because it derived its income from advertising, it was deeply corrupt.

Kraus was convinced that the deterioration of the power to think would have disastrous political consequences: argument would be replaced by emotional slogans exploiting the most primitive human instincts: nationalism, racism, hatred, and violence. The First World War with its brutal hate-propaganda confirmed Kraus's worst fears. He was, mercifully, spared the full horrors of Hitlerism and the Second World War that he had so prophetically predicted.

For his own paper, *Die Fackel*, Kraus accepted no advertising. What is more, he did not publish it at regular weekly or monthly intervals. One of the things that was deeply wrong with the press, he felt, was that it had to fill a certain space regardless of whether there was anything important to say. So he only published when he had some burning topics to discuss. Sometimes the little red-bound brochure came out every few days, sometimes it appeared only once or twice over a period of many months. Sometimes it numbered only a few pages, sometimes hundreds.

Kraus, the fanatic of pure language was not only a dazzling stylist and poet, he was also a frustrated actor and director. Such was the personal magnetism of this figure, and such the loyalty of the *Krausianer*, that he could, from time to time, rent a concert hall and give a solo performance—complete readings of plays by Shakespeare or Nestroy (the great Viennese writer of satirical comedies) in which he played all the parts; or he would recite one of his articles from *Die Fackel*, or speak and sing to piano accompaniment his new adaptations of the libretti of the works of one of his favourite composers, Jacques Offenbach.

Occasionally Kraus would even stage complete performances of works he felt needed support. One of his favourite playwrights was Frank Wedekind (1864–1918) whose play *Die Büchse der Pandora* (Pandora's Box)—the second part of his epic about Lulu, the embodiment of pure female sexuality—had been banned as obscene by the authorities. Kraus organized two 'private' performances of this play in May and June 1905, with Wedekind in the lead. Kraus himself played a small part. (Lulu was played by Tilly Newes, whom Wedekind subsequently married.) Berg, aged 20, attended one of these performances.

Wedekind was also a champion of the works of one of Germany's greatest playwrights, Georg Büchner, who was just being rediscovered after having remained virtually unknown since his death at the age of 23 in 1837. Büchner, a precocious genius, had been a revolutionary against the authorities of his native country, Hessen–Darmstadt. A scientist, he had already reached the position of a lecturer in physiology at the university of Zurich when he died of typhoid fever. As a scientist he was ruthlessly realistic in his writing. Only one of his plays had been published; none was performed in his lifetime. A collected edition of his works did not become available to the general public until towards the end of the century, but even after that it took a long time for the recognition of his genius as a writer of rhythmic prose which, while being strictly realistic, even documentary, read like the most captivating poetry. It was only with the triumph of naturalism in Germany—the breakthrough achieved by writers like Ibsen, Strindberg, and Gerhart Hauptmann—that the true importance and quality of Büchner emerged. Büchner's last unfinished play, *Woyzeck*—at that time still, because of a misreading of his handwriting in the manuscript, called *Wozzeck*—did not get its first performance till almost 80 years after it was written, in 1913 at Munich. This production was briefly brought to Vienna, where Berg saw it in May 1914.

Here too, Kraus's enthusiasm for Wedekind and Wedekind's advocacy of Büchner as his literary and dramatic forerunner and model contributed to shaping Berg's interests and tastes.

Kraus's enthusiasm for Wedekind sprang from his pre-occupation with one of the main topics of debate of the period: the nature of sexuality and the need for a new morality.

Vienna was, perhaps only second to Paris, obsessed with sex. It is no coincidence that Freud's theories about the sexual drive's being the fundamental force in human nature and culture originated there. Arthur Schnitzler (1862–1931), the great Viennese playwright and physician portrayed the sexual mores of the city in plays like *Liebelei* (Dalliance, 1895), *Anatol* (1893) and, above all, *Reigen* (1900), a sequence of ten scenes, at the climax of each of which a black-out covers the sex-act itself. The play thus gives a bitter picture of the feelings 'before' and 'after', and the essential part played by the social position of the partners, whether a soldier and a prostitute, a count and an actress, a poet and a shop-girl, etc. In one of these episodes, the teenage master of a middle-class household seduces (or is seduced by) a servant girl, in the habitual ritual of sexual initiation of young gentlemen. (Berg fathered an illegitimate child on a servant girl at the family's summer home in the country when he was only 17.) For young men it was almost obligatory that they should pick up some shop-girls and make them their mistresses; at the same time, they made it a point of honour to gain the favours of some married middle- or upper-class lady of their acquaintance. (This is the theme of *Liebelei*.) All this took place behind a screen of strict bourgeois morality. Decent middle-class girls had to retain their virginity until marriage, while the men indulged themselves with an array of mistresses and prostitutes. Schnitzler's *Reigen* (made famous in a sugary adaptation as the film *La Ronde*) portrays the sexual merry-go-round of the city.

Wedekind, far more of an aggressive moralist than Schnitzler, the medical man who merely diagnosed and described the state of affairs, played for the German-speaking world in the 1890s and the early years of the new century the part that D. H. Lawrence took upon himself for the English-speaking world 20 or 30 years later: that of the revolutionary advocate of frankness about sex, and a new and more enlightened attitude, particularly to female sexuality.

Kraus enthusiastically joined this fight in the pages of *Die Fackel*. He vehemently exposed the hypocrisy of the press which preached virtue and purity in its editorial columns while coining large sums of money by advertising brothels on its back pages. In long articles Kraus exposed the double standards of a judicial system that persecuted and imprisoned prostitutes while letting their clients go scot-free.

This crusade, however, only formed part of the much larger debate about the nature and role of women in society and the rise of the emancipated 'new woman'. Should women be treated as the intellectual and moral equals of men? Should their capacity to serve as more than mere passive reproductive vessels be recognized, their ability to enjoy sexual pleasure at last acknowledged? Should they be given the same right to take the sexual initiative as men? What, in fact, was the nature of 'Woman'?

Ibsen and Strindberg had initiated this debate. They represented the two opposing poles in the heated discussion which raged with particular intensity in sex-obsessed Vienna.

One of the most spectacular contributions to this debate came from a young Viennese philosopher, much admired by Kraus, Otto Weininger (1880–1903) whose book *Geschlecht und Charakter* (Gender and Character) caused an immense stir and became a bestseller when it appeared in 1901. Weininger argued that all human beings contain elements of the male and female principle, but that while the male principle was creative and positive, the female principle was essentially evil, passive, uncreative, and predatory. (The idea of the bisexual nature of humanity also appeared at about the same time in the work of Freud. Freud's early collaborator Fliess accused Freud of having passed his idea to Weininger. An acrimonious discussion about this appeared in the columns of *Die Fackel*.) Moreover, Weininger, of Jewish origin himself, equated the female principle with Jewishness, and, arguing that the Jews were the most feminine of races, castigated their lack of creativity, cringing servility, and deviousness. (It is said that Weininger was the only Jewish writer whom Hitler admired.) Kraus, also of Jewish background, frequently allowed his self-hatred to inspire anti-semitic diatribes: after all, many of the journalists he so detested were Jews. Weininger became the victim of his own ideas. When he realized that he could not, in his own life, do without dependence on women, he shot himself, at the age of 23.

Wedekind's Lulu plays approach the same problem. In Lulu, Wedekind wanted to display female sexuality in its purest form. But Lulu appears evil merely because in living out her natural instincts of pure sexuality, she comes into conflict with the unnatural and false moral standards of bourgeois society. If the men in Lulu's life had not been conditioned by the false idea that a man's honour derives from his exclusive possession of his female partner, they would not have had to kill themselves when she followed the natural generosity of her sexual drives.

The debate about the essential nature of *Das Weib* (Woman, writ large) was also the central concern of one of Kraus's favourite poets, Peter Altenberg (1859–1919). Altenberg, who became an intimate friend of Alban and Helene Berg, was the vagabond poet, the Verlaine of *fin-de-siècle* Vienna. The son of well-to-do parents, he had tried his hand at medicine, bookselling, and other professions, but had been diagnosed as too sensitive a spirit to follow any of them. So, having dissipated his inheritance, he haunted the cafés and night-spots of Vienna, bizarrely dressed, wearing wooden sandals, and entertaining all and sundry with his witty conversation if they bought him a coffee or a cognac. He wrote short, impressionistic prose poems about his life, sensitive sketches that capture the subtle emotion of a moment: a woman's shoulder glimpsed from a distance, a fragment of overheard conversation. A master of the short form, Altenberg loved writing postcards as well as receiving them. His room in a small hotel in the centre of Vienna was plastered with hundreds of picture post-cards.

Altenberg was enormously susceptible to female charms. He fell in love with multitudes of women of all social classes. He was particularly fond of prostitutes and haunted the all-night cafés where they congregated. To win their friendship he offered to write their love-letters for them.

Prostitutes played an important part in the debate about the nature of Woman. Kraus, Wedekind, and Altenberg regarded them as the least hypocritical of women, truly emancipated in that they freely and openly disposed of their sexuality. And Altenberg, who believed that the equivalent of genius in a man was simply beauty in a woman, included many of these charming but unfortunate creatures in his immense pantheon of goddesses.

Needless to say, Altenberg worshipped his women in a platonic fashion. He had, he said, 'soon enough discovered that copulation was an atavistic, historical, completely inadequate, rude, soulless, and weakling procedure, which could not possibly give ultimate fulfillment to the tender soul of woman, which above all is capable of eternally waiting.' A health fanatic, Altenberg believed that keeping oneself thin and light by eating as little as possible—no meat and fats—and having a good digestion was the pre-condition of developing a poetic soul. Indeed, he maintained, with tongue in cheek and yet with ultimate seriousness, that history was not, as the Marxists maintained, a struggle between the rich and poor, or, as the German nationalists had it, between Aryans and non-Aryans, but in reality an eternal war between the constipated and those with a free-flowing digestion. On the other hand he believed in alcohol as a stimulant of poetic thoughts and sensibilities.

Among the women Altenberg worshipped pride of place went to Helene Berg and Berg's sister Smaragda (who after a brief marriage had openly adopted a lesbian lifestyle and often wore men's clothes—it has been said that she started her life as Lulu and ended it, in 1954, as Geschwitz). He paid similar esteem to Lina Loos, the wife of the great architect Adolf Loos (1870–1933), one of the first to banish non-functional ornament from the facade of buildings, widely hailed as one of the principal originators of modern, functional architecture and also a member of Karl Kraus's intimate circle.

Through Loos, Berg found his way into the circle of the avant-garde painters of Vienna: Gustav Klimt (1862–1918), Egon Schiele (1890–1918), and Richard Gerstl (1883–1908), whose life was so tragically linked with that of Berg's mentor, Arnold Schoenberg. Oskar Kokoschka (1886–1980), the great painter and also the author of some of the earliest expressionist dramas exploring—what else?—the nature of Woman, had been one of Loos's protégés, but drifted away from him when he became romantically linked with Gustav Mahler's wife, Alma (1879–1964), Vienna's most formidable hostess. After the death of her husband she was briefly married to that other great pioneer of functional architecture, Walter Gropius (1883–1969), one of the founders of the Bauhaus, and later became the wife of the poet and novelist, Franz Werfel (1890–1945).

It was in memory of Alma Mahler's daughter by Gropius, Manon Gropius, who had tragically died at the age of 18 that Berg composed his last work, the Violin Concerto. Anna Mahler, Alma's daughter by Gustav Mahler, a talented sculptress, in turn was married for a time to the composer Ernst Krenek (*b*1900), who became a close associate of Berg's. Intellectual and artistic Vienna was a tightly knit society: the literary circles, and groups of painters and sculptors variously overlapped with those of the musical avant-garde. Schoenberg also saw himself as a painter and frequently wrote his own librettos, as, indeed, did Berg.

Alma Mahler, the society hostess, was anathema to Kraus: she presided over a salon that was open to all the major journalists and literati whom Kraus despised and abominated. Yet Berg, never cliquish, maintained good relations with these circles as well. In his earliest days as a composer he had written *Lieder* to texts by Hugo von Hofmannsthal (1874–1929), who became Richard Strauss's principal librettist. This symbolist poet of great subtlety and immense literary culture was closely akin in sensibility to the German poet Stefan George (1868–1933), who was linked to Hofmannsthal in a passionate friendship at the turn of the century, before he was banished home to the Rhineland after the teenage Hofmannsthal's parents had become alarmed about the ardour with which the older man worshipped their precocious son. Berg used George's translations of Baudelaire's poems for his song-cycle *Der Wein*.

After Alma Mahler married Werfel the couple became the Bergs' most intimate friends. Werfel had started his career in his native Prague as a fiery avant-garde expressionist poet and playwright, a brilliant talent. Later, after he had moved to Vienna, he became a Catholic convert and published a series of highly successful popular novels which became international bestsellers and were filmed by Hollywood (*The Song of Bernadette*). The more highbrow critics of the day, on the other hand, felt that Werfel had compromised his talent in the hunt for financial success and wrote him off as a serious creative force. Werfel's sister, Hanna Fuchs-Robettin, in whose house Berg stayed during visits to Prague became Berg's secret love of his latter years.

A novelist whose stature is increasingly being recognised and who was among Berg's best friends was Hermann Broch (1886–1951). He ran a large textile mill, while at the same time studying philosophy and producing experimental novels of great intellectual power and consummate skill, like *Der Tod des Vergil* (The Death of Virgil), a long internal monologue that makes the last days of the Roman epic poet Virgil a metaphor for the death of Western civilisation, which Broch foresaw in the years leading up to Hitler's triumph. This book thus echoes Kraus's vision of the last days of civilisation in a more serene, historicising mood.

A literary personality who linked the circle of Kraus and Altenberg with that of the more fashionable establishment figures was Egon Friedell (1878–1938), Altenberg's friend and protector. He was a phenomenon extremely typical of Viennese cultural life: journalist, cabaret compère, actor, and playwright. Friedell, a massive, towering man of consummate wit, was also a major scholar and author of a brilliant *Cultural History of Modern Times*, a truly breathtaking synthesis of artistic, philosophical and sociological erudition. When, in 1938, Friedell killed himself by jumping out of a window as he heard Nazi stormtroopers entering his apartment to arrest him, he left behind the torso of an equally brilliant cultural history of the ancient world.

Another typical Viennese literary phenomenon of the time was the critic and writer Felix Salten (1896–1945): one of the editors of the literary and artistic sections of the *Neue Freie Presse*, Karl Kraus's favourite target. Salten not only wrote children's books that reached world fame like *Bambi*, the story of a roe-deer immortalized in a Disney animated film, but he was also, almost certainly, the author of one of the most celebrated pornographic books of all time, *Josefine Mutzenbacher*, the life story of a Viennese prostitute as told by herself. This not only constitutes a linguistic tour-de-force in reproducing the authentic idiom of the girl, but also manages the virtuoso feat of making pornographic descriptions hilariously funny. In some ways Josefine M. is a light-hearted version of Lulu in broad Viennese dialect.

The First World War and its conclusion in the collapse of the Habsburg Empire marked a watershed in the life of Vienna and all Viennese. Having been the capital of a large country, a world metropolis, Vienna suddenly found itself reduced to being the *Wasserkopf* (pathologically large head) of a dwarf state. Its two million inhabitants formed a full third of the total population of the post-war remnant of the Habsburg Empire, the little republic of Austria.

Famine, the Spanish influenza, and runaway inflation took their toll. By 1924 a cup of coffee or a bread roll cost thousands of crowns. Most middle-class families who had relied on savings in the bank were suddenly reduced to penury. Only the black-marketeers who had acquired supplies of goods like sugar or timber and who indulged in selling and re-selling these treasures—hence they were called *Schieber* (pushers)—and speculators on the wildly fluctuating stock exchange prospered. Karl Kraus conducted a vicious campaign against some of these and their toadies, the newly jumped-up shady press barons whom they bribed to manipulate public opinion.

Vienna became a city of genteel beggars: the widows of generals and cabinet ministers of the old regime let their large flats to lodgers; in the cafés the needy intellectuals sat for many hours in front of their one cup of coffee and subsequent glasses of water.

The politics of the new republic were accordingly bitter and embattled. Vienna had a socialist—'Red'—city government, the rest of the country a Catholic, clerical—'Black'—majority. Between these two factions there raged an almost continuous civil war, as each had its own private army of uniformed and armed volunteers: the *Schutzbund* (Protection League—Red) and the *Heimwehr* (Home-Guard—Black). The third force, at first in the background, in the 1930s ever more prominent, were the Nazis. These political battles were conducted with immense intensity of hatred and venom. The artists and intellectuals were, willy-nilly, drawn into these fights. The Blacks tended towards old-fashioned conservative literature and music, folksy tunes and sentimental novels about sturdy peasants; the left was 'progressive' and hence tended to side with 'modern' tendencies in architecture, painting, music, and literature. The socialist city council of Vienna, for example, embarked on a vigorous municipal housing programme, using ultra-modern design concepts and adorning the vast new complexes with avant-garde sculpture. While Webern became involved with socialist music-making, Berg, wholly unpolitical in his outlook, remained largely aloof.

After 1925 the economic situation stabilized to a certain extent. The currency was reconstituted and a very modest prosperity attained by the weakened middle class. It was this period—between 1925 and 1933—that saw Berg's rise to international status as a leading avant-garde composer. To an increasing degree his livelihood depended on income from abroad.

In spite of its loss of political importance and its descent into poverty, Vienna retained much of its former status as one of the cultural capitals of Central Europe. One must see Vienna always within the context of its role in that wider milieu. Within the old Empire, Vienna had merely been the first among a group of peers: Prague, Budapest, and Cracow were the satellites that revolved around Vienna, but supplied a brilliant array of talents: Kraus came from Brünn (Brno); Dvořák, Smetana, Janáček, Werfel, Rilke, and Kafka, were from Prague; Budapest supplied an unending stream of operetta composers, dramatists like Molnár and Balàzs, and serious composers like Bartók and Kodály; Cracow produced the eminent playwright Thaddeus Rittner.

But Vienna also fitted into a larger context: within the German-speaking sphere its sister city was Munich, home of Richard Strauss and Wedekind, where the people spoke a dialect very close to the Viennese and had a very similar Catholic–Baroque tradition. Yet Vienna and Munich were at the base of a triangle of which the apex was Berlin. If Vienna was philistine and conservative in its tastes, Berlin was daring and avant-garde, more so than ever in the post-war period. Viennese artists sealed their success by going to Berlin. Max Reinhardt, the leading theatrical innovator of the age, was an Austrian working in Berlin, as were large numbers of prominent actors, writers and designers. Karl Kraus went to Berlin to give his readings. Schoenberg found his place there, as soon as his importance was recognized. And for a musician like Berg, the performance of one of his works in Berlin was the ultimate accolade, the confirmation that he had arrived. The first performance of *Wozzeck* at the Berlin State Opera under Kleiber on 14 December 1925 was the high point of his career.

It is within this context that Berg's life in the post-war period, the period of his rise to success and acceptance, must be seen: he moved freely between Vienna, Prague, Munich and Berlin.

Hitler came to power in January 1933. The subsequent campaign against all modern art as alien and degenerate engulfed Germany and ultimately drove Schoenberg to America. It was a catastrophe for Berg. Vienna remained, at first, free of direct Nazi rule. But instead of uniting against the increasing threat from the north, the two warring Austrian factions erupted in open conflict. In February 1934 the *Heimwehr* clashed with the socialist *Schutzbund* in the course of violent disputes about how to face the Nazi menace. In a brief civil war the large new Viennese housing developments, the strongholds of the Reds, were shelled into submission by the Black artillery. As a result not only the Nazi party, but the Social Democratic Party as well, was outlawed and forced underground.

The Catholic chancellor Dollfuss attempted to establish a mildly Fascist regime, modelled on Mussolini's Italy. In July 1934 Dollfuss was murdered in an abortive Nazi coup. His successor, Schuschnigg, vainly tried to stem the underground activities of the Nazis, who were supported by Hitler across the borders.

Karl Kraus, who had ridiculed the philistine and reactionary Catholic party for decades, realizing that the Schuschnigg regime remained the last barrier against a Nazi take-over, rallied to its defence—much to the disgust of leftists like Bertolt Brecht who had been a close ally of his. So, paradoxically, he found himself on the same side as Franz Werfel, Berg's friend, who as a fervent Catholic convert had become one of the pillars of the regime.

Yet the dominance of the reactionary and conservative Catholic party inevitably had a dampening effect on the more 'progressive' artists. Berg, who had lost ground in Nazi Germany as a representative of 'degenerate' avant-gardism and a *Kulturbolschewist* (cultural Bolshevik), as the Nazis liked to call modernists, was also pointedly neglected by the new Austrian establishment. Yet he refused to take the course Schoenberg had taken and to emigrate outside the Central European orbit.

History took its relentless course: Mussolini, decisively weakened by his Abyssinian adventure, was driven into Hitler's arms and could no longer protect Austria. From 1936 to the spring of 1938 the regime gradually had to recognize and admit Nazi influence. And in March 1938 Hitler's forces occupied Austria. By that time, perhaps mercifully, Berg was dead.

BERG'S CHARACTER REMEMBERED

JOAN ALLEN SMITH

Helene told me that she often locked him in his study and took away the key in order to force him to compose, which he didn't deny. However, in her absence, he explained to me that out of obstinacy, in such cases, he didn't compose but rather took out a flask of cognac that he kept under the sofa for such occasions and consoled himself with it.[1]

The first time that the Austrian writer Soma Morgenstern saw Alban and Helene Berg was on the number 59 tram travelling into the city from the Vienna suburb of Hietzing. He was impressed by their appearance and described this first sighting in a memoir that he later wrote about Berg. The couple sat together in deep contemplation of a score of Gustav Mahler's First Symphony that they held between them. Morgenstern, on his way to a Mahler concert, deduced that the Bergs were going to the same performance. It was clear to him from their equally intense involvement in the score that they were both musicians. With a lay music lover's wistful envy, he watched them immersed in the piece, which to him was then totally unknown. As they bent over the page, Morgenstern was not able to see Berg's bright grey eyes and wide, sensitive mouth. Berg was compressed into a seat too confined for his lanky frame so that he perpetually shifted his long legs. Morgenstern could see that he was a tall man. 'His narrow shoulders, like the unaffected, negligent posture, gave an impression that he took up less space than would be natural to him'.[2] Morgenstern later considered this posture with its psychological implications to be one of Berg's most characteristic features. Helene's girlish style attracted his notice. His overall impression was of an aristocratic and aloof couple.

Two or three years later, Berg and Morgenstern were coincidentally together once again on the number 59 tram. Morgenstern had met Berg briefly a few months before and now debated whether he should extend a greeting. He finally

13

did, and the two arranged to meet at Berg's apartment in the Trauttmansdorff-gasse. This first visit marked the start of a keen and warm friendship which was to last the remainder of Berg's life.

This essay will investigate Berg's character using a defined body of material. The primary source is the unpublished memoir written by Soma Morgenstern. Morgenstern was a prolific reminiscent. As part of a projected autobiography, he wrote two long pieces—one about his school friend, the author Joseph Roth, and one about Alban Berg, whom he describes as 'the dearest in a life very blessed with good friends'. The latter memoir comprises some 300 pages of recollections of the composer and of Viennese culture. It constitutes the major insight we have into Berg's personal life.[3]

Because the Morgenstern material concerns the last ten years of Berg's life, I shall consider primarily Berg the mature man and composer, although material from Berg's early years will be used where appropriate to support this view. In order to avoid reckless speculation, I have chosen to present the picture of Berg as offered by Soma Morgenstern and Berg's other compatriots with a minimum of psychological conjecture. It is nonetheless my personal view, although I hope it is one of which Dr Morgenstern would have approved.

I first met Dr Morgenstern in November 1973 when I interviewed him in New York City for an oral history project on the genesis of the twelve-note idea.[4] His recollections were vivid and perceptive, and more personal than those of many who knew Berg in a more professional setting. This interview, together with material from other interviews conducted with former students and friends of Berg, and material from published and unpublished sources, including the correspondence between Berg and Morgenstern, has also been consulted.

Morgenstern's friendship with Berg extended from their first acquaintance in 1924 until Berg's death in 1935. Their relationship was comprehensive, spanning many activities both literary and informal. Morgenstern covered cultural events and wrote a regular feuilleton column as a cultural correspondent for the *Frankfurter Zeitung*. While thus earning a living, he was engaged in more serious pursuits, and by 1932 he had begun his novel, *Der Sohn des verlorenen Sohnes*, (The Son of the Lost Son) which was to be the first volume of a trilogy.[5] However, the rise of National Socialism interrupted his career, and forced him to flee first to France and later to the United States.

Berg himself found a description of his personality and habits in a fictitious obituary entitled 'Nekrologie' by Alfred Polgar. Berg sent the clipping to Morgenstern, underlining the following sections which he felt best described himself:

> He liked to eat poppyseed cake. He wore only soft hats and didn't feel comfortable until they were quite crushed and crumpled. Sleeping only on the

right side, he used to pull up his right knee ... One hand rested under the pillow, the other ... On the other hand, he loved his piano with great tenderness. When he returned home from a trip, he went to it right away and stroked it as the rider his horse. While playing, he held a cigarette in his mouth and the ashes often fell on the keys. He walked slightly stooped, and when with others, always on the left side, not out of politeness, but because he never felt comfortable on the right (although he could not have said why). In speech he very frequently added the words *nicht wahr?*, and his laugh strangely enough was two octaves lower than his voice. He spoke tenor and laughed bass. He was asthmatic and ... He carried small change in his left pants pocket, his collar size was 40, and his curse: 'Damn it all!' [Zum Teufel noch einmal]. In the movies, he cried easily, although he was ashamed of his tears ... In the margins of the staffpaper on which he wrote his scores, he often drew circles and pentagons and crosshatched painstakingly. He tolerated alcohol in great quantity; ... also he sometimes let his lower lip droop.

To Morgenstern, Berg was a 'true Viennese', which he defined as follows:

The Viennese who is worthy of the name, no matter how seriously he takes himself, does not give himself airs. This noble posture also has its bad side. The consequence of this attitude is that he not only will avoid obstacles, but even turn away from them altogether. And obstacles are present everywhere in abundance. And especially so for a composer who writes 'atonal' music—a theoretically appropriate and yet fatal adjective, which the unknowing immediately fasten on as a warning of a music that deliberately will not sound good. From this it follows that one composes for the drawer. No wonder that one early on gets the reputation of being lazy.

In many ways, Berg's personality and upbringing were typical of the upper-middle-class Viennese of his time. His education was cultural with a strong background in German literature and philosophy. He attended the opera from an early age and was well versed in the symphonic repertoire from playing piano four-hands with his sister. His attitude toward daily life was one of studied casualness. He read, attended concerts and rehearsals, and sat with friends in the cafés which were then an integral part of Viennese gentility. He spent a great deal of time writing letters. He had a voluminous correspondence, and he was fond of receiving personal mail. At the forefront of musical development in his time, he was likewise well acquainted with avant-garde developments in painting, literature, and the theatre.

Berg often made fun of his own laziness and taunted Morgenstern about his, leading to squabbles about who was the more slothful. In fact it is often difficult to see how Berg managed to compose as much as he did. It is well known that Berg was a deliberate composer, slow in process as well as by procrastination. (In a letter to Morgenstern, Berg once remarked in jest that he hoped to finish *Lulu* by the turn of the millennium.)[6] His time was eaten up by the exigencies of family business, work for his teacher Arnold Schoenberg, and the First World War. In the early post-war years, the Society for Private Musical Performances demanded hours of his time. He organized, coached, set up chairs, and attended rehearsals. In the later 1920s, he lost months of work at a time through travelling for performances, mostly of *Wozzeck*. Morgenstern reports that during this time Berg also looked industriously for a new opera libretto. This search must have been a delightful procrastination, an excuse to sit around reading—surely an ideal occupation for the indolent person. As the excerpt at the head of this essay indicates, Berg was perhaps encouraged to work in significant ways by his wife Helene, whose own lack of interesting occupation may have contributed to her vicarious ambitions. In general, though, Berg's habits in Vienna involved working in the morning, often on projects of a more routine nature, such as orchestrating or copying, his first compositional drafts usually having been done in the country during the summers. In the afternoon he often taught.

In person, Berg was fundamentally shy, with a well-developed persona of charm and wit. Pianist Stefan Askenase wrote that Berg was 'one of the most charming men' he ever met. 'Of great intelligence, full of wit and irony, he loved life and company. Still, with all familiarity, he commanded respect'.[7] Eugen Lehner, violist of the Kolisch Quartet, considered Berg a typical Austrian aristocrat with a 'certain nonchalance, great charm, and a certain very man-of-the-world and so on—incredibly handsome, very warm.'[8] Pianist Erna Gál reported that 'he was a wonderful, fine, aristocratic gentleman. Inside and outside ... Berg was ... cooler than Webern towards other people. But very kind, very, very kindhearted and noble, really very, very noble.'[9]

Morgenstern, however, reports that he 'did not have a cheerful disposition'. Nonetheless, 'his strong sense of humour carried him through difficulties'. He was impulsive and excitable, but somewhat aloof. The shyness of his school years appears to have followed him through life, possibly contributing to the impression of coolness, and Morgenstern reports that Berg often needed to drink cognac in order to relax and make light conversation. On the other hand, he loved to gossip, as Morgenstern, who worried that he presented only Berg's virtues, humorously makes clear.

Berg, he tells us, loved gossip, not of the kind that for instance writers write about writers—Tolstoy about Dostoevsky—but quite simply, 'as women gossip'. Morgenstern describes visiting Berg unannounced in order to lend him a book. When he arrived, the window of Berg's study was open. It was tea-time, and Morgenstern heard many women's voices and laughter. He waited until a pause in the conversation and then called Berg to the window. He came 'with rosy cheeks and shining eyes ..., a child receiving presents'. 'Come in, come in quickly!' he cried, forgetting himself. Morgenstern went in and encountered a 'terrible scene'. Five women were there—Helene, Berg's sister Smaragda, her close friend Frau Keller, and two others. The table was spread with pastry and liqueurs, and an atmosphere of great cheer prevailed. In the midst, Berg was 'the only cock of the walk'. He invited Morgenstern to share this honoured position but still obviously considered him an intruder and seemed relieved when he declined. At the door, the excited Berg said, 'I was so pleased to see you that I did not consider how little you would care for such an odd company of women. You cannot imagine what they gossip about! It is really like an intoxication!'[10]

This intense attitude of Berg, the avid observer of human behaviour, is further exemplified by his delight in soccer. Morgenstern, who shared this fervent pastime, felt that Berg's enthusiasm exceeded his knowledge but that he was not unusual in being an intellectual infected by a brother's interest in sports. The two supported different teams and maintained a friendly rivalry.

In his eating and drinking habits, Berg was similarly self-indulgent. He enjoyed good food and excellent cognac. His *Letters to His Wife* are filled with descriptions of meals, and Morgenstern mentions often that Berg kept a bottle of cognac hidden under the couch in his study.[11] This desire for gastronomic comfort is echoed by one of his students, Bruno Seidlhofer, who reports that Berg 'drank coffee with us [his students], which he ground himself with his little Turkish machine. He had these lessons mostly after lunch and then ground coffee.'[12]

Berg's love of food and drink was tempered by a strong bond with nature. This affinity dates from his early years, as he testifies in a letter to Helene of 13 July [1908]: 'This morning for the first time I tried doing some work. Hope I can put into it all the things I am missing here, testifying to my three great loves, Nature, Music and Helene.'[13] Although in his youth he alludes to a fear of nature which causes 'restlessness and dissatisfaction instead of joy',[14] in later life Berg achieved a peace and serenity in the country which allowed him to accomplish his greatest work.

The nature in which Berg grew up, at the Berghof on the Ossiacher See, was relatively civilized. The house itself was large and comfortable and the lake well populated. The surrounding hills supplied pleasant walks without undue strain or fear of wild animals. By the time Berg met Morgenstern the Berghof had been sold and Berg spent his summers either at the Nahowski family home, Trahütten, at a small rented house on the Berghof property, or after 1932 at his own summer cottage, the Waldhaus, not far from the Berghof on the Wörthersee.

Berg's habits on these country sojourns are described in detail by Morgenstern. Berg, who enjoyed the role of host, arose early and brought Morgenstern breakfast in bed. Afterwards everyone worked until twelve o'clock. They went swimming then and again in the evening. Berg was a strong swimmer and felt that swimming was the best exercise for himself: 'Next to my *work*, my greatest pleasure is *life in the water* (at all temperatures). Because my heart is much too small and rather disqualifies me from other forms of physical exercise, swimming and floating in the water are most compatible with my physique.'[15] In the lake, Berg shaved himself without a mirror while he gave Morgenstern strict swimming instructions: 'Ordinarily you're a low-spirited person [*Kopfhänger*]; only in the water do you raise your head high against the sky. That makes you twice as heavy as you are!' After shaving, Berg traditionally dropped part of his shaving gear into the lake, and he and Morgenstern would dive in an attempt to retrieve it. They were always unsuccessful in this and every week Berg bought more shaving equipment in reserve. He had to conceal the daily casualties from Helene as she was 'not a little miserly'.

At home, Berg seems to have found water less appealing. Morgenstern reports an amusing incident concerning Berg's reluctance. He went to visit Berg one morning at eleven o'clock. The maid, Anna Laulitsch, opened the door smirking, and Morgenstern could hear a ruckus in the background, with Helene's voice and Alban's deep breathing as they ran about the apartment. Finally Alban rushed out of the dining room, dressed only in trousers. Behind him came Helene in a white apron with a wet sponge in her raised right hand. Without greeting Morgenstern, Berg rushed up to him, grabbed him, and thrust him in front of himself as a screen. 'She wants to wash me! She wants to wash me!' ['Sie will mi woschen! Sie will mi schon wieda woschen!' Berg spoke a heavy Viennese dialect when excited.] 'He hasn't washed his face in a week!' maintained Helene, with the sponge raised threateningly to Alban, who continued to cower behind his friend. 'She lies!' cried Alban, 'She always lies! Don't believe a word of it, Soma. Last Monday I washed!' 'It was Sunday,' insisted Helene, 'and today is Friday!'

After Helene went back to the kitchen Berg seriously instructed Morgenstern in the dangers of water as an internal or external remedy. He went to his bookcase, took out a biography of Michelangelo, and read a letter in which the father of the master, as Morgenstern quotes, gives his son advice for living: 'Be moderate in all, my son. Wash seldom, and you will remain healthy.' Then Berg appended: 'You know how long Michelangelo lived.'

On the other hand, Berg must have bathed occasionally, as Bruno Seidlhofer maintains: 'This I tell you only as a joke—we spoke also about inspiration and he told me, his best things occurred to him in the bathtub or on the toilet. There he had the best brainstorms.'[16]

One of Berg's most successful brainstorms was the decision, following the success of *Wozzeck*, to purchase an automobile. This car, a dark blue Ford cabriolet christened the 'blue bird', was one of Berg's greatest joys in his later years. Berg kept the car in Carinthia and used it to drive himself and his friends on jaunts through the neighbouring mountains. On one of these, a trip with Erwin Stein and others, Morgenstern discovered Berg the dispenser of largess. Before setting forth Berg purchased a dozen packs of cigarettes, which he kept on the seat next to him. When they drove through a forest near the Berghof, where a group of workers was repairing the road, he slowed down and tossed them cigarettes. The workers already knew him. The ceremony was repeated daily. With some embarrassment Berg explained the scene to Morgenstern, 'I cannot drive by in my car like a capitalist without thanking them at least.' He drove quite slowly, yet quickly enough that he need not await their thanks.

This personal view of politics seems typical of Berg. Although nominally his social views were those of Karl Kraus, he did not take an active role in social issues. Indeed his views in earlier war years reveal an enthusiastic naïveté, and he was distressed by Kraus's pacifist stand during the First World War.[17] For Morgenstern, who ultimately lost his job with the *Frankfurter Zeitung* and was forced to flee the Nazis, the 'Jewish question' was of urgent importance. In assessing Berg's political views, there is little evidence that Berg adopted an anti-Jewish stance, although the Morgenstern document hints that Helene may have held anti-semitic views. That Berg didn't think deeply about politics and allowed himself to be unduly influenced is further suggested by Morgenstern's description of his attitude to the so-called 'Aryan document'. One day, Berg told Morgenstern that he had received a request from the German Music Board to prove his Aryan descent. Asked what he thought he would do, he replied, 'I must get the documents.' 'I suppose you realize that by doing so you take upon yourself the embarrassing task of proving with documents that you are not of the same blood with Schoenberg, Mahler, Karl Kraus, and Altenberg.' He shook his head. 'What should I do? Everyone must do it.' Morgenstern told Berg that Krenek had thrown his form in the waste basket. At that Berg responded, 'Krenek is not married to Helene.' Berg's political attitude in this case seems determined more by a desire for peace at home and a tendency not to act for himself than by wrong political thinking. Certainly Morgenstern did not blame Berg in any way and their friendship continued unabated.

Berg came from a family of mixed religion—his father was Protestant and his mother Catholic. Although Berg himself was raised a Catholic, he appears to have held an ambivalent view of his religion in later life. In an early letter to his future wife, written in August 1909, his attitude appears fervent:

> The triumph of all that is great and holy is not something from my imagination, it is from the reality within me which alone is decisive. After all, when Christ died on the Cross, ... his triumph was not imaginary, but in the reality of his resurrection. And to follow him as best I can, I must seek my salvation in an ideal, pure reality of the spirit, a resurrection from the brutal materialism of ordinary life.[18]

These remarks should perhaps not be taken too seriously. Berg was at this time on the verge of marrying into a Catholic family and eager to impress his sceptical future in-laws of his suitability. When asked if Berg went to church often, his nephew Erich Alban Berg replied, 'Probably he went more often when there were good concerts.'[19] Morgenstern, for whom the religious issue was of great importance, reported that Berg thought himself 'not such a good Catholic'. Morgenstern himself thought that Berg only remembered to be a Catholic when someone died and he had to go to the funeral.

Berg and Morgenstern spoke easily about religious issues as they did about most topics. The freedom with which they discussed their views and ideas was stimulating for both parties. They each possessed a high degree of erudition in their own areas which they were able to share with some mutual understanding. Berg's activities, especially during the composition of the opera *Lulu*, were often literary in nature. He could and did share his problems with the libretto with Morgenstern, consulting him both in the selection process and later in the formidable task of adapting the Lulu plays. Morgenstern in turn discussed his novel with Berg and took him to the theatre.

The following anecdote, describing Berg's first literary discussion with Morgenstern, is revealing both of the passion of Berg's views and of his impulsive, excitable, and somewhat naïve nature. Morgenstern fell into a discussion of Karl Kraus, little knowing that Berg was an ardent admirer of the Viennese satirist, and rashly referred to Kraus's 'lampoon'(*Pasquill*), 'Heinrich Heine und die Folgen', as 'infamous'. Scarcely had he spoken the word 'infamous' when Berg jumped up and ran into the hall. Morgenstern, thinking he was called to the telephone, innocently awaited his return. When Berg came back, he sat down, and with closed eyes, he asked, 'Why lampoon? Why infamous?' Morgenstern explained that the word 'lampoon' is not derogatory but merely a genre of literature. Berg then wanted to know why Kraus's essay was 'infamous'.

'The lampoon against Heine is infamous because here a writer, who owes Heinrich Heine his entire writing existence, scorns his master.'

Berg went to telephone again. When he returned and sat silently for a while, Morgenstern hoped that Berg considered the debate concluded. He felt he was wasting his time arguing with a Kraus fanatic. After a while, however, Berg resumed.

'You are speaking of Kraus as if he were a student of Heine.'

'A Heine follower.'

'Kraus therefore owes his existence to Heine?'

'Yes, in the true sense of the word. Without Heine, the language which he uses against Heine would not exist.'

'It is therefore a betrayal?'

'To speak in the manner of Karl Kraus: he spits in the fountain from which he has drunk.'

The phone now actually rang in the hall, and Morgenstern now realized that Berg had run out previously in order to calm himself. He was busy thinking of a pretext on which to change the subject when Helene came into the room. Slim, light-footed, very beautiful, she was not quite advantageously dressed, Morgenstern thought. She looked at Alban, gave Soma her hand and asked him, 'You were fighting? Naturally you were fighting! I am pleased that you are here. Sit down again. And explain!'

Explanations followed in which Berg accused Morgenstern of trying to 'demolish' Kraus.

'Karl Kraus is a little Heine follower. Didn't you say that?'

'I said "follower", but not "little".'

'Isn't the word "follower" alone already contemptuous?' Alban retorted.
'Not always … '
Helene then intervened. 'What do you want from the Herr Doktor? Karl Kraus
is not everyone's cup of tea. Now let's leave it. I will make you coffee and then
you can scuffle some more.'

This story reveals Berg's sometimes uncritical devotion to the avant-garde
enthusiasms of his time. Like Schoenberg and the other members of his circle,
Berg was heavily influenced by the writings of Kraus. This influence was of a
serious cultural nature. The quality of Berg's literary argument in this and other
excerpts, however, is occasionally more characteristic of adolescent hero-
worship than of the very real cultural ties that informed his creative work. His
remarks on the nature of followers are particularly interesting in view of his
relationship with Schoenberg, and it is worthwhile to speculate about Berg's
own self-image in this light.

From the reports of Berg's literary discussions contained in the Morgenstern
memoir, it is not clear to what degree of literary sophistication Berg's views
extended. His schooling was undistinguished. He had difficulties with his
assignments and often tried to get help from his friends. After numerous
obstacles, including repeating a year, he graduated from a *Realschule* rather
than the *Gymnasium*, with no prospects for university.[20] According to
Morgenstern, he retained all his life a discomfort with foreign words and
perhaps also a sense of inferiority about his education, although Morgenstern
felt that he more than made up for his schooling with a secure feeling for what
was genuine and a refined taste for new values. Nonetheless, he read and
discussed literature avidly, he was full of curiosity, and had a certain self-
confidence in his own ideas.[21]

According to Morgenstern, Berg read mainly novels and lyrical poetry. His
favourite poets were Peter Rosegger and Adalbert Stifter. He also liked to read
Joseph Roth, Robert Musil, and Gottfried Keller. He had a thirst for new
literary pleasures, as Morgenstern found on one occasion when, still during the
lifetime of Franz Kafka, he gave the composer a birthday present of *Der
Landarzt* (The Country Doctor). Berg phoned after two days and asked in great
excitement, 'Why have you never told me about him? Why have I never heard of
him?' Although Morgenstern acknowledges that Berg was a voracious reader, in
the reported literary discussions Berg actually says little of an analytical nature,
and Morgenstern does most of the talking. Berg's contributions are often
intuitive in character—the views of a creative visionary rather than of an
intellectual—but it is clear from his compositional sketches that he was also
capable of sophisticated analytical thinking.

Berg did of course have definite literary tastes, which he shared with
Schoenberg and other of his friends. Besides Karl Kraus, he was a great admirer
of the architect Adolf Loos whom he knew well. A perusal of his small but select
library reveals an interest, also noted by Morgenstern, in reference books, the
mark of a curious man.[22] In addition to a major encyclopaedia and other

reference works, Berg's book collection is heavily weighted toward literature and letters. He possessed complete editions of the works of Ibsen and Strindberg, both of which he annotated heavily. (His annotation style consists primarily of underlining and the use of exclamation marks, although he occasionally drew pictures as well.) There is little psychology (Freud and Weininger) or philosophy (Kierkegaard and Hegel) but considerable correspondence, including the correspondence of Ibsen and of Schopenhauer. A mind more interested in human personalities than factual information seems indicated. (His wife, by contrast, professed serious introspective interest in the work of Rudolf Steiner and various occult writings.)[23] Books on music consist primarily of popular biographies, with few books of a theoretical nature. Other works in his library encompass the writings of Kraus and Loos, Peter Rosegger, Franz Werfel, Knut Hamsun, Poe, Cervantes, and Baudelaire. A number of older books, probably removed from the Berghof, include the collected works of standard authors, including Grillparzer and the Schlegel and Tieck translations of Shakespeare. He had a small library of musical scores, some of which appear to be presentation editions. Composers most represented include Beethoven, Schumann, Schubert, Mahler, Brahms, and Wagner.

While Berg may have played an inferior role in literary discussions, on the subject of music, Morgenstern was of course the listener. According to Morgenstern, Richard Strauss was Berg's *bête noire*. He reports Berg as saying, 'He composes with plasticine', and describes his friend sitting at the piano in order to demonstrate to him 'vulgar' places in Strauss operas, and as contrast, 'noble, refined' places in the music of the misunderstood Alexander von Zemlinsky. He called the *Alpensinfonie* 'Gewittergoy' music.[24]

Of his own music Berg apparently spoke little. He admired the facility of Poulenc and Milhaud and on more than one occasion described his own music to Stefan Askenase as unapproachable by comparison. For instance, during a concert in Berg's honour, after 'cheery and harmless' chamber music pieces by Poulenc and Milhaud which he liked very much, they began to play his Chamber Concerto and Berg said, 'Is this unfriendly music!' Morgenstern also remembers many occasions when Berg asked someone who had just heard a work by him, 'that must have shocked you more than a little, didn't it?'

Perhaps the main charm of Berg's friendship with Morgenstern was its normality. Morgenstern was someone with whom Berg could relax, someone sophisticated enough to provide stimulating conversation, but also someone appropriate for fun. While other relationships in Berg's life were problematic, the friendship with Morgenstern appears to have been continuous and uncomplicated. The two principal relationships of Berg's life, that with his teacher Arnold Schoenberg and that with his wife Helene, were neither.

Berg was the third of four children. He had two older brothers, both more robust than himself, and a younger sister to whom he was close. His father, handsome and refined, suffered from a weak heart. Although a business man (in the import–export business), Berg's father was sensitive and reflective.

Hermann Watznauer (1875–1939), an important friend from Berg's youth, described Berg's father in words that might almost describe Berg himself:

> His pale face was unusually sharp and nobly cut. The eyes lay deep, and unusually wide eyelids ended in a fine-cut semi-circle under the prominent, salt-and-pepper brows ... Each of his movements was formal, quiet and gave evidence of complete gentility. Behind the proud and dignified posture, however, was concealed—noticeable only to the alert observer—a constant fatigue, a not completely concealed exhaustion.[25]

The mother, on the other hand, was a strong healthy woman of statuesque proportions. Given to an overweight robustness, she appeared to be the dominant member of the family. She was described by Watznauer as being 'in health respects just the opposite of the husband. ... [She] could not comprehend that one could be sick. ... She had the fortunate temperament of the healthy, blunt, genuine, agreeable Viennese. Everything that she seized flourished.'[26]

In appearance and health and probably also in character, Berg resembled his father, who died shortly after his son's 15th birthday. Although Watznauer, who was ten years older than Berg, became something of a father figure for him, the loss of his true father at so young an age had a profound effect upon his character. The further influence of the strong mother figure and the relatively weak father upon his later relationships with women is also significant. With the loss of his father, Berg felt little in common with his family.

The dependency in Berg's relationship with his teacher Arnold Schoenberg has been much discussed. When Berg first met Schoenberg, he was talented but inexperienced. Berg's brother Charly's initiative in first presenting Berg's songs to Schoenberg accentuates Berg's passivity and lack of focus at that time. Unlike Webern, who was musically already quite advanced when he went to Schoenberg, Berg can fairly be said to owe essentially his entire musical education to Schoenberg. This fact alone, without Schoenberg's overpowering personality, would have made it hard for Berg to achieve independence. When other factors of Berg's personality are considered, we see that it must have been a struggle indeed. When Berg went to Schoenberg, his father had been dead only four years. During this period, his friend Watznauer had guided his approach to adulthood. But it was Schoenberg who shaped Berg's future, who helped him to find his voice and to focus his creative energy.

Schoenberg was only one year older than Watznauer but with a commanding personality and without the highly personal interest which Watznauer would have felt.[27] He held a kind of fascination for his students. In the earlier years, Berg expresses this dependence clearly in letters to Schoenberg, such as for instance this letter of 24 April 1913: 'You yourself know, dear Herr Schoenberg, that I am always conscious of, and never want to be conscious of anything but: being your student. To follow you in every respect, knowing that everything I do in *opposition* to your wishes is wrong.'[28] For Berg, Schoenberg played the role of the domineering father figure that Berg had never had. In later years it was difficult for Berg to break away or to transform the parental relationship into one of equality. He found it difficult to compose freely when Schoenberg was in town.[29] His letters to Schoenberg are uncandidly designed to please. At the same time, he seems unable to tear himself away. Indeed, as late as 1933 he was writing to his master: 'Now and again I need to be allowed to breathe the air of your study, which seems to me like the inside of a giant brain filled to bursting, to stand at your desk and to savour the other joys of your lovely home.'[30]

The strength and ambivalence of this relationship formed in Morgenstern's view the main problem of Berg's life: 'Already shortly after the beginning of our friendship, I saw that Alban's life problem [Lebensproblem] was the relationship with his friend and teacher Arnold Schoenberg.' Later on in the memoir Morgenstern speaks of Berg's own ambivalent response to a letter suggesting that passages in Wozzeck written when Schoenberg was in Vienna are distinguishable from those composed when he was away. According to Morgenstern, Berg replied: 'You perhaps don't at all suspect that you are touching therewith the problem of my life, a problem that I have carried with me for decades without being able to solve it and which will be my downfall.'

One of the principal influences of Schoenberg upon Berg was of course his use of the twelve-note method of composition. Whereas Schoenberg, and Webern also, came to the twelve-note method from a compositional necessity, Berg adopted the method at least partially because of the closeness of his relationship with Schoenberg. In reality, under the circumstances of their friendship, not to use the method would have been unthinkable. It is clear from Berg's letters as well as his sketches that the twelve-note method was not intuitively easy for him. In a letter to Schoenberg of 13 July 1926, he wrote: 'Gradually, even I am becoming adept in this method of composing, and that is very reassuring. For it would have pained me dreadfully if it had been denied me to express myself musically this way.'[31] Nonetheless, it must be said that, of the three composers, perhaps Berg was the most successful in assimilating the new compositional approach into his previous style. Less strict than Schoenberg and Webern in his adherence to a single set, and possibly less mathematically astute than Schoenberg, Berg was nonetheless extremely rigorous within his own usage. The ambiguities of this situation—of the friendship itself and its demands for twelve-note composition—have been described by Stefan Askenase:

> He could see that it was ... well, I can't say a bad thing, but something etwas was ihn belastete. He had the feeling of a weight—something that [weighed] on him. ... Schoenberg was a very strong personality and he was very much influenced by him. If he had not been influenced, ... let's say even if he had been living in the same period and had not met Schoenberg, I don't think he would have become a twelve-tone composer.[32]

Berg had a further affection for the composer Gustav Mahler. Berg experienced the Mahler epoch in the Vienna State Opera as a young man, and Mahler remained for him the ideal picture of the artist. He was entranced by a new epoch in the history of opera, and he admired not only the composer and the director, but above all the man Mahler—his frankness, the integrity of his character, and the stubbornness of his will. A life-long friend of the composer's widow, Berg adopted an adorational attitude toward the older man. Morgenstern was aware of this hero-worship, and to some extent considered it even more important than the relationship with Schoenberg: 'When he spoke of [Mahler], Alban was rejuvenated physically. His eyes shone, his face lit up, and with youthful movements he hurried to the piano, in order to cite the places from the symphonies which lay especially close to his heart.'

The fervent reverence that Berg felt for the male idols of his life, as well as his Stendhalian attitude toward women exemplified in the *Letters to His Wife*, raises the issue of Berg's romanticism. Is the often spiritually florid prose of these letters typical of his stance toward life? Did it change as he got older? The violinist Felix Galimir, who knew Berg during the time of his friendship with Morgenstern, comments as follows:

> I would say the prototype of Romanticism was Berg. As a person, you know, this dreamer type, a little sicklish, never quite well ... terribly tall ... ideal romanticist. And the whole attitude ... was so romantic. I guess you feel it in the music too. ... The *Letters to His Wife* ... are ... not faked—that's exactly him. And in some way, he was a little bit out of context already then, because there . . . were very few people left of this calibre romanticism as he was.[33]

Berg's personality was indeed 'marked by the imaginative or emotional appeal of the heroic, adventurous, remote, mysterious, or idealized',[34] and he received a general literary education in the grand Romantic tradition. Nonetheless, rather than being a Romantic composer in the historical sense, or some wholesale hold-over from the 19th-century Romantic tradition, Berg was more in actuality a romantic personality type who, in keeping with his nature, shared many of the attributes of the musical Romanticists and the values of the 19th-century Romantics, but who was, on balance, firmly grounded as a composer in the 20th century.

According to Morgenstern, Berg believed in the 'holiness' of art. It is perhaps this romantic view, the passionate embracing of ideas and attachments, as we have seen in Berg's defence of Karl Kraus, that kept Berg young. Berg himself wrote in a letter to his wife: 'At fifty I look like a fifteen-year-old (!) and feel as full of energy as a five-year-old.'[35] Morgenstern, in arguing against the well-known idea that artists and musicians who die young have completed their life's work, remarked: 'Alban Berg lived to be fifty. As a man, he was fifty, and also by the calendar. As an artist, as a composer, he was closer to thirty-five.'

Berg's marriage to the former Helene Nahowski forms one of the most ambiguous relationships in music history. Billed as a perfect love by Berg's early biographers, information has now emerged that indicates that Berg sought frequent solace in the arms of other women.[36] This knowledge has been used to suggest that Berg was bitterly unhappy in his marriage. The key to a reconciliation of these two opposing views, which have been based largely upon Berg's views and actions, lies in the convoluted personality of his wife and in the dependent element of Berg's character. To see this, it is necessary to embark upon a brief acquaintance with Helene Berg. Morgenstern gives us a tender description of her appearance as he saw her that first evening in the number 59 tram:

> She was wearing a little old-fashioned coat with a wide double collar, and she looked like a girl in it. Opulent, ash-blonde, ... carefully but not too severely braided hair surrounded her face with the fluffy fresh colour of a Renoir picture, the mouth still fuller than one finds in such pictures. The prominent cheekbones made the face slavic. ... She had blue eyes which, although they were rather darker than light blue, made me think that the moon, called Luna in Latin, is rightly feminine. As they rose to get off near the last station, I saw that ... the girlish face was only just appropriate to a woman that tall.

Coming from an aristocratic family, Helene had a certain financial and social stature, and Berg, as is plain in the *Letters to His Wife*, had difficulty in gaining permission for her hand. According to Morgenstern, the Bohemian poet Peter Altenberg thought the relationship surprising and advised both parties against it: 'A young artist such as you doesn't marry the daughter of a court official!' 'Such a beautiful, aristocratic girl doesn't marry such a young Bohemian. Nothing will come of it!'

The original bond appears to have been spiritual in a highly romantic vein. Berg's letters to Helene in the early years aboundingly affirm the sanctity and noble nature of their relationship. In an undated letter from 1907, Berg says that he loves 'a woman with great art in her, the art which means everything to me and builds me the finest bridge to exalted humanity: music.'[37] And on 2 June 1907 he writes: 'Love is the condition for everything great and beautiful, ... this has been so from time immemorial and will remain so forever.'[38] This is Berg, the passionate lover of noble thoughts, the fervent believer in grand schemes. In agreeing to marry the young idealist, Helene must have shared this view.

Later on, as Berg travelled more frequently for performances of *Wozzeck*, Helene suffered from nervous complaints and arthritis and spent extensive periods at spas. The correspondence between the two of them is thus unusually long for a married couple. Surprisingly, the tone of the letters does not vary much throughout the term of the marriage, and many of the later letters are as romantic and idealistic as those of the early years. In the later letters, however, the tone often seems forced, as though Berg had to continue in this style in order to reassure Helene and himself of the continued exalted uniqueness of the relationship. Helene appears constantly and obsessively concerned for threats to the marital image: not only for Berg's fidelity but also for his health.[39] When Berg goes on trips Helene packs for him, including medicines which he is supposed to take, and he writes proudly of following her instructions.

Helene had little intellectual stimulation during these years, and the couple had no children. At the time of her marriage she had friends in artistic circles; she was beautiful, intelligent, and enjoyed a modest singing talent. All this was to be sacrificed, as she wrote to Berg in a poignant letter shortly before their wedding: 'Gladly and of my own free will I give up everything that made my girlhood so full of beauty, hope and happiness—my modest "art". I quench my own flame, and shall only exist for and through you.'[40] Berg eventually found a legitimate outlet for his creative idealism in his operas. His obsession with the marriage was tempered by new opportunities for travel and interesting friendships. As Berg was away more and more, Helene, who seldom accompanied him, increasingly took refuge in running the house and in her studies of occult phenomena. It is perhaps no wonder that her frustration expressed itself in overbearing behaviour, nightmares, and other physical and nervous disorders. Although Berg's letters to Schoenberg usually express sympathy for Helene's frequent indispositions, in a letter of 13 September 1912 Berg hints at the disruption such problems caused to his work habits and his peace of mind:

> For how right you are in this, dear Herr Schoenberg, as in everything, everything, that one works best on walks—in the country, naturally—and the reason I didn't work for so long may have been because I didn't get out. Of course I also need great emotional peace and complete mental and physical equilibrium, which I found here—with the obvious exception of my wife's illness.[41]

The composer's nephew, Erich Alban Berg, goes so far as to suggest that Berg was henpecked: 'She dominated him. And he did everything that she wanted. He revenged himself through his amours.'[42]

Erich Alban Berg may well be correct that Berg involved himself with other women in order to avenge himself for his inferior place in the marriage or at least from a need to recover his male integrity. It is certainly well known that Berg had affairs with several women during the course of his marriage, the most notorious (but not the last) being Hanna Fuchs-Robettin, sister of the writer Franz Werfel. It does not follow necessarily from the existence of these affairs, however, that Berg was unhappy in the marriage. The spiritual connection between the two Bergs continued until his death, and beyond it for Helene, who perpetuated the inflated marital image through continued communication with Berg in dreams and through knocking in the bookcase. The physical bond seems also to have endured, as Berg implies in a letter to Helene of 22 February 1934: 'You should take delight in your dear body, just as I enjoy it with my own (far less dear) body.'[43] Helene's shrewd judgement that Berg required extra romantic involvements in order to feed his romantic fantasy may well be true.[44] Whatever the situation, the marriage appeared to suit Berg's character and his upbringing. Like his father, he married a strong woman who dominated him, but perhaps one with an understanding of his needs. On the negative side, her rigidity, especially about money, and her neurotic need for control and reassurance contributed to the difficulties of the marriage, causing Berg much pain, frustration, and, in the end, possibly his life.

This view is supported by Morgenstern in small details—the washing episode or Berg's imprisonment in his study. Helene's reluctance to allow Berg to spend money is graphically echoed by Erich Alban Berg, who describes how Berg often had to borrow money from his mother for necessities when his wife refused it to him.[45] In fact it seems that Berg, in order free himself for composition, doomed himself to a life of financial servitude to the women of his family. In his early years he subsisted on an allowance paid to him by his mother for services rendered in managing the family affairs. Later, although he earned his own money from teaching and performances (chiefly of *Wozzeck*), his wife controlled the purse strings and the illusion at least of financial dependence continued.

Most important was Helene's refusal, at the end of his life, to allow Berg to consult a physician recommended by Morgenstern. Berg was at this time suffering from a boil on his hip. Morgenstern relates that in December of 1935 he was at the Berg's for dinner. Berg, although suffering, seemed of good courage, and both told Morgenstern that the boil, which had already caused much trouble, would now heal. Helene had, as she explained, sterilized a pair of scissors in boiling water and herself opened and expressed the boil. When he had returned home Morgenstern frantically phoned a surgeon friend, Dr Kasper Blond, and informed him of this household operation. As he had feared, Dr Blond told him that this was most dangerous owing to the risk of blood poisoning. On the following day Morgenstern called Berg and told him that he had received the first copies of his novel. He asked if he could bring it to him right away as a pretext to see Berg in order to advise him to consult a doctor immediately. Berg was so pleased by this news that he wanted to go into the city directly in order to fetch the book himself. He had not been to the Café Museum in a long time, he said. They would both come there to afternoon coffee. Morgenstern then called Dr Blond and begged him to come to the Café Museum in order to meet the Bergs. The Bergs arrived punctually.

> Walking, one saw nothing unusual about Alban, but when it came to sitting, he moved ahead to take a seat on a hard chair, not on the sofa. He also sat sideways on the edge the entire time. ... He was immensely pleased with the book. 'That must be celebrated,' he said. I proposed to them to celebrate the evening of December 24, this time at my place. 'Gladly,' said Helene, and Alban added, 'If I can make it. As you see, sitting has become a problem for me.'

Morgenstern informed them that his friend Dr Blond was also in the coffee house and proposed that they hear his opinion and advice. Alban had nothing against it but Helene hesitated. Knowing that Helene was extremely careful with money, Morgenstern assured her that Dr Blond had long treated him and his friends without charge. Helene rejected the idea despite this generosity, saying that she had already consulted a doctor whom Alma Mahler had once recommended to her. Morgenstern was much distressed by Helene's insistence upon controlling a situation that was extremely dangerous and rapidly getting out of hand.

Within two days of this meeting Berg was taken to the Rudolfspital. Morgenstern read of it in the newspaper and went there to find Berg in a room for terminally ill patients. Berg asked him to return the next day, outside normal visiting hours so that they could enjoy a lengthy talk. When Morgenstern arrived, he had to wait to see Berg while a priest was with him. When the priest had left, Morgenstern entered the room; he reports that Berg said to him, 'That was such a nice man—I couldn't say no to him.'

That Berg accepted the last rites of the Catholic Church does not clarify the murky issue of Berg's religious attitudes as his motives for doing so remain unclear. Was Berg the sort of man who would take the last rites in order to please the priest? Would he say that he had done so from embarrassment? One thing at least seems clear: that Berg died as he lived—with courage, grace, and even humour.

In his eulogy for Berg, Morgenstern named five men who were the guiding stars of Berg's life: Peter Altenberg, Gustav Mahler, Karl Kraus, Adolf Loos, and Arnold Schoenberg. According to Morgenstern, Berg did not remove these stars to some distant heaven, but rather 'they were his house gods, and he lived in their presence so modestly that he never once became aware of how, under these his stars, he was a star of equal brilliance.'[46]

A composer's personality is of interest to scholars because of the insight into the compositional process that may be gained. Berg as a person gives the impression of charm and wit, but also of dependency and weakness. However, to consider these traits irreconcilable with the power of Berg's music is to ignore the underlying strength of his character. Berg was lazy but he possessed considerable intellectual energy, as evinced by his compulsive reading, his love of literary discussion, and his interest in intellectual trivia. As a composer, he wrote inconstantly, but when he worked, he worked with loving attention to detail. The sketches abound with careful planning and mathematical calculation of passage work minutiae, which almost certainly remain inaudible. Berg must have harboured resentment—hostility bred in his servile attachments. But he wisely chose opera libretti that allowed scope for his idealism, only to defeat that idealism by a sordid realism, almost as though he were acknowledging for himself the self-deception of his attitudes. It is that deeper self-knowledge, not evident on the surface of Berg's personal life, which gives his music its authority. In the end it seems that, in order to progress from the naïveté of his beginnings with Schoenberg to the complexity and sophistication of *Lulu*—a journey from uncertainty to the mastery of an authentic voice—Berg must have suffered considerable inner struggle.

Notes

1. Soma Morgenstern, 'Alban Berg und seine Idole' (unpublished).
2. Ibid. Unless otherwise stated, all quotations in this essay are from this unpublished memoir by Soma Morgenstern.
3. I am grateful to Soma Morgenstern's son Dr Dan Morgenstern for making this material available to me and to Professor George Perle for kindly putting me in touch with the Morgenstern family. I should also like to thank Dr Rosemary Moravec of the Austrian National Library for sending me copies of Morgenstern's correspondence on deposit there.
4. Much of the material from this study is published in Joan Allen Smith, *Schoenberg and His Circle: a Viennese Portrait* (New York: Schirmer, 1986).
5. The three volumes, all eventually published in English, are: *The Son of the Lost Son*, trans. Josef Leftwich and Peter Gross (Philadelphia: Jewish Publication Society of America, 1946), *In My Father's Pastures*, trans. Ludwig Lewisohn (Philadelphia: Jewish Publication Society of America, 1947); and *The Testament of the Lost Son*, trans. Jacob Sloan in collaboration with Maurice Samuel (Philadelphia: Jewish Publication Society of America, 1950).
6. Berg to Morgenstern, 13 September 1931.
7. Personal correspondence from Stefan Askenase, 27 July 1973.
8. Eugen Lehner, interview with author, Newton Center, Massachusetts, 2 June 1973.
9. Erna Gál, interview with author, London, 11 October 1973.
10. Berg obviously did not succeed in carrying out the promise made to Schoenberg in a letter of late November 1915: 'First of all: to achieve complete independence from my wife's family. To limit dependence on my mother to the support due to me as a result of my administrative work. No more involvement in family quarrels, complete withdrawal from gossip and the like.' Julianne Brand, Christopher Hailey, and Donald Harris, eds and trans., *The Berg–Schoenberg Correspondence: Selected Letters* (New York: W. W. Norton, 1987), p. 257. I am grateful to Ms Brand and Mr Hailey for allowing me to read the manuscript before publication.
11. Stefan Askenase describes Berg's interesting comparison of cooking with composing in Smith, op. cit., pp. 116–18.
12. Bruno Seidlhofer, interview with author, Vienna, 10 November 1973.
13. *Alban Berg: Letters to His Wife*, ed., trans., and annot. Bernard Grun (London: Faber and Faber, 1971), p. 36.
14. Letter of 20 August 1910, *Alban Berg: Letters to His Wife*, p. 112.
15. Berg to Schoenberg, 1 September 1928, Brand, Hailey, and Harris, op. cit., p. 373.
16. Bruno Seidlhofer, interview with author, Vienna, 10 November 1973.
17. For more on Berg's war views see Mark DeVoto, 'Berg and Pacifism', *International Alban Berg Society Newsletter*, no.2 (January 1971), pp. 9–11; Joan Allen Smith 'The Berg–Hohenberg Correspondence', *Alban Berg Symposion Wien 1980: Tagungsbericht*, ed. Rudolf Klein, Alban Berg Studien, vol. 2 (Vienna: Universal Edition, 1981) pp. 192–4.
18. *Alban Berg: Letters to His Wife*, p. 90.
19. Erich Alban Berg, interview with author, August 1986.
20. Berg's difficulties in school have been described in Rosemary Hilmar, *Alban Berg: Leben und Wirken in Wien bis zu seinen ersten Erfolgen als Komponist* (Vienna: Verlag Hermann Böhlaus Nachf., 1978) pp. 20–28. See also Joan Allen Smith, 'The Berg–Hohenberg Correspondence' pp. 189–91.
21. Stefan Askenase describes him as 'very *Gebildet*—of much knowledge', interview

with author, Munich, 5 November 1973. In the correspondence between Berg and Morgenstern, the equal nature of their literary discussion is apparent as Berg makes extensive sylistic comments on Morgenstern's literary efforts.

22. I am grateful to the Alban Berg Stiftung for permission to examine Berg's library and to Frau Adamiak of the Stiftung for her cheerful assistance.

23. Such pursuits were, of course, popular at the time. Berg and Schoenberg both professed interest in numerology, and extra-sensory perception was being investigated by psychologists.

24. *Gewittergoy* was a term in use in central-European theatre circles to refer to men who, even by their physique, exhibited an Aryan bravado. In Vienna of the 1920s, as in New York City today, it was common for non-Jews to use Jewish slang.

25. Hermann Watznauer, Biography of Berg, in Erich Alban Berg, *Der unverbesserliche Romantiker: Alban Berg 1885–1935*, (Vienna: Österreichischer Bundesverlag, 1985), pp. 10–11.

26. Ibid. pp. 12–13.

27. For more on the relationship with Waltznauer see Erich Alban Berg, op. cit.

28. Berg to Schoenberg, 9 July 1913, Brand, Hailey, and Harris, op. cit., p. 182.

29. See, for instance, letters of 28, 29, and 30 June 1921, *Alban Berg: Letters to His Wife*, pp. 289–92.

30. Berg to Schoenberg, 25 January 1933, Brand, Hailey, and Harris, op. cit., p. 439.

31. Berg to Schoenberg, 13 July 1926, ibid., p. 348.

32. Stefan Askenase, interview with author, Munich, 5 November 1973.

33. Felix Galimir, interview with author, New York, 28 March 1972.

34. 'Romantic', *Webster's New Collegiate Dictionary* (Springfield: G. & C. Merriam, 1977).

35. Letter of 24 February 1934, *Alban Berg: Letters to His Wife*, p. 416.

36. See, for example, George Perle, 'The Secret Program of the Lyric Suite', *International Alban Berg Society Newsletter*, no. 5 (June 1977), pp. 4–12.

37. *Alban Berg: Letters to His Wife*, p. 22.

38. Ibid., pp. 24–5.

39. Berg was plagued throughout his life by poor health. He suffered from asthma from an early age. This condition bothered him more in the country than in the city, but it was a life-long problem for him. He was for a time exempt from military service and was eventually confined to the position of a clerk. He suffered from boils long before the attack from which he died and he had serious problems with his teeth. On the other hand, Helene seems to have been obsessive about this and many other things. Berg rarely expresses his concern in an unsympathetic way, but the tone of a letter of 9 June 1927 (Berg, op. cit., pp. 355–6) suggests a growing impatience:

I racked my brains for hours on how I could free you from your madly exaggerated fears, these obsessions about the physical well-being of the few people who are near to you, above all myself. It's only these obsessions that force me to conceal things. If I tell you, for instance, that I took aspirin last night as a precaution (when travelling) you already picture me ending up as a morphine addict in Steinhof. And if, to stop me coughing, I take some harmless drops of codeine, you're afraid I'll die of tuberculosis in Alland. You have no real evidence that I'm iller, frailer, more nervy, thinner today than I was ten years or ten weeks ago. No ordinary doctor, specialist or psychiatrist finds anything which might be disturbing or not quite normal for my age. One can have a bit of bowel trouble even at eighteen. But you have these obsessions about my pegging out, and it's the same with all the other obsessions.

40. Letter of 2 May 1911, Berg, op. cit., p. 123.
41. Berg to Schoenberg, 13 September 1912, Brand, Hailey, and Harris, op. cit., p. 113.
42. Erich Alban Berg, interview with author, August 1986.
43. *Alban Berg: Letters to His Wife*, p. 414.
44. Helene Berg to Alma Mahler, 28 February 1936, George Perle, '"Mein geliebtes Almschi ...": Briefe von Alban und Helene Berg an Alma Mahler Werfel', *Österreichische Musikzeitschrift*, vol. 35 (1980), pp. 8–10.
45. Erich Alban Berg, interview with author, August 1986.
46. Soma Morgenstern, 'Im Trauerhaus', *23: Eine Wiener Musikzeitschrift*, nos 24–5 (1 February 1936), p. 16.

The Songs

BERG THE COMPOSER OF SONGS

MARK DEVOTO

Berg's Youth and Musical Training

'Two things emerged clearly even from Berg's earliest compositions, however awkward they may have been: first, that music was to him a language, and that he really expressed himself in that language; and secondly: overflowing warmth of feeling.' Thus wrote Arnold Schoenberg in 1936 in a memoir intended for, but not printed in, Willi Reich's 1937 memorial volume for Alban Berg.[1] And later, in 1949: 'when I saw the compositions he showed me—songs in a style between Hugo Wolf and Brahms—I recognized at once that he was a real talent.'[2]

Berg was 19 years old in the autumn of 1904 when he began to study with Schoenberg. His musical background was that of a passionate young amateur, in a music-loving household in one of the musical centres of Europe. Yet, aside from a few informal piano lessons, he had had no training of any kind in music, beyond what he could learn as a self-taught composer of songs. By contrast, his friend Anton Webern, who was two years older, but who began his studies with Schoenberg at about the same time, had had a thorough training in music theory and musicology and was an accomplished cellist. For all this inauspicious beginning, the pedagogical relationship turned out to be remarkably fruitful. Schoenberg began at an elementary level with his talented youngster, with voluminous exercises in 16th-century counterpoint, working up to more elaborate efforts in Bach style and classical forms, and finally to fully original works.

The influence of Schoenberg on Berg's life and work is one of the best-known facts about 20th-century music, and yet it is only relatively recently that the extent of this influence has begun to be fully measured. From the correspondence we are now learning that Schoenberg was, until Berg was 30 and even later, the most profound influence in his life. To Berg, Schoenberg was simultaneously a substitute father and Jewish mother, constantly stimulating

35

him to his best efforts and beyond, and constantly expressing a dissatisfaction which Berg endured good-naturedly but with inevitable frustration. From Schoenberg's own theoretical and pedagogical writings, especially his *Harmonielehre* (for which Berg prepared the index in 1911),[3] we get an idea of what an extraordinary teacher he must have been, and Berg's numerous surviving written assignments bear witness not only to the effort and rigour but also the inspired richness of the dialogue between them.[4] There are plenty of the usual type of short cantus firmus pieces in strict counterpoint; but also a number of longer stylistic exercises, choral motets, and chorale preludes in the style of the German Baroque; freely ranging choral pieces and unfinished piano pieces suggestive of Brahms; and instrumental arrangements of piano pieces.

Above all, it must be remembered that the period of Berg's studies with Schoenberg coincides with the years of Schoenberg's own most far-reaching musical evolution. In 1904, when Berg first came to him, Schoenberg was 30 years old, and had already composed *Gurrelieder* and *Pelleas und Melisande*, works which revealed him as a composer of great originality and incredible mastery of technique, but which nevertheless reflect the top-heavy post-Wagnerian grandiosity of their own time. In 1905 Schoenberg began moving in more radical directions, using the smaller instrumental dimensions of the string quartet and chamber orchestra, in an effort to explore the resources of progressively greater complexity in tonal chromaticism and in thematic density of cyclic symphonic forms. The thematic and contrapuntal intensity of Schoenberg's works of this period derives from his obsessive exploration of the possibilities of musical form, and this exploration dominated his works throughout his career. Schoenberg is often called an 'expressionist', and there is no doubt that, especially in his works that have a text, Schoenberg was concerned with achieving a maximum of expressive quality, even to the point of psychological distortion (*Pierrot lunaire, Erwartung, Die glückliche Hand*); yet one always feels that the expression, however strong, is only a logical by-product of the concern for formal integrity and for the utmost concentration of musical ideas.

Like a loving and dutiful son, Berg eagerly absorbed this compositional philosophy, but it reflected his own nature without any doubt, and could hardly fail to influence his own development. The effect on his works is plain enough. Berg's Piano Sonata (1908), for example, is marked by an extraordinary density of motives and themes, all continuously overlapped and combined into a unified, *Tristan*-like progression of events, with the normal outlines of the sonata form unmistakably present but blurred as much as possible. The models for such a tightly-knit, single-movement form are not the works of Brahms, who might have inspired Berg's Piano Variations or early songs, but Schoenberg's String Quartet no. 1 (1905) and Chamber Symphony no. 1 (1906).

Berg's Early Songs

By January 1910, a little more than five years after beginning his studies, Berg was hard at work on his Four Songs op. 2 and his String Quartet op. 3, and Schoenberg could take justifiable pride in the accomplishment of their work together, as we can tell from an impassioned letter to his publisher Hertzka:

> [Alban Berg] is an extraordinarily gifted composer. But the state he was in when he came to me was such that his imagination apparently could not work on anything but *Lieder*. Even the piano accompaniments to them were song-like in style. He was absolutely incapable of writing an instrumental movement or inventing an instrumental theme. You can hardly imagine the lengths I went to in order to remove this defect in his talent. As a rule teachers are absolutely incapable of doing this, because they do not even see where the problem lies, and the result is composers who can think only in terms of a single instrument ... I removed this defect and am convinced that in time Berg will actually become very good at instrumentation.[5]

From this testimony, one can hardly overlook the importance of songs in Berg's early efforts as a composer. Yet Berg himself published only eight of his 'early songs' during his own lifetime, the Seven Early Songs in 1928, and the C major setting of Theodor Storm's 'Schliesse mir die Augen beide' (composed in 1907) only in 1930.[6] By that time, five years before his death, Berg's worldwide reputation had been consolidated with orchestral and chamber works and the opera, *Wozzeck*. By contrast, and for different reasons, his dimension as a composer of songs does not seem to be very large, and yet it is fundamental to his personality nevertheless.

The extent of Berg's early efforts in song composition was hardly even suspected until H. F. Redlich published his Berg biography in 1957, with a tentative enumeration of the unpublished compositions in the possession of Berg's widow, Helene. The list included the titles and poets of some 70 *Jugendlieder*, with date attributions given to Redlich from Frau Berg's own listing.[7] Only one of these songs, 'An Leukon', to a text by Johann Ludwig Gleim, had been published, in Reich's 1937 memorial volume.[8] Very little else about these earliest songs was revealed in the next few years, although a few individual manuscripts came on to the market, with photographs in auction catalogues. These autographs were apparently duplicate copies made by Berg himself, and some by his friend Hermann Watznauer, which Berg had given to friends. Several manuscript songs were donated to the Library of Congress by Frida Semler Seabury, an American who had spent two summers as a guest with the Berg family when she and Berg were in their late teens, and who had written the text for one of Berg's settings ('Traum').[9] Several others turned up with a batch of letters saved by Berg's boyhood friend, Paul Hohenberg, who later emigrated to America;[10] Hohenberg supplied the text for 'Sommertage', which Berg later published as the last of the Seven Early Songs.

An extensive survey of the *Jugendlieder* was undertaken by Nicholas Chadwick for his doctoral dissertation of 1971, with Frau Berg's permission. In an article published the same year, with excerpts from a number of these earliest songs, Chadwick gave a new chronology based on Frau Berg's own index.[11] Rosemary Hilmar's catalogue, published in 1980, provides the most authoritative listing so far, including a partially chronological ordering by Berg himself with opus numbers up to 'op. 16, no. 3' (these numbers of course were later superseded by those of Berg's published works), and some 15 photographs of selected autograph pages of various songs.[12] In 1985 Dietrich Fischer-Dieskau's recording of some 22 unpublished early songs was issued by EMI,[13] and in 1986 and 1987 two volumes of 46 selected songs, edited by Christopher Hailey, were published by Universal Edition.[14]

The most striking characteristic of the recently revealed early songs is that they are better pieces than we might have expected. They show a good deal of youthful ingenuity and imagination, some technical defects notwithstanding; most of all, Berg's songs reveal a charm and naïve gracefulness that are completely lacking in the earliest songs of his friend Webern, or in Schoenberg's contemporaneous *Brettl-Lieder* (cabaret songs), works which their composers also did not choose to publish.

'Ferne Lieder', 'op. 6, no. 3', is typical of the earliest songs; Hilmar's chronology ascribes it to 1903.[15] Its graphic style alone reveals something about Berg's musical knowledge at age 18. It shows some sophistication in the placement of stems and beams, as though Berg had studied piano music closely from this standpoint; yet the key signature is incorrectly laid out (the E♭ to the left of the B♭), and the time signature, with one exception, appears on every system. The music itself is harmonically and expressively conventional, and although sensitive, it shows nothing markedly original or subtle. Another song, 'Vielgeliebte, schöne Frau', 'op. 5, no. 1', ascribed by Hilmar to the autumn of 1902, is musically better, although Berg may have had Mahler's 'Wenn mein Schatz' from *Lieder eines fahrenden Gesellen* in the back of his mind, as well as the 'Garden' melody from Goldmark's 'Rustic Wedding' Symphony.[16] No graphic peculiarities are present in this song, and if the putative chronology is correct, this may be a later copy than 1903.

One supposes that it is the abundant doubling of the vocal line, particularly in the uppermost part, that provoked Schoenberg's remark that 'even the piano accompaniments [to Berg's early songs] were song-like in style.' This is a characteristic of many of the earlier German song composers, including Schubert and Schumann, some of whose finest songs might be perfectly acceptable as piano pieces if the vocal part were omitted. The 18-year-old Berg is hardly different from his older predecessors in this regard. The evolution of *Lied* style during the later 19th century, however, had brought about the possibility of an almost total independence of the voice from the piano accompaniment, so that the vocal line and the piano accompaniment evolved into a kind of partnership like chamber music, in which all kinds of declamatory style, even approaching operatic declamation, became possible for the modest medium of the solo song. The songs of Gustav Mahler and Hugo Wolf were the most obvious contemporary models for what Berg would aspire to, and it was doubtless in the direction of these that Schoenberg wished to steer his pupil.

The Seven Early Songs (1905–8; published 1928)

We can get an idea of the transformation of Berg's technique when we observe the evolution from the earliest songs to a more advanced work, the song 'Die Nachtigall', which is no. 3 of the Seven Early Songs. According to Redlich, this song was composed in the winter of 1905–6, but is certainly no later than '1.12.07', the date given on a fair copy made by Watznauer. Watznauer's copy differs in many small details but in no substantial ways from the version of the 1928 published score, and thus provides a good example of what Berg could do after only two or three years of study with Schoenberg. The smooth accompaniment in the outer sections of a simple da capo form is woven entirely in deft juxtapositions and transformations of a single motive, supported at most of the downbeats by a single bass note. That the motive is mostly triadic in structure does not prevent its being ingeniously bent, echoed, and overlapped in a continuously moving texture that effectively complements the expressive vocal line (Example 1).

'Im Zimmer', dating supposedly from the summer of 1905, is the earliest of the Seven Early Songs, and like 'Die Nachtigall' it employs only a limited chromaticism; its tonal ambiguity, hovering between G minor and B♭ major, derives from a subtle use of irregular resolutions of secondary dominants. All of the other songs in the group are later, dating probably from the summer of 1906 to early 1908 (although one manuscript copy dated by Berg does suggest, not entirely convincingly, that they all date from 1907), and their tonal chromaticism is much richer. In 'Traumgekrönt' of the summer of 1907, there is no stable tonality comparable to that of 'Die Nachtigall'. The key signature of two flats is indicative of G minor, but this is only faintly suggested near the beginning, and is confirmed only by G major (as a Picardy third) at the end; the very first phrase begins with an augmented 6–4–3 chord and an irregular resolution which tonicizes E♭ major. The form of the song as a whole is very simple, strophic in two verses of two paired phrases each. The texture is dominated by the four-note motive that begins the accompaniment. The subtle charm of the tonal chromaticism is partly accounted for by the surprises of the irregular resolutions, but these in turn are assisted by the abundance of chromatic passing notes and suspensions which seem to form part of the harmony itself. Such a harmonic idiom is typical of the contrapuntally-generated chromaticism which gathered such momentum in the 19th century, especially after Wagner. Like much of *Parsifal*, or Bruckner's later symphonies, or Wolf's more anguished songs, Berg's early chromatic harmony is characteristically rich in harmonic progressions that are only vaguely related tonally, but which are strongly connected by stepwise relationships and common tones. This contrapuntal habit is a general phenomenon which I shall

Ex. 1 Seven Early Songs, III (1907 version), bars 7–15

call 'creeping', a convenient designation which has ample applicability to Berg's harmony.[17]

An early instance of extended creeping in Berg's harmony is the passage in Example 2, from 'Geliebte Schöne', from 1904 or 1905, cited by Chadwick. This kind of harmony is typical of the 'hovering tonality' of passages in works such as Liszt's First Mephisto Waltz or Chopin's E minor Prelude, involving differential chromatic descent of the bass against suspensions in the other voices, resolved or unresolved, producing root successions that are usually only distantly related. The most likely models for this kind of harmony, however, are Hugo Wolf's songs, with their frequent and intense modulating chromaticism in relatively short musical spaces.

A particularly apt illustration of creeping is afforded by Example 3, a passage from Berg's 'Schilflied', the second of the Seven Early Songs. The example is drawn from an early manuscript by a copyist, probably dating from no later than

Ex. 2 *Geliebte Schöne*, bars 28–39

1911; a comparison of this passage with the 1928 published piano score will show that Berg's later alterations are insubstantial. This is an illustration of symmetrical creeping with two voices moving chromatically in contrary motion, as the reduction of the outer parts shows; this 'chromatic wedge' was a device that Berg especially loved and which can be found in nearly all of his works.

The most spectacular of the Seven Early Songs is No. 1, 'Nacht'. The whole-tone harmony at the beginning and end is very striking, but it is completely at home with the expressive chromaticism and strong diatonic cadences which dominate the harmony of the remainder of the song. A passage like that shown in Example 4 shows how effectively the whole-tone scale can be accommodated by a series of strongly tonal progressions.

The overall form of 'Nacht' is a *Bogenform*, more complex than that of 'Die Nachtigall', with a varied da capo in the outer sections and an inner section rather like two strophes. Berg showed a remarkable fondness for the *Bogenform*

Ex. 3 Seven Early Songs, II (1908 version), bars 9–12

Ex. 4 Seven Early Songs, I, bars 19–20

principle in nearly all of his subsequent works, including extensive and literal palindromes in several of them. The symmetry of the outer sections of 'Nacht' is especially elegant, with the opening vocal line answered in the reprise by its own melodic inversion (Example 5).

Ex. 5 Seven Early Songs, I, voice only, (a) bars 2–3, (b) bars 27–8

This early instance of Berg's melodic symmetry is no different from the independent thematic inversions of Brahms and Bruckner, or for that matter from the inverted themes found often in Bach's binary forms. Berg would later develop it as a basic premise of his thematic technique, particularly in his twelve-note works, in which prime and inversion forms, and only these forms, generate the serial substance on an approximately equal basis.

Four Songs op. 2 (1909–10)

Berg's first published work was his Piano Sonata, which he had printed at his own expense in 1910 as op. 1. The best evidence suggests that Berg worked on this under Schoenberg's guidance in late 1908 or early 1909, after the latest of the Seven Early Songs. One supposes that Berg would not have attempted to publish the Sonata if Schoenberg had not approved of its publication, and from this one infers that Berg had finally achieved what Schoenberg had aimed for with him—the ability to compose an instrumental work in an extended form on a large scale with a concentrated thematic process: in other words, the antithesis of the *Lied*. Soon he would embark on an even larger instrumental conception, his String Quartet op. 3, completed in 1910, the culminating work of his period of actual study with Schoenberg. When Berg began writing it is not known precisely, but there is some indirect evidence in his sketchbooks that he may have worked on the Quartet at approximately the same time as the Four Songs op. 2, on texts by Hebbel and Mombert, published along with the Piano Sonata in 1910. Clearly Berg was not yet fully ready to stop writing songs in order to work exclusively on larger forms. It is in the Four Songs that Berg weathered his crisis of chromatic tonality, as Schoenberg and Webern had done before him.

In the first song, 'Schlafen, schlafen', Berg provides a key signature of D minor, but this key is established by nothing stronger than a gradually dissolving D minor triad at the beginning and a gradually crystallizing D minor triad at the end, a tonal *Bogenform*. The harmony in between is dominated by extensive creeping, especially with stepwise chromatic motion throughout much of the bass line, but some characteristic chord forms are present, including appoggiatura 13th chords such as Ravel used in *Gaspard de la nuit*, and a climactic chord of five superposed perfect fourths such as Schoenberg used in his Chamber Symphony no. 1 (although Berg had employed this same kind of quartal harmony in his Piano Sonata).

The remaining three songs comprise a trio of texts from *Der Glühende* of Alfred Mombert. The second and third songs, 'Schlafend trägt man mich in mein Heimatland' and 'Nun ich der Riesen Stärksten überwand', form a tonally associated pair (Eb minor and Ab minor) joined by fermata. The second song is even more symmetrical than the first, with its unusual sequence of root-position French sixth chords at beginning and end, mirroring the 'Heimatland' reference in the text. The sequence maps the ascending circle of fourths with the descending chromatic scale; every French sixth chord in the sequence, of course, maps with the whole-tone scale. The combination of interval cycles fits well with the principal structural motive, a three-note cell of ascending minor sixth and descending semitone. The *Bogenform* symmetry of the third song, 'Nun ich der Riesen Stärksten überwand', is hardly prominent, but it does include the same melody at beginning and end in the accompaniment (Example 6(a)), a melody with a family resemblance to a theme in the Piano Sonata (Example 6(b)), which had been adumbrated in an earlier incomplete sketch for 'Sonata no. 3' (Example 6(c)).[18]

The Ab minor harmony of the third song has a certain resemblance to the 'Hagens Wacht' music in Act I of *Götterdämmerung*, but is much more restless and unstable; the centrepiece of the song is a harmony tritonally opposite to Ab, a D minor triad with added superior major sixth degree, supporting 'tolling bells'.[19]

The fourth song, 'Warm die Lüfte', is the largest of the four in scope and declamation; it is about as long as the first song, forming with it a dimensional *Bogenform* that brackets the shorter songs in between. Berg's song follows Mombert's poem very closely in its expressive moods. Instead of an overall cohesive form there is an impressionistic atmosphere unifying the several recitative-like dramatic episodes; the song might almost be regarded as a miniature early-springtime version of Schoenberg's *Erwartung* (1909).

'Warm die Lüfte' is widely held in the published literature to be Berg's first unequivocal essay in atonality, heralded by the elimination of a key signature. Like Schoenberg's setting of 'Entrückung' in the last movement of his String Quartet no. 2 (1908), the first of his works in which atonality is fully evident, this song by Berg has unmistakable vestiges of tonality. The harmony at the beginning of the song is very peculiar, with a strongly tonicizing open fifth C–G in the bass, the C also doubled in the top voice, and what could be heard as a Db major triad in the inner parts, with various neighbour notes; this is not an atonal sonority but a dissonant one strongly suggesting C minor. The bars that follow provide differentially creeping layers of parallel minor sevenths suggesting mixed incomplete dominants, culminating in bar 5 with a stationary sonority

Ex. 6 (a) Four Songs, III, bars 1–2, (b) Piano Sonata, bars 26–7, (c) from 'Sonata no. 3'

(a)

(b)

(c)

Reprinted by permission of Robert Lienau, Berlin

supported by the C–G fifth once again in the bass. It is not that this kind of harmony is strongly tonal in any classical sense; rather it is *paratonal*, tending to attract the ear to a tone-centre by repetition of a particular note and by the prominence of strongly tonal intervals.

It is this kind of tone-centring or paratonal harmony that above all distinguishes Berg's mature music from that of Schoenberg and Webern. In most cases the latter composers intentionally avoided any kind of harmonies or textures that would give prominence to intervals that could be identified triadically. By contrast, Berg's music very often stresses precisely the perception of harmony that can in some way be associated with the classical tonal vocabulary, even to the point of making this harmony a part of the fundamental structure; relatively seldom does his music submerge a paratonal perception in overpowering chromaticism or complex texture.

In the middle section of the song, the harmony is generated by a complex of wedges. As the reduction in Example 7 shows, the right-hand wedge contains two stationary elements, the F♯ and middle C, alternating with other chordal elements which are placed a semitone higher at each subsequent repetition. This kind of wedge might be called *incremental expansion*, progressive expansion of intervals measured from one or more fixed notes.

Ex. 7 Four Songs, IV, bars 12–15, reduction of main progressions in piano

Reprinted by permission of Robert Lienau, Berlin

The expansion leads the vocal line to chromatically successive higher points, up to the climactic G♯ in bar 16. Before this point, the piano has burst out of the systematic wedge in as graphically explicit a manner as possible, with a simultaneous black- and white-key glissando in opposite directions.[20] The culminating chord in the piano part is framed by C in the bass, which connects to the opening measures and to the initiating dyad of the wedge section beginning in bar 11, and B♭ in the uppermost part, which then tumbles down to the bottom register of the piano at bar 18.

The final section begins with a harmonic sequence of appoggiatura 13ths which became a favourite of jazz composers in later decades. It matches a chromatically descending layer with the ascending cycle of perfect fourths, quite similar to the beginning of the second song.[21]

Background to the Altenberg Songs op. 4 (1912)

In the autumn of 1910 Arnold Schoenberg, after years of increasing bitterness about his economic and artistic situation, left Vienna for Berlin in search of better opportunities as a composer and teacher.[22] Berg and Webern, at considerable trouble to themselves, were pressed into service to help Schoenberg pack up his household goods for shipping; later they would be drafted to canvass well-known patrons of music in Vienna in order to establish a fund for Schoenberg's support. Schoenberg's situation did eventually improve in Berlin. Berg was deeply distressed to lose the face-to-face friendship of his teacher whom he had seen almost daily for six years; at the same time, he was ready to assume the independent control not only of his own life but also of his own musical development.

On 24 April 1911, Berg heard the first performance of his Piano Sonata and his String Quartet. He was 26 years old. A little more than a week later, on 3 May, he married Helene Nahowski, whom he had been courting for several years. The couple settled in Vienna the following autumn, not far from the Schönbrunn Palace, at Trauttmansdorffgasse 27 in the Hietzing district, which was to be their home for the rest of their lives.

Berg had obtained a job with Universal Edition; it did not pay much, but it allowed him to work in his own time at home, and it kept him in contact with the music he loved. His first tasks included preparing the piano-vocal score of Franz Schreker's opera *Der ferne Klang* and proofreading and preparing the index for Schoenberg's *Harmonielehre*, which went to press in the spring of 1911. At about this time Berg also began to teach, taking on a few private pupils.

After a lapse of some years, Schoenberg took up work again on the enormous orchestral score of *Gurrelieder*, which he had fully composed in 1901 but had orchestrated only up to the beginning of Part III. A full year before finishing the remaining 60 pages of full score (dated 7 November 1911 on the last page), he asked Berg to begin preparing a piano reduction, and obtained some money from Universal to pay him for the huge task. Berg worked hard on the reduction, which occupied him, along with corrections to the full score, well into the summer of 1912. By that time it was clear that *Gurrelieder* would be performed, perhaps by the late autumn, and Berg's assistance in the huge project would be needed more than ever.

The year 1912 was a busy and important year for music. Schoenberg wrote *Pierrot lunaire*, one of his most radical and perfectly conceived works, during the spring and early summer, while a few hundred miles away in Switzerland Igor Stravinsky was working on *The Rite of Spring*. Spending part of the summer in the country, Berg managed to find enough time to write his first orchestral work, which he called Five Orchestral Songs on Picture-Postcard Texts of Peter

Altenberg, op. 4. This work would turn out to be Berg's greatest achievement in song form, and yet its troubled history doomed it to near-oblivion for nearly 40 years, and even today it has not achieved the full recognition it deserves.

In his choice of texts Berg was already signalling the unusual. Altenberg (1859–1919), whose real name was Richard Engländer, was an eccentric poet, a sort of Viennese Erik Satie in verse, who during his lifetime enjoyed an underground reputation that has not diminished to this day. He was a close friend of both Berg and his wife Helene; Altenberg's collection entitled *Neues Altes* (Something New, Something Old) includes poems dedicated to 'H. N.', works that predate Helene's marriage to Berg. Known affectionately as the 'Socrates of the coffee house', Altenberg enjoyed writing short, epigrammatic, and sometimes scurrilous poems in blank verse on picture postcards, which he sent to his friends. It was five of these poems that Berg chose to set as songs.

It is likely that the immediate impulse for writing an orchestral song cycle came from Berg's experience of hearing the première on 20 November 1911 of Mahler's *Das Lied von der Erde*, under Bruno Walter's direction; Berg was so deeply affected by the work that he wrote to his wife about it twice in the same day while he was returning on the train. (Several pages of Berg's notes on the final song, 'Der Abschied'—whether Berg was writing down his own aural impressions at the performance, or whether he was studying the printed score, is not known—turn up in the middle of a sketchbook for the Altenberg Songs.) But Berg was obviously eager to test his hard-won skills by writing an orchestral work of some size. Coming only two years after the last work of his apprenticeship, the String Quartet, Berg's Altenberg Songs are about as striking a declaration of independence from his teacher as could be imagined—a fact that was unlikely to be, and indeed turned out not to be, entirely pleasing to Schoenberg. For Berg's first attempt at writing for orchestra is as fully forceful, though on a smaller scale, as Schoenberg's had been ten years earlier in *Gurrelieder*, a work that understandably shows a clear influence on Berg's songs. And certainly the Altenberg Songs display a range of expressiveness, from the subtlest to the most explosive, that is fully worthy of comparison with any other music of the time. Beyond these obvious aspects, the Altenberg Songs demonstrate a variety of structural levels that are not only deep and comprehensive, but are also remarkable adumbrations of his own future technique as well as that of his mentor, even when their evolution from Schoenberg is plain.

The larger outlines of the Altenberg Songs, including the intensive use of *Bogenformen* and of cyclic themes, are the most obvious legacies from Schoenberg's *Gurrelieder*, no less than the orchestral prelude, with its polymotivic, almost impressionistic orchestral texture. In his Analytical Guide to *Gurrelieder*, prepared only a short time before the première, Berg repeatedly draws attention to these unifying devices. [23]

Another remarkable aspect of the work is that Berg managed to conceive and realize the songs in all completeness during that hectic summer. The immense amount of activity notwithstanding—Berg's letters to Schoenberg are strewn with comments and questions about the *Gurrelieder* work above all—the summer was especially fortunate for Berg's peace of mind as a composer. As usual, his personal concerns were more clearly revealed in his letters to Anton Webern than in those to his redoubtable master, and he wrote to Webern several times about his own pleasure in composing the songs. No evidence has come to light, however, that Berg was particularly excited about or even aware of the profound artistic significance of what he had accomplished, nor is there any evidence that Webern, to whom Berg showed two of the songs, or Schoenberg, who later received the whole cycle, understood them well, either at first or later on. By the middle of September, Berg was back in Vienna hard at work on the preparations for the coming première of the *Gurrelieder*, and everything else, including the Altenberg Songs, had to be put aside for a while.

Nevertheless, by 6–7 October 1912, Berg could write to Schoenberg, along with a mass of other information in a 16-page letter, that all of the orchestral songs were finished. When he sent them to Schoenberg is not known, but it must have been by early January 1913, when Schoenberg offered to conduct two of the songs at a concert then being planned for late March under the sponsorship of the Akademischer Verband für Literatur und Musik, for which Berg was one of the planners. Berg was overjoyed, and wrote to Schoenberg on 9 January that even though conceived as a cycle, the songs could be performed individually. That estimation was hardly the voice of Berg's considered judgement, but rather his habitual deference to his teacher's wishes, whatever their merits might be. Schoenberg, for his part, sounded a sour note in his letter to Berg of 14 January:

> Above all they seem to be ... remarkably good, and beautifully scored. There is one thing, though, that I find disconcerting: the rather too overt striving to employ new techniques [*neue Mittel*]. Perhaps I will learn to understand better how these techniques connect organically with expressive necessity. But right now they bother me.

Berg responded on 17 January:

> How happy you have made me by your statement that my songs are not all bad, especially concerning their orchestration. When I think of all the unsuccessful first orchestral works [that are written] I was afraid to have made a mistake in every measure. Even the contrary opinion of Webern could not relieve me (he had seen only two of the songs). Only your valuable comments. ... I would like to take advantage of this occasion to say a word about the new techniques whose use frequently displeased me when afterwards I noticed them accumulated one upon another in such great number. When I was composing they followed each other quite naturally. Only afterwards did I realize that I may have given the impression of being pretentious. ... For a short time only have I truly understood the sounds of the orchestra, and only for a short time, equally, have I understood recent compositions. Since it is always the most recent

compositions which I look at, that is, those of the last few years, I instinctively feel those new sonorities which are produced by these new techniques.[24]

Berg was at this time carrying much of the *Gurrelieder* responsibilities on his own shoulders, not the least of which was that of acting as Schoenberg's personal agent, receiving regular instructions by mail. Too late to appease Schoenberg, the Vienna Academy had offered him a professorship; he remained in Berlin, satisfied with conditions there, and was content to allow the ever-willing Berg to handle the arduous task of ensuring that the *Gurrelieder* performance would be up to the highest standards. Berg corrected orchestral parts and supervised rehearsals of the choruses; this was probably the only time in his life that he did any conducting.[25] He also took the time to prepare the Analytical Guide to *Gurrelieder* along with everything else, writing it in a great hurry during December and January. (The Guide was set and printed, 100 pages with 129 engraved examples, in apparently not more than two weeks.) After many difficulties and a postponement, the première of *Gurrelieder* at last took place in Vienna on 23 February 1913 under the direction of Franz Schreker, and was a tremendous success.

It was not enough of a success to persuade Schoenberg to move back to Vienna, for he still rankled over his years of maltreatment by the Viennese musical establishment. But he did return a month later to direct the promised special orchestral concert in the Grosser Saal of the Musikverein. The programme included Schoenberg's Chamber Symphony no. 1; orchestral songs by Alexander von Zemlinsky; the première of Webern's Six Pieces op. 6, for large orchestra; and two of Berg's newly completed Altenberg Songs.

Because of difficulties with a copyist, Berg had not been able to obtain orchestral parts for the complete cycle of five songs, and had had to copy out some of them himself. Because of this, and because, apparently from the start, Schoenberg had not contemplated a complete performance of the cycle, in the end only the second and third songs were actually programmed. A fine opportunity was thus lost. The large orchestra of the Wiener Konzertverein had been hired by the Akademischer Verband for the performance of Webern's Six Pieces, and it was this work that Schoenberg wanted above all to perform. The choice of a singer for Berg's songs was also troublesome. Marya Freund, preferred by both Berg and Schoenberg, was not pleased by the songs she had seen in score, and despite Schoenberg's entreaties she declined to sing them. After another singer proved unsuitable, Berg settled on the tenor Alfred Boruttau, who had sung the part of Klaus the Fool in the *Gurrelieder* première; but clearly Berg was not delighted. It was under these handicaps that Berg, eager nonetheless to hear his first orchestral music played, brought his work before a Viennese public that turned out, true to form, to be thoroughly hostile.

The concert precipitated a scandal comparable to that of the Paris performances of Wagner's *Tannhäuser* in 1861, a portion of the audience being armed in advance with whistles and doorkeys. The audience was peaceable enough during the performance of Zemlinsky's Maeterlinck Songs, but became restive and noisy during the Schoenberg and Webern works. During Berg's songs, which came fairly late in the programme, the audience, reacting probably as much to Altenberg's derisive texts and exotic punctuation as to the finely textured music, lost all restraint. Shouting and whistling drowned out the music, fistfights broke out, and the musicians left the stage; after a time, police were called in to restore order. The final work on the programme, Mahler's *Kindertotenlieder*, could not be performed.

The incident was widely reported in the European press as a disgraceful exhibition of avant-garde excesses, with the Vienna papers the most antagonistic of all. A particularly nasty piece in *Die Zeit* went so far as to suggest that Schoenberg had been compelled, against his own wishes and better nature, to perform Berg's and Webern's works, because these 'well-to-do' (*wohlhabend*) pupils had supported him financially for so long![26] Berg angrily demanded a retraction of this absurd slander, but without success. Things had more or less died down when a court hearing was held and several of the participants in the mêlée were fined, including Berg's friend Erhard Buschbeck, head of the Akademischer Verband, who had to pay a hundred crowns.

The effect of the catastrophe on Berg himself was more extensive. Far from being elated at the prospect of a *succès de scandale*, as was Stravinsky at a much more famous première two months later, Berg was devastated by the public's reaction to his songs. 'The whole thing is so loathsome that one would like to fly far away', he wrote shortly afterward to Webern, who had been in the thick of the fracas.[27]

But what had really hurt Berg was Schoenberg's opinion of the songs. Schoenberg's part in the aftermath of the disaster is still not clear; but two months later, when Berg visited him in Berlin, the meeting proved a shattering experience for Berg. Schoenberg apparently took his pupil heavily to task about the songs, saying that the extreme brevity of some of them was contrary to Berg's expressive nature, and that Berg would do better to work on longer and more developed pieces. Berg's letter to Schoenberg dated 14 June (shortly after their meeting) is a painful confession of self-doubt.[28] Yet he was not quite ready to work in the direction which Schoenberg demanded; between then and the early spring of 1914, Berg worked on several different things, with some apparent frustration, and completed only one work, the relatively brief Four Pieces op. 5, for clarinet and piano.

Unassertive by nature and inexperienced in dealing with public hostility, and especially sensitive to the reproaches of his teacher, Berg never again tried to get the Altenberg Songs performed. On 20 July 1914 he was hard at work on the Three Orchestral Pieces, op. 6, the largest work he had yet composed; still full of uncertainties about his music (and, one may suppose, about the future of Europe, which was soon to explode in war), he wrote to Schoenberg:

> I'm always having to ask myself whether what I'm expressing there [in the

> Three Orchestral Pieces] ... is any better than the last things I wrote. And how
> could I judge this? *Those* I hate—to the extent that I have already been on the
> verge of destroying them—and about these I have no opinion still, because I'm
> stuck right in the middle of them.[29]

This forms an interesting contrast with the more reassuring letter he had written
on 11 July, nine days earlier, to his wife:

> And the Altenberg Songs were after all written for you. If you had heard them
> sung properly and all together—in less disturbing circumstances! I believe you
> would enjoy them, even the ones you disliked sung out of context and rather
> murdered by Boruttau.[30]

In 1916 Berg arranged the fifth song for a *Hausmusik* of piano, violin, cello,
and harmonium, and gave a presentation copy of the arrangement to Alma and
Anna Mahler; no voice part is included, but the text is written in.[31] This
arrangement probably served as the basis for a careful piano-vocal score of the
fifth song which Berg published in 1921 as a supplement in a Dresden periodical,
Menschen.[32] No further performances are known until shortly after Berg's death,
when some of the songs were performed with piano accompaniment at a
memorial concert; a complete performance with orchestra seems not to have
occurred until 1952.

The Structure of the Altenberg Songs

We still do not know very much about the specific circumstances of how Berg
composed the songs; no dated manuscripts are known, and the available
sketches are incomplete. One clue comes from Berg's letter of 5 August, 1912 to
Webern: 'My third song is a big one; it is 2–3 times as long as the other two which
you already know. The fourth one is shorter than all three.'[33] The song that is
'shorter than all three' can only be the one now known as the second song, 'Sahst
du nach dem Gewitterregen'. The 'other two' are presumably the present third
song, 'Über die Grenzen des All', and the fourth song, 'Nichts ist gekommen';
while the 'big one' has to be either the first song, 'Seele, wie bist due schöner', or
the fifth song, 'Hier ist Friede!'. This apparent order of composition suggests
very strongly that Berg only gradually evolved a completely symmetrical formal
conception of the cycle.[34]

The *Bogenform* symmetry is demonstrated in microcosm by the tightness of
formal construction of the second song in only eleven bars. The bulk of
accompanimental material evolves from a single basic cell of major third plus
opposite semitone, or the reverse of these two intervals. The cell ascends in
overlapping statements beginning in bar 3, stabilizing in bar 5, and reaching a
climax in bars 6–7, and descending in reverse for the remainder of the song. The
symmetry is underscored by the initial and final F octaves of the

accompaniment, relating paratonally to the F minor ninth sonority in the middle of the song. The vocal line does not share in much of this motivic process, but the progression of its pitches is intimately connected with the accompaniment, down to the close canon with the bass in the final phrase.

The symmetrical conception is hardly less striking in the third and fourth songs. The third song, the middle of the cycle of five, has a textual symmetry as well, with essentially the same line of text at beginning and end; this is underlined by the same twelve-note chord, in twelve different changing wind instruments at the beginning (the composer Josef Bohuslav Foerster, hearing the abortive première, described this in his memoirs as 'an inimitably dissonant piling-up of sounds')[35] and two octaves higher in string harmonics at the end, with the same melody in the vocal line. The fourth song, the most motivically primitive of the five, is dominated by a chromatically creeping harmony in a thin texture mostly in a high register, but it does nail down the beginning and end with the identical ascending semitone in the flute. It is likely that this song was actually the first that Berg composed in the cycle, before he had formed any broader conception of its overall structural unity.

It is in the two big songs, the first and fifth, that Berg's remarkable sense of formal symmetry is realized in full force. These two songs are vastly different in their larger conception, and yet they are based to a great extent on the same motivic materials, which indeed account for much the largest part of their musical substance. Both are worth a close examination and comparison.

Ex. 8 Altenberg Songs, I, bars 1–2

The first song begins with an impressionistically scored orchestral prelude, a curtain-raiser much like that of Schoenberg's *Gurrelieder*, with a long and gradual crescendo. It is an overlapping, polymetric tapestry of six different motives (Example 8), of which one, designated I in the example, is the most prominent even in *ppp*. With six different metric lengths, this gamelan-like assembly would not come out together again until 158½ bars later. The texture is sustained without change through five bars, or four literal statements of I. Thereafter the entire texture gradually moves upward toward a climax at bars 14–15, with a remarkable series of internal transformations. These transformations chiefly involve the pitch structure of the constituent motives, with nearly every pitch attributable to some identifiable transformational process. Some of the motives move up semitonally, though not at the same speed (II,VI); one motive, III, moves up by an expanding interval cycle, first a semitone, then a whole step, then a minor third, major third, etc., to a settling point (flutes and second violins, bars 12–14). The complex figure IV in the celesta, echoed by harp, transforms rapidly until in bar 9 it becomes an entirely new motive, α, which later achieves stature as a cyclic theme (it reappears as a tiny 'afterthought' in bar 6 of the second song, and is one of the three passacaglia themes of the fifth song).

The treble motive I, as the superior element of the texture and the most intensely scored (piccolo, clarinet, glockenspiel, xylophone, and a 'ghost' of half the first violins), tends to define a paratonal pitch level which may be called a 'compound tone centre', to use George Perle's phrase, with the pitch class G the focusing pitch of the five. The transformations of I begin with its semitonal transposition, followed by gradual internal alteration, and eventually settling on three and then two pitches (E and C♯). If we assume that the integrity of the motive is marked by its initial pitch, then the transformations of I are outlined by the successive states of this first pitch: G, then A♭, then B♭, then C♯, finally E. These five pitch classes themselves constitute a new and independent cyclic motive, β, the most important motive in the entire cycle (Example 9).

Ex. 9

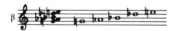

The motivic tapestry just described serves as accompaniment to another important cyclic motive, the expansive theme, δ, which begins in the violas at bar 9. Berg's introduction of this melody is a good illustration of his fondness for incremental repetitions. If these are disregarded, however, the melody is seen to contain precisely twelve different pitch classes. The order numbers are given in Example 10, showing also the overlap, at the climax of the prelude, with motive I.

The climax is also a settling point for all of the accompanimental figures. These achieve harmonic stability by the second half of bar 14. Disregarding the

Ex. 10 Altenberg Songs, I, bars 9–15

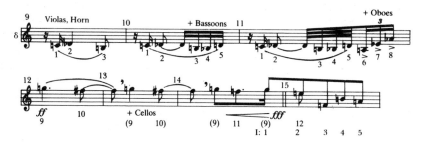

melody δ and all its instrumental doubling, one sees the accompanimental harmony at this point as consisting of just five pitch classes, G, A♭, B♭, D♭, and E (Example 11). These are identical in content with the melodic motive β given above.

Ex. 11 Altenberg Songs, I, bars 14–15, harmonies

The upward-moving crescendo culminates at the downbeat of bar 15 with a complete transformation. The final pitch of δ is also the second pitch of I, as we have already noted. The harmonic basis of the accompaniment now becomes an entirely different pentachord, γ, which is related by semitonal creeping of the four upper pitches upward, and the bottom downward, very much like something arrived at by experimenting with the right hand on the piano keyboard, the thumb moving opposite to the other fingers.

The orchestral realization of this harmonic change coincides with a descent from the climax by means of an ingeniously disintegrating texture. Berg provides a chromatic scale (piccolo and flutes), both species of whole-tone scale together (clarinets), string glissandi overlapping at the tritone, dividing the octave symmetrically (B and F), and the γ chord itself, inverting downwards end over end. Added to this is the harp glissando on a diminished seventh chord, which, because it does not entirely map with the γ chord, commences not on the downbeat but one hemidemisemiquaver after it. (Finally, there is the succession of chords in the piano, the only part of this passage which cannot—so far!—be precisely explained.)

The winding-down of the climax involves the emergence of a simpler, more strongly paratonal, harmony with chromatic wedging in the lower parts and triadic components in the upper. This is the immediate background to the dramatic entrance of the solo voice, with chromatically creeping whole-tone harmonic support. The passage from bar 17 to the middle of bar 24 is the most 'free' part of the song, with the wedging process the most systematic structural aspect.

At the middle of bar 24, a second massive crescendo begins, with an entirely new motivic process, one which, like the prelude, is so systematic and intensive as to provide a thematic basis for nearly every note in the remainder of the song. The orchestral texture is worked out principally with four new motives, but also includes two which were introduced in the prelude. The new motives include an interval series of minor seventh, semitone, minor third, and semitone (VII), a chromatic succession of fourth chords and an augmented triad (VIII), a five-note melody (IX), and a single pitch class, D (X). The interval series does not specify the intervallic direction. Motive VIII is progressively shortened (decremental repetition) through bar 27, then restored at the climax (bar 29). The two motives heard earlier are IV and V, the latter in the form of a single sustained chord in the harmonium. IV is treated rather more radically (Example 12).

Ex. 12 Altenberg Songs, I, bars 1–9, transformations of motive IV

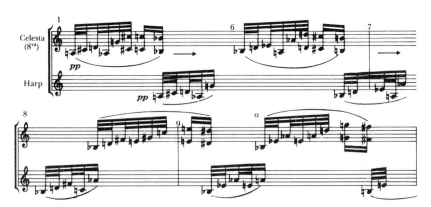

It is especially interesting to see Berg trying out abstract manipulations of pitch-class sequences more than a decade before Schoenberg's twelve-note technique, although of course Schoenberg was also experimenting with similar devices at this time. The noteworthy aspect of these manipulations of IV, however, is that the retrograde IV is specifically arranged to have the same rhythm and characteristic contour as its parent motive, and the retrograded dyads of the next statement preserve at least the original rhythm. For Berg, the integrity of the theme as an actual melody is all-important, from the earliest works to his most advanced serial technique.

All of these motives are piled together in short melodic bursts, with a dramatic gap in the whole texture to allow the harmonium to whisper through, until the violent climax in the middle of bar 29. The final section of the song follows, with the second phrase of the text. The vocal part is constructed on β, successive pitches of the motive alternating with the initial G. As each of these pitches appears, a mini-explosion of the motives of the previous section (IV, V, VII, VIII, IX, and X) accompanies, each motive decrementally repeated until bar 34, beginning a sort of codetta, when the motives appear in farewell gestures one after the other. It is this section that provides the proof that X is really a mono-pitch motive. Example 13 shows it as a pedal point initiated by the octave coincidence of the bass wedges in bar 24, continuing through the climax at 29, and in different registers thereafter. (The various notes for percussion, together with the special noises in the final bars, are included here as details which may be associated with this motive.)

Ex. 13 Altenberg Songs, I, bars 24–38, D pedal

The codetta is built on an extension of β, with a solo violin continuing the line after the last note of the vocal line, expanding the incrementing interval to a fourth, finally a tritone. The VIII motive appears in melodic inversion, as a descending line of chords; then X (cellos, *col legno*, bariolage with open string), followed by VII (ascending piccolo), IV (contrabassoon), and an arpeggiation of the extended β (celesta). The first of the two noises which follow is an indeterminately notated 'Flag. gliss. a. d. E-Saite' (glissando in harmonics on the E string) with a wavy line sloping diagonally upward, *pppp*, and this presumably means artificial harmonics, not the glissando of adjacent natural harmonics that Stravinsky made famous at the beginning of *The Firebird*. The second is notated for the violas, cellos, and basses below the bottom line with an x-shaped note, and the rubric 'Durch Streichen auf dem Löchern des Saitenhalters hervorzubringen!' (produced by bowing on the holes of the tailpiece). These special effects, which are rather more typical of the avant-garde orchestral vocabulary in the 1950s than of 1912, might have been the 'new techniques' that annoyed Schoenberg, who himself was perfectly content to specify such exotic sounds as the rattling chains in *Gurrelieder* or the suspended cymbal bowed with a double bass bow in *Die glückliche Hand* (1913). (Berg wrote one other puzzler in this song, the double bass notes in the treble clef at bars 29–30. Whether Berg meant this to be played by sliding the pinched thumb and forefinger along the string, or by merely pinching the string tightly in a fixed position at the end of the fingerboard and bowing it normally, is not known, but it is the latter that Richard Strauss meant in the decapitation scene in *Salome*.)

All of the extraordinary vocal and orchestral writing makes it the most expressionistic, not to say expressive, of any of Berg's songs. Certainly the gestures are immense, and one wonders how the 1913 audience would have reacted after hearing this cataclysmic song rather than the quiet and subtle pieces it did hear. More than that, one wonders how Schoenberg could have failed to note that this song, much more than the two little songs he conducted, surely qualified as a work of large dimensions, such as for which he suggested Berg's expressive temperament was best suited.

The first Altenberg Song is thus unique in Berg's output for several reasons, but it is nevertheless perfectly complemented by the fifth song, 'Hier ist Friede!', a work of comparable dimensions, with a huge climax involving the full orchestra, but of completely different expressive quality. Where the first song is a kaleidoscope of violent moods, the fifth song has a uniformly steady declamation deriving from its metric regularity as a passacaglia. Like the first song, it starts and finishes very quietly, building to two climaxes in between. And if the dimensional correlation is perfectly obvious, with the first and fifth songs as the large pillars on the outer extremes of the cycle of five, there is an internal thematic correlation as well, one not nearly as obvious but which is nevertheless brilliantly conceived.

The passacaglia structure is laid out on a five-bar pattern, with 55 bars in all. The first five bars announce the five-note theme β, and the next five α (in the bass) and δ (Example 14). The δ of this passacaglia is the simple succession of twelve notes with little rhythmic differentiation, very different from the complex melody of the first song; the α is a theme with a central role here, unlike the basically subsidiary function that it had in the first song, as a temporary

Ex. 14 Altenberg Songs, V, bars 1–12

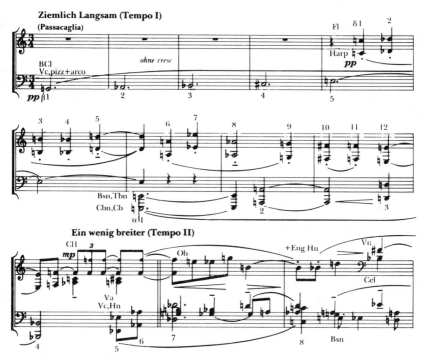

transformation of IV. (The only other correlation of α with the rest of the cycle is its appearance as a momentary detail in the second song.)

In the nine variations that follow, the three themes are supplemented by others (such as the five-note theme of 'Hier ist Friede!', or the oboe melody of bars 10–12, which appears in the third song), but mostly they are worked out together in a close and often abstract development. Within just the space of bars 10–15, for instance, the first full variation, Berg provides the completion of α (in the bass, the last five notes), a complete new statement of δ (horn 1, violas), a close chromatic counterpoint for δ made up of β notes on the downbeats with creeping notes in between (horns 2 and 3, cellos), an overlapping β transposed up a minor third (second violins and celesta, B♭, B, C♯, E, G—in other words, four of the original five pitch classes), plus two different guises of the 'Hier ist Friede!' melody. All of these are worked out together with obviously extreme care and sensitivity to constructing a strongly paratonal harmony, which seems to forecast the most memorable episodes of intense harmonic richness such as the end of Act I in *Wozzeck*, or the 'Invention on a key' in Act III.

The later variations, building toward a first climax at bar 25 and a grand climax at bar 35, are concerned in various ways with manipulations of the themes, but with an equal concern for the overall continuity of line and texture in which the dividing lines between successive variations are often blurred or overlapped. The third variation, for instance, is most clearly marked by the five-note β in the bass, less definitely by the numerous accompanimental figures which are all transpositions of β in the inner parts. The vocal melody δ supported by this texture straddles the previous variation, beginning with the last beat of bar 19, where its first three notes echo the last three of 'Hier ist Friede!' Yet the vocal prominence of this melody is not enough to carry it through to completeness, and it is broken off three notes before the end, on the word 'alles!' on A♭ and G, which pitches serve to connect the vocal line to the next variation, an incremental repetition of β, beginning with the second pitch (A♭ followed by G, bars 25–26). There is even a tonal connection of these pitches with the D♭ and C of α, moving up from the bass just beneath them. These same pitches are re-emphasized as α moves to the uppermost part in the solo violin, remaining on the same two pitches until bars 29–30, when they can be taken over by the initial pitches of δ (all violins), initiating the fifth and climactic variation. All three themes participate equally: α in the bass, and β in the horns, upper woodwind, and violas and cellos, alternating the initial pitch with every subsequent pitch (incremental expansion).

The climax, on the downbeat of bar 35, brings together the fifth pitch of β (E), the twelfth pitch of δ (E), and the seventh pitch of α (D♭, in the bass), to which Berg joyfully adds an A, forming a first-inversion A major triad, as dramatic a paratonal gesture as the C major triad in Act II, scene 1 of *Wozzeck*. The descent from the climax provides the opportunity for a contrast in thematic intensity, with an incidental occurrence of β (harp chord, bar 36) as the only central motive present, and the rest of the variation based entirely on the subsidiary motives noted earlier.

At bar 40, the beginning of the seventh variation, the overlap of 'Hier ist Friede!' with δ is continued by bassoon and piano, with the voice joining in in bar 42 with its final line of text, 'Hier tropft Schnee leise in Wasserlachen' (Example 15). The last word, 'Wasserlachen', is a chromatic-scale extension of the end of δ which ran out with F♯–F–E ('leise in'), but the extension goes down to D♭–C to meet the last two notes of α rising from the bass in the harp. At this point also there is a pedal point on G in the bass which provides not only a paratonal anchor but also serves as the starting point for a penultimate statement of β, beginning in bar 46.

From here to the end is a demonstration of Berg's formal genius at its best. The incremental repetition of β in the first cellos, doubled by first horn, is supported by a finely symmetrical creeping harmony, but it is never completed; in place of the expected appearance of E on the downbeat of bar 50, there is a new chord, marked by a *sforzando* in the horns and tuba. This chord has been heard only once before, at the climax of the first song, where it was identified as γ, the creeping transformation of β (G–A♭–B♭–D♭–E going to F♯–A–B–D–F). Beginning now in bar 50, the γ chord is systematically transformed into β, the fourth trombone taking the lead by downward arpeggiation, reaching the

Ex. 15 Altenberg Songs, V, bars 39–54

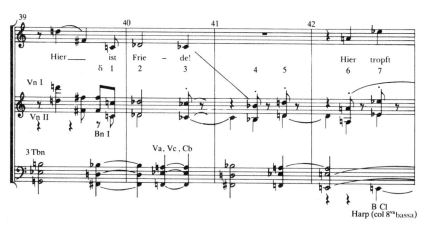

Ex. 15 cont.

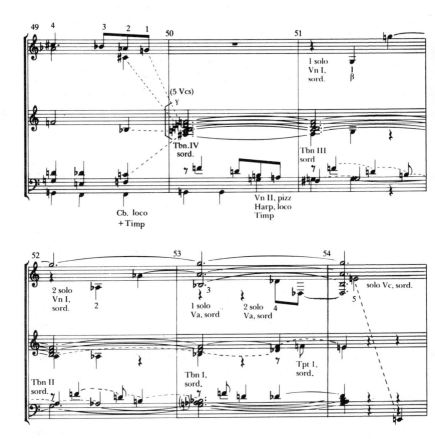

bottom F♯ and then stepping up to G; then the third trombone going almost to the bottom to A and stepping down to A♭; then the second trombone B to B♭, the first D to D♭, and finally just the first trumpet F to E. The trombones sustain their arrival notes until the trumpet provides the last of the five, and then the chord is handed over in *Klangfarbenmelodie* fashion to oboes and bassoons, then flutes and clarinets, then the piano, finally to the harp. (The rhythm of this *Klangfarbenmelodie* is identical with the rhythm of the secondary melody which appeared near the beginning of the song (flute, clarinet, oboe, bar 10), and similarly in the third song. This is an early instance of motivic rhythm such as Berg developed much more intensively in later works, beginning especially with Act III, scene 3 of *Wozzeck*.) While all this has been going on, the G pedal point has crept upward from the bass to just below middle C, and in bar 51 a solo violin picks it up two octaves higher to sustain it as the first pitch of a descending β. A second solo violin takes the second pitch, A♭, up one octave; then a solo viola the B♭, neither up nor down, zero octaves; another solo viola, D♭, down one octave, and finally a solo cello, E down two octaves—a perfect symmetry of registers. The solo-string chord remains to the end, dying away *pppp*. The overall formal symmetry, of course, is what underlies the overall *Bogenform* of the cycle. The transformation of β to γ in bars 14–15 of the first song is perfectly mirrored by the reverse transformation in the final bars of the fifth song.

Conclusion

The Altenberg Songs form a fitting culmination to Berg's career as a composer of songs. He had begun his musical life as an amateur composer; songs were what he could learn to write by himself, and they formed an appropriate vehicle for communicating his own musical expression to the friends of his youth. Now, in 1912, not quite aware of the strength of his new maturity, he had written a masterpiece that turned out to be unapproachable by his own generation. Two years later, on the eve of a continental catastrophe, he would make an intense effort to write a piece that would satisfy his teacher's demands, and in this effort he succeeded, completing in 1915 the Three Orchestral Pieces, the most texturally complex of all his works. That accomplishment, and his experiences in the war, pointed him toward *Wozzeck*, which must have convinced him once and for all that his greatest achievements were to be had in the field of opera. And *Wozzeck* itself, for all its revolutionary transformation of the operatic genre, contains some distinctive episodes which unmistakably show that Berg was a master of the *Lied*, and this is even more true of *Lulu*.

After the Altenberg Songs, Berg would write only two new works that can be called songs. One of these is the second setting of Theodor Storm's *Schliesse mir die Augen beide*, his first complete exercise in twelve-note technique, written in 1925, using the first set of the Lyric Suite.[36] The other is part of the Lyric Suite itself, the final movement, which is a setting of Baudelaire's *De profundis clamavi*, but which for 50 years was known to the world only as an anguished piece for string quartet.[37]

By stretching a point, *Der Wein* might be added to the list. As a concert aria, which is what Berg called it, *Der Wein* is one of the last and certainly one of the most splendid examples of a genre favoured by Mozart (who wrote 60) but that was already obsolete with Beethoven's *Ah perfido!* Nevertheless, it is not hard to see *Der Wein* as a cycle of three connected songs, unified musically by a single row and textually by three 'wine' poems from Baudelaire's *Les fleurs du mal*. The overall form is Berg's beloved *Bogenform*, with an abbreviated *da capo* of the first song at the beginning of the third, and a literal palindrome in the middle of the second song.

In order to fufill the commission for *Der Wein* from the singer Růžena Herlinger in the spring of 1929, Berg had to interrupt the early stages of his composition of *Lulu*, but it does not seem as though he interrupted his compositional state of mind, for the two works share the same lush harmonic and orchestral world. Much of *Der Wein* sounds as though it could have come right out of the first scene of Act I of the opera. The characteristic diatonic aspect of Berg's serial technique in these works seems to go far in supporting the kind of richly expressive melodic line that he favoured for soprano roles. Like the row associated with the figure of Lulu, that of *Der Wein* shows a substantial diatonic-scale segmentation; Lulu's row begins with the first six degrees of a minor scale with a major sixth; that of *Der Wein* with a minor sixth. In both *Lulu* and *Der Wein* the scalewise aspect of the row is the outstanding feature of the principal melodic themes. (The scalewise aspect also turns up in one of the three associatively identical sets of the first movement of the Lyric Suite, but the scale involved is the 'all-combinatorial major hexachord' of the first six degrees of the C major and F♯ major scales.) Another common aspect between *Der Wein* and *Lulu* is jazz, which Berg listened to frequently on the radio, and whose spirit, symbolized especially by the overripe, pungent sound of the alto saxophone, penetrates both works.

We can only surmise that Berg, who in his last years worked chiefly on operatic composition, might have continued from time to time to compose songs had he not been cut off in his prime. As a dramatic composer he has not been surpassed in this century, and the dramatic dimension of his art was a long time in developing. But it is not too much to say that Berg's evolution demonstrates that his origin as a composer of songs is perhaps the most basic part of his personality as a composer. Songs are, after all, monuments to feelings, carved out of the marble of melody. Even the most abstractly conceived moments—the aspects of Berg's works that have the most deeply psychological or intellectual motivation—are indissolubly linked to his instinctive melodic inspiration, which, it may be argued, binds Berg as closely to the world of Schubert and Mahler as Schoenberg's sense of melodic form bound him to Mozart and Brahms.

Notes

1. This was later printed in a revised and abridged version of that memorial volume (see note 8): Willi Reich, *Alban Berg* (Zurich: Atlantis Verlag, 1963); English trans. Cornelius Cardew (London: Thames and Hudson, 1965), pp. 28–30.
2. Hans Ferdinand Redlich, *Alban Berg: Versuch einer Würdigung* (Vienna: Universal Edition, 1957), p. 328.
3. The 1911 edition was the first (Vienna: Universal Edition); the last German edition, the third, was published in 1922. The authoritative English translation is *Theory of Harmony*, trans. Roy E. Carter (Berkeley and Los Angeles: University of California Press, 1978).
4. See Rosemary Hilmar, 'Alban Berg's Studies with Schoenberg', *Journal of the Arnold Schoenberg Institute*, vol. 8, no. 1 (June 1984), pp. 7–29.

5. *Arnold Schoenberg Letters*, sel. and ed. Erwin Stein, trans. Eithne Wilkins and Ernst Kaiser (New York: St Martin's Press, 1965), p. 23.

6. Willi Reich, 'Alban Berg', *Die Musik*, vol. 22 (February 1930), pp. 347–53.

7. Redlich, op. cit., pp. 330–32.

8. Willi Reich, *Alban Berg: mit Bergs eigenen Schriften und Beiträgen von Theodor Wiesengrund-Adorno und Ernst Krenek* (Vienna: Herbert Reichner Verlag, 1937).

9. Frida Semler Seabury, '1903 and 1904', *International Alban Berg Society Newsletter*, no. 1 (December 1968), pp. 3–6; Donald Harris, 'Berg and Miss Frida: further Recollections of his Friendship with an American College Girl', *Alban Berg Symposion Wien 1980: Tagungsbericht*, ed. Rudolf Klein, Alban Berg Studien, vol. 2 (Vienna: Universal Edition, 1981), pp. 198–208.

10. Joan Allen Smith, 'The Berg-Hohenberg Correspondence', *Alban Berg Symposion Wien 1980: Tagungsbericht*, pp. 189–97.

11. Nicholas Chadwick, 'Berg's Unpublished Songs in the Österreichische Nationalbibliothek', *Music and Letters*, vol. 52 (1971), pp. 123–40.

12. Rosemary Hilmar, *Katalog der Musikhandschriften, Schriften und Studien im Fond Alban Berg und der weiteren handschriftlichen Quellen im Besitz der Österreichischen Nationalbibliothek*, Alban Berg Studien, vol. 1 (Vienna: Universal Edition, 1980).

13. EMI Digital 27 0195 1, Dietrich Fischer-Dieskau, baritone, with Aribert Reimann, piano.

14. Alban Berg, *Jugendlieder*, vol. 1 [1901–1904] (Vienna: Universal Edition, no. 18143, 1986); vol. 2 [1904–08] (Vienna: Universal Edition, no. 18144, 1987).

15. Photograph of manuscript in Hilmar, op. cit., p. 163, pl. 6.

16. Photograph of manuscript in Hilmar, op. cit., p. 167, pl. 11a.

17. See Mark DeVoto, 'Alban Berg and Creeping Chromaticism', *Alban Berg: Analytical and Historical Perspectives*, ed. David Gable and Robert Morgan (Oxford University Press, forthcoming).

18. See Hilmar, op. cit., p. 172, pl. 15b.

19. See Mark DeVoto, 'Alban Berg's "Marche Macabre"', *Perspectives of New Music*, vol. 22 (fall–winter 1983, spring–summer 1984), pp. 430–31, ex. 20.

20. Berg's use of the simultaneous black- and white-key glissandi is his earliest-known compositional partitioning of the complete chromatic scale; it precedes Debussy's simultaneous glissandi (in the same direction, descending) in *Feux d'artifice* (*Préludes*, bk II, no. 12) by a year or two. An earlier precedent can be found, however, in Carl Tausig's *Das Geisterschiff*, dating probably from the last 1860s, which has simultaneous ascending glissandi.

21. Stuckenschmidt attempted to show a personal connection between Berg's sequence of 1909 and Debussy's use of the same sequence in no. 4 of his *Six épigraphes antiques* of 1914; see H.H. Stuckenschmidt, 'Debussy or Berg? The Mystery of a Chord Progression', *Musical Quarterly*, vol. 51 (1965), pp. 453–9. A more likely antecedent, if there was any, for Debussy's sequence would be Ravel's *Le Gibet* (from *Gaspard de la nuit*) of 1909; see Walter Piston, *Harmony*, fourth edition, rev. Mark DeVoto, (London: Victor Gollancz, 1978), p. 513.

22. I am grateful to the League of Composers–ISCM, Boston Section, for permission to use some of this historical material which I originally wrote for their publication series in 1985.

23. Alban Berg, *A. Schönberg: Gurrelieder: Führer (Grosse Ausgabe)* (Vienna: Universal Edition no. 3695, 1913).

24. Quoted from Donald Harris, programme note for Berg's Altenberg Songs, *Boston Symphony Orchestra Program Book*, 89 (1969–1970), pp. 551–70.

25. Dmitri Shostakovich's statement that Berg insisted on conducting part of a rehearsal of *Wozzeck* in the Leningrad production of 1927 rather taxes my credulity: *Testimony: the Memoirs of Dmitri Shostakovich*, 'as related to and edited by' Solomon Volkov, trans. Antonina W. Bouis (New York: Harper & Row, 1979), pp. 43–4.

26. Quoted in Rosemary Hilmar, *Alban Berg: Leben und Wirken in Wien bis zu seinen ersten Erfolgen als Komponist* (Vienna: Verlag Hermann Böhlaus Nachf., 1978), p. 97.

27. Reich, *Alban Berg* (1965), p. 41.

28. Redlich, op. cit., p. 90.

29. Redlich, op. cit., p. 358, n. 81.

30. *Alban Berg: Briefe an seine Frau* (Munich and Vienna: Albert Langen and Georg Müller, 1965), p. 254; *Alban Berg: Letters to his Wife*, ed., trans., and annot. Bernard Grun (New York: St Martin's Press 1971), p. 159.

31. The fair copy of this arrangement is in the Moldenhauer Archive of the Bayrische Staatsbibliothek in Munich; publication is expected in the near future. Berg's pencil draft is in the Berg Archive at the Österreichische Nationalbibliothek (F 21 Berg 64).

32. This piano–vocal score was reprinted in René Leibowitz, 'Alban Berg's Five Orchestra Songs', *Musical Quarterly*, vol. 34 (1948), pp. 487–511. When the piano-vocal score of the complete cycle was published in 1953, the *Menschen* score, with some simplification, was incorporated into it. Berg's draft for the *Menschen* score is in the Archive of the Gesellschaft der Musikfreunde in Vienna.

33. Redlich, op. cit., p. 78.

34. A detailed analysis of the Altenberg songs can be found in my dissertation, *Alban Berg's Picture Postcard Songs* (PhD, Princeton University, 1967); a portion of this study, covering principally the first and fifth songs, is published as 'Some Notes on the Unknown *Altenberg Lieder*', *Perspectives of New Music*, vol. 5, no. 1 (fall–winter 1966), pp. 37–74.

35. J.B. Foerster, *Der Pilger*, quoted in Konrad Vogelsang, *Alban Berg: Leben und Werk* (Berlin: Max Hesses Verlag, 1959), pp. 17–18.

36. Joan Allen Smith, 'Some Sources for Berg's *Schliesse mir die Augen beide* II', *International Alban Berg Society Newsletter*, no. 6 (June 1978), pp. 9–13.

37. Douglass M. Green, 'Berg's De Profundis: the Finale of the Lyric Suite', *International Alban Berg Society Newsletter*, no. 5 (June 1977), pp. 13–23; George Perle, 'The Secret Program of the Lyric Suite', *International Alban Berg Society Newsletter*, no. 5. (June 1977), pp. 4–12 ; Perle's article appeared in slightly revised form in *Musical Times*, vol. 118 (August–October 1977), pp. 629–32, 709–13, 809–13.

A CONSERVATIVE REVOLUTION:
THE MUSIC OF THE FOUR SONGS OP. 2

STEPHEN W. KETT

Arnold Schoenberg's contemporaries frequently singled him out as a forward-looking composer, one who broke with the harmonic and melodic traditions of the past: a 'revolutionary' of musical composition. Schoenberg himself, however, was always quick to point out that this epithet needed considerable clarification. On several occasions he denied his purely 'revolutionary' status by painstakingly demonstrating that his greatest musical innovations stemmed from the melodic and harmonic implications inherent in the works of Bach, Mozart, Beethoven, Brahms, and Wagner. For Schoenberg, his 'truly new' music was founded upon an intimate knowledge and love of the Germanic tradition. He was a 'conservative' revolutionary', a composer who did not destroy, but preserved and continued the practices of the past. This colourful oxymoron points up Schoenberg's belief that his music was not only a logical continuation of the tradition but its historically inevitable end-result.

Berg has generally come to be known as the 'Romantic' of the Second Viennese School, or even the 'poet of the atonal'.[1] With his lyrical melodic writing and his highly idiomatic use of a harmonic language that is not so far removed from the chromatic tonal harmony of the late 19th century, Berg could be deemed a musical 'conservative'—at least, when compared to the 'revolutionary' Schoenberg and the 'progressive' Anton Webern.

In this regard it is worth remembering a comment that Schoenberg himself made about Berg's operatic works.:

> In his operas [Berg] mixed pieces or parts of pieces of a distinct tonality with those which were distinctly non-tonal. He explained this apologetically by contending that as an opera composer he could not ... renounce the contrast furnished by a change from major to minor. Though he was right as a composer he was wrong theoretically.[2]

Schoenberg immediately proceeds to point out that—as he 'had proved' in his operas *Von Heute auf Morgen* and *Moses und Aron*—the expressive and dramatic contrast provided by the change from major to minor mode was, in essence, no longer necessary since it could now be produced using 'the style of free dissonance'.[3] One begins to envisage the creative but inept younger composer, Berg, 'apologetically' explaining his sad predicament to the stern but forgiving mentor Schoenberg.

Implicit in Schoenberg's remarks is a judgement about Berg and his music that has been, and is still, widely held. It holds that Berg's use of familiar tonal sounds and progressions in his twelve-note compositions (such as *Lulu*) and his other 'non-tonal' mature works (such as *Wozzeck* and the Chamber Concerto) reveal not only his underlying 'Romantic' compositional inclinations but perhaps even his *inability* to escape from the tonal world of the late 19th century.

While this long-standing view of Berg's music accurately describes one integral aspect of his mature style—that is, Berg does freely utilize chromatic tonal resources—such a limited understanding has unfortunately led many to conclude that his musical language is not 'progressive' and, most importantly, that its implications are not relevant to the work of later composers. Only recently has this assessment of Berg's work been widely re-examined.[4]

In all his mature compositions Berg integrates tonal and non-tonal elements into his musical language. And yet while this language is both tonal and atonal it is neither one nor the other exclusively. The composer's mature work thus presents a unique challenge to contemporary analysts, whose methodologies are best suited to either the tonal or the atonal repertoires. These analytical difficulties are mitigated somewhat in the twelve-note works, where an underlying dodecaphonic structure provides a convenient point of departure for critical study. In the earlier mature works, however—from the Altenberg Songs to the Chamber Concerto—the tonal–atonal harmonic world which Berg explores defies a comprehensive analysis by any single method and the initial approach to an analysis of it is, at best, unclear.

In some ways the most analytically challenging are the compositions of Berg's earliest maturity: the Piano Sonata op. 1, the Four Songs op. 2, and the String Quartet op. 3. These works are also revealing in that they shed light on Berg's early development as a composer and on the genesis of his mature style. Given their important position in Berg's rather small corpus of published compositions, they have, however, received surprisingly little critical attention to date.[5] Studies of these works would not only help to provide a compositional context for Berg's apprenticeship with Schoenberg, but would help to clarify some of the more elusive aspects of his mature musical language.

The focus of this chapter will be the Four Songs op. 2. The goals of the present study are: first, to place the songs in a context within Berg's life; second, to isolate those formal, melodic, and other structural aspects of Berg's early compositional style that would later characterize his fully mature musical language; and third, to suggest that, while the music of Brahms, Wagner, and Mahler had a powerful influence on the young composer, his developing musical language was highly individual and even 'revolutionary'.

Origins and Context

It is, of course, impossible to identify the creative origins of any artistic work precisely. Fortunately in the case of the Four Songs we have, in addition to the texts Berg chose, some of the earliest sketches for the songs to help date the beginning of the compositional process and a curious allegorical painting by the Secessionist painter Josef Engelhart, which may have provided some initial creative inspiration.[6] Our knowledge of the other songs that Berg composed during his apprenticeship with Schoenberg also informs our understanding of the genesis of the Four Songs.

Let us first briefly examine the poetic texts selected by the composer for the Four Songs. These are part of two larger poetic cycles by two poets: Friedrich Hebbel (1813–1863) and Alfred Mombert (1872–1942). The Hebbel poem, used in the first song, was published in 1842 as the fourth in a cycle of eleven poems entitled *Dem Schmerz sein Recht*. The three Mombert texts used in the remaining songs form part of an extended cycle (nos. 56, 57, and 70 respectively) of 87 poems entitled *Der Glühende*, published in 1896. It is not clear whether Berg used published editions of these poetic cycles as the sources for his song texts or whether he discovered them as individual works in a contemporary literary magazine or anthology.[7]

Stylistically, the poets could hardly be less alike: Hebbel, the early 19th-century Romantic, and Mombert, the early 20th-century pre-expressionist. The four texts chosen by Berg, however, are unified by a central theme: a psychological exploration of, and journey to, a distant world of 'sleep–death' as an escape from reality. While the theme is a common one in 19th-century Germanic culture—Wagner's *Tristan und Isolde* being only the most famous treatment of it—in the Four Songs some of the more disturbing aspects of this idea are explored and made explicit.

The first three poems in the song cycle (that is, the Hebbel text and the first two Mombert poems) comprise a single group unified around the idea of sleep as a metaphor for death and as an escape from reality. In the fourth text, an explicit and dramatic juxtaposition of life and death is presented against a bleak naturalistic background. This 3 + 1 textual substructure is relevant to a study of the musical structure of the song cycle, and is itself, perhaps, revelatory of its original inspiration.

The evidence of the sketches and complete working drafts indicates that Berg began work on the second and third songs first, as early as the summer of 1908. He began work on the first while refining and completing the drafts of the second and third, and sketched ideas for the fourth as late as the spring of 1910. In addition to the numerous small changes (of a kind that one would expect) made to all the songs during this two-year compositional process, Berg changed his mind more than once about the transposition level of the second song and about the key signatures of both the second and third. These seemingly small changes provide important clues to the cyclical structure and tonal interrelationships of the work.[8]

The possibility that a contemporary allegorical painting originally inspired Berg to compose the Hebbel song was first suggested by Rosemary Hilmar in the catalogue of the Berg Exhibition held in Vienna in 1985. The painting, *Die Schlafenden* by the Viennese Secessionist painter Josef Engelhart (1864–1941), was completed in 1897 and first exhibited at the Second Exhibition of the Secession in 1898. More suggestive than the similarity between the title of the painting and the words and subject of the Hebbel text is the striking similarity between the structure of the painting and that of the complete cycle of four poems as arranged by Berg. The 3 + 1 substructure of the Berg can be seen as a mirror of that of Engelhart's canvas in which three sleeping women in the left foreground, are watched by a menacing and half-hidden faun-like creature in the right background.

It perhaps seems unlikely that the inspiration for Berg's first song cycle should have come from a painting exhibited in 1898 when he was 13 years old. *Die Schlafenden* was, however, later included in an exhibition devoted exclusively to Engelhart's work—the 34th Exhibition of the Secession in 1909, the year when Berg was in the middle of his work on these songs. According to the composer's nephew, Erich Alban Berg, Berg was very familiar with Engelhart's works and was a friend of the Engelhart family.[9] It is possible, therefore, that there exists a relationship between *Die Schlafenden*, a characteristic product of the *fin-de-siècle* Viennese artistic culture in which Berg grew up and composed the works of his early maturity, and the creative origins of the Four Songs.

As a precocious self-taught young composer and later as a student of Schoenberg, Berg was drawn to the genre of the *Lied*. Largely unknown today, Berg's *Jugendlieder* (numbering more than 80 songs), provide the most consistent and revealing compositional record of his development up to the completion of the Four Songs—his first, and only published, song cycle for voice and piano.

To judge from many of Schoenberg's own remarks, Berg's proclivity for the *Lied* exasperated his teacher.[10] Yet however exasperated Schoenberg might have been, his influence on the young composer's musical style was profound and unmistakable. Schoenberg provided a rigorous foundation in harmony and counterpoint and, as Rosemary Hilmar has pointed out, insisted on extreme motivic economy and 'developing variation' (that is to say, that the melodic and harmonic materials of a work undergo a process of continuous development) in the compositional exercises and the free works of his students.[11] In comparison with his earliest songs, Berg's later *Jugendlieder* and the Four Songs provide excellent examples of the dense motivic style of composition nurtured by Schoenberg.[12]

Another pervasive feature of both Berg's earliest *Lieder* and his later published works is a practice that Mark DeVoto has referred to as chromatic 'creeping'—that is, the use of chromatic linear motion in some or all harmonic voices as a means of creating, prolonging, and moving between harmonies.[13] Often, in Berg's early works, extensions of such chromatic and linear motions result in novel prolongational or 'passing' chords. In Berg's earliest songs these new harmonies most frequently behave as they would in tonal compositions of the 18th and 19th centuries. In the later *Jugendlieder*, the Piano Sonata, the Four Songs, and the String Quartet, these same chords no longer serve only to prolong or move between 'familiar' (major, minor, augmented, diminished) sonorities but rather become important goals themselves.[14]

Given Berg's early proclivity for song composition it is somewhat surprising that after the composition of the Four Songs he never again published a cycle of songs for voice and piano. They are the final product of that early compositional period during which Berg composed *Lieder* almost exclusively.

Harmonic and Motivic Structure

A single pitch collection or chord unifies the entire cycle of the Four Songs; an incomplete minor seventh, with both a major and minor third, that I shall call Chord 'B' (Example 1). The chord is first introduced in bar 5 of the first song and reappears in the closing bars of the fourth, as both the short-term goal of bars 20–22 and, at bar 25, as the final harmonic goal of the entire cycle.

Ex. 1

B

Because of its bi-modal (major–minor) colour, this *B* chord has a very striking expressive potential. Rather than alternating a minor (with its traditionally sombre and dark associations) and a major chord (with its traditionally self-confident and bright associations), Berg's *B* chord provides a combination of both. It is, as we shall see, difficult to imagine a tonal sonority better suited to expressing the final lines of Mombert's text in the fourth song.

Berg highlights the tonal implications of this chord in the opening song of the cycle. Once the *B* chord is reached in bar 5, the composer immediately develops the simple progression shown in Example 2. Given the strong bass motion underpinning this short *A*–*B* progression it is at least possible to hear the *A* chord as the dominant and the *B* chord as the tonic of a traditional V–I cadential progression. In fact, the *A* chord is an incomplete dominant seventh of D minor with an added major sixth. The alteration of a dominant seventh chord by the addition of a major (or minor) sixth was, of course, common practice in the 19th century. Evidence of Berg's particular love of this added-sixth sound can be found in many of his *Jugendlieder*, where most of the dominant sevenths are altered by the addition of either a major or minor sixth.

Ex. 2 Four Songs, I, bars 5–9

Reprinted by permission of Robert Lienau, Berlin

This interpretation of both the *A* and *B* chords in the first song sheds light on bars 20–22 of the fourth, the piano accompaniment to which consists entirely of a sequentially extended version of the *A–B* progression of the first song (Example 3). Although it is difficult to understand the full harmonic and structural significance of this progression outside the context of the fourth song and the entire cycle, its inherent tonal implications—including those recalled from the first song—are immediately apparent. Indeed, Berg gives additional meaning to this 'tonal' sequential progression by placing it in the explicitly atonal context of the fourth song. I shall consider this passage in greater detail later but we may, in general, observe here that the tonal/atonal duality of such a passage is entirely characteristic of Berg's early mature musical language.

In order to understand how the second and third songs use the material set out in the first and prepare for the penultimate sequential progression in the fourth it is necessary to divide the *A–B* progression into its two constituent parts: the sequence of ascending perfect fourth intervals from B♭ to B natural (marked Y

Ex. 3 Four Songs, IV, bars 20–22

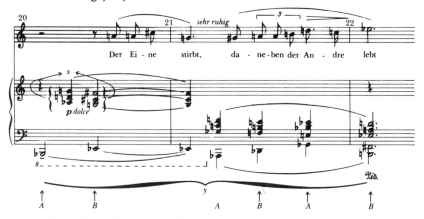

Reprinted by permission of Robert Lienau, Berlin

in Example 3) and the three-note collections (marked X) which represent the element that chords A and B have in common. The bass pattern Y—a familiar 'circle of fifths' progression in tonal music—first appears in bars 1–3 of the second song; although the four-note chords in these bars are neither A nor B chords, the sequential progression is distinctive enough to be easily recognizable when it returns in the closing bars of the last song.

Berg incorporates a horizontal statement of the three-note pitch collection X into the principal accompanimental motive of the third song (Example 4). Such economy of motivic and harmonic material, a hallmark of Berg's mature style, is evidence of the powerful influence of Schoenberg's compositional philosophy on the young composer.

Ex. 4 Four Songs, III, bar 1

Reprinted by permission of Robert Lienau, Berlin

The penultimate progression of the fourth song, incorporating the A and B chords of the first and the 'x' and 'y' motives of the second and third songs, thus acts as a modified recapitulation of the entire cycle and yet, at the same time, transforms this earlier material.

Formal Design

The first three songs employ A-B-A designs. As Figure 1 illustrates, the modified ternary form plan of the first song is defined by texture and dynamics as well as piano and vocal tessitura. Berg emphasises the arch shape by incorporating a modified palindrome of bars 1–5 in the final bars of the song (Example 5). To my knowlege, this admittedly short passage is the composer's earliest published example of a formal device—the palindrome—that pre-occupied him in many of his later works.[15]

Figure 1

		textural arch		dynamic arch
bar		no. of voices		
1	1 [2]		ppp	
2		3		
3		4		p
11		5		mf
12		6		
16		7		f
18		6		mf
		5		
19		4		mp
		6		
		5		
21		4		p
22		5		pp
23		3		ppp
30	1 [2]		pppp	

The second and third songs, whose combined length equals that of the first, are also short A-B-A forms with similarly modified, or condensed, recapitulations—recapitulations in which the subtle but significant changes again demonstrate the influence of Schoenberg's belief that similar musical material should be continuously changed and developed even within such short compositions.

The free form of the fourth song differs markedly from those of the first three. As the miniature drama of the Mombert text unfolds, the music grows in dynamic and registral intensity until simultaneous white- and black-note glissandi in bar 15 mark the first climax. Immediately following this high point,

Ex. 5 Four Songs, I, (a) bars 1–5, (b) bars 26–30

Reprinted by permission of Robert Lienau, Berlin

the piano accompaniment moves rapidly through a four-octave registral descent until it finally reaches the instrument's lowest B♭. It is at this point that the passage that includes the sequential progression of *A* and *B* chords (see Example 3) begins.

In terms of proportions, then, the larger structure of the Four Songs is made up of three sections of roughly equal bar counts: 30 bars for the first song, 30 bars for the second and third together, and 25 bars for the fourth. As we shall see, the second and third songs are directly connected rhythmically, harmonically, and in other ways.[16] Thus, even before a more detailed analysis of the songs is undertaken, Berg's intricate web of harmonic, motivic, and formal relationships in the cycle begins to emerge.

One more characteristic of Berg's early harmonic–contrapuntal style should be mentioned here: his fondness for harmonic wedge patterns.[17] As the name suggests, a wedge pattern is a relatively systematic motion, either implied in a single line or made explicit in two or more contrapuntal lines, outward from a central pitch. Such a wedge pattern serves as the structural basis of bars 12–14 of the fourth song and is followed by what is aurally and visually the most explicit wedge passage of the entire cycle: the diverging right- and left-hand glissandi in the piano part at bar 15. Throughout the work Berg employs both large- and small-scale wedge patterns to prepare climaxes and articulate important points in the structure.

The goal of the following, more detailed, examination of each of the songs is not to provide a comprehensive study of each song but rather to focus on moments that reveal how Berg develops the larger musical structure and that highlight the 'progressive' nature of his early mature compositional language.

'Schlafen, schlafen, nichts als schlafen!'

Although it was probably not the first to be composed, Berg selected the Hebbel song to open the cycle. The characteristic world-weariness of the 19th-century Romantic text is transformed in Berg's setting into an unsettling lullaby. His treatment of the opening lines of Hebbel's text, combining compound duple metre, *sehr langsam* and *ppp* markings, and a rocking bass ostinato, conforms to the musical conventions of the *Wiegenlied* or lullaby. As the protagonist's sleep becomes more fitful in later lines, however, the carefully established elements of the musical lullaby are also disturbed, and the music moves to a dramatic climax in bars 16–17. Subsequently, as the opening mood of tranquillity is gradually restored (mirroring, perhaps, our own real experiences of sleep), the music of the opening section returns. Berg's use of a modified palindrome of the opening in the closing bars is, therefore, a device that expresses an element of the poetic text.

The song can be subdivided into three (overlapping) principal sections: A (bars 1–10), B (bars 10–19), and A1 (bars 19–24) followed by a short coda (bars 24–30). Berg does not, however, simply bridge the major sections; he carefully (and characteristically) blurs the distinctions at these points of formal juncture.

An examination of one of these passages will illustrate the point and demonstrate Berg's economy of motivic material. In the opening five bars of the song the voice imitates the piano at the interval of a dotted crotchet (Example 6). The voice thus sounds only on the weak second half of each bar. The pattern changes for the first time on the downbeat of bar 5. The resulting melodic idea, created by joining the metrically accented descending semitone in bar 5 to its ascending disjunct anacrusis in bar 4 constitutes the principal motivic shape (labelled *m* in Example 6) of the entire song. This *m* motive appears in various transformations (inverted, retrograde, and rhythmic augmentation and diminution) throughout the song.

Ex. 6 Four Songs, I, bars 1–5

Reprinted by permission of Robert Lienau, Berlin

To bridge the A and B sections of the song Berg incorporates *m* into the hemidemisemiquaver ascending figure that signals the beginning of the second section (Example 7). This transition is also smoothly effected by the accelerando from bar 10 to bar 11 and by the extension of the chromatic rocking motion from E♭ to D to C♯ in the bass. Finally a figure closely related to *m* is used in the vocal line at the outset of the B section ('Jener Wehen'). Such variation and integration of a limited amount of motivic and thematic material is very characteristic and appears throughout the cycle.

Ex. 7 Four Songs, I, bars 10–11

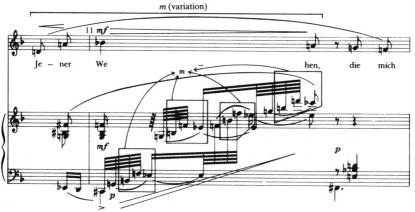

Reprinted by permission of Robert Lienau, Berlin

The harmonic structure of the song is equally subtle and intricate in its design. The opening bars lead us to expect a piece in D minor, yet D minor is never established since no explicit dominant chord is presented in these bars. Because of the listener's past experience of tonal works that begin in a similar way, the implicit dominant within the ostinato bass figure inevitably suggests D minor, but it is a D minor that is, perhaps, 'recalled' rather than strictly established. That is to say that Berg is here exploiting his listener's experience of tonal music to create expectations that are then modified throughout the song. As we shall see, these expectations are further manipulated throughout the entire cycle. In fact, much of the impact of the closing six bars of the final song results from Berg's manipulation, transformation, and integration of several previously introduced tonal segments into whole-tone and atonal contexts. This careful control of recollection, expectation, and transformation, combined with the juxtaposition and integration of tonal recollections and new atonal harmonic and melodic formations, is a definitive feature of Berg's mature musical style and one that is first apparent in the Four Songs.

The linear–harmonic progression of bars 2–5, while excluding an explicit dominant chord, moves away from the 'tonic' D minor to the first *B* chord in bar

5. After the bass ostinato is introduced in bar 1 and the full D minor triad presented in bar 2, Berg initiates a small chromatic wedge pattern, the A in the right hand of the piano part on the second beat of bar 2 ascending to B♭ (second beat, bar 3), B♮ (second beat, bar 4), and finally C (first beat, bar 5) (Example 8). This chromatic creeping leads to the *B* chord on the downbeat of bar 5, concurrently with the first downbeat in the vocal line as the *m* motive is introduced.

Ex. 8 Four Songs, I, bars 1–4

Reprinted by permission of Robert Lienau, Berlin

In bar 6 a new chromatic linear motion in the voice and accompaniment is initiated, resulting in the semitone transposition of the *B* chord up to E♭ in bar 7 (Example 9). Whereas previously in bars 1–6 the tonic D had remained the fixed pitch within the bass ostinato, in bar 7 it is the upper A that remains fixed. This seemingly small point is of some importance since the three-note *x* chord created by the upward semitone transposition in bar 7 is now, in bar 8, aligned with the A♮ of the bass to produce chord *A*. Finally, the first *A–B* progression in bars 8–9 provides the entire A section with a somewhat 'traditional' V–I cadence. It is important to remember that Berg generates the *B* chord out of an explicitly tonal context: when a transposition of this four-note *B* chord reappears at the close of the final song, part of its meaning and relevance to the text derives from its origins in the 'recollected' D minor tonality of the opening song of the cycle.

'Schlafend trägt man mich in mein Heimatland', 'Nun ich der Riesen Stärksten überwand'

While the first song is a highly chromatic tonal piece centring on the key of D minor, the first two Mombert settings are written in a freely extended tonal

Ex. 9 Four Songs, I, bars 6–9

Reprinted by permission of Robert Lienau, Berlin

language and move through several harmonic areas. The second and third songs function as the central structural unit of the cycle. Together they are, as we have seen, exactly equivalent in their total number of bars to the first song. Berg develops ideas from the first song in both, as well as introducing new melodic and harmonic material. The second and third songs are musically joined to one another in three ways: by (1) a fermata over the final double barline of the second song; by (2) the final chord of the second song, which acts as a dominant chord to the initial A♭ minor 'tonic' of the third; and by (3) the rhythmic motive (Example 10) that first appears in the final bar of the second song and reappears in the third and again in the fourth.[18]

Ex. 10

Most important for the purposes of the present analysis, the two songs together comprise the central tonal block of the cycle on E♭. The key signatures of the two songs, of six and seven flats respectively, are not signatures in the traditional sense—that is, they do not indicate the key and mode of the piece. Rather, they indicate the antecedent–consequent (dominant–tonic) relationship of the two songs within this central structure. It is perhaps worth noting that in an unfinished early draft of the second song Berg indicated a signature of three flats and notated the entire song a major third higher than in the final published version. It is, therefore, fair to conclude that, in both the early and final versions of the song the key area of E♭ major–E♭ minor played some part in his tonal plan for the complete cycle.

The opening chord of the second song has been the object of considerable previous study,[19] partly because the chord (labelled *C* in Example 11) is the enharmonic equivalent of a familiar augmented sixth chord—the French sixth.

Ex. 11 Four Songs, II, bar 1

Typically the French sixth chord functions as a cadential embellishment of a dominant chord. But no firm tonic key (with a dominant) is established at the beginning of the second song. However, it is impossible to defend a tonal analysis of the *C* chord only when the song is considered outside the context of the entire cycle. While the 'French sixth' chord of the second song does not serve as a dominant coloration and does not subsequently resolve as it might in a tonal composition, perhaps Berg uses the *C* chord at this point in the cycle to provide a harmonic link between the distantly related D minor key of the first song and the E♭ tonal area of the second and third—the chord being both a modified dominant seventh of E♭ and the 'French sixth' of the D minor tonic of the first song. After five years of intensive study with Schoenberg, Berg was certainly aware that the French sixth could be reinterpreted in this way and could therefore be used to connect such distantly related tonal areas. Schoenberg's own colourful comments in his *Harmonielehre* on the French sixth and other 'vagrant' chords are particularly relevant here. In the chapter entitled 'At the Frontiers of Tonality' Schoenberg states that:

> Later, the pupil will best take all these vagrant chords for what they are, without tracing them back to a key or a degree: homeless phenomena, unbelievably adaptable and unbelievably lacking in independence; spies, who ferret out weaknesses and use them to cause confusion; turncoats, to whom abandonment of their individuality is an end in itself; agitators in every respect, but above all: most amusing fellows.[20]

If we consider the opening lines of Mombert's text for the second song, 'Schlafend trägt man mich in mein Heimatland' ('Sleeping, I am carried to my homeland'), Schoenberg's further remarks seem particularly appropriate:

> Once we abandon the desire to explain the derivation of these chords, their

effect becomes much clearer. We understand then that it is not absolutely necessary for such chords to appear just in the function their derivation calls for, since the climate of their homeland has no influence on their character. They flourish in every climate.[21]

As was the case with the *B* chord, the implicit tonal potential of the *C* chord is perhaps more revelatory of its function in the work as a whole than is its explicit pitch structure considered only within the context of the second song. The *C* chord is made up of four pitches of a whole-tone scale arranged as two tritones separated by a major third (Example 12). As a result the vagrant *C* chord, like the *B* chord, is deliberately ambiguous and can function in tonal, whole-tone, and atonal contexts. In his important article on the second song Craig Ayrey has said that, 'The first Mombert song … can tolerate a double historical focus'.[22] This 'double focus' results from Berg's particular use of this and other closely related chords throughout the song.[23]

Ex. 12

C

The harmonic vocabulary of the third song is highly chromatic but less whole-tone orientated than that of the second. The tonal scheme of the song is based on three principal key areas: A♭ minor, D minor, and E♭ major. Like the thematic links mentioned above, this tonal structure thus refers back to the first song, directly links the third with the second, and closes the large-scale tonal movement of the first three songs from D minor to E♭.

Unlike the second song, where no firm tonic key is apparent in the entire A section, the A♭ key area of the third (the key indicated by the key signature and the 'tonic' of the modified dominant seventh *C* chord at the end of the preceding song) is introduced immediately. The music then moves, via an enharmonic modulation, from A♭ to D minor, the tonic key of the first song. The relationship of this section to the earlier song is also made clear thematically through the reappearance of the bass ostinato figure of the first song in the falling perfect fifth in the upper part of the piano at bars 6–8 (imitating the sound of the bells mentioned in the text) and the simultaneous reference in the piano to the falling sixth to which the word 'Schlafen' was set in the first song.

After the final cadence on E♭ is reached at bar 11 the semiquaver A♭ falling to the low E♭ in the accompaniment comes as something of a surprise. This accompanimental A♭ both mirrors the final cadential motion of the vocal line in bar 11 and recalls the repeated falling perfect fifth 'bell' figures in bars 6–8. It can also be understood as a last reference to the opening A♭ key area of the song.[24] The end of the third song thus provides a thematic and harmonic conclusion both to the first and the central structural group of the second and third. The intricate web of tonal interrelationships generated in the second and third songs is summarized in Figure 2.

Figure 2

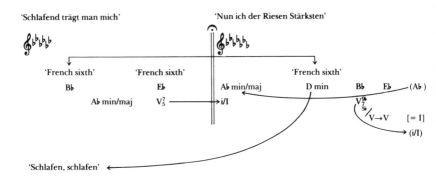

'Warm die Lüfte'

The last song of the cycle is immediately and strikingly different in harmonic vocabulary and vocal style from the three previous songs.[25] Frequently cited as Berg's first freely atonal composition, this highly dissonant and tonally experimental song is most reminiscent of Schoenberg's roughly contemporaneous song cycle *Das Buch der hängenden Gärten* (1909). Although the vocal and accompanimental styles are undeniably influenced by Schoenberg's song cycle, Berg's musical language clearly distinguishes his work from that of his teacher.

In the very first bars the composer effectively 'distances' this song from those that precede it in the cycle. Unlike what has gone before, the harmonic vocabulary of this song is based on the two whole-tone scales or hexachords. While the C chord of the second song is made up of pitches from one whole-tone hexachord, the high level of dissonance in the fourth results from the simultaneous use of both hexachords (Example 13). Thus in bars 1–2 the opening chord employs the notes of one whole-tone hexachord (hexachord I) in the voice and the piano right hand and the other (hexachord II) in the left hand of the piano part. Although the lowest note (C♮) does not belong to hexachord II, it is sounded together with the low G as an anticipation of the downbeats of bars 1–3. The interval of the perfect fifth, so central to the thematic and harmonic design of the preceding songs, is thus presented here as a simultaneity.

Ex. 13 Four Songs, IV, bars 1–2

hexachord I

hexachord II
(incomplete)

perfect 5th
(as dyad)

Reprinted by permission of Robert Lienau, Berlin

The vocal style of 'Warm die Lüfte' is also unique in the cycle. Unlike the first three songs, where lyrical and arched vocal lines are usually doubled in the accompaniment, in the fourth song the voice is rarely doubled by the piano and the highly disjunct vocal line moves freely between registers: the short vocal 'display' at bars 7–8 (expressing the text 'Ich will singen'—'I want to sing'), for example, is accompanied by a piano figuration that simply alternates between two pitches a tritone apart. A particularly striking moment in the vocal line occurs in bar 19 (following the principal climax in bar 15) with the low and *tonlos* (without pitch) setting of the exclamation 'Stirb!' ('Die!') where Berg probably intended something similar to the Schoenbergian *Sprechstimme* effect. Like the unusual white- and black-note piano glissandi at the climax, this proto-*Sprechstimme* vocal effect suggests that the last of the Four Songs was a kind of compositional laboratory for the young Berg of 1908–10.

The metric and rhythmic structure of the fourth song is similarly free, a regular metre appearing only in the opening two to three bars; subsequently, the composer consistently blurs metrical distinctions. Characteristically Bergian are the notated *ritardandi* and *accelerandi* throughout. Thus, the spectacular piano descent to the low B♭ at bar 18 incorporates a notated *accelerando* (which is further reinforced by the *accel.* indicated by Berg's tempo markings) while the piano part at bars 7–9 consists of a written out *ritardando* on the repeated E♭–A tritone. Finally, the word 'singen' in the vocal part at this same point employs the rhythmic motive from the second and third songs.

Perhaps the most remarkable passage in the final Mombert song is the last six bars. Here Berg transforms and integrates the most important harmonic elements of the first three songs. In these bars Berg not only reintroduces chords and chord progressions that had previously had strong tonal harmonic implications, but does so within a fundamentally different and atonal context. The earlier chords and progressions thus change—or, perhaps more accurately, 'expand'—their meaning. The full significance of this final passage is a result of the dual nature of these simultaneously tonal and atonal chords.

If we now, with an awareness of its relationship to the first three songs, re-examine the closing section of the fourth, we can significantly improve our earlier understanding. All of the elements of the harmonic structure are now easily identifiable. The *C* chord—that is, the French Sixth—of the second song is, as I pointed out earlier, the basis of the written-out *accelerando* at bar 17. While in the opening bars of the second song the *C* chord can be regarded as two tritones separated by a major third, in the fourth song the chord is repartitioned as two major thirds separated by a tritone.

In bars 20–22 Berg extends the *A–B* progression of the first song using the ascending sequence of perfect fourths (*y*) from the opening bass line of the second song. The goal of this new progression is the *B* chord (including the perfect fifth dyad in the bass) reached on the downbeat of bar 22. Finally, three 'cadences' in the accompaniment follow (bars 22, 23, 24) in successively lower registers, each culminating in the *B* chord (Example 14). Each of the three non-*B* cadential chords consists of a major triad and a minor triad separated by a major third. The tonal and symbolic implications of both the three non-*B* cadential chords and the *B* chord itself are thus clear, given Berg's use of these sonorities to set the last two lines of Mombert's text: 'Der Eine *stirbt*, daneben der Andre *lebt*. Das macht die Welt so *tief-schön*' ('The one *dies* while, nearby, the other *lives*. This makes the world so *deeply beautiful*').

The final transpositional level of the *B* chord in the closing bars is of some significance. Interpreting it as a modified seventh chord with both a major and minor third, the pitch that defines the chord's 'minor' modality is D♮, the pitch that defines the chord's 'major' modality is D♯ (spelled as E♭ by Berg). In this way, within the final *B* chord of the fourth song, Berg makes reference to (or, perhaps better, subsumes) the tonic key of the first (D minor) and the central tonal area (E♭) of the second and third. These final nine bars thus constitute both the musical and dramatic dénouement of the entire cycle.

Whether arrived at by instinct or conscious calculation, a great part of the musical and dramatic impact of the closing bars derives from a powerful tonal–atonal duality. While Berg obviously refined his compositional techniques throughout his creative life (so that many of the stylistic feature that are only nascent in the Four Songs find their ultimate realisation in mature masterpieces such as *Lulu* and the Violin Concerto), it is also clear that even in these early songs Berg was struggling with those same tonal–atonal compositional issues that preoccupied his teacher, Schoenberg, for several years. The solutions that Berg arrived at in the Four Songs are hardly those of a composer 'unable' to escape the world of late-19th-century harmony and Romanticism. Rather, they are solutions that both look back to the German tradition of Beethoven, Brahms, and Wagner and contain within them the seeds of future developments—the seeds of Berg's own, highly idiomatic and far-reaching 'conservative revolution'.

Ex. 14 Four Songs, IV, bars 17–25

Reprinted by permission of Robert Lienau, Berlin

Notes

1. René Leibowitz, *Schoenberg and his School: the Contemporary Stage of the Language of Music*, trans. Dika Newlin (New York: Philosophical Library, 1949), pp. 137–67.
2. Arnold Schoenberg, 'Addendum 1946' to 'Composition with Twelve Tones (1)', *Style and Idea: Selected Writings of Arnold Schoenberg*, ed. Leonard Stein, trans. Leo Black (Berkeley and Los Angeles: University of California Press, 1984), p. 245.
3. Ibid.
4. For examples of this traditional view see Willi Reich, *Alban Berg*, trans. Cornelius Cardew (London: Thames and Hudson, 1965) and Hans Ferdinand Redlich, *Alban Berg: the Man and his Music* (London: John Calder, 1957). For some time George Perle has actively fought this view in his published articles and books on the composer: see, for example, *The Operas of Alban Berg*, vols 1 and 2 (Berkeley and Los Angeles: University of California Press, 1980, 1985).

5. I do not mean to suggest that no work has been or is being done on Berg's opp. 1–3. A recent example is Janet Schmalfeldt's excellent work on the Piano Sonata in her paper 'Berg's Path to Atonality: the Piano Sonata op. 1', delivered at the University of Chicago International Alban Berg Symposium, 22 February 1985.

6. Mark DeVoto first alerted me to the existence of unidentified sketch materials for the first, second, and fourth of the Four Songs in the Austrian National Library. I have subsequently uncovered other sketches for parts of these songs as well as a sketch of the third.

7. Nicholas Chadwick states that Berg used the second, revised edition of *Der Glühende* (Minden in Westfalen, 1902) as the source of the Mombert texts. The evidence on which he bases this statement is, however, never made clear. See 'A Survey of the Early Songs of Alban Berg' (BLitt, Oxford University, 1971), p. 82.

8. For a detailed discussion of the sketches and a comprehensive analysis of the cycle see Stephen Kett, 'Alban Berg's *Vier Lieder* op. 2: an Analytical, Contextual and Source-critical Study' (PhD, Harvard University, in progress).

9. Personal communication from the composer's nephew, Erich Alban Berg, 28 February 1986.

10. See Mark DeVoto's contribution to this volume.

11. Rosemary Hilmar, 'Alban Berg's Studies with Schoenberg', *Journal of the Arnold Schoenberg Institute*, vol. 8, no. 1 (June 1984), pp. 7–29.

12. The far-reaching changes in Berg's early *Lied* style can be seen by comparing the early song 'Abschied' of *c*1901 (published in Reich, op. cit.) and the later 'Nacht' of *c*1907–8 which was published in 1928 as one of the Seven Early Songs. (An edition of the Seven Early Songs by Christopher Hailey is now being completed for the *Alban Berg Gesamtausgabe*.)

13. See Mark DeVoto's contribution to this volume and his 'Creeping Chromaticism', a paper delivered at the University of Chicago International Alban Berg Symposium, 23 February 1985.

14. For examples of two new chords generated in this way see the discussion of chords *A* and *B* below.

15. For a discussion of Berg's use of palindromic forms see Robert Morgan's paper in *Alban Berg: Analytical and Historical Perspectives*, ed. David Gable and Robert Morgan (Oxford University Press, forthcoming).

16. It may not be coincidental that the texts for these two songs are also adjacent (nos 56 and 57 respectively) in Mombert's cycle.

17. See Bruce Archibald's contribution to this volume. The first full description of this aspect of Berg's harmonic–contrapuntal style is to be found in Archibald, 'Harmonic Practice in the Early Music of Alban Berg' (PhD, Harvard University, 1967).

18. The use of this rhythmic motive in the Four Songs was first pointed out by Douglas Jarman, *The Music of Alban Berg* (London: Faber and Faber, 1979), pp. 147-8. Berg's use of much more complex and abstract rhythmic patterns is a well-known characteristic of his later mature compositions.

19. While the opening chord of the second song has been mentioned in all of the major monographs on the composer, the most extensive analysis of the song itself appears in Craig Ayrey, 'Berg's "Scheideweg": Analytical Issues in op. 2/ii', *Music Analysis*, vol. 1 (1982), pp. 189–202.

20. Arnold Schoenberg, *Theory of Harmony*, trans. Roy E. Carter (Berkeley and Los Angeles: University of California Press, 1978), p. 258.

21. Ibid.

22. Ayrey, op. cit., p. 190.

23. Note that in the published score of the second song the recapitulation in the latter half of bar 15 has two notes different from the original statement in bars 1–2. Berg corrected the C on the last quaver of bar 15 to read C♭ (thus making it the same as the B♮ at the equivalent point in bar 2) in a personal copy. It seems highly likely that the B on the second half of the second beat of bar 15 should also be corrected to match the equivalent A in bar 1.

24. In fact, in a fair copy of this song made by Kemperling, Berg's copyist, this low A♭ was either 'corrected' or inadvertantly changed to the more traditional (and 'expected') cadential B♭. There is no evidence in any of Berg's own corrected copies of the published score that the note should be changed.

25. This song was published (together with one song each by Schoenberg and Webern) in 1909 in the *Blaue Reiter Almanac*, ed. Franz Marc and Wassily Kandinsky.

The Instrumental Music

BERG'S DEVELOPMENT AS AN INSTRUMENTAL COMPOSER

BRUCE ARCHIBALD

(In the following essay middle C is designated as c′, with octaves above as c″, c‴ etc, and octaves below as c, C, C′etc. Octaves are reckoned from C upwards.)

Until he began to study with Arnold Schoenberg at the age of 19, Alban Berg was essentially self-taught as a composer. His pre-student works are entirely songs, over 70 of them. Part of Schoenberg's task was to lead Berg into instrumental composition. The known instrumental works written under Schoenberg's tutelage include the Twelve Variations on an Original Theme, for piano, the Sonata op. 1 for piano, and the String Quartet op. 3.[1] Following his formal studies came the Four Pieces op. 5, for clarinet and piano and the Three Orchestral Pieces op. 6. These works present a remarkable development over a mere eight years, from 1907 to 1915.

If the Piano Variations were composed no earlier than 1907 as is generally assumed (they were performed on 18 November 1908), then the greatest leap is from there to the Piano Sonata of 1908. The Variations are in the language— tonal, textural, and gestural—of Brahms and Schumann. The theme is a single binary form of 8 + 8 bars. The first half is solidly diatonic in C major while the second hints at the chromatic language of the Piano Sonata (Example 1). The variations themselves are arranged to emphasize variety and they show considerable charm and virtuosity. And there are flourishes of contrapuntal adroitness: Variation 3 is a two-voice canon at the octave, Variation 5 is freely canonic at the octave, and Variation 6 is a triple canon. Variation 12 is greatly expanded into an appropriately climactic Finale.[2]

Sonata op. 1, for piano

In the Piano Sonata we come upon an entirely new harmonic language for Berg, one that reflects the strong influence of the mentor's music, specifically the Chamber Symphony no. 1. Schoenberg's work adds two new elements to highly

Ex. 1 Piano Variations, bars 9–16

chromatic tonality: whole-tone harmonies and harmonies based on perfect fourths. The importance of these elements to Schoenberg is reinforced by the fact that he devotes chapters to them near the end of his *Harmonielehre* of 1911: Chapter 20, 'The Whole-tone Scale and Related Five and Six-part Chords', and Chapter 21, 'Chords Constructed in Fourths.'[3] The Chamber Symphony opens with three chords: the first a six-note chord built on perfect fourths, the second a six-note chord containing five notes of the same whole-tone scale with one note doubled, and finally an F major triad (Example 2). The voice-leading consists entirely of semitones and common tones. The progression is a cadence in F, and by working backwards from the triad we hear the whole-tone chord as a dominant major ninth with added Gb and ab'. The ab' functions as a g#' by leading upward to ab'. It can be thought of as a raised fifth of the dominant ninth while the Gb is a lowered fifth. Such an interpretation coincides with material in Schoenberg's Chapter 20. The first chord, the quartal chord, serves the function of dominant preparation and—with its G, f and bb—in fact is rather like a supertonic seventh. In Chapter 21 Schoenberg does not specifically give this interpretation, but when he gives examples of resolutions of six-note quartal chords (p. 406) they tend to resolve to dominant-type chords. So, in short, we have here a ii–V–I cadence in F major (no matter that the piece is in E major) with a different sonorous quality for each chord.

Berg knew the Chamber Symphony well—in fact he wrote an analysis of it for Universal Edition, as he also did of Schoenberg's *Gurrelieder* and *Pelleas und Melisande*. The harmony of the Chamber Symphony is the source and fibre of Berg's Piano Sonata. The one-movement Sonata is in B minor—and indeed there is a signature of two sharps throughout—but also there is an accidental in front of almost every note. Only at the end of the first phrase and at the end of

Ex. 2 Schoenberg, Chamber Symphony no. 1, first three chords

the piece is there a dominant resolving to a tonic triad. In fact, there are no other dominants resolved directly to appropriate triads in any key during the Sonata, although dominant-type sonorities are constantly present. The harmony floats in a state of what Schoenberg called 'suspended tonality' that derives from Wagner and his followers, to which is added the two distinct elements discussed above.[4]

The opening phrase presents the musical material of the piece (Example 3). The melody alone presents the material: a quartal triad (g^{ι}–c''–$f\sharp''$), an augmented triad implying whole-tone harmony (g''–eb''–b'), and the descending semitone representing chromaticism (d''–$c\sharp''$, also heard in diminution in the alto). The voice-leading is entirely descending semitones connecting a ii^7 to forms of dominant in bar 3 to the first of two B minor tonics. As the exposition is to be repeated we actually hear the V–i in B minor three times.

Ex. 3 Piano Sonata, bars 1–4

Reprinted by permission of Robert Lienau, Berlin

In this first phrase quartal harmony is only represented by the opening melodic gesture, which becomes the primary motive, in all its permutations, of the Sonata. However, this motive is not made up of perfect fourths as in the Chamber Symphony but a perfect fourth and an augmented fourth covering a major seventh rather than minor seventh. This three-note cell is so frequently used by the Schoenberg circle in these years of late tonal and early so-called atonal music that it has been given the nickname 'the atonal triad'. Berg uses it almost exclusively as a melodic figure, and when he turns to chords of fourths the fourths are perfect. In the Chamber Symphony Schoenberg used the six-note perfect fourth chords at points of climax, most notably at the climax at the end of the development, which becomes the transition to the slow-movement section (bars 356–77).[5] Berg places the fourth chords at the climaxes of large subsections. Example 4 is from the second large subsection of the exposition. The harmony leading into this excerpt has been the prevailing seventh-plus chords with whole-tone flavouring and in semitone voice-leading. Fourths gradually emerge until they are full-blown on the downbeat of bar 44. The melodic motion continues into the climax in bar 45 where a full six-note chord emerges (third beat). Harmonically the bar is a ii^7 in B minor that is explicit and traditional on the downbeat and then is transformed into the quartal chord on the third beat—a possible confirmation of my interpretation of the first chord of the Chamber Symphony.

Ex. 4 Piano Sonata, bars 44–5

Reprinted by permission of Robert Lienau, Berlin

As implied above, Berg's Sonata is in sonata form, and indeed it is a nicely balanced one with each of the three sections itself divided into three subsections. Each subsection is shaped as a gradual building-up to a climax and a rapid decay. In terms of number of bars, the sections and subsections are as follows:

exposition	$29 + 20 + 7 = 56$
development	$14 + 30 + 11 = 55$
recapitulation	$26 + 30 + 13 = 69$

In the exposition the subsections correspond to the traditional A group, B group, codetta. Appropriately, the codetta is much shorter than the other two subsections; it is very restful, quiet and slow (*Viel langsamer*, quasi Adagio)—the calm after the two storms. In the recapitulation the codetta is expanded to round out the movement as there is no coda. In the development it is the central subsection that is the largest and attains the most impassioned—indeed the ultimate—climax of the Sonata. Only here does Berg resort to *fortississimo* (*ffff*).

Whole-tone harmony in Berg's Piano Sonata is so pervasive that almost any excerpt would present it. Often whole-tone sounds occur in conjunction with more traditional seventh and ninth chords. In these cases there is an ebb and flow between sonorities that are almost but not quite whole-tone and those that are purely so. An example is the beginning of the second subsection or *B* group of the exposition (Example 5). Here is a prolonged and embellished dominant of D major. The first chord is built entirely from one whole-tone hexachord except for the melody note e″. However, the notes of the following bar (bar 31) are entirely from the hexachord containing A.

Ex. 5 Piano Sonata, bars 30–32

Reprinted by permission of Robert Lienau, Berlin

The beginning of the codetta is purely whole-tone (Example 6). The prevailing harmonic motion of descending semitones moves the chords back and forth from the one hexachord to the other. The chords themselves are dominant sevenths with raised or lowered fifths.

Ex. 6 Piano Sonata, bars 50–52

Reprinted by permission of Robert Lienau, Berlin

The Berg Sonata is comfortable for the hands and gratifying to play, although it is not without considerable difficulties. The greater counterpoint of the development can be a finger twister and a challenge as to rhythm and weighting or balancing. The whole Sonata is replete with octaves for both hands. The beginning of the recapitulation adds to the opening phrases an ascending overlapping of the primary motive in the left hand that requires skill and dexterity (sinisterity) for clear articulation. Berg was a pianist but rarely performed in public. In his early years he would play his songs while his brother Charly or his sister Smaragda would sing, but this was usually in private. On 7 November 1907, in a concert by Schoenberg's pupils, Berg played the piano for his own Double Fugue, for string quartet with piano accompaniment (manuscript lost), but on the same programme he did not play for three of his Seven Early Songs. There is no record of his ever playing his Sonata in public, nor his Chamber Concerto, for violin, piano, and 13 wind instruments. While the early Piano Variations have awkward moments for the fingers, the two major keyboard works are pianistically idiomatic but difficult. Berg loved to play piano four-hands which he did with Smaragda and later with his wife Helene. In his student years the Berg family had a large library of four-hand music. He jokingly liked to call himself 'the last of the great four-hand players'.

String Quartet op. 3

With Berg's next work, the Four Songs op. 2, completed in 1910, he again followed in the footsteps of the master. Like Schoenberg's String Quartet no. 2 (1908), the Four Songs begin in chromatic tonality but finally reach out beyond the grasp of tonal centres, as if feeling 'air from other planets'. The following work, the two-movement String Quartet op. 3, begins the exploration of this new-found land.

Carried over from the Sonata and other earlier works is a predominance of whole-tone harmonies and patterns. Quartal figurations consist almost exclusively of the 'atonal triad'—there are few chords of purely perfect fourths. An important chord that pervades the String Quartet is the major third plus perfect fifth, outlining a major seventh, and its permutations. The medium of the string quartet brings forth an even greater contrapuntal intensity than is found in the earlier works.

In the absence of the unifying force of tonality, Schoenberg, Berg, and Webern held firm to the musical motive as a source of unity. In this they felt themselves in the tradition of Beethoven and Brahms. By motive they meant not just the rhythm and pitch order of a musical figure but also the pitch content abstracted into other rhythms or orderings or into simultaneities. An example in the String Quartet is the melodic pattern e^1–f–ab^1 (minor second–minor third) first heard in bars 10 and 11 and recurring intact and in permutations throughout the first movement. In Berg's post-tonal music there are two interrelated characteristic features: the use of wedge-like patterns and an intervallic consistency of voice-leading. The first is fairly obvious but the second is best presented by an example from the opening of the Quartet (Example 7). The lower two voices in bars 2 and 3 are consistently descending minor seconds (viola) over descending perfect fourths (cello). The result is a wedge-like pattern in similar motion, with each voice maintaining its specific interval. I shall return to this second characteristic feature in more detail shortly.

Ex. 7 String Quartet, I, bars 1–13

More common wedge formations in the String Quartet and later works are those of contrary motion. A hint of this is found in bar 4 where the major seventh G–f♯ is embellished by neighbour notes, first minor seconds and then major seconds. Another wedge occurs in the melody (second violin) where the sustained b (bars 2–3) splits apart by semitone steps: b–c^l–c♯^{l}–d^l against b–b♭–a (bars 3–6).

Whole-tone content can be heard in the opening motive where five of the six notes come from the same whole-tone hexachord, and even the interloper c^l can be heard as a chromatic passing note between d♭^{l} and b. The following wedge-like figure cancels whole-tone sound and introduces two permutations of another important cell mentioned above, the major third plus perfect fifth (bar 3: c–g–b and G–b–f♯). Whole-tone sound returns with the return of the initial

motive in bar 5 (viola). In this bar plus upbeat all but three brief notes (cello G
and viola e♭ and f) are from one hexachord. The first entrance of the first violin
introduces a new motive of strongly whole-tone flavour as its first six notes
present five notes from one hexachord with c♯″ repeated. Additionally, the
lower three voices reinforce this same hexachord.

Ex. 8 String Quartet, I, (a) bars 41–4, (b) bars 48–9

The first two phrases of the second theme group (bars 41ff. and bars 48ff.)
more thoroughly integrate whole-tone sound with the major third–perfect fifth
cell. (Example 8). In the first phrase the major thirds and the minor seventh in
the violins give the impression of moving back and forth between whole-tone
hexachords. At the same time these melodic voices connect with one or the other
note in the ostinato to form the three-note cell as marked in the example. The
beginning of the second phrase is essentially a four-note segment of a whole-tone
scale. But again, with its supporting voices we find a combination of whole-tone
and major third–perfect fifth.

A short time later these initial motives of the *B* group are contrapuntally
combined. The result is very strongly whole-tone (Example 9). I have encircled
only the notes of the hexachord in which the melody participates. (Obviously

the non-circled notes participate in the other hexachord.) The result is a rich overlapping and interlocking of the alternation of whole-tone hexachords in a fluid, cloud-like flow.

Ex. 9 String Quartet, I, bars 63–5

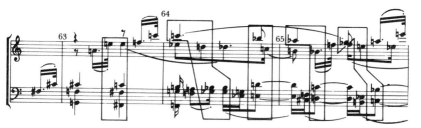

Returning to wedge-like patterns, possibly the most spectacular display of wedges is the opening bars of the second movement (Example 10). Here is vigorous, dissonant, angular music whose wildness is focused toward the strong

Ex. 10 String Quartet, II, bars 1–3

Ex. 10 cont.

arrival on a unison d′ in bar 4. Embedded in this turbulence are two melodic figures important for the rest of the movement. These are the first four beats of violin 1 and the triplets of violin 2 beginning on the third beat of bar 2. But giving focus to the seeming chaos are several wedge patterns, the three most obvious of which are: (1) the pizzicato notes in violin 2 and cello that move inward by semitones to e′ (bars 1–2); (2) a melodic compound-line wedge in violin 1 moving outward by semitone and whole-tone steps (bar 2, beat 2 to bar 3, beat 2); (3) the rapid inward wedge to d′ at the end of bar 3. The last is in effect the summation of a large-scale wedge as indicated by the minim note-heads in Example 10 (b). The lower component comes from the angular line in viola; the upper component begins as the lower part of violin 1's melodic wedge. Another more subtle and complex wedge is found in the lower register and, thus, formed by notes in viola and cello. It begins in viola as the minor third d–f expands to the perfect fourth c♯–f♯. Then five beats later this perfect fourth is transplanted down an octave in cello and expanded further to the perfect fifth C–G. Another view of this wedge is to place it in the context of a larger one wherein the fourth c♯–f♯ resolves to the fifth c–g twice in two different octaves. And, in addition, another wedge occurs—the minor seventh b over c♯ expands to the octave c–c′ (Example 10(c)). To push this into more abstract theoretical territory: there is a primary wedge on the large scale and in diminution inward to the arrival note d′. There are two secondary wedges—one inward to e′ in the pizzicato instruments and the other outward to C in the lower register with the C appearing in three octaves (C, c, c′). These two secondary-wedge patterns focus on the whole-tone step above and below the destination d′ and thus act as a large-scale tonal wedge moving inward by major seconds: in short, a cadence by symmetry.

Related to wedge patterns and symmetry is the intervallic consistency of voice-leading mentioned earlier. In 1972 while contemplating the numerous examples in Berg's music of what I then called intervallic harmony I devised a chart that gives an abstract of the possibilities of intervallic consistency (Example 11). Over a C pedal there is a line for each interval up to a tritone. As each line moves upward by its specific interval, larger intervals above smaller, it forms a chord with the other lines at each step of the way. Each chord contains only a single kind of interval and these chords increase in size from all minor seconds to all major seconds to all minor thirds etc. As the lines continue after the tritone chord, each chord is built of the octave inversions of the previous intervals in reverse order (perfect fifth, minor sixth, etc.). Thus a symmetrical chart is formed that reveals a unity of line and chord, or of melody and harmony, or, to misquote Heraclitus, 'The way up and the way across are the same'.

Ex. 11

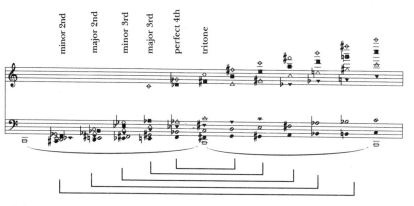

◇ tritone
■ perfect 4th
△ major 3rd
▼ minor 3rd
𝑜 major 2nd
● minor 2nd
□ unison

A short time after devising this chart I showed it to George Perle and he in turn showed me a copy of a letter Berg had written to Schoenberg on 27 July 1920 which contained a very similar diagram. The only significant difference is that Berg includes all twelve intervals from minor second to perfect octave (and no C pedal, though it also starts on C). In addition Berg marks both the horizontal symmetry around the tritone and the vertical symmetry. His letter reads: 'Dear Friend, I came upon the above peculiarity by chance. A theoretical frivolity.'[6]

Berg's belittling of his chart masks what is certainly a strong element in his creative instincts. The chart is a concise abstraction of a kind of pure spiritual source from which many concrete passages of his music emerge throughout the rest of his career. Of the numerous examples in the String Quartet, let me mention only two more. The opening idea of the first movement (Example 7, bars 1–3) returns two octaves higher to close the movement but with an added voice in the wedge-like figure. This is a middle voice (viola) that begins on the same f″ as the descending-fourths line and descends by major seconds: f″–eb″– db″. The resulting final chord is sustained (diminuendo, *pppp*, non vibrato) and is a quartal chord built as an atonal triad and a perfect-fourth triad that share two notes: from the top down, b″–f#″–db″–g′.

Finally, from early in the second movement, an important melody is introduced in the viola with three-voice harmony below it (Example 12). In bar 10 two of the accompanimental lines move by semitones and the lowest voice by whole tones. There is a brief instant of a pure perfect-fourth chord so rare in the work. In the harmony of bar 11 the outer two voices descend by semitones (viola, cello) while the middle voice, which becomes the top voice, ascends by perfect fourths (violin 1). At the end, over the barline, there is an exchange of intervals and directions between the upper two lines. The resulting chords are consistently whole-tone, alternating between the two hexachords on each quarter note. The melody (violin 2) adds a touch of dissonance by conflicting with one hexachord for a quaver while anticipating the next hexachord by a quaver. Thus, whole-tone harmony is maintained and decorated by consistent intervallic motion using the only three intervals (exclusive of their inversions) that move from one whole-tone hexachord to the other: minor second, minor

Ex. 12 String Quartet, II, bars 10–11

third, and perfect fourth.

The two movements of the String Quartet are both in sonata forms of about ten minutes' duration. The first movement is lyrical, but in spite of a basic tempo mark of *langsam* there is sufficient richness of detail and activity not to give it the feel of a slow movement. However, the second creates a sharp contrast with its vigorous tempi and generally much higher dynamic level. Only in the lush and broadly lyrical second theme (bars 55ff. and 201ff.) does the tension relax somewhat.

In the String Quartet the sonata forms are merged with perpetual development in highly contrapuntal textures. The work is an organic being constantly growing, recombining, evolving. The sectional divisions of sonata form here are well-balanced and clearly indicated in spite of the continual ongoing nature of the music. As is appropriate in slow-movement sonata form (if we hear it as a slow movement) the development section is quite short in comparison with exposition and recapitulation, which are themselves nicely balanced: in number of bars, 80 (40 + 40), 24, and 82 (43 + 39). One might think of the last five bars as a coda. In the second movement all three sections are similar in size except that they show on the large structural level the constant growth that is found moment to moment: in number of bars, 72 (55 + 17), 79 (47 + 32), and 81 (49 + 32).

Figure 1

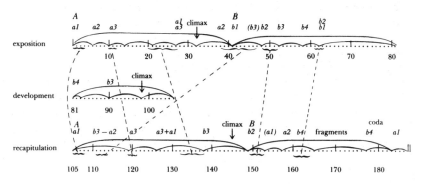

A brief look at the first movement will serve as an introduction to the interacting of sonata form structure with perpetual development. In Figure 1, which summarizes the form of the movement, I have placed the exposition directly above the recapitulation so that parallelisms can be seen. The lines connecting the two sections show similar material's being used in a somewhat similar manner, but in no cases are the parallelisms exact. For instance, the return of the first three bars at bars 105–7 has the wedge-like figure rhythmically dislocated: the ab–g–f♯ begin on the downbeat of bar 106 but the fourths f–c–G begin a quaver later. In the exposition all the material of the A group (bars 1–40)

is presented in the first eleven bars, in which three themes – *a1*, *a2*, and *a3* – appear (see Example 7); the remaining bars develop these ideas. Most especially worked over is *a3*, which is heard in various rhythms and variations and in inversion. As the climax is approached (bars 28–32), *a3* in diminution is played below the opening motive of *a1*, combined to form an outward wedge of mostly whole tones (specifically b″–c♯‴–e♭‴–f♯‴ over G♯–F♯–E–D–C). The two whole-tone scale fragments conflict—that is, represent opposing hexachords—but the skip of a minor third in the upper line brings them together on a C–f♯‴ tritone for the climax.

In the *B* section of the exposition the materials are presented in a more leisurely way, but basically *b3* and *b4* (see Example 13) are variants of the descending whole-tone scale fragment of *b2* (see Example 8). This descending whole-tone motion dominates the section. In the recapitulation the demarcation of the end of *A* and beginning of *B* is less obvious because contrapuntal-developmental action is even more intense. I have indicated *B* as beginning in bar 149 where *b2* returns in a form most like its first appearance in bars 48–9. However, bars 138-48 have a great contrapuntal expansion and climax on the *b3* figure which is gradually transformed into *b2*. Thus the *B* section might be thought to begin in bar 138.

Ex. 13 String Quartet, I, themes

These are only hints of the extraordinary developmental richness of the String Quartet. Finally, I would like to mention a tonal element in the second movement that has ramifications in later works, especially the Three Orchestral Pieces and *Wozzeck*. When Berg emphasizes a tonal centre, either as a single pitch or as an actual key, it often is D or D minor. We saw in Example 10 that the focus at the beginning of the second movement was toward an emphatic d′. This pitch remains as a pedal for six bars. The notes d″ and d‴ return at bar 23, d′ at bars 65–72 and 166–72, and five octaves (d‴′, d‴, d″, d′, d) at bars 218–27. Finally, in the last seven bars (bars 227–33) a traditional vii[7] of D minor is evolved (C♯–G–e–b♭) to which is added a tonic d′. The flourish of the final bar (Example 14) is both tonal and non-tonal: the rapidly ascending chords and the final down-bow crunch are quite atonal and dissonant, but the first beat and the first half of the third beat present a vii[7]–i cadence in D minor. Thus D is a significant tonal reference point in the second movement. More on D minor later.

Ex. 14 String Quartet, II, bar 232

Berg's String Quartet is a love song to Helene just as some 16 years later his other string quartet, the Lyric Suite, would be a love song to Hanna. Berg was working on the String Quartet during the passionate period of his love and courtship of Helene Nahowski, and the emotional excitement of the time can be felt in the music. The première of the Quartet came on 24 April 1911 just days before their marriage on 3 May. The players were an *ad hoc* group and not a functioning string quartet with ensemble experience together. The poorly received performance was inevitable, with a thrown-together group's having to deal with the considerable difficulties of the piece. The work uses the full range of special string techniques such as playing near the bridge or the fingerboard, harmonics, pizzicato, non vibrato, and some very dramatic bowings. But most problematic for such an ensemble must have been the constant and extreme rubato—rarely does a single bar maintain a single tempo. Twelve years later the work received a proper performance by the Havemann Quartet on 2 August 1923 in conjunction with the first chamber music festival of the International Society for Contemporary Music. There it was received with great enthusiasm.

> They played with indescribable beauty, and I can tell you, though only you, that despite my great excitement (I was sitting in the second row, next to Rufer, rather hidden, unrecognized by the audience) I revelled in the lovely sounds, the solemn sweetness and ecstasy of the music. You can't imagine it by what you've heard so far. The 'wildest' and 'most daring' passages were sheer harmony in the classical sense.
>
> The first movement ended in an elevated atmosphere; complete stillness in the audience, a short breath for the players, and it went on.
>
> At the end there was almost frantic general applause. The quartet themselves came back twice, and kept looking for me in the audience. The third time I was called for, stepped on to the platform quite by myself, and was received with terrific enthusiasm by the *whole* audience—not one sound of booing. The applause continued, and once more the five of us went up on to the platform. Quite an important success for Salzburg and for such a small work of chamber music.[7]

Four Pieces op. 5, for clarinet and piano

The Four Pieces for clarinet and piano hold the unique place in Berg's works of being his only miniatures, of the sort preferred by Webern especially during this period: Four Pieces op. 7, for violin and piano (1910), Six Bagatelles op. 9, for string quartet (1913) which is dedicated to Berg, Three Little Pieces op. 11, for cello and piano (1914). Berg's Altenberg Songs are considered miniatures by some, but their brevity is a logical outcome of the short 'picture-postcard' poems he was setting; also the first and last songs have a breadth of melody that takes them out of the realm of miniatures.

The Four Pieces were written in 1913, but it is not clear exactly when in that year. The score indicates spring: so does Willi Reich on p. 41 of the English translation of his *Alban Berg* (1963); but Reich on p. 113 of the same book and Redlich on p. 291 of his English-language *Alban Berg: the Man and his Music* give summer. In Berg's *Letters to his Wife* the date is June 1913 in a chronology given on p. 127: this would set them in the same month that Berg travelled to Berlin to visit Schoenberg.[8] This visit was both a joy and a trauma.

The joy was Berg's first encounter with Schoenberg's *Pierrot lunaire*, which was composed and premiered in 1912. Schoenberg arranged a rehearsal of *Pierrot* for Berg. Over a year later, on 20 July 1914, Berg wrote to Schoenberg: 'I only know that on the two occasions when I heard *Pierrot* I was conscious of the deepest impression *ever* made on me by a work of art, and that the enigmatic power of these pieces has left *indelible* traces on my mind.'[9]

The trauma came in the form of Schoenberg's strong criticism of Berg's recent work and possibly even of his personality. Reich and others feel that Schoenberg's criticism, which had a profound effect on the ex-student, centred on Berg's turn to writing miniatures. This seems ironic in that the Four Pieces were strongly influenced by Schoenberg's own miniatures, the Six Little Piano Pieces op. 19, composed in February and June of 1911. The sixth of these pieces, the one composed in June, was inspired by the visionary sight of a ray of sunlight breaking through the clouds at Mahler's funeral. Many writers have pointed out a clear similarity between the second pieces in both sets: an ostinato of a repeated major third, g^L-b' mostly staccato in the Schoenberg and d–f♯ very legato in the Berg. While both pieces are in 4/4 metre, are very soft and slow (Schoenberg, *pp*, *langsam*; Berg, *ppp*, *sehr langsam*), and both are nine bars long, the character of each is quite different. The Schoenberg is cool, fragmented and in a steady pulse with a kind of repressed expressivity; the Berg is warm, with rich sustained harmonies and much rubato, and presents a single broad phrase of overtly expressive melody.

Certainly Schoenberg's criticism was more complex and profound than simply that Berg was writing miniatures. We do not know of his criticizing Webern, who brought miniaturism to its extremes. Whatever the details of the confrontation might have been, we know it had a powerful impact on Berg.

After returning to Vienna from Berlin he wrote to Schoenberg on 14 June 1913:

> But I must thank you for your censure just as much as for everything you ever gave me, in the full knowledge that it is meant well—and for my own good. I need not tell you, my dear Mr. Schoenberg, that the great pain it caused me is a guarantee that I have taken your criticism to heart.[10]

Even more remarkable than the scale of the Four Pieces is their pitch content. In Berg's first four works with opus numbers we can recognize melodies and motives and their recurrences and transformations. This is not the case in the Four Pieces, where the surface gives the impression of constant change. Unity of pitch content is buried deep in the music and is found only after many hearings and some private investigation. Recent research finds the interaction of small groupings of notes, usually called cells or sets, to be helpful in understanding the unity. A cell or set is an unordered group of from three to eight notes or pitch classes.[11] That is, for example, the pitches may appear as a chord, as a melody, as voices in counterpoint, etc. Douglas Jarman points out how the opening, mostly unaccompanied, melody in the clarinet (one and a half bars) presents the primary pitch relationships for all four pieces.[12] The melody is in two short sub-phrases of six and three notes respectively: a♭″–e♭″–g′–a′–c″–e″ and a″–d″–f♯′. Together there are eight different pitches, with A (a′,a″) appearing in both phraselets. Thus there is a six-note set, a three-note set, and a combined eight-note set. Jarman demonstrates how the second piece opens with the eight-note set, the third with the eight-note set transposed a major third higher, and the last piece with the six-note set at pitch.

Unlike the pointillistic nature of Webern's miniatures, and to a much lesser extent Schoenberg's Six Little Piano Pieces, Berg's Four Pieces are like large Romantic gestures confined to small chambers. The music dramatically cries out to be freed. The first and last pieces are the largest of the four, and they both build to horrendous, almost wailing, climaxes and then settle back to a state of resignation, possibly despair. The shorter middle pieces do similar things on smaller scales. The second piece, *sehr langsam*, is a single arching melody. The third is a scherzo-like piece in four tiny sections, each of which is a portion of the rise and fall shapes of the other three pieces. Putting it in over simple terms, the four sections alternate ascent and descent.

The fact that the second piece is slow, the third is scherzo-like, and the outer pieces are larger has led many writers to feel that the work is a four-movement sonata in disguise. Furthermore, the fourth piece has been likened to a rondo-finale with the return of the initial chord in bar 11. The first piece is a far cry from a sonata-allegro movement, but there is a hint of recapitulation in bar 9 when on beats 2 and 3 the piano right hand plays the opening three notes of the clarinet transposed a tritone; overlapping by half a beat, the clarinet plays the piano's first three notes at pitch (repeated two beats later by the clarinet in bar 2).

In a most perceptive study of the Four Pieces in terms of performance

William DeFotis trenchantly describes Berg's solution to the problem of composing

in small forms with materials recognizably derived from large ones ... Consistent with his penchant for setting up a counterpoint of intentions for himself, he solved the problem by simultaneously using two opposing approaches: 1) omitting the expected continuations and resolutions of those materials, thereby constantly creating unconsummated beginnings; 2) interpolating transformations of the materials, dwelling upon pivotal moments of those transformations. Thus, the pieces are simultaneously abridged and extended with regard to the *tendencies* of their materials.[13]

Dynamics and rubato are two of the elements discussed that realize these opposing approaches. Not only are the two instruments almost constantly performing different dynamics, but often the piano alone is dealing with different dynamic levels between the hands. As in the String Quartet, rubato is in constant motion, notated in meticulous detail with complexity and subtlety in the contrapuntal interactions of the rhythms' overlapping ebbs and flows.

Harmonic–melodic materials found in the immediately preceding works are present in the Four Pieces in still greater integration. Whole-tone sounds are heard more with foreign intruders than in pure states. An example of a more integrated whole-tone texture is found in the second piece. Example 15 shows a reduction of the entire piece to its pure pitch structure: the whole-tone hexachord of the prominent major third d–f♯ is written in empty noteheads and the hexachord of the secondary major third f–a in black noteheads. The whole-tone harmony creates a kind of ternary *A-B-A* form within the single arching melody.

Quartal sonorities are common, especially the 'atonal triad'. Probably the most constant presence from before is the wedge pattern. In the first piece alone there are approximately ten separate, often overlapping, examples of wedge-like motions. Example 16 shows two examples: from the first piece a somewhat free wedge and from the third piece a strict one.

A new element in Berg's style, found prominently in the Altenberg Songs is the complex chord, the subject of Chapter 22 in Schoenberg's *Harmonielehre*.[14] It remains an important element through the rest of his music. In the Four Pieces it is most prominent at the end of the first piece where it consists of a semi-symmetrical pile of three 'atonal triads' over a low B♯ (Example 17).

The last piece has a harmonic shape based on three successive chords all built on C (C′, C, c′). They move from a five-note chord to a darkly dissonant six-note chord to a pure and transcendent four-note C major major-seventh chord (Example 18).

Berg was not to hear his Four Pieces for some six years. In November 1918 Schoenberg, now back in Vienna, founded the Verein für musikalische Privataufführungen (Society for Private Musical Performances) for the purpose of presenting well-rehearsed performances of recent music and frequent

Ex. 15 Four Pieces, II

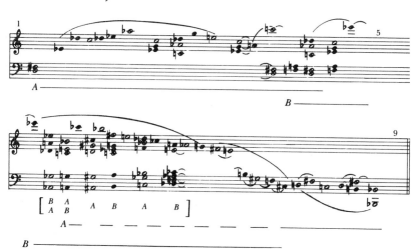

Ex. 16 Four Pieces, (a) I, bars 3–5 (piano only), (b) III, bars 15–16 (piano only)

(a) (♩ = ca. 58)

(b)

Ex. 17 Four Pieces, I, end

Ex. 18 Four Pieces, IV

repetitions of these works to a private audience of Society members. Berg was made Director of Performances, which basically meant he did all the work. In February 1919 he wrote a prospectus for the Society, part of which can be found on pp. 46–9 of Willi Reich's book (English translation). On 17 October 1919 the Four Pieces were premièred at a Society meeting and numerous performances followed. After the highly successful performance of his String Quartet at the ISCM in 1923, Berg wrote to Helene on 4 August: 'A clarinet player introduced himself to me enthusiastically. He had played the Clarinet Pieces (which he said were beautifully written for the instrument) in Heidelberg and Mannheim; and he would be doing them next in other German cities.'[15]

Three Orchestral Pieces op. 6.

> I have once more played through Mahler's Ninth. The first movement is the most glorious he ever wrote. It expresses an extraordinary love of this earth, for Nature; the longing to live on it in peace, to enjoy it completely, to the very heart of one's being, before death comes, as irresistibly it does. The whole movement is based on a premonition of death, which is constantly recurring. All earthly dreams up to this peak; that is why the tenderest passages are followed by tremendous climaxes like new eruptions of a volcano. This, of course, is most obvious of all in the place where the premonition of death becomes certain knowledge, where in the most profound and anguished love of life death appears 'mit höchster Gewalt'; then the ghostly solo of violin and viola, and those sounds of chivalry: death in armour. Against that there is no resistance left, and I see what follows as a sort of resignation. Always, though, with the thought of 'the other side', which we can see in the *misterioso* on pages 44–45, as if in the pure air above the mountains, in the ether itself.[16]

In this undated letter to Helene, thought to be from autumn 1912, we sense the power of Mahler's music, and particularly the Ninth Symphony, over Berg. This great force manifests itself most clearly in the Three Orchestral Pieces op. 6. Shortly after his confrontation with Schoenberg in early June 1913, almost as penance, Berg began an extended orchestral work, possibly meant to be a symphony or a 'gay suite' to be dedicated to Schoenberg for his 40th birthday on

13 September 1914. Berg had been contemplating a Mahlerian symphony based on the Swedenborgian novel *Seraphita* by Balzac. At that time, in mid-1912, Schoenberg was planning an operatic trilogy on the same novel. In the Mahler tradition, Berg's symphony would end with a vocal solo—a boy's voice from the gallery singing text from Balzac's novel. It was long assumed that a fragment of this music was later used in the orchestral interlude in Act III of *Wozzeck*, the 'Invention on a Key'.[17]

The orchestral interlude in *Wozzeck* is in D minor, a key central to Berg's early works. Its prominence in Berg's works may represent a superficial influence of the first movement of Mahler's Ninth, where D minor is second to D major as the most important tonal area. We have seen the importance of D in the String Quartet both as a note and as a minor triad. It is important as a note in the Four Pieces. The first of the Four Songs op. 2 is in D minor and in the third song the key abruptly reappears in an otherwise amorphous realm of Ab minor. D is prominent in all of the Three Orchestral Pieces. In 'Präludium' there is a strong final cadence to a D minor triad with an added Bᵇ (bars 48–9). Also the climactic chord (bar 36) has D'as its bass. In 'Reigen' it is heard early on (bars 6–7) as a minor triad with linear elements above implying a C♯ minor triad. The same sonority is heard and sustained for over six measures at the end of the exposition (bars 41–8), approached through a large-scale cadence. At the end it is an important bass note (bars 108–10), prepared a bar and a half earlier by a sustained octave A–A'in the bass (bars 105–6). In 'Marsch', D is briefly heard as a minor triad plus Bᵇ (as in 'Präludium'; here bar 91) but strongly heard as pitch pedals in many if not all possible octaves (bars 134–5, 139–43, 155–60, 164–70). Coming near the end of the piece these pedals have a powerful sense of resolution, especially the shattering timpani hammer blows at bars 142–3, the downright tonal cadence fortississimo leading into bar 155, and the final long-repeated d' (pizzicato strings to harp harmonics), approached via a gigantic inward chromatic wedge of quartal chords.

Berg worked on 'Präludium' and 'Marsch' from the summer of 1913 through the summer of 1914, and was able to send Schoenberg the completed scores of both pieces on 8 September 1913, in time for his 40th birthday on 13 September. Considering the unity of the three pieces and the sense of growth from one to the next, it is surprising, even amazing, that he composed the middle piece, 'Reigen', last. 'Reigen' was sent to Schoenberg almost a year later, on 5 August 1915. The pieces grow in size (approximately 4, 5, and 9 minutes; 56, 121, and 174 bars) and in complexity of structure and texture from first to last. The basic three-note cell in 'Präludium' (eᴸ–gᴸ–aᵇ' and dᴸ–eᵇᴸ–gᵇ' in bar 8) generates the first theme in both 'Präludium' and 'Reigen' and is the first motive heard in 'Marsch' (G–Aᵇ–B, cellos). From the climax of 'Präludium' emerge two melodic ideas that dominate 'Reigen' and are very important in 'Marsch'.

Of the Three Orchestral Pieces, 'Präludium' shows most clearly the influence of the first movement of Mahler's Ninth. Both are arch-shaped, beginning in near silence with motivic fragments that gradually lead into a melody. Both reach a horrendous climax followed by a gradual return to fragments that die out to silence. Both are in 4/4 metre and have a distinct rhythmic motive that is used throughout and especially at the climax: in Mahler where the 'höchste Kraft' is followed 'mit höchster Gewalt' (bars 308–20), and in Berg inside the climactic complex chord (bars 36–7). Mahler introduces the rhythm in the first bar (Example 19(a)); Berg slowly prepares it until it takes its first form in bar 9 (Example 19 (b)), and its full form in darksome repeated chords in bars 14–15 (Example 19 (c)). The opening melodies of both works, which gradually evolve from the initial motivic fragments, themselves show an evolving quality (Example 20). The immediate continuation of Berg's melody has Mahlerian shape and rhythm as can be seen when compared to a later version of Mahler's second theme (Example 21).

Ex. 19

Ex. 20 (a) Mahler, Symphony no. 9, I, bars 7–10, (b) Three Orchestral Pieces, I, bars 16–17

Unlike the Mahler first movement the symmetry of Berg's 'Präludium' is quite literal. In the first eight bars there are soft percussion noises beginning with a stroke on the large tam-tam, the timpani introduce specific pitches until we have three chords in a small portion of the orchestra, and finally two overlapping permutations of the basic three-note cell found throughout the work. The last eight bars present the same materials in almost exact reverse order. This is one of the first examples of Berg's use of near-literal retrograde and it is a procedure he was to use on larger scales in later works.[18] In the third of the Altenberg Songs there is a hint of retrograde or at least symmetry in that the opening twelve-note chord is erased from bottom to top and at the end is reconstituted in the same direction but two octaves higher.[19] 'Reigen' (Round Dances) is also arch-shaped and symmetrical in a more general way in that the opening and closing sections in duple metre frame the triple-metre *Ländler* that is the main part of the piece.

Central to the music of the Three Orchestral Pieces are complex chords and complex sonorities. These were found in the Four Pieces, but their most elegant early examples are in the Altenberg Songs.[20] In the Three Orchestral Pieces

Ex. 21 (a) Mahler, Symphony no. 9, I, bars 211–14, (b) Three Orchestral Pieces, I, bars 18–19

chords of five and six different pitch classes are the norm and chords of more than six pitches are common. Chords of twelve different pitches are found but these are saved for climaxes. A prime example is the climactic chord of 'Reigen' (bar 66), which is constructed entirely of perfect fourths (Example 22 (a)). The symmetry of the chord is emphasized in that it is built outward from its central perfect fourth, g^L–$c^{''}$, over a time-span of 6½ bars. It is erased rapidly, in about four beats, and the central fourth is in turn reduced wedge-like by semitones: g^L–$c^{''}$ to $g\#^L$–$b^{'}$ to a^L–$b\flat^{'}$. The climactic chord of 'Präludium' is primarily of perfect fourths with eight different pitch classes and C heavily doubled ($c, c^{'}, c^{''}, c^{'''}, c^{''''}$). It is symmetrical only in that the perfect fourths are roughly central surrounded by major sixths, one on top and two on the botom (Example 22 (b)). In both 'Präludium' and 'Reigen' these climactic chords occur between the middle and the Golden Section of their respective structures.

Ex. 22 Three Orchestral Pieces, (a) II, bars 59–68, (b) I, bar 36

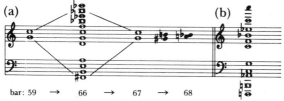

bar: 59 → 66 → 67 → 68

Complex chords also operate the moment-to-moment activities. At the beginning of 'Präludium' ten chords are introduced in three groups of three, three, and four chords respectively: first, the three mentioned above with the primary three-note cell heard over the third (bars 6–8), secondly, three chords under a high $e\flat^{'}$ in solo trombone presenting the first version of the rhythmic cell (bars 9–11), and finally, four dark, low, and densely spaced chords arranged in an asymmetrical inward wedge, the last of which states the second form of the rhythmic cell (bars 11–15). As the first melody unfolds, the first three chords are the harmonic basis of the first phrase (bars 15–19), and the second three chords transposed up a minor third are the basis for the second phrase (bars 19–21), and transposed up another semitone for the next phrase (bars 21–3). About half way from there to the climax the last chord of the group of four occurs at pitch but with considerable octave expansion (bar 28, from bars 13–15). The climactic chord itself has, as its principal component, the first of the four-chord group at pitch (bar 36, from bars 11–12).

Following the climax of 'Präludium' two new motives are introduced that are important in the rest of the work. For convenience I am labelling the first *A* (bars 37–9, upper strings and winds, two trumpets), which emphasizes major thirds, and the second *B* (bars 44–6, tremolando violins, celesta), which emphasizes minor thirds. *B* also very strongly focuses on, even cadences on, D (d′) owing to the melodic outlining of a vii⁷ of D minor (e″–c♯″–b♭′–g′) followed by the strong inward wedge to d′(g′–g♭′–f′–d′ over a–b♭–b♮–d′) (Example 23).

Ex. 23 Three Orchestral Pieces, I, (a) bars 37–9, (b) bars 44–6

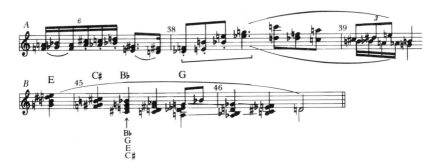

The beginning of 'Reigen', the duple-metre introduction to the *Ländler*, is like a fantasy on these two motives. The motives are combined in a complex yet delicate and shimmering texture. The harmonic background of the second part of this 19-bar introduction (bars 14–19) is generated from the ascending triplet figure of the *A* motive. From this figure eight possible five-note chords are available (Example 24) and some of these produce the harmonic background for the latter part of this gossamer texture and also produce the chords for the accompanying vamp of the *Ländler* proper (bars 20ff.).

Ex. 24

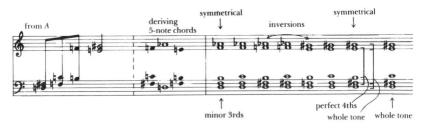

Balancing the complex sonority of the introduction is another sonority for the coda built exclusively from the *B* motive. When duple metre returns in bar 111 a stretto on *B* begins in the upper register, in the order of oboes, muted violins six beats later, clarinets four beats later than the violins, and flutes two beats later than the clarinets. Each entry is increasingly truncated and each ends with an oscillation that accelerates to a trill. In the lower register there is an augmentation of *B* as a melody in the tuba without the four-note chords, and from each note of the augmentation there rises an inversion of the *B* melody with each ending in a tremolo. The result of all this is a complex chord of eleven different pitch names with C♯ omitted, possibly because it had been a long-held pedal below the beginning of the stretto and then became the first note of the tuba's augmentation. The chord is repeated in the basic rhythm from the beginning of 'Präludium' and in the middle of the chord appears the ascending triplet figure of *A* in horns and trumpets. The final major third c″–e″ of this figure is sustained beyond the termination of the eleven-note chord (Example 25). The major third contrasts with the predominantly minor thirds of the complex chord. The tertial chord, in turn, contrasts with the quartal chord near the centre of the piece.

Ex. 25 Three Orchestral Pieces, II, bars 119–21

Possibly the most extraordinary complex sonority in 'Reigen', and even in the whole work, is a passage that occurs twice in succession at the end of the development and overlaps into the beginning of the recapitulation. The sonority consists of four melodic strands, each a short fragment of an earlier melody repeated several times. The lower two lines come from a theme near the end of the exposition (bars 37–8). The bass (bassoon, harp) plays seven quavers of the theme repeated in the manner of a tape loop. The tenor (violas, cellos) plays eleven quavers of the same theme. The alto (horns, celesta) plays the closing theme of the exposition (bars 38–9), which is heard there and here as two voices in parallel sixths or sevenths, and here as eight notes in triplet quavers. Since these lines are of different lengths, their repetitions are heard in constant realignment, kaleidoscope-like (bars 83–7). After two bars of this ever-changing sound the ascending fragment of *A* is introduced as the topmost voice in trumpets, oboes, and pizzicato violins (bars 85–8). This latter motive has bar 88 to itself, sustaining the major third f″–a″.

This total-pattern technique is immediately repeated at differing trans-positions for each line and in a vastly expanded register that includes the entire large orchestra. Stravinsky, in 1959, expressed great admiration for the Three Orchestral Pieces and especially this passage:

> Berg's orchestral imagination and orchestral skill are phenomenal, especially in creating orchestral blocks, by which I mean balancing the whole orchestra in several polyphonic planes. One of the most remarkable noises he ever imagined is at bar 89 in *Reigen*, but there are many other striking sonorous inventions ...[21]

The fanfare-like motive from *A* now rises to the major third $c^{\underline{}}e'$ decorated by upper neighbours $d\flat^{\underline{}}f'$. (The major third $f''\!-\!a''$ of 85–8 had been decorated by lower neighbours $e''\!-\!g\sharp''$.) The oscillation of $c^{\underline{}}e'$ and $d\flat^{\underline{}}f'$ accelerates into the opening theme of the *Ländler* at bar 94, at the pitch level of the opening of the exposition (bars 20ff.). Thus the recapitulation emerges from the complex sonority admired by Stravinsky and, as the theme continues, the sonority gradually dissolves and the accompanying vamp returns.

I have been describing 'Reigen' in terms of sonata form as I feel it accounts best for the large-scale structure of the piece. Figure 2 summarizes the form of the movement; Example 26 presents the main themes. The exposition, emerging out of the complex sonority of the introduction, begins with the *Ländler* theme and its vamp (bars 20ff.), to which are added counterpoints, most notably derived from *A*. A new *Ländler* theme, *b*, motivically related to *a1*, begins in bar 33 and, while it continues, a closing theme, *c*, made up of parallel sixths and sevenths, enters below it in bar 38. The large cadence to the long-held D minor is completed by the end of bar 41 and there is harmonic stasis for several bars— the end of the exposition. The development begins with *a2* (bar 45), a motive heard in the duple-metre introduction but not in the *Ländler* (exposition) itself. But the development quickly becomes more rhythmically active, more contrapuntal, and texturally wilder than anything heard thus far. Its midpoint is the twelve-note quartal chord and its close the extraordinary sonority described above. The recapitulation, appropriately, is more complex in harmony and counterpoint than the exposition, including the addition of several variants of *B*. A new complex sonority is achieved in bars 105–8 which has as a strong basis a dominant of D minor, resolved in bar 108 to a D pedal in the bass. The coda (upbeat to bars 111ff.) has been described above. It is very un-Classical for both the exposition and the recapitulation to end in the same 'key', but these are points of articulation. Sonata form is not governed here by tonal structure as it was in its roots and at birth, but by melodies, developmental processes, and the balanced structuring of complex sonorities—as might be expected after a century and a half of adventures.[22]

'Marsch' is the ultimate experience in Berg's use of complex sonorities. None of his later works have textures as densely contrapuntal as those in 'Marsch'. The opening large phrase is relatively simple compared to what follows. Four motives are introduced, one per bar, to produce four levels of repeating and changing lines of counterpoint. The violins add a melody above this texture. As

Figure 2

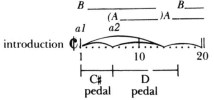

introduction

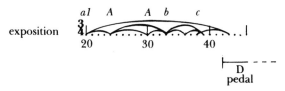

exposition

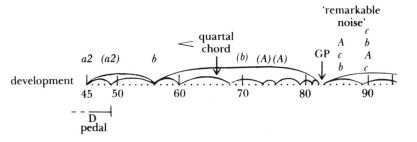

development

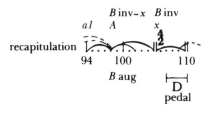

recapitulation

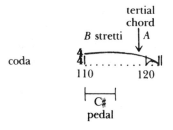

coda

the melody sweepingly unfolds, the underlying strands of motives expand into parallel thirds and parallel triads, creating a considerable density by bars 10–12 that settles back so as to begin again. But at more intense points there can be several three-voice canons overlapping one another with additional lines, some in parallel chords, many in parallel octaves, creating a cacophony of polyphony (bars 115–25).

Mahler is strongly felt in 'Marsch', but here he is the Mahler of the Sixth Symphony. Most striking is Berg's borrowing of the hammer blows, from the

Ex. 26 Three Orchestral Pieces, II, themes

finale of the Sixth. Like Mahler, Berg asks that the hammer be made of wood and not metal (*mit nichtmetallischem Klang*). Berg combines the blow with a low D in the timpani (requiring the largest, 30-inch, drum) played with two sticks, and the drum continues with an angry expansion of the original rhythmic motive.

Berg's lifelong preoccupation with the idea of a rhythmic motive (*Hauptrhythmus*) probably came from Mahler's Sixth, where the concept of a rhythmic pattern as a primary motivic cell has its fullest workout since Wagner. The extraordinary intermesh of motives from which the elaborate, seemingly chaotic, formal structure takes shape derives also from the finale of Mahler's Sixth. In both there is a pervading spirit of sonata form buried in a formal fantasy where developments begin before expositions end, and where forms overlap and are interrupted as if in preparation for *Lulu*. In both there is progressive clarification as the end nears. Berg resolves the chaos, partially shattered by the hammer blows, with a strong unison line in low brass that creates a powerful cadence in D minor (bars 149–55). George Perle puts the tragic force of 'Marsch' in historical perspective and summarizes its essence most eloquently:

> The *Marsch* was completed in the weeks immediately following the assassination at Sarajevo and is, in its feeling of doom and catastrophe, an ideal, if unintentional, musical expression of the ominous implications of that event. Fragmentary rhythmic and melodic figures typical of an orthodox military march repeatedly coalesce into polyphonic episodes of incredible density that surge to frenzied climaxes, then fall apart. It is not a march, but music *about* a march, or rather about *the* march, just as Ravel's *La Valse* is music in which *the* waltz is similarly reduced to its minimum characteristic elements.[23]

It might be surmised from all of the above, and correctly so, that Berg uses a very large orchestra. The winds are mostly in fours: four flutes, all of whom are asked to play piccolos as well; four oboes, one of whom is asked to play English horn; four clarinets plus a bass clarinet; three bassoons and a contrabassoon. The brass consists of six horns, four trumpets, four trombones (three tenors and a bass, with the first trombone possibly playing alto trombone for the high eb ″s in 'Präludium', bars 9–11) and contrabass tuba. For the percussion: four timpani, snare drum, bass drum, field drum, a pair of cymbals and a suspended cymbal, large and small tam-tams, triangle, glockenspiel, and a large hammer. There are also two harps and celesta. The string section must be appropriately large; the listing of instruments reads *stark besetzt*. The influence of Mahler is again felt in the infinite variety found in the scoring, ranging from solos and small choirs of similar or contrasting instruments to full tutti. The latter can be powerful unison-type statements as in 'Marsch', bars 149–55, or the many imaginative inventions like the 'remarkable noise' in 'Reigen'.

While many events in the Three Orchestral Pieces presage Berg's great opera *Wozzeck*, they are also a culmination. In his only purely orchestral, even symphonic, work he brings together into a grand unity the many explorations and inspirations of a mere eight years of growth since his Piano Variations and Piano Sonata. Stravinsky's perspective from 1959 holds true today:

> If I were able to penetrate the barrier of style (Berg's radically alien emotional climate [to Stravinsky]) I suspect he would appear to me as the most gifted constructor in form of the composers of this century. He transcends even his

own most overt modeling. In fact, he is the only one to have achieved large-scale development-type forms without a suggestion of 'neoclassic' dissimulation. ... Berg's forms are thematic (in which respect, as in most others, he is Webern's opposite); the essence of his work and the thematic structure are responsible for the immediacy of one form. However complex, however 'mathematical' the latter are, they are always 'free' thematic forms born of 'pure feeling' and 'expression.' The perfect work in which to study this and, I think, the essential work, with *Wozzeck*, for the study of all of his music – is the Three Pieces for Orchestra, op. 6. Berg's personality is mature in these pieces, and they seem to me a richer and freer expression of his talent than the twelve-note serial pieces. When one considers their early date—1914; Berg was twenty-nine—they are something of a miracle.[24]

Notes

1. The recently published catalogue of Berg manuscripts in the Austrian National Library also includes a large number of pieces and fragments for string quartet as well as scherzos, impromptus, sonata movements, and other pieces for piano written during the years of Berg's apprenticeship with Schoenberg. See Rosemary Hilmar, *Katalog der Musikhandschriften, Schriften und Studien im Fond Alban Berg und der weiteren handschriftlichen Quellen im Besitz der Österreichischen Nationalbibliothek*, Alban Berg Studien, vol. 1 (Vienna: Universal Edition, 1980). These pieces will be published shortly in the *Alban Berg Gesamtausgabe*.

2. The Variations were published in 1985 by Universal Edition. Until then they were only available as an appendix to Hans Ferdinand Redlich, *Alban Berg: Versuch einer Würdigung* (Vienna: Universal Edition, 1957), pp. 393–404, or in the English version, *Alban Berg: the Man and his Music* (London: John Calder, 1957), pp. 249–59.

3. Arnold Schoenberg, *Theory of Harmony*, trans. Roy E. Carter (Berkeley and Los Angeles: University of California Press, 1978), pp. 390–410.

4. In view of its harmony, rubato, and basic expression, John Kirkpatrick once described the Sonata as the pianist's *Tristan*.

5. The form of Schoenberg's Chamber Symphony no. 1 is of a one-movement symphony that contains elements of a multi-movement symphony in a symmetrical format: sonata exposition—transitional/developmental—scherzo—development—slow movement—sonata recapitulation in reverse order.

6. George Perle reproduces the letter on p.5 of his article 'Berg's Master Array of the Interval Cycles', *Musical Quarterly*, vol. 63 (1977), pp. 1–30, where he discusses ramifications of this diagram in detail.

7. *Alban Berg: Letters to his Wife*, ed., trans., and annot. Bernard Grun (New York: St Martin's Press, 1971), p. 326.

8. Douglas Jarman feels that the date in the score, spring 1913, is probably correct; see *The Music of Alban Berg* (London: Faber and Faber, 1979), pp. 6–7.

9. Redlich (English version), op. cit., p. 233.

10. Willi Reich, *Alban Berg*, trans. Cornelius Cardew (London: Thames and Hudson, 1965), p. 41.

11. A pitch class is a letter name note in any octave—for instance, $D''/D'/D/d/d'd''/d'''$ etc.

comprise one pitch class, D.

12. Douglas Jarman, op. cit., pp. 23–7. A detailed study of the third piece can be found in Christopher Lewis, 'Tonal Focus in Atonal Music: Berg's Op.5/3', *Music Theory Spectrum*, vol. 3 (1981), pp. 84–97.

13. William DeFotis, 'Berg's Op.5: Rehearsal instructions', *Perspectives of New Music*, vol. 17, no. 1 (fall–winter 1978), p. 131.

14. 'Aesthetic Evaluation of Chords with Six or More Tones', *Theory of Harmony*, pp. 411–22.

15. *Alban Berg: Letters to his Wife*, pp. 326–7.

16. Ibid., p. 147.

17. See Redlich (English version), op. cit., pp. 65–6. The recent publication of the sketches for the projected Symphony shows that this assumption was incorrect; the D minor Interlude of *Wozzeck* has its origins in an early piano sonata ('Sonata V') the manuscript of which is now amongst those in the Berg collection of the Austrian National Library.

18. See Stephen Kett's contribution to this volume for a description of an earlier example in the Four Songs.

19. The *Klangfarben* technique used on the first of these chords is discussed in Robert Erickson, *Sound Structure in Music* (Berkeley and Los Angeles: University of California Press, 1975), pp. 166–8.

20. A thorough account of the remarkable sonority that begins the first of the Altenberg Songs can be found in Mark DeVoto, 'Some Notes on the Unknown *Altenberg Lieder*', *Perspectives of New Music*, vol. 5, no. 1 (fall–winter 1966), pp. 37–74, especially pp. 41–52.

21. Igor Stravinsky and Robert Craft, *Conversations with Igor Stravinsky* (New York: Doubleday, 1959), p. 81.

22. For a more detailed account of 'Reigen' see Bruce Archibald, 'The Harmony of Berg's *Reigen*', *Perspectives of New Music*, vol. 6, no. 2 (spring–summer 1968), pp. 73–91.

23. George Perle, *The Operas of Alban Berg*, vol. 1: *Wozzeck* (Berkeley and Los Angeles: University of California Press, 1980), p. 18. Also quoted on p. 386 of Mark DeVoto's thorough and perceptive study of 'Marsch': 'Alban Berg's "Marche Macabre"', *Perspectives of New Music*, vol. 22 (fall–winter 1983, spring–summer 1984), pp. 386–447.

24. Stravinsky and Craft, op. cit., pp. 79–80.

MUSICAL PROGRESSION IN THE 'PRÄLUDIUM' OF THE THREE ORCHESTRAL PIECES OP. 6

MICHAEL TAYLOR

The music of Alban Berg has always presented a particularly intriguing paradox, a seeming contradiction between the directness of its expression and the complexity of its surface, a problem compounded by the composer's fondness for number schemes, abstract patterning, and programmatic reference. The Three Orchestral Pieces op. 6 epitomize this conundrum: they are notated with almost fanatical precision, yet they convey (for the most part) the impression of a simple, inevitable progression both within the individual pieces and across the whole work. This essay has a twofold purpose: to attempt to elucidate the meaning of 'progression' in this context, and to examine the relationship subsisting between this progression and the detail of the score. Stated more simply, it will probe the link between what is heard and how this emerges from the text. The approach will be empirical, based upon repeated listening followed up with a detailed study of the score, but always with the ear as final arbiter.[1] Within the confines of an essay of this length it would be impossible to undertake such a task for more than a small section of one piece, so I have chosen the opening of the first, the 'Präludium'. This offers a very clear example of the interdependence of detail and onward movement. I also include a briefer consideration of the end of the 'Präludium' in order to examine the use of the same material in a different context.

Berg began the composition of the Three Orchestral Pieces—'Präludium', 'Reigen', and 'Marsch'—in the summer of 1913, and completed them the following August, according to the date at the end of the score. From the extant material (located in the music collection of the Austrian National Library) it appears that he followed his customary procedure of noting down ideas in small sketch books (only a few entries survive for the Three Orchestral Pieces) working these over in a number of drafts (none of which is known), before the preparation of a short score containing numerous instrumental indications, which was subsequently orchestrated. The short score also contains a piano version of the early part of the 'Präludium', but which was written first is not clear. The existence of drafts may be inferred from the transformation of the isolated jottings of the sketches into the extensively worked and connected short score, as well as from Berg's practice in other, more fully documented works. The first two pieces were given under Webern's direction in 1923; the first complete performance (for which Berg undertook a thorough revision of the score) did not take place until 1930.

This was Berg's first purely orchestral work, yet it displays an accomplished grasp not only of orchestral technique, but of the functional use of orchestration to clarify its often complex musical processes. If the orchestral sounds of the earlier Altenberg Songs are more extravagantly coloured, those of the Three Orchestral Pieces demonstrate an ability not only to think in much longer spans than the relatively short-breathed songs, but also to realize the larger structures in a coherently thought-out orchestral sound.

The first sound (event 1) seems to present little information: a single deep gong stroke, quiet, metallic, allowed to reverberate undamped, followed by a relatively long period of inactivity before the second event. (Although our means of measuring it is not yet established, the score indicates here that a five-quaver silence precedes, and a four-quaver one succeeds the gong, but this could only be apparent from the sight of the conductor beating from the beginning of the first bar. The beginning of the arithmetical progression satisfies only Berg's number fetish.)

The gong is struck again, but this time twice before resonating; to this is added a quieter, higher cymbal tremolando which appears to amplify the ringing of the gong. The two strokes provide the first opportunity to establish some temporal measurement, though only in terms of relatively longer/shorter. The absence of a definite pulse unit denies the possibility of anything more sophisticated at this juncture. The gap between events 2 and 3 can thus be assessed as smaller than that between events 1 and 2.

The complementary pairing of measured gong strokes and unmeasured cymbal tremolando (both metal sounds) is imitated in event 3 by the addition of a similar pairing of skin percussion: bass drum (low, measured) and muffled side drum (higher, unmeasured), but a slight delaying of the side drum entry and the acceleration of the gong strokes introduce rhythmic complexity. The total duration of activity is again extended and the punctuating silence further reduced. (For 'silence' from here to event 10, read 'absence of activity': the percussion sounds on through the written rests.)

It is already possible to hear across this span of music a definite progression from the first gong stroke towards events of increasing duration and frequency. On one level this is achieved by the progressive lengthening of sounds and corresponding shortening of the intervening silences (Example 1) but the implications of pitch definition carried by the low (gong, bass drum)/higher (cymbal, side drum) distinction, and dynamic (in the sense of volume) produced by the addition of layers of sound, indicate further lines of development and, consequently, scale. The speed at which the progression unfolds is not uniform:

on the basis of events 1 and 2, the bass drum would be added in event 3 and the side drum in event 4, instead of which these two notional events are elided. Considering the sequence negatively it is apparent that the lengthening/ shortening process cannot continue indefinitely if the sense of progression is to depend upon it alone and the addition of much further percussion would lead to confusion.

Ex. 1

Event 4 has the same overall duration as event 3 but adds to the ensemble four timpani, the rhythmic articulation of which, building on the complexity of event 3, directs attention to the final quaver, the first time two notes are struck together (Example 2). The arrival of the new sonority is enhanced by a simplification of the untuned percussion parts, pushing them into the background. After a two-quaver silence the timpani themselves are subsumed into the general character of event 5 by the acceleration of the content of their first appearance into a slow tremolando, while a second, higher-pitched gong joins the ensemble, beating out four quavers (this is marked *deutlich* (clearly) in the score, but is frequently inaudible), resuming the expansion of activity. For the first time there is a swelling and dying away, directed to the final quaver as in event 4; the silence is reduced to a single quaver.

The ways in which these two events build upon the first three may be summarized as follows:

(1) the expansion/contraction is continued;
(2) new sonorities introduced in one event are synthesized into the general sound in the next;
(3) the tendency to progress from the simplicity of the first gong stroke through increasingly complex rhythmic superimpositions (polyrhythm) towards tremolando;
(4) the development of the low/higher opposition (gong, cymbal and drums) into the noise-coloured pitches of the timpani (the specified leather sticks emphasizing the noise element). The outward-wedging arrangement of pitches marks a further elaboration of the tendency to open out (Example 2).

The principal vehicle for movement in the piece thus far has been the percussion. Having launched the 'Präludium', they retreat further into the background in event 6, all executing a fading tremolando as the first instrumental sounds are heard. The polyrhythmic layering is taken over by the

Ex. 2

flute, horns, violins, violas, and cellos, using a repositioning of the timpani pitches from event four (G–F–Bb–Eb), many 'coloured' by the use of mutes, fluttertongue, or pizzicato on the fingerboard. The respective durations of event and silence remain as before. Of the string sounds in event 6, the pizzicato violins and cellos are intended to dominate (*p*, *voll* as opposed to the *pp* of the violas) but in event 7 the situation is reversed, the pizzicatos retreating into the background (together with the percussion), while attention is focused on the violas, which enhance the general tendency towards the final quaver by adding an acceleration to the same point. Plucked sounds are retained, however, by the simultaneous phasing-in of a harp playing the same notes.

The assumption of the timpani pitches by the non-percussion instruments, the establishment of a spacing for them, and retention of that spacing into the following event, have completed the evolution of the first harmony of the piece (Example 3).[2] Its line of derivation from the first gong stroke is quite clear, as is the rough timbral transition:

noise ————————————————————————————→ pitch
gong + cymbal → bass drum + side drum → timpani → pizz. strings → harp

The first sounds have also established the timbres of flute, horns, percussion, harp, and violas, a polyrhythmic ensemble, and a dynamic envelope associated with the chord, but whereas these elements have reached a degree of fulfilment, the persistent tendency of each event towards its final quaver creates a feeling of imbalance implying continuation. One possibility would be the reversal of the process but this would seem a weak response to the growing momentum of the chord, a failure to recognize that the process which led to its establishment has assumed the role of instigator of harmonic movement.

Ex. 3

a

Considering each event in isolation and subsequently in relation to its immediate neighbours, it is possible to arrive at an understanding of the generation of directed movement at the beginning of the 'Präludium'. In functional terms it is clear that the sequence serves to prepare the chord in meticulous detail, as a succession of increasingly elaborate orchestrations of the initial gong stroke. The absence of melodic detail, the very tightly circumscribed textures, and the gradual unfolding of the process allow the ear to absorb the subtle changes which gradually define the object of the progression with increasing precision.

The restatement of the chord a at the beginning of event 8 is almost free of reminders of its percussive origin, the attendant percussion ensemble having been reduced to cymbal and the two gongs. Fractionally after it begins, the bassoon enters above the fluttertongued flute Eb at the top of the chord and almost immediately the chord itself changes. All other aspects of the event remain as before and after the fade at the end there is a brief silence.

Hitherto, movement has been generated within the developing chord a but now that process has been taken a stage further, the chord itself being subject to movement while retaining the texture of the sequence. The triggering effect of the new bassoon note is quite clear, as is its apartness from the chordal material: it begins after the chord (thus enabling a to register), it does not partake of the polyrhythmic ensemble or the dynamic envelope, and it sounds on after the harmonic movement. The stimulation provided by the bassoon arises partly from its distinctness and partly from the transformation it wreaks on the referential sonority. Chord a, which has been in existence for the last four events, has a repertoire of intervals consisting of perfect fourths, minor sevenths, a minor third, and a minor sixth (see Example 3), and the bassoon Ab both 'belongs' to this collection, forming another perfect fourth (F–Bb–Eb–Ab) with the upper notes, and, simultaneously, introduces a new 'dissonant' element (the semitone G–Ab) with the lowest.[3] The separation of the three upper notes from the lowest makes this plain, as well as creating a space for bass movement. The appearance of this interval provokes the upward movement of the bass and other parts of a creating a new chord, b, against which the Ab continues to sound momentarily. The composition of this chord, notably the absence of an intruding semitone, attempts to restore something approaching the intervallic balance of a (Example 4).

Ex. 4

b

However, as this new chord is patently not *a*, the feeling of closure at the end of event 8, already under threat from the continuing push created by the unequal swelling and fading and the accelerating viola figure, is further weakened.[4] Any feeling of a decisive move on to *b* is prevented by the failure of the dynamic envelope to co-ordinate with the harmonic shift (Example 5). (In the example the barlines are placed where they are heard, rather than where they are notated in the score.) The emergence of a new timbre (bassoon) at a higher register, with melodic potential (hence the demarcation from the chordal texture which now seems to retreat) signals a significant new stage in the chain, event 8 representing both the outcome of its seven predecessors and the beginning of a new group.

Ex. 5

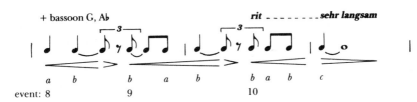

Event 9 begins with *b* before reverting to *a* (supported now by just the two gongs). The bassoon re-enters with a note just under its previous one, squeezing back up to A♭ as *b* returns. This event is longer than event 8 and the acceleration begins to appear in other parts (horn and harp) while the viola has a more complex acceleration–slowing–acceleration pattern; a very brief silence again.

Continuing with *b* heightens the tension by denying the immediate return to *a* which, when it does arrive, lasts only one quaver. The short bassoon G, also slightly dissociated in time from *a*, levers on to the A♭ (transposing the original G–A♭, separated by two octaves, between the bass of *a* and the bassoon, into an adjacency) thus creating a feeling of upbeat–downbeat, the latter being confirmed by the simultaneous move on to *b* (see Example 5).

The arrival on this second *b* in event 9 is much more emphatic than that in event 8,[5] and marks an important stage in the development from duration (of sound and silence) towards metre. (The occurrence of the barline here is probably coincidental, but this is the first audible barline of the piece.) Once again, however, the dynamic profile fails to confirm *b* as completely secure; the swelling on the bassoon A♭ and the 'extra' acceleration of the viola increase the propulsive force.

Event 10 resumes on *b*, as did its predecessor, but by shortening the duration of each chord the *b–a–b* sequence is restated within the acceleration (depriving the final *b* of pre-eminence) impelling the music on to a new goal (see Example 5). Percussion support for *a* is limited to a small gong stroke, reflecting the waning role for both chord and percussion.

For the first time the concerted drive of acceleration and swelling, aided here by a slowing of the overall tempo, is allowed an unequivocal fulfilment. The inference from the score would seem to be that, because of the unequal swelling and fading, events 8, 9, and 10 each begin a little louder, producing an intensification across all three culminating in the arrival on *c*. This moment is marked not only by harmonic change but also by new highest and lowest notes B♭ and E, new timbres of unmuted horn in its top register and clarinet, dislodging the ever-present flute E♭ (which shifts up to join the horn on B♭, still fluttertonguing) and by a strong downbeat, upstaging the end of event 9 completely. Contextually this moment already assumes a greater aural significance as the outcome of the piece to date, not merely the local progression, for, as has been seen, no other implication has been allowed so clear a realization. The subsequent extension of *c* into the longest uninterrupted flow and the melodic burgeoning confirm rather than establishes its credentials.

This event sees the complete transformation of *a* from the principal focus into a passing chord in the drive towards *c*. The local and gestural implications combine to produce a cadential point, a formal juncture, which invests the third chord with a functional relationship to the first analogous to that of dominant/ tonic.[6] The novelty of the third chord (after the intervallic similarities of the first two) strengthens this link (the forcible association of the D minor and B♭ major triads at the opening of Beethoven's Ninth Symphony offers a parallel), but does not disguise the ways in which it capitalizes on the accumulated expectations (Example 6).

Ex. 6

The bassoon A♭, G–A♭ is continued upwards by the horn and flutes to B♭, the registral and directional continuity crowned by the change of timbre (marking B♭ as goal); two notes—F♯ and B—are retained from *b*, while its lowest note C♯ rises by step to D and is supplanted by the drop to E, a compensating reaction to the bass rise from *a* to *b*, which, taken with the treble, forms an emphatic wedge outwards on to *c*: see Example 6. The tritone E–B♭, outlining the registral extremes of this chord, is part of the whole-tone component D–E– F♯–B♭, against which is pitted the B–B♭ clash.

The upward continuation of the G–A♭ by the horn frees the bassoon to repeat the G–A♭ motive, prefacing it with an E. This triggers a responding (and also rising) melodic shape: D–E♭–G♭ played by the muted trumpet (another new timbre) which complements the bassoon intervallically and rhythmically

(Example 7). These two rhythmic shapes underlie much of the 'Präludium' and their exposition at this crucial point reflects their importance. Similarly, the two minor thirds E–G (bassoon) and Eb–Gb (trumpet), presented in such proximity, highlight the new melodic development. The combined upward pressure of the two rising parts, the accelerating reiteration of the bassoon Ab (three quavers, two quavers, one quaver), the resulting accretion of whole tones at the top of the chord—Gb and Ab plus the still-sounding Bb—and the gradual increase in volume of the accompanying parts which counters the dynamic resolution on to *c* initiated by the bassoon, disturb the stability of the chord. A further slowing at the end of the chord increases the desire for continuation.

Ex. 7

The brief caesura cuts across the mounting impetus at the end of event 10 and the subsequent failure to continue the polyrhythmic texture and its accumulated attributes (bassoon and muted trumpet, most notably) places all these implications in abeyance. In addition, the novelty of the scoring—one timbre per note—invests the new chord *d* with a clarity, distinctness, and hence definition hitherto unknown in the piece. Above and slightly after the new sonority an irregularly repeated note sounds four times, the chord changes (*e*), the reiterated note begins again but the harmony changes (*f*) before the fourth statement. The high note appears again after a slightly longer pause, but without repetition, dying away. Silence.

Whereas the textural implications of event 10 and its predecessors are abrogated by the continuation, registral expansion is continued at both extremes, the upper Bb proceeding to C and the bass E falling to D. The placing of the high trombone pitch (Eb) one quaver after *d* is strongly reminiscent of the bassoon entry of event 8, a memory further underscored by the semitone D–Eb it creates with the bass (compare G–Ab in event 8, where the bass also moves upwards) and the colouring of the sound by small gong strokes and celesta tremolando. The minor third formed between the trombone Eb and the C at the top of *d* furnishes an intervallic link with the preceding bassoon and trumpet figures. The rhythmic and dynamic articulation of the Eb (and its repetition above the harmonic movement) establishes a larger unit of temporal measurement, particularly noticeable after the stretching associated with *c*, allowing awareness of the slight feeling of acceleration which underpins the closing wedge of the *d–e–f* sequence beneath (Example 8).

Ex. 8

Even without the restoration of strict tempo at this point, the shorter duration of *d* represents the first reversal of the expansionist trend. The suspension of the Eb above the complementary closing gesture deprives the close of some of its effect,[7] and, at the same time, arrests further upward movement. It forms an audible pitch anchor with the flute Eb which was prominent from event 6 the ear being led through the upper progression (Example 9) and retaining the trombone sonority, it will bridge a fall of two octaves and an abrupt change of texture and dynamics into the succeeding section.

Ex. 9

flute bassoon   horn viola trombone

The second group of chords is, like its predecessor, united by texture, but the distinctness of the two textures militates against a functional complementation of opening and closing gestures. In composition, *d–e–f* offers little that is new, the spreading out from *c* robbing *d* of the impact it might otherwise have had. The contraction of registers is accompanied by a systematic reduction in the number of notes in each chord (6 to 5 to 4) towards the relative simplicity of *f* in which semitones, present in all three chords, are particularly noticeable. The reduction in the rate of contraction between *e* and *f*, relative to *d* and *e*, helps to mark *f* as the goal of the local progression rather than an intermediate stage; its extension (contrary to the shortening of *e* compared with *d*) and the delaying of the final trombone Eb confirming this.

The sudden increase in volume and drop in register sound disproportionate to previous events, but the variation of the polyrhythmic texture and the sound of the perfect fourths offer some sense of return. The melody (clarinets and horns), after one leap up, moves slowly downwards, avoiding co-ordination with the chord progression beneath until its final note which is prolonged by the clarinets after the abrupt cut-off of the last chord by the brass.

Considering the consistent registral flow of the first two sections (*a–b–c* and *d–e–f*), the gradual expansion and contraction, the location of this unit in such a pronounced low range creates an upper registral vacuum which offsets the other features, stressing the recapitulatory bias indicating possible conclusion. In *g* the placing of the only element inconsistent with the prevailing perfect fourth sonority at the bottom of such a deep chord renders its effect one of vague disturbance of the sound, although the stepwise continuation upwards, culminating in a leap, is a vital part of the profile of the sequence. The precise chording of the trombones, tuba, and second double basses articulates another accelerating closing wedge, both of these features recalling the second section (*d–e–f*); the composition of the chords with its heavy bias towards fourths and seconds, and the rather amorphous texture created by the bassoons, cellos, and first basses recall the first, as does the thematic statement, its being entirely constructed from minor thirds and semitones (compare bassoon and trumpet, event 10) (Example 10).

Ex. 10

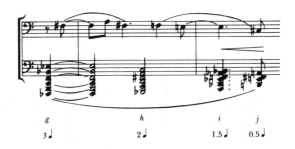

The integration of this melody with the chordal progression is achieved by means of an expansion of the relationship between the trombone E♭ and the viola C at the top of chord *d* into an elaborate network of minor thirds between the upper part of the chords and the melody (see Example 10).[8] The syncopation of the melody allows the chords to retain their identity and create the intervallic connections; only at *j* are chord and melody notes attacked simultaneously, at which point the latter becomes absorbed into the final sonority.

The chord sequence itself displays a more emphatic realization of the closing wedge pattern found in the second section but, unlike *d, e,* and *f,* the individual chords make less of an impact, the drive towards *j* being paramount. The contrary motion of the extreme voices is smooth and strongly defined, the bass (possibly more difficult to hear) being amplified by the two parts immediately above it moving in parallel fourths. The contraction of interval size exhibited by the top part also serves to intensify the feeling of closing towards *j* as do the increasingly directed semitonal movement and the final swelling and slowing. The octave duplications created by the internal stepwise progression and the vacillation of the second and third trombones between F♯–A and F–A♭ further undermine h and i as independent chords. Although achieving a degree of finality by virtue of its close position and rhythmic articulation, the pitch content of j gives it a somewhat ambiguous sound, a balance between the fourths, sevenths, and seconds of the opening of the work and the thirds that have become increasingly important in the intervening bars.

For j to function satisfactorily, if temporarily, as a punctuation point it requires further emphasis than is imparted by the abrupt cut-off of the brass. The exposure of the woodwind, sustaining the identical chord, begins this process, but the dynamic exaggeration given to the C♯ by the clarinets' *ff-p* (specifically one quaver after the arrival on j, the bassoons already *p*) triggers a characterisitically Bergian distortion of the chord by means of semitone inflection which, while it takes its cue from the final move on to j, (especially the double-bass parts: the F–B of the second basses is continued as B–F by the firsts, and the tuba B♭–B by the seconds) is established as an important generator of pseudo-harmonic movement in the following section (Example 11). Here it is used to produce not only a bending of j into a strong reference to the minor thirds of the preceding bars, but also embryonic melodic units which are taken up soon after (bar 15).

The way in which the notes of the chord are sustained until the melodic movement reaches them is another fingerprint of Berg's style.[9] Berg is here concerned to establish the principle of departure from, and return to, the chord and he marks the return by restoring the low brass and reviving the rhythmic figure associated with the high trombone E♭. (The prefiguring of this rhythm in the previous bar seems a rather redundant feature.) In retrospect this suggests a 'resolution' of the E♭ (so prominent in the first two sections and the beginning of the third) to the C♯ which is now heavily emphasized. As before, the loud statement of j is cut off to reveal a quietly sustained version of the same chord,

Ex. 11

j j

this time an octave higher and wholly on clarinets, but its function is different. The elongation of *j* has become more pronounced and the absence of a downbeat, coupled with the harp echo of *j* (this, together with the two statements of the rhythm is very similar to *d–e–f*) increases this feeling. The migration up an octave contains a suggestion of change, but at first the figures on bass clarinet and cellos bring more repetition (compare these with the double bassoon and double basses in Example 11). With the entries of the horn, cor anglais, and bassoons the decisive move is made into the main body of the movement.

Figure 1 summarizes the 'Präludium', showing how the passage discussed in detail above sits within the complete piece. The remainder of this essay deals with the conclusion of the movement in a necessarily rather more descriptive fashion, examining the ways in which the repetition of material functions to form the closure.

Figure 1

bars
1–15	introduction	Langsam (Tempo I)

1–8	section 1
9–11	section 2
11–15	section 3

16–41	principal section	Ein wenig bewegter (Tempo II)

16–24	antecedent

25–35	consequent and intensification	
36–39	climax	Ziemlich breit
40–41	lead back	(rit.)

42–56	conclusion	Tempo der korrespond. Stelle (Takt 9)
42–44	section 2 recapitulated	
45–48	interpolation	Etwas belebter
49–56	section 1 (reversed) recapitulated	Sehr langsam (wie die korrespond. Stelle (Takt 8))

The return of *d–e–f* follows the climax of the piece and the introduction of new material which will be taken up in 'Reigen'. The restatement is, however, not literal, for, while the chords remain the same they happen at a higher dynamic level and use an homogeneous texture (strings, with each change coloured by horns: *d*, six horns for three quavers; *e*, five horns for two quavers;

f, four horns for one quaver). The most noticeable difference, however, is the high E♭ which now occurs an octave lower, placing it within rather than above the chords; the trombone is replaced by four flutes and three bassoons. The new context for *d–e–f* means that instead of following an opening, it now functions within the large-scale closing gesture signalled by the abrupt descent after the climax, and the lowering of the E♭ allows the closing wedge an unimpeded expression. In terms of balance there is a lopsided feel to the equation of the inexorable registral expansion (which occupies almost two-thirds of the piece) towards the apogee, and the ensuing collapse which lasts just a few bars. The subsequent closing gestures reverberate like aftershocks from the climax.

The final statement of the E♭ is disturbed by a four-part violin tremolando (using the upper three notes of *f* and the E♭) and the contracting shape of the wedge is contradicted by the transfer of the lowest note of the chord to a lower octave (horns) (Example 12).

Ex. 12

The violin tremolando rises an octave, the complement of the horn fall, and becomes the beginning of a new descending motive, the new texture (tremolando shadowed by celesta) and faster tempo conveying the sense of interruption of the larger-scale closing tendency (the downward inclination of this motive is, of course, consonant with the larger progression). The addition of oboes to the end of this idea highlights the last four notes: B♭–G♭–F–D, which are slowed, giving further emphasis. The rising bassoon figure (again faster) contradicts the general trend downwards, and contains the residuum of the material introduced after the climax but reduced in distinction to the point where it becomes a punctuating detail rather than the dramatic gesture it was. The sequence of absorption is as follows: bar 37, trumpets introduce sextuplet figure; bar 39, repeated by strings and wind; bar 40, splitting begins in trumpets; bar 41, sextuplet figure slowed and divided into two voices (second and third trombones); bar 46, skeletal version in bassoons; bar 48, final reduction (second trombone). (All stages are marked *Hauptstimme* or *Nebenstimme*.)

The tempo slows again and the final three notes of the oboe/violin figure are restated by cellos doubled by celesta, but rhythmically the crotchet–crotchet–

minim pattern is replaced by a minim–crotchet–semibreve one, augmented versions of the two shapes from event 10. The accompanying parts begin to assume the character of the polyrhythmic texture associated with *a–b–c*. The trombone states the final derivation of the sextuplet figure, now reduced to a slow oscillation and small leap, at which point *c* is restated.

Although a polyrhythmic texture is employed it is not the same as that of the beginning of the piece. A number of the component voices of *c* use falling melodic fragments (at the corresponding point in the early events most of the melodic units were rising) and the solo double bass doubled by celesta, beginning from the same pitch as the cellos' version of the violin/oboe figure, alters its internal composition from step–leap to leap–step (see Example 14 below). Muted trumpet (doubled by harp harmonics) presents a faster version of the original shape, beginning higher than the bass G♭:A♭–G–E. The trumpet restates its A♭–G, causing the chord to shift to *b*, the double bass entering with the last two notes of its previous entry, E♭–D. While *b* is still sounding the trumpet returns to its A♭, fluttertonguing, and the reversal of the original progression is completed by the appearance of *a* (marked by the entry of the timpani). The double bass restates its E♭ and there is a brief silence.

To describe what happens here as a retrograde playing of *a–b–c* may be factually correct as far as it goes, but it hardly does justice to the complete rethinking of the articulation of the sequence, in keeping with its position in the closing gesture. The immediately preceding music gradually approaches and prepares the return of *c* and the inward wedging onto the actual chord makes the move conclusive (Example 13).

Ex. 13

The new motive introduced by the violins and celesta is subjected to the demands of the closure not by absorbing it into the texture, as was the case with the sextuplet, but by transforming it into descending versions of the bassoon and trumpet figures from event 10 (Example 14). Each chord has a different orchestral colour, the sequence remaining unbroken until the silence after *a*. In the same way that melodic tensions were used at the opening to produce movement, the trumpet and double bass clash with the chords; for example, over *b* the trumpet moves from the 'stable' A♭ to the 'unstable' G before returning to the A♭, while the double bass does the same from E♭ ('stable') to D ('unstable') without returning to E♭ before the change of chord to *a*. The retention of the trumpet A♭ across this change prevents immediate closure (see Example 14).

Ex. 14

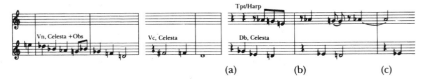

(a)   (b)   (c)

The resumption brings a rapid presentation of *b–a* with the trumpet A♭ still at the top. A second, overlapping statement of *a*+A♭ uses a different instrumental group (including gong), swelling and fading, followed by another short silence. The new group begins *a* again, fading, but is itself overlapped by a third (at the top of which the bassoon takes over the A♭), swelling and fading into a short silence. Many details of the texture are becoming faster or more noise-coloured, and a side drum is added. Group three yields, fading to a fourth, featuring a bassoon (but minus the A♭) and suspended cymbal. The swelling and fading is more noticeable in the percussion here and the gap between this event and the next doubles. The fading entry of this fourth group and the entry of the final groups are almost obliterated by the swelling and fading of the percussion. The upper notes of *a* are gradually disappearing from the completely pitched instruments and appearing on the timpani (leather sticks). The duration of the silence again increases. All non-percussion sounds have ceased by the next event, the length of which is reduced and that of the following silence further increased. In the next event the percussion is reduced, supporting two falling timpani notes, and an even longer silence highlights the shrinking sounds. A final gong stroke fades into silence.

The reversal of the opening transition from silence to sound, noise to pitch, duration to rhythm, etc. is achieved by a different, but no less cogent, process, summed up in Figure 2. The use of overlapping produces an effect akin to breathing: this creates an impression of movement within the successive entries of *a* until this process is itself overtaken by the rise to prominence of the percussion. The gradual lowering of the upper register produces a tapering-off effect towards the percussion.

It is worth noting that, while the overall effect of this final section of the piece is that of a mirror image of the opening, this is achieved by detailed processes which become more specifically related to the impression they create. The statement of *d–e–f* in correct—not reverse—order is made part of the closing gesture by the transposition of the E♭, and its separation from *a–b–c* by new material, far from breaking the relationship established at the opening, rejigs it to prepare the actual retrograde statement: *c–b–a*. Even then the process is recomposed in the light of the overall closing, resulting in a tighter, less systematic progression, achieving a satisfactory balance without recourse to mechanical repetition.

Figure 2

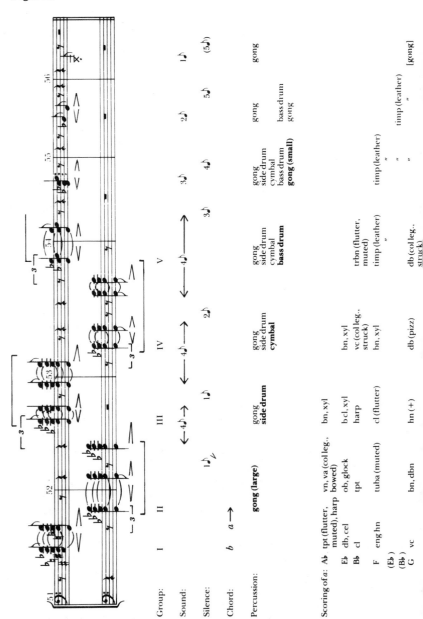

For her unfailing help and encouragement throughout the writing of this essay I am greatly indebted to Angela Rohan.

Notes

1. A caveat must be entered at this point for, in my opinion, none of the recorded performances I have been able to hear (Boulez (1967, 1986), Karajan, Davis, Dorati, Abbado, and Levine) provides more than a partial realization of Berg's intentions. A performance is a compromise between a conductor's or player's understanding (intuitive or conscious) of the score and his or her ability to execute its demands accurately; ideally both aspects would be perfect but in practice this level is rarely approached. The recordings demonstrate that accuracy without understanding is not enough to allow the shaping processes of the piece to emerge.
2. The lettering of the chords in Example 3 and subsequent examples is adopted from Berg's sketches.
3. Dissonant in the sense of not belonging to the intervallic content of a.
4. An apposite analogy would be a phrase in a Classical work's closing on—rather than in—the dominant, leaving open the option of an immediate return to the tonic or continuation in the new key.
5. Here the analogy would be, perhaps, a tonicized dominant.
6. Looked at in reverse, the establishment of the dominant in a Classical work's needs a similar affirmation of its function, rather than the passive assumption that because it is the dominant it will be perceived to function as such.
7. Compare the use of the same material at bars 42–4, where the pedal does not cover the progression, thus allowing its closing tendency much stronger expression.
8. Some of the points in this discussion, but not the main thrust of the argument, were anticipated in Bruce Archibald, 'Harmony in the Early Works of Alban Berg' (PhD diss., Harvard University, 1965).
9. It may be compared to the 'erasing' by the descending clarinet line of the piano chord in bar 7 of the second of the Four Pieces for clarinet and piano; to the mutation of the chord sustained in bar 50 in the fifth of the Altenberg Songs into that of bar 54 by means of the trombone figuration; and to the dismantling of the death chord in the final scene of *Lulu*.

'FREUNDSCHAFT, LIEBE, UND WELT': THE SECRET PROGRAMME OF THE CHAMBER CONCERTO

BRENDA DALEN

Early in 1925, the Viennese periodical *Pult und Taktstock* printed the 'Open Letter' in which Berg unveiled the dedication of his newly completed Chamber Concerto for piano, violin, and 13 wind instruments.[1] According to this letter, the concerto was intended first and foremost as a tribute, albeit belated, for Schoenberg's 50th birthday, celebrated on 13 September 1924. Both the holograph fair copy[2]—which Berg eventually presented to Schoenberg—and the published score bear the dedication 'Arnold Schönberg zum fünfzigsten Geburtstag'. Second, the completion of the concerto marked the occasion of Berg's own 40th birthday, 9 February 1925.[3] Third, the work commemorated the 20-year friendship enjoyed by the three central figures of the Second Viennese School: Arnold Schoenberg, Anton Webern, and Alban Berg.[4]

As Berg explains in the opening paragraph of the dedicatory letter, this threefold jubilee or 'trinity of events' was captured musically in the concerto's introductory motto, which derives from pitch-class equivalents for letters in the names 'Arnold Schönberg', 'Anton Webern', and 'Alban Berg' (Example 1).[5] The three ciphers in effect complete the maxim 'Aller guten Dinge ...', which has been entered in the score without its predicate 'sind drei'. In this way, Berg conveyed musically the familiar birthday greeting also expressed in the 'Open Letter': '... all the good things that I wish for you come in threes'.[6] His analytical comments reveal that the introductory motto and the number three, symbols of friendship and spiritual unity, play a significant role in the thematic development and overall structure of the concerto. The motto features prominently in the theme of the first movement, and the number three has determined virtually every aspect of the concerto's construction, including the length and number of the movements and the subsections within each movement, the duration, the instrumentation, the organization of rhythm and metre, the types of thematic and harmonic material, the formal structures, and the methods used to amalgamate the first two movements in the finale.[7]

Anticipating how readily this emphasis on number symbolism might be

Ex. 1 Chamber Concerto, introductory motto

misconstrued by his critics ('I know that—insofar as I make this generally known—my reputation as a mathematician will rise in proportion ... to the square of the distance that my reputation as a composer falls'),[8] Berg added a spirited apologia alluding to an underlying secret programme for the Chamber Concerto.

> But seriously: if in this analysis I have spoken almost exclusively of things connected with the number three, this is first, because they are the very events that would be overlooked by everyone (in favour of all the other musical events); second, because as an author it is much easier to speak of such external matters than of the inner processes, in which respect this concerto is certainly no poorer than any other music. I tell you, dearest friend, if it were known exactly what I have smuggled into these three movements of friendship, love, and world, in the way of human–spiritual references, the adherents of programme music—if indeed there still are such—would be most delighted.[9]

Other source documents for the Chamber Concerto corroborate Berg's remarks concerning its secret programme. In a programmatic outline that may be contemporaneous with the draft of the 'Open Letter', Berg has subtitled the three movements 'Freundschaft', 'Liebe', and 'Welt' (friendship, love and world),[10] and has given some indication of the ways in which these associations are embodied in the music (Figure 1).[11]

The finale ('Rondo ritmico con introduzione'), combining aspects of sonata and rondo forms, represents the world and life in a kaleidoscopic reprise of the two preceding movements ('Thema scherzoso con variazioni' and Adagio), and therefore takes its meaning from their extra-musical references.[12] (The tabular survey included in Berg's 'Open Letter' and reproduced in translation as Figure 2 provides an overview of the concerto's formal structure.)

As the programmatic outline shows, the first movement, a theme and variations, represents friendship within the Schoenberg circle. Schoenberg, Webern, and Berg ('A.S., A.W., A.B.') are depicted in the three-part theme,

Figure 1 Berg's programmatic outline of the Chamber Concerto (ÖNB Musiksammlung, F21 Berg 74/II, fol.2

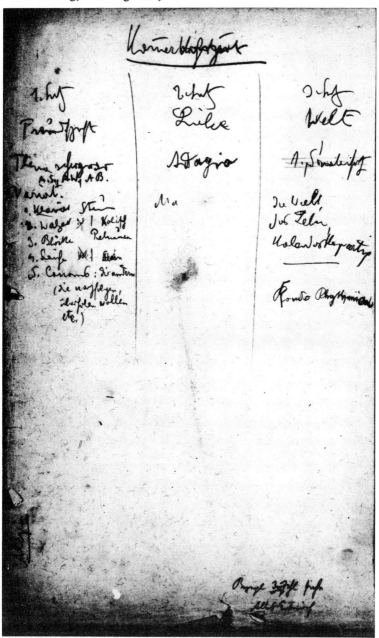

Figure 2 Tabular Survey from Berg's 'Open Letter'

Tabular Survey

	Thema	Var.1	II	III	IV	V	number of bars
	in the basic shape		retrograde	inversion	retrograde inversion	basic shape (2nd Reprise)	
	(Exposition)	(1st Reprise)		(Development)			
I Thema scherzoso con variazioni	bars: 30	30	60	30	30	60	240
II Adagio	A_1 $\quad$ 19 11 $\mid$ 12 $\mid$ A^1 A^2 $\mid$ B^1 $\mid$ 12	B $\quad$ 36 39 B^2 $\mid$ 12 9 B^3	A_2 (inversion of A_1) $\quad$ 30 $\mid$ 19 11 $\mid$ A^1 A^2 $\mid$ B^3 $\mid$ 12 9	A_2 $\quad$ 30 19 11 $\mid$ A^2 A^1 $\mid$ B^3 $\mid$ 12 9	B (Mirror form of preceding B) $\quad$ 36 39 B^2	A_1 $\quad$ 30 11 19 $\mid$ A^2 A^1 $\mid$ B^1 $\mid$ 12 12	
	Ternary		Retrograde				
III (= I plus II) Rondo ritmico con introduzione	Introduction (Cadenza for violin and piano)	Exposition	(da capo)	Development		2nd Reprise or Coda	
	bars: 54	96		79		76	305

number of bars braces: 240, 480, 960, 480, 305

while Eduard Steuermann ('Steuer'), Rudolf Kolisch ('Kolisch'), Josef Polnauer ('Polnauer'), and Erwin Stein ('Stein')[13]—also former pupils and trusted friends of Schoenberg[14]—are portrayed in the first four variations.[15] Beside the name of each dedicatee, Berg has noted a musical characteristic or variational procedure, which presumably reflects some aspect of that dedicatee's activities or personality. Some of these associations are self-evident; about others we can merely speculate. The first two variations, designated 'Klavier' and 'Walzer', are dedicated to the pianist Eduard Steuermann and the violinist Rudolf Kolisch, both avid performers of the music of the Schoenberg circle. Steuermann and Kolisch were the soloists for the Viennese première of the Chamber Concerto, which Webern conducted on 31 March 1927. The connection between the solo piano variation and Steuermann is obvious. The single pizzicato entry for the violin in bars 111–12 of the second variation refers to Kolisch's trademark, the ritual touching of the open strings before a performance.[16] The burly Josef Polnauer had gained a considerable reputation for protecting Schoenberg and his friends in the violent disturbances that often erupted during public performances of their works,[17] and perhaps the percussive figuration for the piano in the third variation ('Blöcke') symbolizes his unique contribution to promoting their music. It is not clear just how the 'runs' ('Läufe') in the fourth variation are connected with Erwin Stein; they may represent some aspect of his character or of his activities in Schoenberg's Society for Private Musical Performances.

In the fifth variation, a series of *stretti* or canons between the piano and wind ensemble unfolds in such a way that 'a group of voices that enters later tries to overtake another group that entered first, succeeds in doing this, flies past and leaves the first group far behind'.[18] Berg allots this variation to 'the others (who follow after, want to overtake, etc.)'.[19] Although he has not named these 'others' in the programmatic outline, a remark made in a letter to Webern in August 1923 shows obvious animosity towards certain of Schoenberg's pupils, whose compositions evidently had enjoyed greater public success than had those of Berg and Webern: 'Specht, in a speech about music in Austria, called special attention—*quite out of the ordinary*—to the two of us (you and me) in contrast to the Pseudo-Schoenberg pupils—Wellesz, Reti, Pisk, etc.—who weren't mentioned once.'[20]

Berg's outline furnishes a single enigmatic clue to the extra-musical impulse behind the second movement. Under the words 'Liebe' and 'Adagio'—in alignment with the programmatic notations for the outer movements—he has written the letters 'Ma'.

The preliminary sketches for the Chamber Concerto reveal that the Adagio may from its inception have connoted 'Liebe'. In the earliest formal overview of the concerto this movement is defined as a simple ternary structure, the opening section of which is 'tender, melancholic, and romantic'.[21] Elsewhere, the middle section is characterized as 'an intimate song'.[22] In other early formal sketches, however, Berg made no further reference to the mood or character of the Adagio, but concentrated exclusively on forging the palindromic design, which, according to his description in the 'Open Letter', is based on

> 'da capo song form': A_1–B–A_2, where A_2 is the inversion of A_1. The repetition of the first half of the movement, comprising 120 bars, occurs in retrograde, partly in a free formation of the reversed thematic material, but partly, as for example throughout the middle section (B), in exact mirror image.[23]

In fact, the secret programme for the Adagio is inextricably bound up in this palindromic design, the main features of which are summarized in the tabular survey in Figure 2,[24] Each of the distinct subsections within the movement presents a different twelve-note series; the subsections are also differentiated by changes in tempo, which result in a gradual acceleration towards the climax near the end of subsection B^2 in the first half.

There has been considerable speculation about the origin of Berg's fascination with large-scale retrogrades and palindromes as well as about the symbolic significance that he apparently attached to them. Commentators on Berg's music generally agree that he possessed a certain psychological pre-disposition for symmetrical designs. Hans Redlich attributes this interest in the palindrome to an inherent

> spiritual escapism which at times craved for suspension of the present and for the magical reversal of time. Berg's deep-seated fear of the evanescence of life found a kind of safety valve in the return of the end of a musical structure to its very source by, as it were, musical black magic, by the use of mirror reflection, inversion and retrograde motion.[25]

Spiritual escapism, which was widespread among artists and intellectuals during the 1920s and 1930s, reflected a growing disillusionment with economic, political, and social unrest as well with scientific and technological advancement. This era, haunted as no other by the fear of its own transience, became intensely preoccupied with the fleeting 'now', and was often tempted to shout with Goethe's Faust to the passing moment: 'Stay awhile, you are so fair!'[26] Ironically, Berg's interest in retrograde and palindromic structures may even have been sparked by contemporary developments in film and radio, which had made the 'play-back' technically possible. In Theodor Adorno's estimation, Berg's inclination for quasi-spatial symmetries and large-scale inverted and retrograde formations stemmed as much from the strong visual dimension in his thinking as from his acquaintance with Schoenberg's twelve-note method.[27] Retrograde movement is fundamentally anti-temporal, and its frequent occurrence within the context of compositions otherwise firmly entrenched in the tradition of developing variation points up a peculiarly static aspect of Berg's musical genius, which Adorno likens to 'the hesitant marking of time'.[28] Misha Donat's view is similar to Adorno's: he believes that while Berg's fascination with retrograde and palindromic movement may have been stimulated by the formulation of the twelve-note method, the tendency itself must already have been latent in his personality.[29] Donat regards the pervasive use of mirror and retrograde formations as an element of Berg's interest in mathematical mysticism, and suggests that in his music 'retrograde movement represents almost a view of life'.[30] Douglas Jarman has framed the most persuasive argument about Berg's obsessional interest in symmetry. He contends that 'the circular, palindromic and other symmetrical designs which play so large a role in Berg's music are not simply technical conceits but, like his use of ciphers and number symbolism, are objective intellectual restraints which hide a deeply subjective significance'.[31]

In fact all the large-scale retrogrades and palindromes in Berg's mature works carry symbolic meanings, often related to ideas of time and predestination. The large-scale retrograde framing the opening scene of *Wozzeck* suggests the image of the endlessly turning mill-wheel that symbolizes the Captain's obsession with time and his fear of eternity. Palindromic and retrograde figurations are also connected with Wozzeck's forebodings of disaster. In Act I, scene 2, Wozzeck senses an ominous message in the toadstool rings near the pond in which he will eventually drown. In scene 4, in conversation with the doctor, he describes these toadstool rings and the message that he believes them to contain, and the setting of his words, 'Lines, circles, and strange figures—would that one could read them', unfolds as a palindromic variation within the Passacaglia. Jarman has pointed out that although Wozzeck cannot read these strange figures, he 'instinctively feels a terror of the predestined course which the musical palindromes reveal to be the message of the toadstool rings'.[32]

Both the large-scale palindromes in *Lulu* symbolize fate. In the Sextet (Act I, scene 3, 'A theatre dressing room') Lulu engages in a heated debate with her wardrobe mistress, Alwa, Dr Schön, the African prince, and the theatre director over her refusal to dance in the presence of Schön's fiancée. The palindromic structure of the Sextet signifies her victory in this debate and foreshadows the outcome of her ensuing confrontation with Dr Schön—the breaking-off of his engagement. The palindromic 'Film Music' Ostinato at the centre of the opera marks the turning-point in the drama, symbolizing the reversal in Lulu's fortunes and the beginning of the downward path that leads to her murder at the end of Act III.

In *Der Wein*, the palindrome spanning the end of the second song and the orchestral interlude that follows 'is to correspond to the return from the realm of [the second] song into that of the third song, which is the same as that of the first'.[33] More specifically, this palindrome may have been inspired by the text for the last stanza of the second song: 'Let us fly, sister, breast to breast, without rest, without stay to the land of my dreams!';[34] its turning-point coincides with the end of the stanza.

Finally, the annotated score of the Lyric Suite reveals that the large-scale retrograde in the third movement commemorated Berg's fated first encounter with Hanna Fuchs-Robettin.[35]

Ex. 2 Chamber Concerto, II, bars 357–64: the turning-point

Ex. 2 cont.

Berg took great pains to ensure that the turning-points of his palindromes were aurally and visually conspicuous. As Hans Redlich has remarked, the seriousness with which Berg regarded these fateful leaps into the world of mirrors is evident in the mystical, almost solemn atmosphere surrounding each musical reversal.[36] Distinctive melodic, harmonic, and rhythmic features, and sharp contrasts in tempo, dynamics, register, instrumentation, and texture set the turning-points in relief, creating the impression of suspended animation or momentary stasis. In Berg's scores the turning-points invariably occur either precisely in the middle of the bar, or between two bars. At the turning-point of the *Lulu* Ostinato, for example, 'the second half of the bar, where the retrograde begins, mirrors the first half graphically, as well as musically, so that the fermata, in the full score, stands *between* the last note of the first half of the Film Music and the first note of the second half.'[37] Berg instructed the printer to place the central points of the palindromes in the *Lulu* Suite and *Der Wein* 'in the middle of the page and to arrange the bars on either side symmetrically around this point'.[38] One of Berg's copyists, Eugene Wolf, recalls that the composer advised him to lay out certain bars of the Lyric Suite symmetrically, so that the two inside pages would be 'like each other—like a mirror'.[39]

The moment at which the palindromic structure of the Adagio begins to move in retrograde (Example 2) is perhaps the most dramatic in the entire Chamber Concerto. The minimal melodic movement, the slowing down of the harmonic rhythm, the introduction of a pedal point, the augmentation of rhythmic values, the decrease in dynamics and tempo, the abrupt shifts in register, and the reduction of the instrumental force account for the eerie atmosphere that characterizes the six central bars. Particularly striking in a movement otherwise scored for violin and wind is the entry of the piano with 'twelve mysterious chimes of low C sharp ... which ring in the hour of musical ghosts'.[40]

Documents pertaining to the publication of the Chamber Concerto attest to Berg's preoccupation with rendering the turning-point of the Adagio visually prominent. The first edition of the full score was simply a photographic reproduction of the holograph fair copy, which had been prepared for presentation to Schoenberg.[41] In this manuscript, as Example 3 shows,[42] Berg copied the five-bar units on either side of the turning-point in perfect symmetry, on adjacent facing pages. To ensure that these bars would also appear on a single opening in the facsimile edition, he instructed his publisher to follow the precise disposition of even and odd page numbers pencilled in the autograph. However else the pagination might be altered, the original correspondence between even-numbered and left-hand (verso) pages, and between odd-numbered and right-hand (recto) pages was to be strictly maintained.[43]

Berg's pupil, Fritz Heinrich Klein, prepared the piano reduction of the Chamber Concerto, and his autograph, heavily corrected by Berg, served as the *Stichvorlage* (engraver's copy) for the first edition.[44] In his supplementary instructions for the engraver, Berg called attention to notations that he had glued into the *Stichvorlage*, and that pertained specifically to the layout of the

Ex. 3 Chamber Concerto, II, bars 356–65: the turning-point in the holograph
fair copy

Ex. 3 cont.

score.[45] Attached to the margin of the page containing the turning-point of the Adagio is Berg's note advising the engraver to amend Klein's layout so as to project clearly the mirror image:

> The engraving of these pages is to be arranged in such a way that bars 357–60 occur as the last system on an *even-numbered* page (that is, left-hand side), while bars 361–4 occur as the top system on the following odd [-numbered] page (that is, right-hand side). In this way, the symmetry of the two four-bar units (mirror image!) is plainly visible. Moreover, bars 355–6 and 365–6 are also symmetrical (or in mirror image!).[46]

This attentiveness to visual detail dates back to Berg's composition draft of the Adagio.[47] Marginalia in the earliest continuity draft of the 'turning-point' or 'centre' ('Wendepunkt' or 'Mittelpunkt'), seen in Figure 3, stipulate that 'this turning-point must produce an *image*' and that the six central bars (bars 118–23 in the draft, and 358–63 in the published score) 'must appear on *one* page'.[48] The image delineated here attained its definitive form in a subsequent revised draft. As Figure 4 shows, Berg made a fair-hand copy of these six bars, arranging them in perfect symmetry around the centre of the page.[49]

The key to unriddling the meaning of the Adagio is a cipher first encountered in the formal diagram in the 'envelope' sketch reproduced as Figure 5.[50] At the centre of this diagram, on the envelope's lower flap, Berg has jotted down a capsule description of the turning-point:

Ein Bild	An image
Auf Höhepunkt (Angelpunkt)	At the climax (pivot)
Klavier Bass	Piano bass
dazu Math Thema	in addition Math theme
Ahde edhA	Ahde edhA

The palindromic configuration designated as the 'Math Thema' constitutes the *Hauptstimme* for the first horn in the turning-point bars (see bars 358–63 in Example 2). The precedent established by the ciphers in the concerto's introductory motto reinforces the notion that the 'Math Thema' also represents a cipher, the derivation of which is a person's name. 'Math' appears to be an abbreviation for this name, and 'a', 'h', 'd', and 'e' are the only letters for which there are musical equivalents. Conflated, the two sets of letters yield the series 'Mathde'.

Additional references to the 'Math Thema' occur throughout the composition draft of the Adagio.[51] Underneath the preliminary sketch in Figure 6,[52] Berg has scribbled a word, which resembles 'Mathde' in contour, but which is illegible beyond the initial letters 'Ma'. Below this sketch, on left-hand side of the page, is an alphabetical chart displaying the Schoenberg and 'Math' ciphers in vertical alignment. The chart's two-level presentation of the 'Math' cipher betrays the numerical scheme by which the two ciphers are related. To obtain the letters 'ahde' in correct order, Berg has extracted the first letter and every subsequent

Figure 3 Earliest continuity draft of the turning-point (ÖNB Musiksammlung, F21 Berg 74/VII [A], fol. 9)

Figure 4 Fair copy of the turning-point (ÖNB Musiksammlung, F21 Berg 74/ VII [B], fol. 12v)

Figure 5 The 'envelope' sketch of the 'Math Thema' (ÖNB Musiksammlung, F21 Berg 74/III, fols. 2–3)

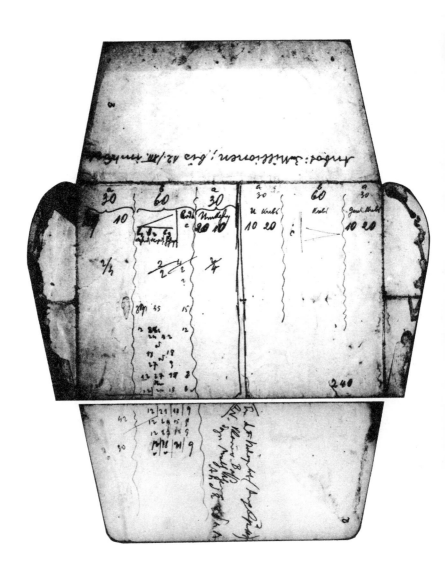

Figure 6 Preliminary sketch of the 'Math Thema' (ÖNB Musiksammlung, F21 Berg 74/VII [B], fol. 26)

fifth letter from successive statements of the Schoenberg cipher.

The 'Math' cipher is decoded for us in the discarded sketch of the turning-point reproduced in Figure 7.[53] Above the harmonic elaboration of the 'Math Thema' found on the third staff, the letters 'Ma–h–d–e' are plainly visible. Upon closer inspection, it becomes apparent that the letter 'h' is covering the underlying syllable 'thil', which completes the word 'Mathilde'. Further confirmation of this reading is found in the first draft of the turning-point (see Figure 3, bars 118–20). Here 'Mathilde' is easily legible in the distribution 'Ma–thil–d–e' below the pitches of the 'Math Thema'. Given the explicit connection between the Schoenberg and 'Math' ciphers in the alphabetical chart, we may with certainty identify the person behind the 'Math Thema' as Mathilde Schoenberg (née Zemlinsky), Arnold Schoenberg's first wife.

There is a logical explanation for this hidden reference to Mathilde Schoenberg at the turning-point of the palindromic Adagio. When the Schoenbergs left Vienna on 1 June 1923 for their annual summer vacation in Traunkirchen,[54] Mathilde may already have been seriously ill. Berg visited them there in early August and found her in very poor health.[55] She suffered from an ailment that a succession of doctors seemed unable to diagnose or treat properly. Berg was sufficiently disturbed by his own firsthand observations of her condition to request a detailed report from the Schoenbergs' son-in-law, Felix Greissle, upon returning to Trahütten. When no reply was forthcoming, he appealed directly to Schoenberg.

> We are very worried about Mathilde. Since my visit in Traunkirchen we have heard nothing about her condition, and though we tell each other that your dear wife naturally has no inclination to write letters and that you don't have time for it, your silence nonetheless makes us very uneasy. We now hope to hear something about Mathilde and all of you from Greissle, to whom I wrote twelve days ago. Perhaps you will be so kind as to encourage him to write me a short letter.[56]

Greissle's letter, which arrived on 5 September, informed Berg that a diagnosis had finally been reached: Mathilde's illness was attributed to an acute gall bladder disorder.[57]

Despite the steady deterioration in Mathilde's condition and her failure to respond to treatment, the family and friends remained optimistic that she would regain her health. Berg chose not to mention the subject in his birthday letter to Schoenberg, but Helene added a postscript expressing her fervent wish for Mathilde's complete recovery in the coming year: 'today, on your birthday—of the many, many warm wishes, which I have for you now and always, there is one I must express. Namely: that the new year brings the complete recovery of your dear good Mathilde.'[58] A few days later, however, the Bergs received an alarming communication from Webern, who had just visited Traunkirchen.

Figure 7 Discarded sketch of the turning-point (ÖNB Musiksammlung, F21 Berg 74/VII [B], fol. 11v)

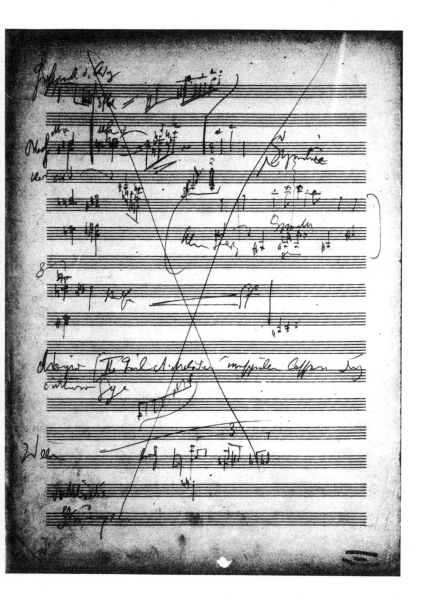

The appearance and condition of Mrs Schoenberg fill me with *great worry*. About fourteen days ago, her suffering was finally diagnosed: sickness of the gall bladder and liver. The latter extremely large and inflamed. An operation may be necessary. For weeks she has been in bed constantly and she is enormously weak. That *worries* me *greatly*. For weeks Schoenberg hasn't moved from her bed. I had no idea. It is terrible. Completely indescribable.[59]

On 20 September 1923, the Schoenbergs returned to Vienna; Mathilde was admitted directly to the Auersperg Sanatorium, where she died on 18 October, the Schoenbergs' 22nd wedding anniversary.[60] A tumour of the adrenal gland was cited on the death certificate as the cause of death.

The palindromic design of the Adagio, though conceived several months previously—in the late spring or early summer of 1923[61]—clearly came to symbolize Mathilde Schoenberg's death, which occurred shortly after Berg had embarked on the composition of the movement. It is in fact possible to establish a direct link between her death and the genesis of the turning-point. The 'envelope' sketch (Figure 5) provides the earliest record of Berg's decision to integrate the 'Math' cipher into the turning-point bars. Although the postmark on this envelope is no longer legible, and the date provided in the notation on its upper flap—'Offer: 300 million; until 12./XII. in writing'[62]—is inconclusive, internal evidence within the sketch itself and information regarding the compositional history of the Adagio indicate that this decision may even have been made after Mathilde's death.

The 'envelope' sketch constitutes the first detailed formal plan of the movement. Numerical calculations entered on this plan suggest that when it was drawn up Berg may already have drafted the first 40-odd bars: the lengths of the first three subsections A^1, A^2, and B^1 (bars 1–42) are fixed, whereas the lengths of the remaining subsections within section B had yet to be determined. The composition draft of the Adagio preserves a coherent draft and partial revision of bars 1–46, at which point—owing to compositional difficulties encountered in subsection B^2—the draft breaks off.[63]

There is little reason to believe that in the autumn of 1923, the Adagio would have advanced beyond bar 46. In fact Berg may not have sketched more than the first 15 bars.[64] The first movement of the Chamber Concerto had been completed by 1 September, and, eager to accomplish as much as possible before his vacation ended, Berg immediately set to work on the second movement.[65] Its composition proceeded very slowly, however, for, as he confessed to both Schoenberg and Webern, the fine weather and pleasant surroundings at Trahütten distracted him more than was good for his work.[66] When he wrote to Webern on 16 September, Berg was unable to report any significant progress in his work, and neither his impending departure for Vienna nor his anxiety about Mathilde Schoenberg's health augured well for its continuation: 'About myself, I can report nothing new. The mood of departure engulfs me. A true uneasiness as to just what will be wrong in Vienna. Under these circumstances, the continuation of my work won't go well.'[67] With Berg's arrival in Vienna on 20 September,[68] the composition of the Adagio almost certainly came to a standstill; the general turmoil of readjusting to city life, arranging his teaching schedule, settling his business affairs, and attending to the needs of the Schoenbergs would have occupied him fully for several weeks. Although Berg may have worked on the movement sporadically later that autumn, he did not actively resume its composition until late February or early March 1924.[69]

Several additional programmatic references, gleaned from both the sketches and the score itself, shed further light on the secret programme for the Adagio. These references support the interpretation of the palindrome as a symbol of Mathilde Schoenberg's death, and make it possible to reconstruct in the music a partial scenario of her struggle against illness.

Figure 8

	'Math Thema'			'Melisande' theme	
statement	bars	form	bars	form	
1	261–4	prime	260–70	prime	
2	274–5	prime	270–79	prime	
3	300–301	prime			
4	314-17	prime			
			350–60	inversion	
5-6	358–63	prime, retrograde			
			361–71	retrograde-inversion	
7	404–7	retrograde			
8	420–21	retrograde			
9	446–7	retrograde	442-50	retrograde	
10	457–60	retrograde	451–61	retrograde	
11	461–4	transposed retrograde			
12	464–5	transposed retrograde			

All told, the Adagio contains twelve statements of the 'Math Thema' (see Figure 8). The first ten statements, which occur at the primary pitch level ('A–H–D–E' or 'E–D–H–A'), unfold symmetrically in prime and retrograde pairs according to the palindromic design; the eleventh and twelfth statements, which have been transposed, are without antecedents in the first half of the movement. Apart from its purely horizontal presentation in the second and ninth statements, where it constitutes the incipit of the main theme for subsection B[1],[70] the 'Math Thema' comprises a twelve-note succession of four trichords, whose highest pitches spell the 'Math' cipher. As Example 4 shows, the Schoenberg cipher is also embedded in this succession.

The 'Math Thema', generally associated with a pedal point and scored for brass instruments, is further emphasized through rhythmic elongation, heavier articulation, and a subtle increase in dynamic level. Unlike the concerto's introductory motto, however, it is not readily audible, except at the turning-point. Its identity is chiefly harmonic rather than melodic, and its significance is structural rather than thematic or motivic. The 'Math Thema' underscores the major points of articulation in the formal structure, appearing at the juncture between the two subsections within section A, at the midpoint in each half of the palindrome, at the climax of the movement, and at the turning-point.

Ex. 4 Chamber Concerto, II, bars 358–60, brass: the 'Schönberg' cipher within the 'Math Thema'

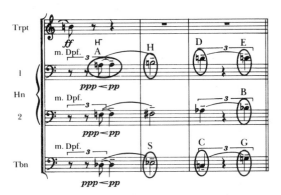

The scenario of Mathilde's struggle against illness and death begins with the entry of the *Hauptrhythmus* (Example 5), an obvious symbol of fate.[71] This rhythmic motive, which originates in the melodic figuration for solo violin in bars 294–6, is concentrated in subsection B^2, in the bars directly leading to the climax of the movement (see bars 294–313, and bars 408–27 in the retrograde). The *Hauptrhythmus* is characteristically scored for pairs of wind instruments in low register, and is consistently given out on the pitch class A, the first pitch in the 'Math' cipher. In bars 299–300 (bars 420–1 in the retrograde), it frames a complete statement of the cipher. The final repetitions of the *Hauptrhythmus* in the first half of the movement (bars 306–8) occur on the pitch class C♯ to prefigure the death knell sounded by the piano at the turning-point.

Ex. 5

The climax ('Höhepunkt') of the Adagio, reached in bar 314, incorporates the penultimate statement of the 'Math Thema' within the first half of the movement. Given Berg's fondness for numerological conceits, it can hardly be a

Figure 9 Berg's formal overview of the Rondo ritmico (ÖNB Musik-sammulung, F21 Berg 74/XIII, fol. 1)

coincidence that this statement of the 'Math Thema' (bars 314–17) and its retrograde counterpart (bars 404–7)—the fourth and seventh statements respectively—occur 47 bars on either side of the turning-point.[72] Mathilde Schoenberg, who was born on 7 September 1877, died shortly after her 46th birthday, or at the beginning of her 47th year.[73]

In several formal sketches for the Rondo ritmico, the short coda to the B section of the Adagio, subsection B^3 (bars 322–30, and bars 391–9 in the retrograde), is designated 'Resigniertes' (Figure 9).[74] The programmatic implication of this label is self-evident, since spiritual resignation informs every detail of the coda's construction. From the outset, the ostinato accompaniment threatens to overpower the plaintive melody in the *Hauptstimme*, and, by the end of the coda, the melody has been absorbed into the accompaniment.

The transition from the Adagio to the Rondo ritmico is effected through significant changes in the final repetition of the A section of the Adagio in retrograde. Berg has worked two extra statements of the 'Math Thema' on 'G–F–D–C' and 'B♭–A♭–F–E♭' into this section. Together with the regular entry at the primary pitch level ('E–D–H–A'), these transpositions form a succession of statements (see statements ten to twelve, bars 457–465), whose initial pitches (E, G, and B♭) derive from the first trichord in the retrograde form of the 'Math Thema'—coincidentally the last three pitches of the Schoenberg cipher. As the violin and accompanying winds fade away in the last five bars of the Adagio, the piano enters unobtrusively with a complete statement of the Schoenberg cipher. In the overall formal design, this statement of the cipher—which ushers in the cadenza preceding the Rondo ritmico—corresponds to the concerto's introductory motto. Perhaps its appearance here, together with the transposed statements of the 'Math Thema' several bars earlier, signifies the end of Schoenberg's mourning and his readiness once again to embrace life and the world.[75]

Finally, a programmatic reference, which—like the reference 'Resigniertes' —crops up in the formal sketches for the Rondo ritmico, suggests another related interpretation of the symbolism in the Adagio.[76] These sketches attach the label 'Melisande' to the second theme of the Adagio, introduced in the last eleven bars of section A (see the *Hauptstimme* in Example 6) and subsequently repeated in inversion, retrograde inversion, and retrograde over the movement. As the formal overview reproduced in Figure 9 shows, Berg specifically designates the inverted and retrograde transformations of this theme 'Umkehrung d. Melisande' and 'Melisande Krebs' respectively.[77] The 'Melisande' theme is not restricted to the A section of the Adagio but appears in the B section as well. A rhythmically augmented version serves as the *cantus firmus* for the fugato that unfolds in subsection B^1 (see the *Nebenstimme*, bars 270–79, and the trombone part, bars 442–50 in the retrograde). Moreover, there is a marked similarity between the opening gesture of Berg's 'Melisande' theme and the opening gesture of the theme whose prime and inverted forms are featured in subsection B^2 (Example 7).[78]

Ex. 6 Chamber Concerto, II, bars 260–70: the 'Melisande' theme

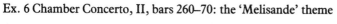

Ex. 7 (a) 'Melisande' theme, (b) main theme of subsection B² (prime), (c) main theme of subsection B² (inversion)

(a)

(b)

(c)

The label 'Melisande' presumably refers to Maurice Maeterlinck's symbolist drama *Pelléas et Mélisande*, the plot of which hinges on a love triangle involving Prince Golaud, his young bride, Mélisande, and his half-brother, Pelléas. Upon discovering that he has been betrayed by Pelléas and Mélisande, Golaud kills Pelléas outright, also wounding himself and Mélisande, who later dies. Although the sketches fail to clarify the significance of this literary allusion, the music itself offers an important clue. Throughout the Adagio, each statement of the theme which Berg designated as 'Melisande' is coupled with a statement of the 'Math Thema' (see Figure 8). This implicit connection between Mélisande and Mathilde may have been intended as an indirect reference to Mathilde Schoenberg's tragic affair with the expressionist painter, Richard Gerstl.[79]

The Schoenbergs became acquainted with this gifted young artist through Mathilde's brother, Alexander von Zemlinsky, sometime in 1907. From 1907 to 1908 Gerstl rented a studio in the tenement house also occupied by the Schoenbergs and the Zemlinskys, and he soon became a part of the family. He gave painting lessons to both the Schoenbergs and painted them in several well-known individual and family portraits. During this period the Schoenbergs experienced marital difficulties and Mathilde became romantically involved with Gerstl. In the summer of 1908 she left her husband and children. Mutual friends of the Schoenbergs—most notably Webern—eventually persuaded her to return home, an action which may have precipitated Gerstl's suicide in November 1908.[80]

In the aftermath of this tragedy Mathilde Schoenberg seems to have suffered a complete psychological breakdown from which she never fully recovered. From this time onward she became increasingly silent and even reclusive. She seldom participated in her husband's social life, preferring rather to withdraw to her room whenever company appeared, under the pretext of not wishing to make any new acquaintances.[81] One visitor to the Schoenberg house recalls Mathilde as 'a frail, sick-looking woman who sat silently in the corner of the couch, always wrapped in a shawl.'[82]

The musical symbolism of the Adagio can be reinterpreted in terms of Mathilde's ill-fated affair with Gerstl. The palindrome symbolizes the Schoenbergs' estrangement and eventual reconciliation as well as Mathilde's spiritual death and gradual retreat from the world following Gerstl's suicide. Moreover, the twelve fateful strokes for the piano at the turning-point may recall the moment at which the fate of Pelléas and Mélisande is sealed in Maeterlinck's drama. In Act II, scene 1 ('A fountain in the park'), the young lovers find themselves sitting together at the edge of a fountain. As they talk, Mélisande removes her wedding ring and playfully tosses it into the air over the water. Just as the clock is striking noon the ring falls into the fountain.[83] On the twelfth stroke Golaud, who is out hunting in a nearby forest, is suddenly thrown from his horse. Later, in relating this mishap to Mélisande, Golaud says, 'I fell, and he [the horse] must have fallen on me. I thought I had the whole forest on my breast; I thought my heart was crushed.'[84]

Knowing Berg's penchant for musical quotation, it seems reasonable that the Adagio might contain references to either of two compositions based on Maeterlinck's drama: Debussy's opera, *Pelléas et Mélisande*, and Schoenberg's symphonic poem, *Pelleas und Melisande*. Hans Redlich has suggested a possible connection between Debussy's opera and the second theme of the Adagio (see Example 6): 'The vaguely cadential series of chromatically altered ninth chords above a pedal point for bassoon on C—already clearly anticipating the twelve bell strokes on low C♯ later in the movement—sounds like a distant echo from Debussy's *Pelléas*'.[85] If the harmonic parallel drawn between these two works fails to convince, it is nevertheless uncanny that Redlich should have perceived a 'distant' echo of *Pelléas* in the very passage that Berg himself associated with Mélisande.

Schoenberg's symphonic poem proves a more likely source for allusive quotation in the Adagio. Two of the leitmotifs identified in Berg's thematic guide to Schoenberg's *Pelleas und Melisande*[86] are reproduced in Example 8, together with the passage that leads to the turning-point of the Adagio, and that Berg designated as the 'Umkehrung d. Melisande' in his sketches.[87] It is possible to detect a loose paraphrase of the leitmotif 'Melisande' in the *Nebenstimme*—the prime and inverted forms of the 'Melisande' theme of the Adagio are present in the *Nebenstimme* and *Hauptstimme* respectively—and of the leitmotif 'Das Sterbegemach Melisandes' (Mélisande's gentle death) in the accompanying triplet figuration.[88] A more exact paraphrase of the 'Melisande'

Ex. 8 (a) Leitmotifs from Berg's guide to Schoenberg's *Pelleas und Melisande*, (b) Chamber Concerto, II, bars 350–55: 'Umkehrung d. Melisande'

Ex. 8 (b)

leitmotif occurs at the climax of the Adagio in subsection B², where the inverted form of the theme that is related to the movement's 'Melisande' theme permeates the texture (Example 9).[89]

The Adagio also incorporates two brief quotations from Act III of *Wozzeck*, which seem to pertain to Mathilde's affair with Gerstl (Example 10). Both quotations refer to Wozzeck's blood-stained hands, the symbol for his guilt over Marie's murder. The statement of the *Hauptrhythmus* allotted to the violin in

Ex. 9 Chamber Concerto, II, bars 314–17: *Höhepunkt*

Ex. 9 cont.

bars 303–5 of the Adagio (bars 416–18 in the retrograde) may allude to Margret's discovery of the blood on Wozzeck's hands in the tavern scene (Act III, scene 3, 'Invention on a Rhythm', bars 185ff.). The arpeggiation preceding this statement of the *Hauptrhythmus* may recall Wozzeck's futile attempts to wash the blood from his hands upon having returned to the scene of his crime to search for the murder weapon (Act III, scene 4, 'Invention on a Chord', bars 274 ff.).

Considering their programmatic implications, it is hardly surprising that neither the thematic references to *Pelleas und Melisande* nor the quotations from *Wozzeck* are readily audible in the Adagio. It is inconceivable that Berg would have risked any but the most obscure allusion to the Gerstl affair; the Chamber Concerto was intended to bring Schoenberg 'all good things' on his birthday, and he certainly would not have tolerated an overt reference to such a painful episode in his life, much less accepted it 'in a spirit of friendship'.[90]

Nor would it have been appropriate for Berg to have confided the deeply personal programme of the Adagio to the readers of *Pult und Taktstock*. His memorial to Mathilde's death might well have been taken as a criticism of Schoenberg's recent remarriage. On 28 August 1924, just ten months after Mathilde's death, Schoenberg had married Rudolf Kolisch's sister Gertrud in a private ceremony in Mödling, and in February 1925, when Berg was writing the 'Open Letter', the Schoenbergs were enjoying a delayed honeymoon in Italy.[91]

There is no evidence that Berg ever revealed the secret significance of the Adagio to Schoenberg, or that Schoenberg apprehended it on his own. Schoenberg did not become familiar with the Chamber Concerto until he attended the première given in Berlin on 19 March 1927.[92] A couple of months later, he wrote to Berg:

> Soon after your last stay in Berlin I looked at your Chamber Concerto several times and after the performance I found that suddenly I, too, could read it quite easily and was very impressed by it. It is certainly a *very beautiful piece* and I'm

Ex. 10 (a) Chamber Concerto, II, bars 303–5, violin *Hauptrhythmus*, (b) *Wozzeck*, Act III, bars 274–7, (c) *Wozzeck*, Act III, bars 185–91

Ex. 10 (b)

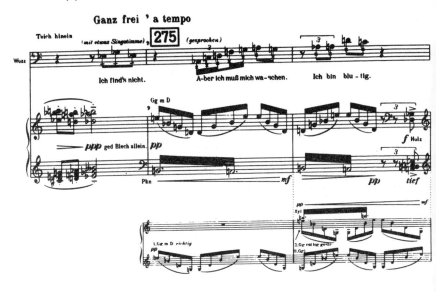

Ex. 10 (c)

very sorry I couldn't hear Webern's performance of it. It would be perfect if Webern could do it here too.[93]

When Berg stated in the 'Open Letter' that as an author he found it much easier to speak about 'external matters' than about 'inner processes', he was clearly distinguishing between the public and private aspects of the programme or the Chamber Concerto. In the letter, Berg the author announced the threefold dedication of the concerto and revealed how this dedication was embodied in certain 'external' features of the music. In the concerto itself, Berg the composer, through secret programmatic processes, expressed those private matters that he could not otherwise have uttered.

A shorter version of this essay, entitled 'The Dedication of Berg's *Chamber Concerto*: Enigmas in the "Open Letter"', was presented at the national meeting of the American Musicological Society in Cleveland, Ohio on 6 November 1986. An expanded version is included in my PhD dissertation, 'A Study of Berg's *Chamber Concerto* Based on the Source Documents' (Yale University, in progress).

Notes

1. Alban Berg, 'Alban Bergs Kammerkonzert für Geige und Klavier mit Begleitung von dreizehn Bläsern', *Pult und Taktstock*, vol. 2 (February–March 1925), pp. 23–8. The 'Open Letter' is reprinted in Willi Reich, *Alban Berg: mit Bergs eigenen Schriften und Beiträgen von Theodor Wiesengrund-Adorno und Ernst Krenek* (Vienna: Herbert Reichner Verlag, 1937), pp. 86–91; rev. and abridged as *Alban Berg* (Zurich: Atlantis Verlag, 1963), pp. 135–40; trans. Cornelius Cardew (London: Thames and Hudson, 1965), pp. 143–8. It is also translated in Juliane Brand, Christopher Hailey, and Donald Harris, eds and trans., *The Berg–Schoenberg Correspondence: Selected Letters* (New York: W. W. Norton, 1987), pp. 334–7.
2. Preserved in the archives of the Arnold Schoenberg Institute, Los Angeles (CASG86–C389). I wish to thank Wayne Shoaf, acting archivist, for his assistance.
3. In fact only the short score would have been finished by 9 February 1925; the orchestration dragged on until the following summer. The draft of the full score (preserved in the Stadtbibliothek, Winterthur, Switzerland) is dated 23 July 1925. In 1935, ten years after completing the Chamber Concerto, Berg arranged the Adagio for violin, clarinet, and piano. This trio arrangement was performed at the celebration given by his publisher, Universal Edition, in honour of his 50th birthday. For more on the trio arrangement, see David Congdon, '*Kammerkonzert*: Evolution of the Adagio and the Trio Transcription', *Alban Berg Symposion Wien 1980: Tagungsbericht*, ed. Rudolf Klein, Alban Berg Studien, vol. 2 (Vienna: Universal Edition, 1981), pp. 145–60.
4. This friendship dated back to 1904, the year in which Webern and Berg began their compositional studies with Schoenberg.
5. In German musical terminology, the pitch classes E♭, B, and B♭ are equivalent to the letters S (Es), H, and B respectively.
6. Brand, Hailey, and Harris, op. cit., p. 335.

7. Ibid., p. 334–7; also Reich, *Alban Berg*, trans. Cardew, pp. 143–7.

8. My translation. Compare with the translations in Reich, op. cit., p. 147, and Brand, Hailey, and Harris, op. cit., pp. 336–7.

9. My translation. There are significant differences between my translation of this passage and those in Reich, op. cit., pp. 147–8, and Brand, Hailey, and Harris, op. cit., p. 337.

10. In an earlier sketch (ÖNB Musiksammlung, F21 Berg 74/X, fol. 7) Berg designated the three movements as 'Freundschaft, Liebe, Welt (Natur, Menschheit, die Menschen)'.

11. ÖNB Musiksammlung, F21 Berg 74/II, fol. 2. See Rosemary Hilmar, *Katalog der Musikhandschriften, Schriften und Studien Alban Bergs im Fond Alban Berg und der weiteren handschriftlichen Quellen im Besitz der Österreichischen Nationalbibliothek*, Alban Berg Studien, vol. 1 (Vienna: Universal Edition, 1980), pp. 53–7. I wish to thank Dr Günter Brosche for permission to study the sketches and Dr Rosemary (Hilmar) Moravec for her kind assistance during my many visits to the library.
    The type of paper used for the programmatic outline is the same as that of the draft of the 'Open Letter' (F21 Berg 74/I, fols 9–18v), which is dated 7 February 1925. The notation 'Bezugl. *3er* Zahl siehe Altes Entwurf' ('With respect to the number 3, see old sketch') in the lower right-hand corner of F21 Berg 74/II, fol. 2 may be a cross-reference to the list on F21 Berg 74/III, fol. 5, which does not seem to have been compiled until at least the first two movements of the concerto had been completed. The contents of F21 Berg 74/II, fol. iv (which belongs to the same leaf as fol. 2), headed 'Rhythmische Möglichkeiten', pertain to the discussion of rhythm included in the 'Open Letter'. Furthermore, Berg does not refer to the finale as a 'Rondo rhythmico' until the later stages of its composition. 'Rondo rhythmico' is used as the title of the finale in the first edition of the Chamber Concerto; in subsequent editions, however, the movement is entitled 'Rondo ritmico'.

12. On the programmatic outline (ÖNB Musiksammlung, F21 Berg 74/II, fol. 2) Berg has designated the finale both as '1. Sonatensatz' (first movement sonata form) and 'Rondo rhythmico' and summarized its programmatic content in the notations 'die Welt', 'das Leben', and 'kaleidoskopartig'.

13. The second and fourth variations were originally also intended for Berg and Webern. However, the notations 'ich' and 'Web' have been crossed out.

14. Steuermann studied with Schoenberg 1912–14, Kolisch 1919–22, Polnauer 1909–11, and Stein 1906–10. Polnauer also studied with Berg 1911–13. Steuermann, Kolisch, Polnauer, and Stein, like Berg and Webern, were active in Schoenberg's Society for Private Musical Performances, which was in existence 1918–21. Webern, Berg, Steuermann, and later Stein served as rehearsal directors; Polnauer was the archivist. Stein also served as president when Schoenberg went to Holland in 1921. Steuermann and Kolisch frequently performed in the Society's concerts. For further information about Schoenberg's activities as a teacher and the Society for Private Musical Performances, see Joan Allen Smith, *Schoenberg and His Circle: a Viennese Portrait* (New York: Schirmer Books, 1986).

15. In the 'Open Letter' Berg states that each of the thematic transformations in the first movement has its own 'face' or 'physiognomy'. As the tabular survey in Figure 2 shows, each of the variations presents a different twelve-note transformation of the theme. It appears in prime form in the first variation, in retrograde form in the second, in inverted form in the third, and in inverted retrograde form in the fourth. In the fifth variation the theme returns in prime form.

16. Douglass M. Green, conversation with the author, 6 November 1986.

17. Polnauer's reputation dated from the first performance of Berg's Seven Early Songs on 7 November 1907: see Reich, op. cit., p. 24. Marcel Dick recalls that at this performance Polnauer had risen to the defence of Gustav Mahler, who was involved in a heated argument with another member of the audience. In retaliation for the healthy blow dealt him by Polnauer's fist, Mahler's adversary drew a knife and sliced Polnauer's face open. The resulting scar was apparently a source of great pride to Polnauer: see Smith, op. cit., p. 70.

18. Reich, op. cit., p. 144.

19. ÖNB Musiksammlung, F21 Berg 74/II, fol. 2. The original text reads '... die andern (die nachfolgen, überholen wollen etc.)'.

20. Berg to Webern, 19 August 1923, Wiener Stadtbibliothek, Handschriftensammlung, IN 185.629. My translation.

21. ÖNB Musiksammlung, F21 Berg 74/III, fol. 1. The original text reads 'zart, melanchol[isch], romantisch'.

22. ÖNB Musiksammlung, F21 Berg 74/V, fol. 26v. The original text reads 'ein inniger Gesang'. It is evident from other notations on this folio that Berg is describing subsection B^1 (bars 171–82) of the Adagio.

23. My translation. Compare with the translations in Reich, op. cit., pp. 144–5, and Brand, Hailey, and Harris, op. cit., p. 335.

24. Berg's tabular survey misrepresents the Adagio's true structure by dividing section B into three subsections containing 12, 36, and 12 bars respectively, rather than 12, 39, and 9 bars (9, 39, and 12 bars in the retrograde). While this numerical discrepancy might easily have been the fault of the printer, evidence in the first draft of the survey (see ÖNB Musiksammlung, F21 Berg 74/I, fol. 3) suggests that Berg himself intentionally juggled the numbers, possibly to convey the impression of uniform proportional relations among the three movements, or to create the illusion of perfect symmetry within each half of the palindrome. The lengths of the subsections within section B are correct in Berg's earlier diagrams of the Adagio (see F21 Berg 74/X, fol. 6v; 74/V, fol. 15). In Figure 2 I have entered the correct lengths of the subsections of the Adagio, and have added the letters A^1, A^2, B^1, B^2, and B^3, used in this essay to designate the subsections. I have retained the letters A_1, B, and A_2 used by Berg to designate the sections.

25. Hans Ferdinand Redlich, *Alban Berg: the Man and his Music* (London: John Calder, 1957), p. 113. Redlich's discussion of the meaning of the palindrome in Berg's music is abridged from that presented in the German edition of his book, *Versuch einer Würdigung* (Vienna: Universal Edition, 1957), pp. 156–7. In summarizing Redlich's views in this essay, I have relied on the German edition.

26. Redlich, *Alban Berg: Versuch einer Würdigung*, p. 156.

27. Theodor Adorno, *Alban Berg: Der Meister des kleinsten Übergangs* (Vienna: Elisabeth Lafite Verlag, 1968), p.21.

28. Ibid., p.22.

29. Misha Donat, 'Mathematical Mysticism', *The Listener* (2 April 1970), p. 458.

30. Ibid.

31. Douglas Jarman, *The Music of Alban Berg* (London: Faber and Faber, 1979), p. 241. For further discussion of the significance of symmetrical designs in Berg's music, see Jarman's chapters 'Formal Structures', pp. 175–222 and 'Conclusions', pp. 223–41.

32. Ibid., p. 239.

33. Berg to Schoenberg, 16 February 1932, Brand, Hailey, and Harris, op. cit., p. 431. I am grateful to Juliane Brand and Christopher Hailey for kindly providing me with their transcription and translation of this and other letters from the Berg–Schoenberg

correspondence before they appeared in published form.

34. The meaning of this palindrome is explained more fully in the 'authorized' analysis of *Der Wein* in Reich, op. cit., p. 153.

35. George Perle, 'The Secret Program of the Lyric Suite', *International Alban Berg Society Newsletter*, no. 5 (June 1977), pp. 8–9.

36. Redlich, *Alban Berg: the Man and his Music*, p. 113.

37. George Perle, *The Operas of Alban Berg*, vol. 2: *Lulu* (Berkeley and Los Angeles: University of California Press, 1985), p. 150. Perle points out that 'Berg's intentions as shown in his fair copy of the full score are correctly represented in the published score of the *Lulu* Suite, only partially represented in the published score of the opera, and entirely misrepresented in the piano reduction.'

38. Jarman, op. cit., p. 240.

39. Joan Allen Smith, 'Interview with Eugene Wolf, 1984', *International Alban Berg Society Newsletter*, no. 13 (spring–summer 1985), p. 8. Wolf must be referring to the brief palindromic conceit in bars 22–5 of the final movement of the Lyric Suite.

40. Redlich, op. cit., p. 113.

41 The publisher's notice, 'Reproduktion nach der Handschrift des Komponisten' ('Reproduction from the composer's manuscript') appears on the title page of the first edition: copies of this edition are in ÖNB Musiksammlung, F21 Berg 75. In his 'Anweisungen für die photographische Vervielfältigung' ('Instructions concerning the photographic reproduction') (F21 Berg 75, fol. 1v), Berg advised the publisher to be extremely careful in handling the manuscript, which, as the only fair copy, represented the dedication copy. The full score of the Chamber Concerto was published by Universal Edition on 29 December 1925: see Hilmar, op. cit., p. 56.

42. Reproduced from the holograph fair copy of the full score of the Chamber Concerto: archives of the Arnold Schoenberg Institute, Los Angeles, CASG86–C389.

43. See Berg, 'Anweisungen für die photographische Vervielfältigung'. Wayne Shoaf reports that Berg's autograph in the Schoenberg Institute contains traces of these pencilled page numbers. In the autograph the turning-point bars would have appeared on pp. 84 (left-hand) and 85 (right-hand). In the facsimile edition they appear on pp. 82 (left-hand) and 83 (right-hand). Berg's instructions regarding the layout of the turning-point were also followed in subsequent engraved editions of the full score (see Example 2).

44. Klein's autograph, designated as the 'Komplette Stichvorlage', is preserved as MH 14308/C in the archives of Universal Edition in the Musiksammlung, Wiener Stadtbibliothek. This manuscript, written with chemical ink, had previously been used for Klein's private edition of the piano reduction: for more information about this see Klein to Berg, 12 August 1925 and 19 August 1925, ÖNB Musiksammlung, F21 Berg 935. The piano reduction of the Chamber Concerto was published by Universal Edition on 19 November 1926: see Hilmar, op. cit., p. 56.

45. See 'Alban Bergs Kammerkonzert-Anweisungen f. d. Stecher', ÖNB Musiksammlung, F21 Berg 20, fols 21–21v.

46. Klein, 'Komplette Stichvorlage', p. 53. My translation. In both this note and the score, Berg, for emphasis, has drawn squares around bars 357–60 with red pencil and around bars 361–4 with blue pencil.

47. ÖNB Musiksammlung, F21 Berg 74/VII. Although on the front cover (fol. 1) there are the notations 'II. Allererste erledigte Skizze' ('II. First completed sketches') and 'Adagio I. Hälfte I. Entwurf' ('Adagio first half, first draft'), this manuscript—a collection of loose sketches and partial drafts representing various stages in the development of the movement—constitutes the composition draft of the entire

Adagio. The manuscript has been given two sets of folio numbers. The first nine leaves are numbered 1–9v; the remaining 28 leaves are numbered 4–31v. In this essay, to distinguish the two sets of folio numbers the first set will be labelled [A] and the second [B].

48. ÖNB Musiksammlung, F21 Berg 74/VII [A], fol. 9. Berg's notations in the left-hand and bottom margins read 'diese Wedepunkt muss ein *Bild* ergeben' and 'das muss auf *einer* Seite'.

49. ÖNB Musiksammlung, F21 Berg 74/VII [B], fol. 12v.

50. ÖNB Musiksammlung, F21 Berg 74/III, fols 2–3.

51. For a complete list of references to the 'Math Thema' in the Chamber Concerto sketch materials, see the expanded version of this essay in my PhD dissertation, 'A Study of Berg's *Chamber Concerto* Based on the Source Documents' (Yale University, in progress).

52. ÖNB Musiksammlung, Berg 74/VII [B], fol. 26. This sketch represents a preliminary version of the 'Math Thema' as it appears in bar 300 of subsection B^2.

53. Ibid., fol. 11v. This sketch is entitled 'Höhepunkt d. Adg.'. Throughout the composition draft of the Adagio the word 'Höhepunkt' is used to designate both the turning-point (bars 360–61) and the climax (bar 314).

54. H. H. Stuckenschmidt, *Schoenberg: his Life, World and Work*, trans. Humphrey Searle (New York: Schirmer Books, 1978), p. 291.

55. Berg to Webern, 10 August 1923, Wiener Stadtbibliothek, Handschriftensammlung, IN 185.628. Berg visited the Schoenbergs 8–9 August after having attended a performance of his String Quartet at the Salzburg Chamber Music Festival.

56. Berg to Schoenberg, 2 September 1923, Brand, Hailey, and Harris, op. cit., pp. 328–9.

57. Felix Greissle to Berg, 1 September 1923, ÖNB Musiksammlung, F21 Berg 795/6.

58. Berg to Schoenberg, 10 September 1923, Library of Congress. Translation provided by Juliane Brand and Christopher Hailey.

59. Webern to Berg, 12 September 1923, ÖNB Musiksammlung, L6 Webern 29. My translation.

60. Death certificate for Mathilde Schoenberg, Los Angeles, Schoenberg Institute. See also Heinz Schöny, 'Schönberg genealogisch betrachtet', *Arnold Schoenberg Gedenkausstellung 1974*, ed. Ernst Hilmar (Vienna: Universal Edition, 1974), p. 19. Felix Greissle reports that during Mathilde's final illness the Schoenberg family stayed with a friend who had a large house near the sanatorium. After Mathilde's death Schoenberg in gratitude presented the friend with the manuscript of his String Quartet no. 2, which he had dedicated to his wife: see Smith, *Schoenberg and His Circle*, pp. 180–81.

61. The basic concept of the palindrome emerges in a series of plans for the overall structure of the concerto (see ÖNB Musiksammlung, F21 Berg 74/XIII, fols 11, 12v; F21 Berg 74/IV, fols 9, 13), which Berg drew up during the spring or early summer of 1923, before he began to sketch the first movement. During the autumn, when he was ready to proceed with the composition of the second movement, he expanded the dimensions of the palindrome and refined its internal structure: see F21 Berg 74/III, fol. 4; F21 Berg 74/IV, fols 4v, 12–12v.

62. ÖNB Musiksammlung, F21 Berg 74/III, fol. 3. The envelope is addressed to Berg's parents-in-law, the Nahowskis.

63. See ÖNB Musiksammlung, F21 Berg 74/VII [A], fols 2–3, 4v–5; F21 Berg 74/VII [B], fols 26v–29.

64. Berg's sketchbook (ÖNB Musiksammlung, F21 Berg 74/V) preserves a single-line

continuity sketch (fol. 20) and an elaborated piano sketch (fol. 25) of bars 1–15.

65. Berg to Webern, 1 September 1923, Wiener Stadtbibliothek, Handschriftensamm-lung, IN 185.630; Berg to Schoenberg, 2 September 1923, Library of Congress.

66. Berg to Webern, 1 September 1923, Berg to Schoenberg, 2 September 1923.

67. Berg to Webern, 16 September 1923, Wiener Stadtbibliothek, Handschriftensamm-lung, IN 185.632. My translation.

68. Berg to Webern, 21 September 1923, Wiener Stadtbibliothek, Handschriftensamm-lung, IN 185.633. See also the entry for 20 September 1923 in Berg's calendar, ÖNB Musiksammlung, F21 Berg 432/20 (1923), fol. 14.

69. There is no further mention of the Chamber Concerto in the correspondence until 25 March 1924, when Berg informed Schoenberg that he had resumed its composition a few weeks earlier. However, the contents of a set of sketches (ÖNB Musiksammlung, F21 Berg 74/XIV, fols 15–17v) dating from mid-April 1924 or later (fol. 15, which is a mailing envelope for *Pult and Taktstock*, bears the postmark 12 April 1924) indicate that Berg was just completing the Adagio and starting to mull over ideas for the cadenza preceding the Rondo ritmico. The Adagio seems to have been completed by 11 May 1924. On that day (according to a brief notation found on F21 Berg 74/III, fol. 5v) Berg apparently read through the Adagio and determined that it would last approximately 15 minutes.

70. In the initial statement of the main theme for subsection B^1 (see the violin part, bars 276ff.), the 'Math Thema' is transposed. In the second statement or 'answer' (see the trumpet part, bars 274ff.), the 'Math Thema' appears at original pitch.

71. For further discussion of Berg's 'fate' rhythms, see Redlich, op. cit., pp. 70, 178–9; Jarman, op. cit., pp. 147–74.

72. Evidence in the first draft of the tabular survey (ÖNB Musiksammlung, Berg 74/I, fol. 3) indicates that Berg was well aware of the numerological conceit. In this draft he has noted the distance from the turning-point to the end of the climax in the retrograde (the seventh statement of the 'Math Thema') as being 47 bars. Furthermore, successive drafts of the climax preserved in the composition draft (compare F21 Berg 74/VII [B], fols 28v, 29) suggest that it was pushed back four bars from its original position in bar 78 (bar 318) to bar 74 (bar 314).

73. Mathilde Schoenberg, death certificate; Schöny, op. cit., p. 19.

74. See ÖNB Musiksammlung, F21 Berg 74/XIII, fol. 1; F21 Berg 74/X, fols 1v–2; F21 Berg 74/VI, fols 11v, 12–12v.

75. The weeks following Mathilde's death were extremely difficult for Schoenberg. For further information regarding his general irritability, his unpredictable and frequently violent changes of mood, his various addictions, and his strained relations with family and friends, see Schoenberg to Alma Mahler, 11 November 1923, *Arnold Schoenberg Letters*, sel. and ed. Erwin Stein, trans. Eithne Wilkins and Ernst Kaiser (New York: St Martin's Press, 1965), pp. 102–3; Alban Berg to Helene Berg, 22, 25, 26, 28 November 1923, *Alban Berg: Letters to his Wife*, ed., trans., and annot. Bernard Grun (New York: St Martin's Press, 1971), pp. 330, 332, 333, 334–5; Eberhart Freitag, *Arnold Schönberg in Selbstzeugnissen und Bilddokumenten* (Reinbeck bei Hamburg: Rowohlt Taschenbuch Verlag, 1973), p. 115; Felix Greissle's interview with Hans Keller, cited in Smith, op. cit., p. 175.

76. See ÖNB Musiksammlung, F21 Berg 74/XIII, fol. 1; F21 Berg 74/X, fols 1v–2.

77. ÖNB Musiksammlung, F21 Berg 74/XIII, fol. 1.

78. Berg has not specifically designated the latter theme as 'Melisande' in the sketches.

79. For further information concerning Mathilde Schoenberg's affair with Gerstl, see Smith, op. cit., pp. 174–81; Stuckenschmidt, op. cit., pp. 93–7.

80. Smith, op. cit., p. 174.
81. Freitag, op. cit., p. 115.
82. Salka Viertel, *The Kindness of Strangers* (New York: Holt, Rinehart and Winston, 1969), p. 57.
83. Maurice Maeterlinck, *Pelléas et Mélisande and Other Plays*, trans. Richard Hovey (New York: Dodd, Mead and Company, 1913), pp. 34–40.
84. Ibid., p. 41.
85. Redlich, *Versuch einer Würdigung*, pp. 170–71. My translation. Redlich's observation is accompanied by a musical example containing a reduction of bars 265–9 of the Adagio.
86. Alban Berg, 'Thementafel zu Arnold Schönbergs *Pelleas und Melisande*', *Pelleas und Melisande (nach dem Drama von Maurice Maeterlinck) symphonische Dichtung für Orchester von Arnold Schönberg, Op. 5: Kurze Thematische Analyse* (Vienna: Universal Edition, n.d.). Berg received the commission to produce a guide to Schoenberg's *Pelleas und Melisande* from Universal Edition in December 1919. It was completed in late February or early March 1920. See Rosemary Hilmar, *Alban Berg: Leben und Wirken in Wien bis zu seinen ersten Erfolgen als Komponist* (Vienna: Verlag Hermann Böhlaus Nachf., 1979), pp. 152–3; Berg to his mother, 28 December 1919, Berg to Helene Berg, 20 February 1920, *Alban Berg: Briefe an seine Frau* (Munich and Vienna: Albert Langen and Georg Müller, 1965), pp. 414, 449.
87. The leitmotif 'Melisande' first appears in Schoenberg's symphonic poem at rehearsal number 1; 'Das Sterbegemach Melisandes' is prominent at rehearsal number 59ff.
88. This triplet figuration does not accompany any other presentation of the 'Melisande' theme.
89. Berg has not designated the theme that occurs at this climax as 'Melisande', however. See note 78.
90. Understandably, Schoenberg remained sensitive about matters related to Gerstl long after Mathilde's death. In a short essay, written on 11 February 1938, Schoenberg categorically denied Gerstl's having had any influence on his painting style: Arnold Schoenberg, 'Painting Influences', *Journal of the Arnold Schoenberg Institute*, vol. 2 (June 1978), p. 238.
91. Stuckenschmidt, op. cit., pp. 294–7, 303–4. Ena Steiner observes ('Mödling Revisited', *Journal of the Arnold Schoenberg Institute*, vol. 1 (February 1977), p. 83) that:

> as late as 1950 Schoenberg, who may have felt that at the time he had surprised the world by his re-marriage only ten months after Mathilde's death, wrote down for posterity that during all the years that Rudolf Kolisch had been his pupil, he had never known his parents and sisters, and that he had met Gertrud, his future wife, during the New Year celebrations 1923/24.

92. The première of the Chamber Concerto was conducted by Hermann Scherchen and performed by Stefi Geyer (violin), Walter Frey (piano), and wind players from the Berlin Philharmonic.
93. Schoenberg to Berg, 12 May 1927, Brand, Hailey, and Harris, op. cit., p. 362. Alban and Helene Berg had visited Berlin 13–22 January 1927: ibid., p. 358.

ALBAN BERG, WILHELM FLIESS, AND THE SECRET PROGRAMME OF THE VIOLIN CONCERTO

DOUGLAS JARMAN

Berg's interest in numerology and his belief in the fateful significance of the number 23 are well known, as is his fondness for using this and other 'significant' numbers as a means of determining certain aspects of his musical structures. Although in using numbers in this way Berg was working within a long-established artistic and especially musical tradition,[1] Berg's intentions in using such number symbolism often seem quite different from those of other artists and composers who have indulged in such conceits. In a work such as *The Magic Flute* the significance of the number three would have been clear (and was intended to be clear) to those of Mozart's fellow masons who chanced to notice its occurrence. Similarly, in the music of the Renaissance and the Middle Ages the symbolic arithmology employed had a meaning and made reference to a body of knowledge that, if not generally well known, was at least familiar to the cognoscenti.[2] The numbers employed in Berg's music, on the other hand, have no such generally understood significance. Whatever Berg's numbers symbolize, they represent something that is purely personal: even when the private significance of a number is known, Berg's reasons for choosing it often remain obscure. For example, the significance of the number ten in the Lyric Suite remained, until recently, a secret. Although we now know of its association with Hanna Fuchs-Robettin we can still only guess as to why Berg chose to represent Hanna by this, rather than another, number.[3]

In practice Berg's numerical schemes have the effect of acting as an abstract, objective means of determining musical proportions. It is clear from the annotations in the score of the Lyric Suite and from the 'Open Letter' on the Chamber Concerto, however, that the numbers upon which he based these schemes had, for Berg, a deeply subjective and almost mystical significance.

Berg's apparent belief in the mystical significance of numbers was not, at that time, an idiosyncratic peculiarity. The early years of the 20th century saw an enormous growth of interest in numerology, astrology, the occult, and in mystical and quasi-mystical religions such as Madame Blavatsky's theosophy (which itself laid emphasis upon symbolic numerology). It was, as Stefan Zweig observed of these inter-war years, a period in which 'occultism, spiritualism, somnambulism, anthroposophy, palm-reading, graphology, yoga and Paracelsism ... every extravagant idea that was not subject to regulations reaped a golden harvest'.[4]

Although spread throughout Europe, an interest in the occult was particularly strong in Germany and Austria, and seems to have attracted many people in those circles of Viennese society within which Berg moved. Schoenberg may have been acquainted with the ideas of Madame Blavatsky[5] and certainly believed in numerology to the extent of regarding the number 13 as his own fateful number. Helene Berg, we know, was interested in spiritualism and the occult[6] and there is at least some evidence that Berg's own interest may have been more far-reaching than has been generally thought. In a passage that is said to have been written for, though never published in, his 1968 book on Berg, T. W. Adorno, who advised Thomas Mann on the musical portions of his *Doktor Faustus*, remarked on the extent to which the composer in Mann's book was modelled on Berg and described how 'the analogous features of Leverkühn's music were copied from such games as Berg's play on the initials AB and HF in the third movement of the *Lyric Suite* and touched on both his liking for number mysticism and astrology.'[7] Berg's interest in astrology may well have been stimulated by his acquaintance with Schoenberg's close friend Oskar Adler, at whose house in the Lichtensteinstrasse were held chamber music evenings which Berg attended. A doctor and a professional violinist, Adler was also deeply interested in astrology and published four books on the subject. Louis Krasner has described Adler as a 'quiet but deep influence' upon the Schoenberg circle. Adler's role 'amongst the active, creative artists, and intellectuals in the Vienna of the 1930s', Krasner has said, 'was not unlike that of Karl Kraus. They were all conscious of his presence and of the vibrations that emanated from him ... and his astrological charts were sought by all the twelve-tone circle. I have no doubt that Berg was familiar with all of Adler's work.'[8]

In the Germany and Austria of Berg's day the existence of paranormal phenomena was taken seriously by even the most eminent scientists. The distinguished Viennese biologist Paul Kammerer, for example, whose main research was concerned with the inheritance of acquired characteristics in the salamander and the midwife toad, devoted much of his time to the study of 'meaningful coincidences' in an attempt to discover the numerological rules which, he believed, governed the occurrence of such chance events. When the results of Kammerer's investigations of coincidence were published in 1919 in his book *Das Gesetz der Serie* ('The Law of Seriality') no less a figure than Albert Einstein was prepared to declare the work 'original and by no means absurd'.[9] Berg, who was five years younger than Kammerer, was acquainted with the biologist (either through Peter Altenberg, of whose circle Kammerer was a habitué, or through Alma Mahler who acted as Kammerer's assistant for a period in 1911) and was certainly aware of Kammerer's work as a research biologist, even though he had a low opinion of it.[10]

In his attempts to establish the existence of some universal principle governing the occurrence of chance events, Kammerer devoted one chapter of *Das Gesetz der Serie* to a study of those theories which dealt with the existence of significant recurring periods. Amongst the theories considered by Kammerer are those of Wilhelm Fliess, a writer whose works seem to have had an enormous influence on Berg's own numerological beliefs.

Fliess's theories were expounded in two books, *Der Ablauf des Lebens* ('The Rhythm of Life', 1906) and *Vom Leben und Tod* ('Of Life and Death', 1909), that created something of a stir in Vienna and Berlin when they were first published. It was Fliess's contention that, as he declares at the beginning of *Vom Leben und Tod*, 'all life is controlled by a periodic rhythm through a mechanism that exists in the living substance itself—a mechanism that is exactly the same for human beings, for animals and for plants; a mechanism that informs the hour of our birth with the same certainity as that of our death'. Life, claimed Fliess, was governed by laws as strict as those of planetary motion. Through his analysis of the dates of the menstrual and other periodic cycles, he had been able to discover that the whole of life was governed by two constant numbers: the number 28, which was associated with women, and the number 23, which referred to men. 'These numbers,' says Fliess, 'were not invented by me but were discovered by me in nature. They are, therefore, not the products of fantasy but of the experience of the direct observation of nature.'[11]

Berg seems to have become acquainted with Fliess's work in the summer of 1914, by which time he had already noted 'the strange coincidences surrounding the number 23' and had persuaded himself that the number played an important role in his life. Whatever the origins of Berg's belief in the personal significance of this number, his discovery of Fliess's work—containing, as it did, what appeared to be scientific evidence—confirmed him in his belief. Berg broached the topic of Fliess in a letter to Schoenberg dated 20 June 1914. Clearly Berg had already discussed his belief in a 'fateful' number with Schoenberg, who had told him to take himself in hand and make himself independent of such 'lucky' and 'unlucky' numbers. In replying to this criticism and declaring his intentions of following Schoenberg's advice ('Your advice makes me realize that it is possible to unravel one's own fate: as a result I now believe that I can and will manage to do so!') Berg was unable to resist the temptation of telling his teacher that there was, nonetheless, scientific support for his belief in the number 23:

> In this connection, Herr Schoenberg, I must nevertheless tell you briefly about a book that I had never heard of before and that I came across by chance last summer, that seemed to confirm my old belief in the number 23. *Vom Leben und Tod* is by the well-known Berlin scholar Wilhelm Fliess and is based on biological experiments in which he shows that life and all phases in the lives of all living creatures run in periods and give rise to cycles which are always divisible by 28 and 23.

As evidence Berg then cited two of the examples given in Fliess's book which show the way in which such cycles affect the development of both plants and animals:

A Clivia, for example, has four new shoots which appear on the

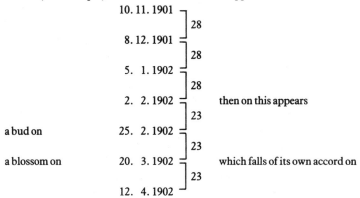

	10. 11. 1901 ┐	
	28	
	8. 12. 1901 ┤	
	28	
	5. 1. 1902 ┤	
	28	
	2. 2. 1902 ┤	then on this appears
	23	
a bud on	25. 2. 1902 ┤	
	23	
a blossom on	20. 3. 1902 ┤	which falls of its own accord on
	23	
	12. 4. 1902 ┘	

Similarly if one looks up Brehm's *Animal Life* one finds that a female ostrich laid on Jan. 15, '57 and Jan. 18, '58 (368 days = 16 × 23 days) and the same ostrich began its brood on July 2, '57 and March 12, '58 (253 days = 11 × 23 days).

Fliess, observed Berg, had demonstrated that such cycles apply equally to human beings:

and not only to individual human beings but also to the dates of birth and death, periods of life, stages in the illness of whole families, generations and even states. From the birth and death dates of men and women, families and countries etc., Fliess concludes that the woman's number is 28, the man's 23.

Despite the bizarre, and often absurd, conclusions to which Fliess's numerological theories lead him in the second half of *Vom Leben und Tod*,[12] Berg was not alone in taking these theories seriously. Just as Einstein regarded Kammerer's law of seriality as being 'by no means absurd' so Freud for many years shared Fliess's belief in the significance of the numbers 23 and 28. Only in the early 1920s did Freud begin to entertain doubts about Fliess's theories; before that time Freud was fully prepared to declare that Fliess had made a 'fundamental biological discovery'[13] in unravelling the numerals that governed the periodic cycles.

Knowledge of Berg's acquaintance with and interest in Fliess's theories raises a number of questions about Berg's music and about the Violin Concerto in particular. It is well known that Berg conceived the Violin Concerto as a memorial to Manon Gropius, the daughter of Alma Mahler and Walter Gropius and a close and much-loved friend of the Bergs, who died of infantile paralysis in April 1935. All commentators on the Violin Concerto have drawn attention to the requiem-like character of the piece, established verbally by the dedication 'To the memory of an angel' and musically by the use of the Bach funeral chorale *Es ist genug* in the final pages of the work. Most commentators have repeated the description of the programme of the work given by Willi Reich, a description based on information provided by the composer himself, according to which the first part of the work seeks 'to translate features of the young girl's character into musical terms'[14] and to capture 'the vision of the lovely girl in a graceful dance which alternates between a delicate and dreamy character and the rustic character of a Kärtner folk tune', while the second part depicts the catastrophe of her death in which 'groans and strident cries for help are heard' until the chorale and a 'plaint' or 'dirge' intoned by the solo violin 'gradually struggles towards the light' and an 'indescribably melancholy reprise of the Kärtner folk tune reminds us once more of the image of the lovely girl.'[15]

The main features of what Reich at one point calls a 'tone poem' and, at another, a 'latent drama' are obvious to the listener and support for this reading of the programme is to be found in Berg's own sketches for the concerto in which appear many of the terms ('sighs', 'groans', 'cry', 'dirge'), that Reich himself uses to describe the piece.[16]

Alongside these clearly audible elements, however, the score of the Violin Concerto contains a number of less audible features that are not easily related to the programme given by Reich. Writing about Berg's obsession with the number 23 George Perle has remarked that 'only in the *Lyric Suite* does Berg's supposedly fateful number play a consistent role in the work itself'.[17] While it is true that no other work is dominated by the number 23 to such an extent as the Lyric Suite, Berg's fateful number plays a very important role in Part II of the Violin Concerto. Part II of the concerto is a movement of 230 bars, with an opening tempo of crotchet = 69 (3 × 23) and a *Hauptrhythmus*, or fate rhythm, that enters for the first time at bar 23. Beginning at bar 157, the 23rd bar of the chorale, the notes B♭, A, G, E (the letters of Berg's name that can be represented musically and that form the 'Alban Berg' part of the motto theme of the earlier Chamber Concerto) appear prominently in the horns, with the marking 'misterioso'.[18] The appearance of Berg's musical cipher at this point may be a coincidence, but Berg is hardly likely to have failed to notice the important role played by his fateful number elsewhere in the movement. And yet why should the number 23 feature so prominently in this movement? Why, in a movement that depicts the tragic death of Manon Gropius, should the inaudible numerological elements suggest that the movement is also about Berg himself?

Two other significant numbers play an important role in the structure of the Violin Concerto: ten and 28. The number ten is, of course, associated with Hanna Fuchs-Robettin in the Lyric Suite. Its importance in the Violin Concerto is signalled from the outset by Berg's own indication which stands at the head of the opening bars of the work: 'Introduction (10 bars)'.[19] In view of the associations established in the Lyric Suite, and of the oblique references to Hanna that appear in both *Der Wein* and *Lulu*,[20] the ten-bar structure of this introduction may, with certainty, be interpreted as a further allusion to Hanna Fuchs-Robettin. The number 28 is the second, the 'female', of Fliess's two periodic numbers. It is a number that appears constantly in the numerical calculations that cover the margins of Berg's sketches for the concerto. A sketch for bars 228–39 of Part I, for example, has the following subtractions in the margin:

$$
\begin{array}{cc}
232 & 210 \\
175 & 175 \\
\hline
57 = 28 & 35 \\
& 28
\end{array}
$$

while two pages later there appears the following (rather questionable) addition:

$$
\begin{array}{c}
16+ \\
13 \\
\hline
28
\end{array}
$$

Calculations based on multiples of ten and 23 also appear in the margins of the sketches.

While it is, admittedly, difficult to understand the meaning of Berg's marginal calculations, the number 28 does play a clear role in the work. The metronome markings of the Andante and Allegretto which form Part I of the concerto, for example, are crotchet = 56 (2×28) and crotchet = 112 (4×28) respectively; the bridge passage of the Andante begins at bar 28; the 'tempo primo' which marks the beginning of the codetta starts at bar 84 (3×28) and the 'ritmico' figuration of the Allegretto is first introduced at bar 140 (5×28).[21] As evidence of the further roles played by Hanna's and Berg's own numbers, Figure 1 shows how every important structural point and every indication and direction in the final Adagio initiates and concludes a unit of 23, 28, or 10 (or a multiple of 10) bars.[22]

Without more definite evidence regarding Berg's calculations, such as we have in the annotated score of the Lyric Suite, such bar counting is, of course, inconclusive. The constant use of ten- and 23-bar units throughout the work, however, does strongly suggest that, in addition to the stated programme about Manon, the Violin Concerto has another and more secret programme that, in some way, involves both Hanna Fuchs-Robettin and Berg himself. Similarly, in view of the association with, and the significance allotted to, the numbers 23 and 28 in Fliess's theories, the presence of both numbers in the Concerto (with 28 appearing to operate in Part I and 23 in Part II) suggests that the division of the

Figure 1 Bar Analysis of the Adagio

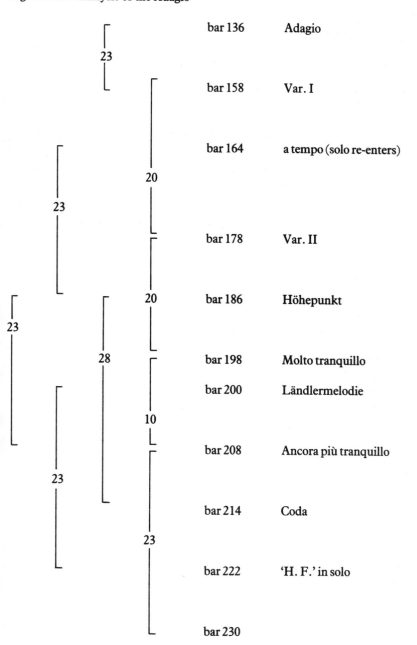

bar 136   Adagio

bar 158   Var. I

bar 164   a tempo (solo re-enters)

bar 178   Var. II

bar 186   Höhepunkt

bar 198   Molto tranquillo

bar 200   Ländlermelodie

bar 208   Ancora più tranquillo

bar 214   Coda

bar 222   'H. F.' in solo

bar 230

work into two parts, rather than into four movements, might itself reflect a female–male division.

That some numerological element is operating in the Violin Concerto is clear from the description of the work which appears in Reich's 1937 book on Berg, in which he refers (in an essay 'authorized by Berg himself') to 'secret relationships of the numbers of bars, as in the Chamber Concerto'.[23] Puzzled by this statement and unable to find anything in the Violin Concerto as systematic as the number symbolism operating in the Chamber Concerto, I wrote to Willi Reich asking for clarification. In a letter dated 8 March 1979 Reich replied, 'I'm afraid that I must disappoint you. After more than 40 years I cannot, with the best will in the world, remember which "secret relationships" were mentioned in my discussions with Alban Berg about the Violin Concerto.'

The existence of another programme in addition to that which concerns Manon Gropius is confirmed by other features of the Violin Concerto. At the upbeat to bar 214 of Part I there appears a *Ländler* melody which reappears, in what Reich called 'an indescribably melancholy reprise—as if in the distance', in the closing pages of the work. We now know, as Reich apparently did not, that this tune is not simply a folk-like melody composed by Berg himself but the tune of a real Carinthian folk song, the text of which, in the translation of Mosco Carner, runs:[24]

> A bird on the plum tree has wakened me,
> Tridie, tridie, iri, tulilei!
> Otherwise I would have overslept in Mizzi's bed,
> Tridie etc.,
> If everybody wants a rich and handsome girl,
> Tridie etc.,
> Where ought the devil take the ugly one?
> Tridie etc.,
> The girl is Catholic and I am Protestant,
> Tridie etc.,
> She will surely put away the rosary in bed!
> Tridie etc.

Discussing the two pre-existing melodies that Berg employs in the Violin Concerto, Herwig Knaus has observed:

> Berg would scarcely have chosen a chorale with a text that was not suited to the programmatic content of his Violin Concerto. That is not, however, the case with the Carinthian folk song. Here the composer did not make a text generally available but referred to it only as being 'in the manner of a Carinthian folk song' ... Berg doubtless took the folk song from the little book of Carinthian folk songs published by U.E. in 1931/32 ... and we can with some certainty rule out the possibility that the composer did not know the text. If Berg did know the text one can infer that, in this case, he was concerned only with the melody

of the song and that the vague reference to a 'popular Carinthian air' was made so as to avoid giving rise to a mistaken interpretation to which the text could have led.[25]

There is nothing in the whole of Berg's output that would encourage one to make such an assumption. On the contrary, in every case where Berg quotes in one work from another the quotation always has some specific programmatic significance. When the music quoted is (in its original form) associated with a text, that text—whether stated or not—always has a clear relevance to the programme or the dramatic situation of the work in which it is quoted. The unstated text of the quotation from Zemlinsky's Lyric Symphony in the Lyric Suite, for example, has a quite specific programmatic significance as has the 'hidden' Baudelaire text that underlies the final 'Largo desolato' of that work. The text of the Bach chorale in the Violin Concerto is given in the score and has a clear relevance to the programme which concerns the death of the girl to whom the work is dedicated; the text of the Wedekind Lautenlied, 'Konfession', which forms the structural backbone of Act III of Lulu does not appear in the work nor is it stated in the score but it has an obvious bearing on the dramatic situation in Act III of the opera.[26] Even the most fleeting and apparently accidental reference to another work in Berg's music can be shown to have textual, programmatic, or dramatic significance. Eric Simon has discussed the relationship between a musical figuration in Marie's Lullaby in Act I of Wozzeck and a similar figuration in the popular Viennese song 'Wann I' von Wean wegga geh'' and has observed that the words of the first and third lines of the song's third stanza are almost identical to the opening words of the Lullaby;[27] Glen Watkins has recently pointed out the dramatic appropriateness of the musical reference to Mahler's song, 'Revelge', in the vocal line of the Trio to the Military March in the same scene of Wozzeck.[28] Given the use of quotations and oblique references elsewhere in his music it is impossible to believe that Berg could have been aware of the text of the Carinthian folk song and yet have chosen to use the melody in spite of its associated text.

If, however, the unstated text of the song was one of the reasons for Berg's choosing to use this, rather than another, folk melody, the text can clearly have no relevance to Manon Gropius (though Berg probably enjoyed the play on words inherent in the similarity between the song's 'Mizzi' and Manon's pet-name of 'Mutzi'). Nor can we regard the 'Mizzi', the Carinthian peasant girl of the folk song, as being a reference to Hanna Fuchs-Robettin. We know, however, that Berg as an adolescent did have a relationship with a peasant girl who worked at the Berg family's summer home in Carinthia. As a 17-year-old youth Berg became the father of an illegitimate daughter. The mother of Berg's daughter was a girl who worked in the kitchen of the Berghof and who was named Marie Scheuchl.[29] 'Mizzi' is the common Austrian nickname for 'Marie'. As a servant in the Berg household Marie Scheuchl may have been addressed as 'Mizzi' by the family; it would almost certainly have been the pet-name for

Marie used by the young Alban.

The daughter of Marie Scheuchl and Alban Berg was born on 4 December 1902 and was named Albine. Berg certainly kept in touch with his daughter to the extent of sending her a ticket for the first Vienna performance of *Wozzeck*. In a letter to his wife Helene, written while he was working on *Wozzeck*, Berg remarked 'There is something of me in this *Wozzeck*'.[30] If this remark refers to the similarities between the position of the poor soldier Wozzeck and that in which Berg found himself during the First War it also points to a more profound relationship between the composer and his operatic 'hero' for the similarity between the name of the opera's Marie, the mother of Wozzeck's illegitimate child, and the name of Marie Scheuchl, the mother of his own illegitimate child, can hardly have escaped Berg's attention.

Berg's motives in hiding the source of the folk song in the Violin Concerto are now clear. He did, indeed, want to avoid drawing attention to the text, not because (as Knaus has suggested) a knowledge of it might give rise to a 'false interpretation', but because the text was too revealing of his reasons for choosing this melody.

The bar analysis given in Figure 1 has shown the extent to which the structure of the chorale variations of Part II of the concerto can be seen as being based on multiples of Hanna's ten and Berg's own 23. As puzzling, and as inexplicable in terms of the Manon programme as the choice of the folk song, are the expression markings associated with the Bach chorale and these variations. Beginning ten bars after the *Höhepunkt* of the Allegro, the Bach chorale carries a series of expression markings that are so curious, so precise and so consistently maintained as themselves to suggest some kind of extra-musical programme. Each line of the chorale is allotted its own expression mark: the three phrases of the first line are marked respectively 'deciso', 'doloroso', and 'dolce'; the repetition of this line on the wind instruments bears the same markings but has the additional heading 'poco più mosso ma religioso'; the third line, again on the solo violin, is marked 'risoluto' as is its repetition by the wind; the final line of the chorale carries the marking 'molto espressivo e amoroso'. Each line retains its own individual expression marking throughout the variations that follow.

Most of these markings are perhaps explicable in terms of the text of the chorale but the curious, and apparently inappropriate, marking 'amoroso', which appears far more frequently than any other expression mark, can be explained only as a reference to Hanna. It is an explanation that is confirmed by the music itself. On its first appearance the 'amoroso' phrase is immediately followed by a double bar and the beginning of the first chorale variation—the 'misterioso' variation which, beginning at the 23rd bar of the Adagio, unfolds in the upper parts the notes of Berg's own name. At bar 194 five statements of the inverted 'amoroso' motive (all of them marked as such in the full score) lead to a reprise of the Carinthian folk song of Part I. Although the 14-bar melody is repeated in its entirety, its first four bars act as a bridge ('ubergehen in die Ländlermelodie') from the final chorale variation; the last ten bars of the tune are separated from these four transitional bars by a short caesura. Finally, preceded by a statement of Hanna's initials on the solo violin at bar 222, the 'amoroso' phrase returns in its prime form at the tenth bar of the coda.

None of the features which refer to Berg, Hanna, and Marie make sense within the context of the accepted 'Manon' programme of the Violin Concerto. That the concerto is 'about' Manon Gropius is indisputable and it is to this programme that the dedication refers. But the 'public' programme of the Violin Concerto conceals an equally authentic, but more private, alternative programme.

Many writers on the Violin Concerto have remarked on how, in writing a requiem for Manon Gropius, Berg also wrote what in the event proved to be his own requiem. The Violin Concerto is indeed a requiem for the composer, though not, as commentators have assumed, because his death so soon after its completion left this as his last completed work, but because Berg *planned* it as both a requiem for Manon and, on a completely independent level, as a requiem for himself.[31] The two programmes are like 'a jigsaw puzzle whose different pieces can be put together in different ways to make two completely different pictures'.[32] The Bach chorale, for example, refers on an obvious and audible level to the death of Manon and, once the hidden programme is known, to Berg's own death. On a less audible (indeed, inaudible) level it refers through its number symbolism to both Manon and Hanna in its use of Fliess's 28, to Hanna through its 'amoroso' expression marks, its use of her initials and multiples of her number ten, to Berg through the appearance of his musical cipher at the 23rd bar of the Adagio and finally to both Berg and Hanna in that the movement as a whole has 230 bars. Similarly, the Carinthian folk song is both a portrait of Manon and, at the same time, a reference—through its unstated text—to Marie. The two appearances of the Carinthian folk song refer respectively to Berg's first love affair with Marie, the servant at the Berg home in Carinthia who bore his child, and to his last love affair with Hanna Fuchs.

In a private letter to the author about this matter George Perle observed:

> The relation between the two programmes suggests the relation between the surface and the hidden metaphors in *Wozzeck* and *Lulu*, but there is still a difference because the keys to the hidden metaphors in the operas are intrinsic to the music even if they have no direct meaning in terms of auditory perception. But in the concerto we are dependent on totally extrinsic knowledge ... The situation is not at all the same as the *Lyric Suite*. That a programme is implied in the *Lyric Suite* has always been known, as even the titles of the movements show, not to speak of Berg's letters to Kolisch, the writings of Adorno, Redlich, Carner etc. But for the concerto there was no mystery since we do have a programme with nothing secret or insufficient about it.

In the light of this second, hidden, programme the final pages of the Violin Concerto—in which (introduced by Hanna's initials) the 'amoroso' phrase, accompanied by inner parts that are still marked 'religioso', gradually fades into eternity—acquire a new and deeply moving significance. What in the public programme of the work may be interpreted as a gesture of acceptance and resignation now, in the alternative programme, becomes an expression of those private feelings to which Berg gave voice in his letters to Hanna and at the end of *Lulu*, when his own and Hanna's initials together follow the final words of the dying Countess Geschwitz: 'Ich bin dir nah, bleibt dir nah, in Ewigkeit'.[33]

I am deeply indebted to Michael Taylor and George Perle without whose help this essay could not have been written. Many of the ideas were discussed at an early stage with Michael Taylor who contributed to their development through his own suggestions and comments. Mr Taylor also helped in obtaining copies of Fliess's writing and of the Berg–Schoenberg letters quoted above. Professor Perle, with whom I corresponded for many months about this matter, not only gave me the benefit of his own insights and kept me informed of his own discoveries but was instrumental in arriving at a solution. I am glad of this opportunity to thank them for their generous help.

Notes

1. Berg could hardly have been aware of this tradition, however, for although ciphers and cryptograms continued to be sporadically employed in the music of 19th-century composers, number symbolism fell into disrepute and almost disappeared from European music during the Baroque. The extent to which number symbolism was an inherent part of the artistic thought of the Middle Ages and the Renaissance has only become clear in the years following Berg's death.

2. We may agree with Peter Stadlen that 'even the cognoscenti only just knew that this desirable sort of thing was going on, but by no means exactly what and how in any given case'. Peter Stadlen, 'Berg's Cryptography', *Alban Berg Symposion Wien 1980: Tagungsbericht*, ed. Rudolf Klein, Alban Berg Studien, vol. 2 (Vienna: Universal Edition, 1981), p. 173.

3. See George Perle, 'The Secret Program of the Lyric Suite', *International Alban Berg Society Newsletter*, no. 5 (June 1977), pp. 4–12 and *Musical Times*, vol. 118 (August–October 1977), pp. 629–32, 709–13, 809–13.

4. Stefan Zweig, *The World of Yesterday* (London: Cassell, 1943), p. 301.

5. See H. H. Stuckenschmidt, *Arnold Schoenberg* (London: John Calder, 1977), pp. 243–4.

6. Helene Berg's own interest is confirmed by her own words in a letter of 2 August, 1930 in which she tells her Alma Mahler that she is deeply involved in her occult books. See George Perle, 'Mein geliebtes Almschi ...', *International Alban Berg Society Newsletter*, no. 7 (fall 1978), p. 6.

7. T. W. Adorno quoted in Metzger and Riehn, 'Statt eines Nachworts zur Kontroverse', Alban Berg Kammermusik II, *Musik Konzepte*, vol. 9 (July 1979), p. 10. It is perhaps worth observing that Leverkühn (who, according to Adorno, had 'more of Berg than of Schoenberg in him') was supposed to have been born in 'the blossom time of 1885', the year of Berg's own birth.

8. Louis Krasner in a private letter to the author.

9. Einstein quoted in Arthur Koestler, *The Case of the Midwife Toad* (London: Pan Books, 1974), p. 138. A summary of Kammerer's book appears as Appendix I of Koestler.

10. See Berg's letter of 18 July 1909 to Helene in *Alban Berg: Briefe an seine Frau*, (Munich and Vienna: Albert Langen and Georg Müller, 1965), pp. 72–4. This and all the other passages in which Berg refers to Kammerer have been omitted from the English edition of the *Briefe*.

11. Wilhelm Fliess, *Vom Leben und Tod* (Vienna: Diedrichs, 1909), p. 1.

12. In the fifth part of *Vom Leben und Tod*, for example, Fliess's theories lead him to a discussion of bisexuality. Reflecting on the binary nature of the male and female dichotomy and of his two periodic cycles, Fliess proposes that, in truth, all such dichotomies have a single origin, the clue to which can be found in the familiar dichotomy of right- and left-handedness. The right hand, declares Fliess, represents the masculinity of men and the femininity of women while the left hand represents those characteristics of the opposite sex that are present in any one individual. 'Left-handed men,' says Fliess, 'are always more effeminate, left-handed women more masculine than their right-handed counterparts ... if one hears of a man who, in his youth, played with his sister's dolls and now takes a particular interest in his wife's toilette, who is perhaps very musical, draws prettily and has a gracious, lithe figure you may be sure that he is left handed. If you meet a 'modern' authoress or a lady interested in women's rights, who is in favour of votes for both sexes, climbs mountains, you can be a hundred-to-one sure that she will be left handed.' (Fliess, op. cit., p. 68)

13. Paul Roazen, *Freud and his Followers* (London: Allen Lane, 1976), p. 108.

14. Willi Reich, *Alban Berg*, trans. Cornelius Cardew (London: Thames and Hudson, 1965), p. 100.

15. Ibid., p. 178.

16. See Constantin Floros, 'Die Skizzen zum Violinkonzert von Alban Berg', *Alban Berg Symposon Wien 1980: Tagungsbericht*, pp. 129–33.

17. George Perle, op. cit., 'The Secret Program of the Lyric Suite', p. 5.

18. cf. A. Pernye, 'Alban Berg und die Zahlen', *Studia musicologica*, vol. 9 (1967) pp. 155–6.

19. I am grateful to Michael Taylor for drawing my attention to the significance of this opening indication.

20. See George Perle, 'Der Tod der Geschwitz', *Österreichische Musikzeitschrift*, vol. 36 (January 1981), pp. 20–21.

21. I am grateful to Michael Taylor for drawing my attention to some of the occurrences listed here.

22. I am indebted to George Perle for much of the information contained in this chart.

23. Willi Reich, *Alban Berg: mit Bergs eigenen Schriften und Beiträgen von Theodor Wiesengrund-Adorno und Ernst Krenek* (Vienna: Herbert Reichner Verlag, 1937), p. 31.

24. Herwig Knaus, 'Berg's Carinthian Folk Tune', *Musical Times*, vol. 147 (June 1976), p. 487.

25. Herwig Knaus, 'Kompositionstechnik und Semantik in Alban Berg Konzertarie *Der Wein* nebst einem Anhang zum Violinkonzert', *Alban Berg Symposon Wien 1980: Tagungsbericht*, p. 143.

26. See Douglas Jarman, *The Music of Alban Berg* (London: Faber and Faber, 1979), Appendix II, pp. 245–8.

27. Eric Simon, 'A Chance Discovery', *International Alban Berg Society Newsletter*, no. 10 (Summer 1981), p. 11.
28. Glen Watkins, 'New Perspectives on Mahler and Berg', *Michigan Quarterly Review* (Spring 1981), p. 142.
29. See Erich Alban Berg, 'Eine naturliche Tochter: zur biographie Alban Bergs', *Frankfurter Allgemeine Zeitung*, 21 May 1979 and 'Bergiana', *Schweizerische Musikzeitung*, no. 3 (May/June 1980), pp. 147–9.
30. See *Alban Berg: Letters to his Wife*, ed., trans., and annot. Bernard Grun (London: Faber and Faber, 1971), p. 229.
31. Louis Krasner recalls how Helene Berg recounted 'again and again' how 'Alban ill in bed and tortured with pain, worked frantically and without interruption to conclude the composition of his Violin Concerto. Refusing to stop for food or sleep, he drove his hand on relentlessly and in fever. "I must continue," Berg responded to his wife's pleading, "I cannot stop—I do not have the time".' Louis Krasner, 'The Origins of Alban Berg's Violin Concerto', *Alban Berg Symposion Wien 1980: Tagungsbericht*, p. 108.
32. George Perle in a private letter to the author.
33. See George Perle, 'Der Tod des Geschwitz', *Österreichische Musikzeitschrift*, vol. 36 (January 1981), pp. 20–22.

The Operas

BERG AND GERMAN OPERA

DERRICK PUFFETT

A Passage from *Wozzeck*

The moment when Wozzeck kills Marie, in the third act of Berg's opera, is one of terrifying power (Example 1). Berg himself described it as follows:

> When finally the murder of Marie is committed to the sound of the *ff* drum beats on 'B', all the motives connected with her are sounded precipitately. They pass through her mind with lightning speed and in distorted form, like the images of life which may well pass through the mind at the moment of death: the Lullaby from Act 1 ([*A* in Example 1], bar 104); suggestions of the trinket scene of Act 2 ([*B*], bar 104); the Drum Major himself ([*C*], the same bar); the motive of Marie bemoaning her wretched life ([*D*], bar 105), which finally fades away in the moment of her last breath with the motive of dreamy fifths ..., the motive of waiting in vain ([*E*], bars 106–7).[1]

The list can be extended: as well as those motives already cited, there is the motive of Wozzeck's entrance and exit (*F*, bars 101 and 107), the motive of Marie's fear (*G*, bar 103), the A minor arpeggios associated with her 'waiting' motive (*H*, bar 103), and a reference to the seduction scene of Act I (*J*, bar 104). Even the pedal note B, which pervades the entire scene, refers to an earlier moment in the opera: the last note of Act II, with its tam-tam stroke that tells us that Marie's fate is sealed.

Many writers have commented on this passage. George Perle draws attention to the complementary relationship of the notes B and F. These are used as what he calls a 'dyadic tone-center' throughout the work, controlling the pitch at which some of the principal leitmotifs appear. In the murder scene, which Berg called an 'Invention on a Note', B is maintained as an ostinato—heard in the form of pulsating timpani crotchets at the moment of the murder itself—while F is prominent in the vocal line ('Ich nicht, Marie!') and elsewhere. The relationship between B and F also establishes a connection with the scene of

Ex. 1 *Wozzeck*, Act III, bars 101–7

Ex. 1 cont.

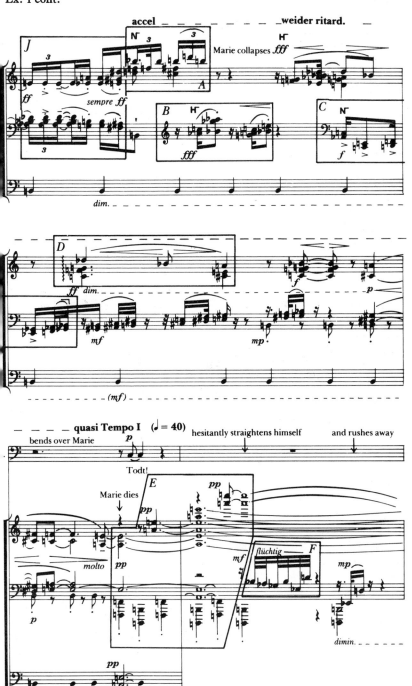

Wozzeck's death.[2]

Douglas Jarman focuses on Marie's 'waiting' motive. In its original form—as it first appears in Act I, scene 3—it uses the notes F, A, C, and E, with C in the bass. Later in the scene C slips down to B, creating a tritone with F (the 'dyadic tone-center' again). Whenever the motive appears subsequently it takes this 'variant' form, until the murder scene, when original and variant forms are combined: at the very moment of Marie's death (fourth crotchet of bar 106), the orchestra plays the variant form (F–A–B–E) while Wozzeck adds the missing C on the word 'Tod!'.[3]

Most recently Janet Schmalfeldt has undertaken an exhaustive analysis of pitch relations in the work. Of particular interest here is her observation that the intervals embodied in Marie's 'waiting' motive are already present in the cello and trombone figures of bar 102. This lends a 'ruthless irony' to Wozzeck's last words to her ('If not me, Marie, then no one else!'), for, 'unlike Marie, we have known for some time now that Marie's "waiting" will, in the words of the composer, "find its end only in her death"'.[4]

Analysis of this kind allows the most subtle understanding (and no opera has been analysed more than *Wozzeck*). Yet a work may be understood in many ways, and one way of approaching Berg's operas—an approach which has perhaps been neglected amid all the more detailed work—is to consider them in relation to the tradition in which they were composed. Even a short passage, such as that quoted above, tells us a considerable amount about Berg's historical background. The whole idea of music as a symbolic language, 'music as metaphor', comes from German operatic tradition, in particular from Wagner. (More remote antecedents in Bach and Schubert need not concern us here.) When Wozzeck plunges the knife into Marie the orchestra sums up her reactions: fear (bar 103); recollections of her seduction by the Drum Major, of her child, and of the earrings the Drum Major gave her (bar 104); a surge of self-pity (bar 105); a final image of 'waiting' (bar 106). This is the practice of music drama. Carl Dahlhaus has shown how, in Berg's article 'The "Problem of Opera"' (1928), written as a defence of *Wozzeck*, 'the argument that in opera the music is obliged to "serve the drama"—the argument of Wagner, or of Gluck—is taken for granted as if there were no more need to quarrel about it'.[5] For all the differences between *Wozzeck* and Wagner (the position concerning *Lulu* is more complex)[6] this basic allegiance is clear. And with this allegiance go certain formal and aesthetic assumptions: the use of leitmotifs, the continuous musical texture, the ever-changing relationship between voice and orchestra. Berg's use of leitmotifs may lack the complexity of Wagner's most ambitious examples, as seen in *Götterdämmerung* and *Parsifal*, yet it is capable of extraordinary power, as the episode of Marie's death shows; and an understanding of that power depends partly on a recognition of Berg's debt to the past.

The pacing of *Wozzeck*, however, is closer to Strauss. Not for Berg the expansive monologues of Gurnemanz! His dramatic timing seems to stem from *Salome* and *Elektra*. Berg's response to these works varied throughout his life:

he attended the Austrian première of *Salome* in 1906, along with Mahler, Schoenberg, Zemlinsky, and many other distinguished artists, and was initially enthusiastic; but twelve years later (at the time he was composing *Wozzeck*, in other words) he confessed to finding *Elektra* 'rather boring'.[7] Yet the debt to Strauss is obvious enough. The kaleidoscopic textures of Example 1 are unified by the pedal point, and in particular by the *crescendo* and *decrescendo*, which impose a pattern of tension and relaxation on what might otherwise appear a random sequence of events. Strauss uses a similar technique in *Salome*, as in the passage beginning at rehearsal number 300 and ending two bars after rehearsal number 304.

Vocal writing in *Wozzeck* constantly betrays its historical models. Marie's tremulous figure in the first bar of Example 1—'Was zitterst?'—recalls Schoenberg's *Erwartung* as surely as does the chord for four trumpets that accompanies it. Wozzeck's 'Ich nicht, Marie!' could occur in either Wagner or Strauss, but the Wagnerian nature of the declamation is unmistakable. Marie's two-octave cry of 'Hilfe!' surpasses by one tone Kundry's famous outburst in *Parsifal* ('Ich sah Ihn ... und *lachte*'); there are further precedents in *Erwartung*. The final, single-note phrase in the extract, Wozzeck's 'Tod!', has something Hugo Wolf-like about it: the hesitant, off-beat entry, as if Wozzeck is reluctant to acknowledge that Marie is dead. Orchestration, too, reveals Wagnerian–Straussian models: the forceful use of trombones (bars 102–3) and horns (first beat of 104); the 'shrieking' presentation of the Lullaby theme, with four piccolos on top (bar 104); the unison doubling of cellos and first violins for the recollection of the earrings (bars 104–6); the perfect fifths in divided strings, subtly interlaid with soft flutes and brass, for Marie's 'waiting' (bars 106–7).

Finally there are echoes of an even more specific kind. The most obvious in this passage is the xylophone thirds in bar 101, recalling similar moments in *Salome* (rehearsal number 329, with the thirds in trumpets, or, for the same music with xylophone, seven bars after rehearsal letter h in Salome's Dance). The pulsating timpani echo many a Mahlerian funeral march, though this is to widen the scope of enquiry considerably: whole essays could be written on the influence of Mahler alone. And the A minor arpeggios in bar 103 look not only backwards to Act I but forwards to the *Tumultuoso* music in Act II of *Lulu*.

The highlighting of reminiscences and anticipations can never replace analysis as a means of 'getting into' a work, especially one as complex as *Wozzeck*. Yet the concentration on analysis in recent studies of Berg has had the effect of isolating *Wozzeck* and *Lulu* from their operatic environment, of turning them into 'masterpieces' without a context. This essay will try to recreate some of the operatic background to the works.

German Opera 1900–1920

German opera around 1900 was dominated by the influence of Wagner.[8] (For the purposes of this essay 'German opera' means 'opera in the German-speaking countries': Germany, Austria, and Switzerland shared a common operatic tradition.) To call a work like Pfitzner's *Der arme Heinrich* (1891–3) 'post-Wagnerian'—a common term of abuse in the years immediately following the First World War—is both to state the obvious and to deny the work its particularity. Wagner's purely musical influence—the expansion of tonal and harmonic resources, the vastly extended time-scale, the increased orchestral possibilities, the formal and expressive significance of the leitmotif—was not, of course, confined to opera. At the same time his influence on opera composers was by no means purely musical: they were also influenced by his choice of subject matter. *Tristan*, *Parsifal*, and *The Ring* inspired many works based on myth and legend (an area that reached into fairy tale, as in the operas of Humperdinck: Dahlhaus describes such works as 'an attempt to succeed Wagner by circumvention');[9] *Tannhäuser* and *Lohengrin*, aided by Italian models such as *Rigoletto*, led to a passion for Medieval and Renaissance costume drama; and *Die Meistersinger* became the most important single model for Romantic comedies.[10] Against the background of all this Wagnerizing, a work like Wolf's *Der Corregidor* (1895), even though written by one of Wagner's leading disciples, suggests the beginning of a reaction, a conscious 'Mediterraneanizing' which would have pleased Nietzsche. Later, with the influence of verismo, the reaction was to become stronger, in such works as d'Albert's *Tiefland* (1902–3) and more pervasively in the operas of Schreker and Korngold. All in all it was a time of immense productivity; with opera houses in most of the major cities, and with seemingly unlimited financial support, the art flourished as rarely before.

Richard Strauss's first opera, *Guntram* (1892–3), was firmly within the Wagnerian tradition. Its themes of chivalry and renunciation mix uneasily with the doggerel libretto (by Strauss himself), though the work contains one truly original character in the Fool, a prototype for similar characters in Schreker and Zemlinsky; even Berg, when writing the part of the Idiot in *Wozzeck*, may have remembered him. The final duet shows Strauss's ability to think in long paragraphs and to devise musical material to suit (including a theme he considered worth quoting in *Ein Heldenleben*). But the work has never achieved widespread success. His next opera, *Feuersnot* (1900–1901), was more original. Although its 'old German' setting owes much to *Die Meistersinger*, the comedy has a satirical edge, and the music a folklike quality, which Wagner's work lacks. The satirical element, which Strauss was simultaneously cultivating in his tone poems (an opera on the subject of Till Eulenspiegel was mooted but abandoned), was to become a hallmark of his later works. The folklike quality was important too, not only for Strauss: Berg remembered it, though not necessarily in its Straussian context, when composing the songs of Andres in

Wozzeck, songs that required a 'popular' flavour in order to stand out from their chromatic surround.

Strauss's first major success in the operatic field, however, was *Salome* (1903–5), based on Wilde. It was bound to cause a scandal, not only because of the erotic subject matter (another connection with Berg, especially if one takes into account his letter of 1907 concerning Wedekind and the 'sensual' in art)[11] but because the music is some of Strauss's most extreme: extreme in volume, extreme in its vocal demands, extreme in its contrasts between diatonicism and chromaticism. *Elektra* (1906–8) took the composer even further down the same road. Another 'antique' setting evoked music of astonishing imaginative power, the climaxes heavier than those of *Salome*, the chromaticism still more subversive, the diatonic passages equally bland. The central monologue for Klytämnestra—'my boldest passage harmonically', according to Strauss[12]—became a prototype for musical 'expressionism', with its violent changes of mood, its 'realistic' declamation, and its orchestral pictorialism, though it is impossible to define the precise extent to which Schoenberg and Berg were influenced by it. The final pages, however—an orgiastic waltz in which Elektra dances herself to death—are a purely orchestral apotheosis, a gesture as thoroughly traditional as the invocation of Valhalla at the end of *Götterdämmerung* or (in its very different way) the last interlude in *Wozzeck*.

Elektra was Strauss's first collaboration with Hugo von Hofmannsthal. Their next project, *Der Rosenkavalier* (1909–10), established Strauss as the leading German operatic composer of the age. At the same time it marked an end of cordial relations between Strauss and the Schoenberg school, who considered that Strauss had betrayed the modernist cause. The idea that *Der Rosenkavalier*, still one of Strauss's best-loved works, constitutes a stylistic 'retreat' has since become critical orthodoxy; whether Berg, for one, really accepted it is difficult to say. His written comments[13] suggest that he did; his music suggests otherwise. More on this later. What is important here is to note the changed role of dissonance in Strauss. Now that comedy is of the essence, dissonance is subdued to the point where a waltz no longer seems incongruous, and extreme dissonance reserved for mock-expressionist outbursts (Ochs's discomfiture in Act II)—a case of Strauss's amusedly turning his style back on itself. Berg himself seems to adopt a similar position, *mutatis mutandis*, in parts of *Lulu*.

Expressionism has been such a vital force in 20th-century music that it comes as a shock to realise there was no tradition of expressionist opera before the 1920s, when expressionism in the other arts had largely exhausted itself. Schoenberg's one-act operas *Erwartung* (1909) and *Die glückliche Hand* (1910–13)—works central to any discussion of expressionism in music—were not staged until 1924, though they were known to musicians in the Schoenberg circle; Berg's *Wozzeck*, composed in 1917–22, was premièred only in 1925. For the first 20 years of this century, and indeed until *Wozzeck*'s triumphant reception, Schoenberg and Berg were overshadowed, as opera composers, by lesser men—not only Strauss, but also Schreker, Pfitzner, and Korngold.

Schreker (1878–1934) is probably the most interesting of these. An exceptionally cultivated man, he drew inspiration from German fairy tale (now invested with a post-Freudian concern with sexuality and the bizarre), French naturalism, and Italian verismo. He wrote his own libretti. His first success, *Der ferne Klang* (1901–10), was produced in 1912 to general acclaim. At this time Schreker was close to Schoenberg, whose *Gurrelieder* he premièred in 1913; but from now on they began to move apart, though their careers continued to overlap in various ways. Schreker's two greatest successes, *Die Gezeichneten* (1913–15) and *Der Schatzgräber* (1915–18), combined fantastic plots with spectacular stage effects and music recalling such diverse models as Strauss, Debussy, and Puccini. After 1920, however, Schreker's star waned. The new generation—composers such as Hindemith and Weill—had no time for his extravaganzas, which in a period of gross inflation seemed impossibly pretentious. The première of *Christophorus* (1924–7), an allegory of the artist's role in society, was cancelled because of the threat of Nazi demonstrations; ironically, it was one of Schreker's most forward-looking works (not for nothing was it dedicated to Schoenberg).

Another distinguished treatment of the artist theme was Pfitzner's *Palestrina* (1912–15). Pfitzner (1869–1949), who, like Schreker, wrote his own texts, had moved from a position that could be described as vaguely progressive (he revered Wagner and had assisted Mahler) to one of extreme conservatism. This new position, later pilloried by Berg in a famous pamphlet,[14] was embodied in his opera, a glowing tribute to the past as symbolized by Baini's hero. Music of astonishing vehemence invokes the Council of Trent, but the opera ends quietly, with Palestrina left alone: nostalgia is tempered by realism. The Austro-Hungarian Franz Schmidt (1874–1939), who lived in Vienna from 1888, produced two operas, *Notre Dame* (composed 1902–4, premièred 1914) and *Fredigundis* (1916–21). Within the limitations of his essentially symphonic style, both contain music of the utmost radiance, the cathedral scene from the latter recalling *Lohengrin*. *Notre Dame* is an unbelievable travesty of Hugo, notable mainly for its brilliant carnival scene and its vivid characterisation of the gypsy girl (Schmidt's Hungarian background pays dividends here). Twenty-two years younger than Schmidt, but of the same general sensibility, was the prodigy Erich Wolfgang Korngold (1897–1957). His one-act operas *Der Ring des Polykrates* and *Violanta* caused a critical sensation when they were premièred together in 1916; the style is a heady mixture of Strauss and Puccini, but with a rhythmic vitality unusual in German opera of this time. Four years later came *Die tote Stadt* ('indescribable music', according to Berg).[15] The modern setting is noteworthy, anticipating the 'topical' works produced later in the 1920s, but the theatrical effects are more like Meyerbeer: in the last act a ghostly procession seems to enter the hero's room. In 1934 Korngold was to leave Europe for Hollywood.

In the context of such works Schoenberg's *Erwartung* seems more original than ever. Its expressionist aspects are now well documented: the concentration on a single, unnamed character; the projection of the most intense emotions; the absence of any conventional structural device (no repetition except on the smallest scale); the violent contrasts; the breathless delivery of the text. The music has until very recently resisted analysis, and even techniques as sophisticated as set theory seem inadequate when placed beside the extraordinary *expressive* power of the work. The most rewarding approach for the naïve listener is through the text and the stage directions, which, as always in Schoenberg, are of fascinating detail; the music then makes its dreamlike effect. The stage directions in *Die glückliche Hand* are even more fascinating: here is the perfect musical equivalent of Kandinsky, complete with 'colour crescendo' (an effect fully notated in the score). Interestingly, the formal structure of the work is more easily grasped than that of *Erwartung*; Schoenberg evidently felt that the earlier work, with its sense of continuous improvisation, was an unrepeatable experiment. From now on conventional structural devices return to his music with ever greater frequency.

The combination of apparent spontaneity and formal artifice is in fact more characteristic of expressionism than is spontaneity *tout court*. For this reason *Wozzeck*, a more 'universal' work than *Erwartung* because of its family relationships, may be considered the expressionist masterpiece. Berg's formal contrivances, which include a fugue, a sonata movement, and a set of variations, have become a byword for musical constructivism (Perle writes of the work's 'form-consciousness')[16] and as such belong firmly in the 1920s. But the impact of *Wozzeck* is overwhelmingly emotional, a type of experience recognized by anyone familiar with Wagner and Strauss. The more specific echoes merely confirm this. So many scholarly words have been written about Berg that it is easy to forget he has entered the operatic repertory in a way no other composer has since Puccini. Schoenberg's reservations about *Wozzeck*[17] may have been prompted partly by jealousy.

As a postscript to this section, mention must be made of another composer in the Schoenberg circle, Alexander von Zemlinsky (1871–1942), whose operatic career actually spans a longer period than either Schoenberg's or Berg's. His first opera, *Sarema* (1895), has not held its place in the repertory, but the next 40 years saw a steady output of works, some of which have recently been revived. They include *Kleider machen Leute* (1908), *Eine florentinische Tragödie* (1915–16), and *Der Zwerg* (1920–21); all are known to have impressed Berg. As a conductor Zemlinsky performed excerpts from *Wozzeck* before the première of the complete work. His Lyric Symphony (1923) was of course a model for Berg's Lyric Suite.[18]

Wozzeck Reconsidered

In its general dramatic conception, *Wozzeck* stands a little outside the tradition just outlined. Büchner wrote 26 scenes which were presumably to be played in straight succession; intervals would have dissipated the tension. Berg reduced the number of scenes to 15, divided into three acts of five scenes each. In doing so he imposed a conventional dramatic framework on a less conventional one[19] (though he constantly turned the three-act structure to his advantage, as Perle has shown). Yet the work still retains some of the structural character of the original. In its succession of short scenes *Wozzeck* has more in common with Goethe's *Faust*, Part I (which Berg once contemplated setting to music)[20] and a work influenced by it, Ibsen's *Peer Gynt*, than with many of its operatic forbears. The short scenes give the work an epic, open-ended quality which looks forward to the cinema. The time scale, as in some works of Shakespeare, is left unclear, so that, for example, we do not know exactly how much time has passed between Acts I and II (and, consequently, whether Marie has slept with the Drum Major once or many times). Even the sequence of scenes, for all of Berg's manic organization, has a slightly haphazard quality, recalling Boulez's comment on *Götterdämmerung*, Act I ('one day I would like to perform it with the scenes in the wrong order and see if anyone notices'). The link with Wagner—again!—is no accident. It was part of Berg's intention to give each of his scenes a strong and individual character, and because he succeeded so well the order can seem confused. Wagner, too, liked to characterize each scene as sharply as possible (the four related-but-different scenes in *Das Rheingold* being a good example).

On the consequences of having so many scenes, Berg wrote:

> A further compelling necessity for musical variety arose with the comparatively large number of orchestral interludes. ... To have written here symphonic transitions or intermezzi throughout (such [as] I was to observe later in another contemporary opera with many changes of scene) would have been at variance with my own conception of musical drama. So I was compelled to aim at contrast and variety by making these interludes partly transitional bridge-passages, and partly giving them the forms of coda to the preceding scene, or prelude to the following scene, or even both at once.[21]

When Berg refers to 'another contemporary opera' he almost certainly means Debussy's *Pelléas et Mélisande*, which in any case he had already studied while composing *Wozzeck*.[22] This is indeed the *only* work, among those which form a regular part of the repertory, that would have provided a model for the many short interludes he required (*Pelléas* also is in 15 scenes). Yet the dramatic function of the interludes in *Pelléas* is quite different from that of the interludes in *Wozzeck*. Robin Holloway has shown how Debussy's interludes serve to articulate the pain and loneliness which the characters cannot express.[23] Berg's characters are not lost for words—far from it—and his interludes have much more the role of continuing dramatic and thematic arguments already carried on at length within the scenes themselves. A better comparison might be with the interludes in Strauss's almost exactly contemporaneous opera *Die Frau ohne Schatten* (1914–18). Strauss's work hinges on the contrast between upper and lower worlds, associated with chamber orchestra and full orchestra respectively: the transition from one to the other is an important means of formal articulation. When at the end of the first scene—transparent chamber sonorities, textures deliberately kept thin so that important information can be conveyed—Strauss decides to give the orchestra its head, the effect is startlingly reminiscent of the first interlude in *Wozzeck*.

Berg attributed his use of conventional forms in *Wozzeck* to a search for 'structural cohesion': 'As I tried to achieve variety of musical means by avoiding the Wagnerian recipe of "through-composing" each scene in similar manner, nothing else was left to me than to give a different shape to each of the opera's fifteen scenes.'[24] Berg's attempt to read an *A-B-A* form into the structure of the work as a whole,[25] however, fails to convince. Even the chart published by Reich, which, he says, Berg 'suggested to him'[26] and which has since enjoyed massive circulation, is more useful as a guide to the composer's psychology than as an indication of how the music actually sounds.[27] How many listeners would recognize a five-movement symphony in Act II, for instance, without Berg's help? (The addition of a fantasia and fugue as an 'extra' movement is not exactly common in symphonic works.)

Another point that needs to be questioned is the claim, also frequently encountered,[28] that Berg borrowed the idea for this 'symphony' from Schreker's *Der ferne Klang*. Berg may have thought he was doing so, but his second act, unconventional as it is, is in fact much more of a symphony than Schreker's. (As Hans Keller pointed out, its structure is related to that of Schoenberg's Chamber Symphony no. 1.)[29] Schreker's 'symphony' collapses at the two points where it should be strongest, namely the 'first movement' and 'finale': there is no trace of sonata form in Schreker's scheme (nor is it necessary for the sake of the drama). In addition, his 'slow movement' and 'scherzo', represented respectively by the ballad 'Die glühende Krone' and the song about the flower girl of Sorrento, stand outside the main dramatic argument—except in the trivial sense that both are performed in a song contest. The claim that the act is a symphony seems to have originated with Schreker himself, who wrote under the influence of 19th-century aesthetics and analysed his music in terms of sonata form whenever he saw the chance.[30] Berg's symphonic movements, by contrast, adhere to Classical precedent (with a sonata-form first movement and rondo finale) and are closely tied in with the drama.

A further point often made in connection with Schreker, most persuasively by Nicholas Chadwick, is that Berg was influenced by the orchestration of *Der ferne Klang*, whose vocal score he prepared.[31] If someone lives with a work for months in this way it is reasonable to suppose he will be influenced by it. Yet Chadwick's examples show no technique that Berg could have derived *only* from

Schreker: he could equally have been influenced by Schoenberg or Mahler. Chadwick is right to point out, at the end of his article, that Berg's orchestration is more rigorously thematic than that of Schreker, whose decorative textures show affinities with *Jugendstil*.[32] Berg's orchestration is rarely decorative in this way. One moment in Schreker which has a definite Bergian *frisson*, however, is Greta surrounded by her admirers in *Der ferne Klang*, Act II—a moment that looks forward to *Lulu* as surely as it looks back to Lehár's *Merry Widow*. And perhaps the moment in *Wozzeck* when Marie tries on her earrings, to the accompaniment of flutes, celesta, and four solo violins, is a reference to Schreker's sound-world (Example 2).

Ex. 2 *Wozzeck*, Act II, bars 60–3

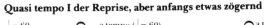

Quasi tempo I der Reprise, aber anfangs etwas zögernd

Other specific echoes can be dealt with more briefly. Berg's Act I, scene 2 is his first extended homage to *Erwartung* (though the repeated use of three main chords is not a Schoenbergian device), enlarging the expressive vocabulary through the use of *Sprechstimme*. *Erwartung* was a most fertile source for Berg. The Eb minor triad, with fifth on top, that bursts into the middle of Act I, scene 4 recalls the opening 'fateful' chord of *Götterdämmerung*; it returns in Act II (bar 589). Jarman has pointed out that the triad of Eb minor with added D is associated with the word 'Blut'.[33] At the end of Act I, scene 4 (bars 642ff.), the motivic liquidation over the pedal D♯ recalls the end of the opening scene of *Elektra* (rehearsal number 34). Another echo of *Elektra* is the harp glissando introducing Act II, scene 2: this recalls the unforgettable moment just before the murder of Aegisth (six bars after rehearsal number 212a).

Act II, as well as being a symphony, is an extended tribute to *Der Rosenkavalier*. Whatever Berg's expressed opinion of this work, the music of Example 3 could hardly be anything other than affectionate parody. 'I too have known love', warbles the Captain, almost imitating Ochs's falsetto.[34] This is surely the key to an earlier passage (Act I, bars 39–40), where the waltz rhythms, together with violins in thirds and sixths, summon up *Der Rosenkavalier* again. The most famous allusion to this work, however, comes in the tavern scene of Act II (bars 430ff., echoing Ochs's 'Ohne mich'). The allusion to the offstage band in Strauss's third act has also been widely acknowledged. More original is

Ex. 3 *Wozzeck*, Act II, bars 326–9

the orchestra *within* an orchestra in Berg's Act II, scene 3: borrowing the ensemble used in Schoenberg's Chamber Symphony no. 1, he pits chamber orchestra against full orchestra for this central scene ('central' in both senses: it is pivotal to the drama, in introducing the idea of the knife, and it occurs at the very centre of the work). As Wozzeck and Marie angrily confront each other, the use of two opposed instrumental groups vividly portrays their non-communication. Another, more trivial, reference comes towards the end of the act (bars 738ff.), where the solo double bass, piercing through the choral snores, recalls Salome's lustful pantings (seven bars after rehearsal number 304 of the Strauss).

Act III, scene 1, with Marie reading the Bible, presents two worlds (perusal and comment, matter-of-fact *Sprechstimme* and anguished cantabile); and perhaps the F minor 'island', within a sea of chromaticism, is to be understood in the light of diatonic–chromatic contrasts in Wagner. (The 'two worlds' of *Die Frau ohne Schatten* are another possible model.) Chromaticism is carried to its limits in the scene of Wozzeck's drowning. Nearly 40 years ago Hans Keller likened this passage to the final part of *Erwartung*,[35] which Berg described as 'terrific both in range and in expression'.[36] (Chadwick likens it to the dawn chorus in *Der ferne Klang*.)[37] The 'blood-red' moon that rises in bar 262—another link with *Salome*—is not, of course, Berg's invention. The function of Berg's final interlude has already been remarked on, though not its function as formal recapitulation, which is one Wagnerian aspect of a passage whose emotional effect, as Joseph Kerman has suggested, is anything but Wagnerian.[38] Kerman also refers to the closing scene as 'pure Ravel',[39] but he cannot have noticed the *Tristan* chords in bars 375ff.

One could go on. But the further one goes in this direction, the more conjectural the whole thing becomes. The enquiry is hampered by sheer lack of evidence. We simply do not know what Berg thought of the operas of Schmidt, for instance; and even if we did, the value of such knowledge would be questionable. What Berg said to one person, on such and such a day, might not be what he would have said to a different person on another day, or to the same person in different circumstances. Most often we are likely to come up against contradictions, suggesting ambivalence. It is better to concentrate on specific relationships. We might consider *Wozzeck*, for example, in relation to two works closely contemporary with it: Schreker's *Die Gezeichneten* and Zemlinsky's *Der Zwerg*.

> The hero of *Die Gezeichneten* (The Marked Ones) ... is an ugly and crippled young nobleman, named Alviano Salvago. Denied the normal pleasures of life, he creates a paradise-island of aesthetic artifice ('Elysium') which he never visits himself, but which his more fortunately endowed friends use as a secret venue for unbridled orgies, for the purpose of which they kidnap Genoa's fairest daughters. In a belated attempt to expiate their crimes, however, the creator of Elysium throws it open to the general public. Not only are its delights

all too much for *them*; it is precisely at the height of the opening celebrations on the island that the one woman Alviano thought to have returned his love is ravished to the point of death by one of his handsome young friends. What is more, she enjoyed every moment, and reveals as much as she dies, to the elemental anguish of Alviano. As a painter (with a weak heart) she had really been interested in him only as an artistic subject![40]

Der Zwerg (The Dwarf), on the other hand, is based on Wilde's fairy tale *The Birthday of the Infanta*, which Schreker had already turned into a ballet (1908). On her 18th birthday the Infanta, the beautiful but heartless Donna Clara, is given the present of a dwarf. A charcoal-burner's son in Wilde, the gift from a sultan in Zemlinsky, the dwarf is dressed like a dandy, complete with dagger; and he has never seen himself in a mirror. Naturally, he falls in love with the Infanta. She is amused by the situation and plays with him. Eventually, when he is left alone, he comes upon a mirror and sees how grotesque he is. As he dies of a broken heart, the Infanta returns to the dance.

The two works are intimately related. Zemlinsky, who was sensitive about his personal appearance (Alma Mahler describes him unflatteringly in her memoirs),[41] asked Schreker to write a libretto for him about the 'tragedy of the ugly man'. Schreker was so pleased with the result that he kept it for himself: it became *Die Gezeichneten*.[42] Whether Berg knew the Schreker we do not know (presumably he did, since it was a huge success). He certainly knew *Der Zwerg*, and admired it, as we know from two letters that he wrote to his wife in 1923.[43] Musical links exist between *Wozzeck* and the other two works. But these are not really the point. What matters is to recognise the general cultural connection, which draws attention to aspects of the Berg not sufficiently acknowledged.

Seen in the context of the Schreker and the Zemlinsky, *Wozzeck* does indeed emerge in a different light. The characters of *Wozzeck* are simply those of the two other works translated to a more modern setting. The brutality of Alviano's friend Vitellozzo, who rapes his beloved Carlotta, is that of the Drum Major, while Wozzeck himself has much in common with the dwarf and the hunchback who are persecuted, or feel themselves to be persecuted, because of their disability. 'Normality never asserts itself in connection with the characters of the opera', Joseph Kerman says of *Wozzeck*.[44] Douglas Jarman has written:

> The three characters who are instrumental in bringing about the final catastrophe are either (as in the case of the Captain and the Doctor) grotesques, obsessed by their own fixations, or (as with the figure of the Drum Major) mere ciphers. The spectator is thus forced, not simply to identify with Wozzeck, but to see events through his eyes.[45]

I would argue, however, that not only the Captain and the Doctor but also Wozzeck himself is portrayed as a grotesque. Is his behaviour in Act I, scene 2 'normal'? Is his response to Marie's infidelity 'normal', come to that? The only 'normal' character in the opera is Marie (who is herself something of a Gretchen figure). Wozzeck, the Captain, and the Doctor are common victims of what

Jarman calls a 'malicious or, at best, indifferent universe',[46] which Berg controls at his will. He is every bit the puppet-master here that he is in *Lulu*; and this is borne out by the black comedy of the scenes in which the Captain and the Doctor torment Wozzeck.[47] The comedy is not in Büchner; it is Berg's original contribution, and it constitutes a comment on the dramatic situation as significant as the final interlude. This 'opera of protest and compassion'[48] is also a sadistic exploitation of human weakness.

German Opera 1920–35

The reaction against Romanticism that followed the First World War had profound effects on German opera. Although opera houses continued to employ large orchestras, so that the works of Wagner and Strauss were never wholly absent from the repertory, there was an increasing feeling that such extravagance went ill with the times. Schreker and Korngold lost their following; the new opera had to be tougher, more economical, more in tune with everyday events. 'Topicality' became the catchword; even Zemlinsky found himself writing jazz, or something like it (*Der Kreidekreis*, 1932). Influenced by Busoni (whose *Arlecchino* and *Turandot*, both written during the war, introduced what he called a 'Young Classicism') and Stravinsky (whose *Histoire du soldat* reached Weimar in 1923, when it impressed the young Weill),[49] composers sought to instil into opera the values of 'absolute' music: from now on there would be as many passacaglias in the theatre as in the concert hall (Hindemith's *Cardillac* contains a good example). Another important figure— as much an impresario as a conductor—was Otto Klemperer; in his years at the Kroll Opera in Berlin (1926–31) he became almost synonymous with the modern movement, performing works by Schoenberg, Stravinsky, Hindemith, Weill, and Janáček among others.[50]

Cardillac (1926), for all its 'modernisms', was in fact simply another version of the artist theme, one that placed Hindemith (1895–1963) in the same idealist tradition as Schreker and Pfitzner. This theme was to remain his lifelong preoccupation: *Mathis der Maler* (1934–5), a study of the painter Grünewald, and his much later Kepler opera, *Die Harmonie der Welt* (1956–7), both returned to it. Such works indeed tended to isolate Hindemith from his contemporaries. Those operas of his which received most publicity at the time were *Hin und zurück* (1927), in which the action proceeds to a central point and then runs back on itself—such constructivist conceits were the delight of the 1920s—and the 'topical opera' to end all topical operas, *Neues vom Tage* (1928–9).

Another composer who achieved notoriety at this time, but later became a staunch traditionalist, was Ernst Krenek (*b* 1900), a Viennese pupil of Schreker. His *Der Sprung über den Schatten* (1923) was the first German opera to use jazz; Schoenberg detested it.[51] But the work with which Krenek made his name was

Jonny spielt auf (1925–6), whose main character is actually a jazz musician. After these successes Krenek turned out a series of dull, respectable works, including the operas *Leben des Orest* (1928–9)—its Classical subject matter influenced by Stravinsky's *Oedipus Rex*—and *Karl V* (1930–33). Another admirer of *Oedipus* was Kurt Weill (1900–1950), who reviewed a Kroll performance of it in 1928. Before that he had already written two brilliant one-act operas, *Der Protagonist* (1924–5) and *Der Zar lässt sich photographieren* (1927), which anticipate the busy contrapuntal manner of Hindemith as well as being 'topical' almost to excess (though Weill deplored topicality as such, as did Berg and Schoenberg). *Der Zar* also includes a tango, showing that Weill's 'popular' style was not invented by Brecht. (In fact the crucial influence seems to have been *Histoire du soldat*.) The major Brecht collaborations were *Die Dreigroschenoper* (1928) and *Aufstieg und Fall der Stadt Mahagonny* (1927–9). *Mahagonny* is a full-length opera, sung virtually from beginning to end; *Die Bürgschaft*, written in 1931 to words by Caspar Neher, completes the process, and here the Stravinsky influence (but the 'monumental' style of *Oedipus* rather than the dance rhythms of *Histoire*) holds full sway. 'Monumental' and 'popular' styles come together in Weill's last German opera, *Der Silbersee* (strictly a 'play with music', not an opera), composed in 1932 in collaboration with Georg Kaiser. The following year Weill left the country, first for Paris and then for New York.

Strauss's last 30 years were a story of growing isolation. *Intermezzo* (1918–23) was in fact the very first 'topical opera', a semi-autobiographical piece which shocked the fastidious Hofmannsthal; for this Strauss had to write his own words. The operas of the next 20 years alternate between Classical tragedy and Romantic comedy, the comedies (*Arabella*, 1929–32; *Die schweigsame Frau*, 1933–4) perhaps emerging as the more successful. Strauss's problems were increased by his decision to stay in Germany during the Third Reich. Another isolated figure, much influenced by Strauss, was the Swiss composer Othmar Schoeck (1886–1957). After a series of early works on Romantic subjects (including *Venus*, 1919–20, after Mérimée and Eichendorff) he moved on to Classical tragedy with a setting of Kleist's *Penthesilea* (1924—5). This is an extraordinary work, which employs some of the same musical techniques as *Wozzeck*.[52] Berg, in turn, was to be deeply affected by Schoeck's song cycle *Notturno* towards the end of his life.[53]

Schoenberg, in the 1920s, was planning his two late operas, *Von Heute auf Morgen* (1928–9), a satire on all things topical, and *Moses und Aron* (1930–32, first performed in 1954). The biblical work seems far removed from the typical operatic concerns of the time; but in fact it is yet another treatment of the artist theme, combined with Schoenberg's ever-increasing absorption in religion. Schoenberg the visionary (= Moses) is here seen to be at odds with Schoenberg the composer (= Aron); it is as if his lifelong fascination with technique had led him to distrust it. The work ends in silence, for Act III was never written; and Moses' last words in Act II are a howl of frustration, a lament at the inadequacy of speech (or of music). It is a far cry from Berg's *Lulu*, another work of which

Schoenberg disapproved. Berg began the composition in 1929 but had not finished the orchestration at the time of his death (1935); a two-act version was performed in 1937, the completed score not until 1979.

Lulu Reconsidered

This section focuses on three aspects of the work: vocal writing, formal symmetry, and Berg's peculiar handling of musical 'expression'.

Lulu is notable for its variety of vocal styles. These range from extravagant coloratura writing for Lulu herself (a traditional device for portraying female 'flightiness'—compare Strauss's Zerbinetta) through the less extravagant but still lyrical music of Alwa and the Painter to various types of declamation (including *Sprechstimme* and ordinary speech).[54] The variety of vocal styles presupposes certain decisions about the nature of the orchestral accompaniment (and indeed about the size of the orchestra, which is smaller than that of *Wozzeck*), which in turn are related to the work's setting, its subject matter, and so on.

In all this Berg may well have been influenced by Strauss's *Intermezzo*. When Strauss published his opera in 1924 he included a lengthy preface, setting out his intentions in composing a comedy about middle-class family life. He drew attention to the variety of vocal techniques used, ranging from pure spoken dialogue to *bel canto*. The prime consideration was the audibility of every word, an aim not achieved in *Guntram* but realized, so he claimed, in ideal performances of *Salome* and *Elektra* (!). 'It was in the first act of *Ariadne*', he wrote, 'that I first used with full assurance, in the alternation between ordinary prose, *recitativo secco* and *recitativo accompagnato*, the vocal style which I have now, in *Intermezzo*, carried to its logical conclusion.'[55] All this sounds very much like Berg, whose *Lulu*, if not a 'bourgeois comedy', is at least a drama of 'middle-class family life' in which the clear delivery of the text is of utmost importance. Whether Strauss would have recognised the work as fulfilling his aims is more doubtful.

Formal symmetry is one of the most widely discussed aspects of *Lulu*.[56] But it is by no means unique to that work, or even unusual in music of the period, though it is probably true to say that Berg carries the idea to unprecedented lengths. The 'schematic work' is a genre. In the field of opera it embraces such diverse examples as Bartók's *Bluebeard's Castle* (1911), with its sevenfold repetition of the same dramatic situation, Schoeck's *Von Fischer un syner Fru* (1928–30), organized as a set of variations with prologue and epilogue, certain works of Hindemith already mentioned, and even Ravel's *L'Heure espagnole* (1907–9).

The best comparison, however, is with the second act of Weill's *Mahagonny*, in which four scenes depict the various 'pleasures' of that city, interspersed with statements of an orchestral refrain. Berg's sonata, rondo, and variation schemes, as efficiently fused with the dramatic situation as any of the forms in *Wozzeck*, are clearly related to Weill in this respect, not to mention Berg's use of the saxophone (his vibraphone, on the other hand, could be heard as a last echo of Schreker's 'distant sound'). The variations in Berg's third act, with street organ borrowed from *Die Dreigroschenoper*, are perhaps the closest parallel.

Berg's handling of musical 'expression'—the inverted commas are necessary—has been recognized as 'peculiar' only in recent years; since the first performance of Act III, in fact. In the Prologue (actually the last part of the work to be composed) music serves a traditional expressive purpose. As the Animal Trainer calls out the names of the various beasts, we hear the leitmotifs associated with the characters in the opera. The music 'illuminates' the text because it is conceived as complementary to it. Later, in Act I, 'expression' becomes 'expressionism', every idea in the text evoking its spontaneous musical image (as in Lulu's conversation with Dr Schön). But in Act II, as Robin Holloway has shown, Berg turns the style against itself: expressionist gestures are used 'almost in inverted commas (as in Schön's asides ... when he returns to find the house full of Lulu's lovers)', and the music 'undermines its listeners' instinctive obedience to emotive instructions'.[57] Act III is more puzzling still: here there seems to be a deliberate dislocation of gesture from its normal expressive workings. When the music formerly associated with Schön—'the only man I ever loved', according to Lulu—returns to accompany her bargainings with Jack the Ripper, the expressive effect is far from clear.

Still more recently Douglas Jarman has argued that *Lulu* is a work of epic theatre. It seems that Berg, who attended rehearsals for *Mahagonny*, wrote a criticism of traditional opera into his last stage work, in which, in a final wry twist of the artist theme, he has Alwa (a composer, specifically identified as Berg himself) confusing art and reality 'to such an extent that he eventually succeeds in getting himself killed in the last scene of his own opera'.[58] Actually, the means by which this comes about—what might be called a subversion of the expressionist aesthetic—is already present in Weill. When Jimmy Mahoney, towards the end of the first act of *Mahagonny* (vocal score, p. 97), says that he is bored, the orchestra comments with a violence out of all proportion to the seriousness of the situation. The gesture is surely intended to parody Strauss or 'expressionist' Schoenberg—or perhaps even *Wozzeck* (a work that Weill admired, while insisting that it marked an end and not a new beginning).[59] Hearing himself parodied in this way, Berg might well have felt that he could do the job better.[60]

Conclusion

It would be pointless now to try to return to Berg's sources and to concentrate our attention on the years around 1900. Berg has, as it were, destroyed those sources by his own progress as a composer and they remain his own secret, which cannot ever be discovered, though we may clear the surrounding landscape. We should be on our guard against nostalgia for the past: the work grown richer with time, as a river is enriched by alluvial tributaries. The interesting thing is to regard the composer's labour as the point of departure for another adventure, the adventure undertaken by those who make the work their own. What is valuable is not discovering the composer, but discovering ourselves through him. The difference hardly matters as long as it is fruitful.[61]

Boulez, of course; and though he is speaking of Berg's literary sources, what he says applies equally well to the musical ones. We can never recreate the state of a composer's mind. Talk of 'influence', musical 'echoes', and the like remains speculative, perhaps even irresponsible, inasmuch as such things cannot be proved. Either one hears them or one does not.

Yet there is something to be said for 'clearing the landscape'. No composer writes in a vacuum, least of all a composer like Berg, to whom music was food and drink. Berg's 'eclecticism' is best summed up in his famous exchange with Gershwin, whom he met in 1928:

Gershwin: How can you possibly like my music when you write the kind of music you do?
Berg: Music is music.[62]

For those who want to make *Wozzeck* and *Lulu* 'their own' there is no substitute for analysis. But some knowledge of the historical context in which they were written can only enrich the experience.

Notes

1. Berg's lecture on *Wozzeck* (1929), trans. in Hans Ferdinand Redlich, *Alban Berg: the Man and his Music* (London: John Calder, 1957), pp. 280–81; I have amended the translation where necessary. Berg also refers to the murder scene in his article 'The Preparation and Staging of *Wozzeck*', trans. as Appendix I of George Perle, *The Operas of Alban Berg*, vol. 1: *Wozzeck* (Berkeley and Los Angeles: University of California Press, 1980), p. 206.
2. Perle, op. cit., pp. 139–40. See also Douglas Jarman, *The Music of Alban Berg* (London: Faber and Faber, 1979), pp. 48–9.
3. Jarman, op. cit., pp. 63–5.
4. Janet Schmalfeldt, *Berg's 'Wozzeck': Harmonic Language and Dramatic Design* (New Haven: Yale University Press, 1983), p. 220. Other writers who have commented on the passage are Gerd Ploebsch, *Alban Bergs 'Wozzeck': Dramaturgie und musikalischer*

Aufbau (Baden-Baden: P. H. Heitz Verlag, 1968), p. 82, and Josef-Horst Lederer, 'Zu Alban Bergs Invention über den Ton H', *50 Jahre Wozzeck von Alban Berg*, ed. Otto Kolleritsch (Graz: Universal Edition, 1978), pp. 57–67.

5. Carl Dahlhaus, *Esthetics of Music*, trans. William Austin (Cambridge: Cambridge University Press, 1982), p. 64. Berg's article is translated in Willi Reich, *Alban Berg*, trans. Cornelius Cardew (London: Thames and Hudson, 1965), pp. 63–6.

6. See Douglas Jarman, 'Weill and Berg: *Lulu* as Epic Opera', *The New Orpheus: Essays on Kurt Weill*, ed. Kim H. Kowalke (New Haven: Yale University Press, 1986), pp. 147–56.

7. On Berg's initial enthusiasm for *Salome*, see Mosco Carner, *Alban Berg: The Man and The Work* (London:Duckworth, 1975), p. 6. Lederer (op. cit., p. 66, n. 17) writes as if Berg retained his enthusiasm, but Schmalfeldt (op. cit., p. 262, n. 10) says he became critical: neither author gives a source. See also Reich, op. cit., p. 38. For Berg's 1918 reaction to *Elektra* see *Alban Berg: Letters to his Wife*, ed., trans., and annot. Bernard Grun (London: Faber and Faber, 1971), p. 243.

8. The 'narrative' sections of this essay draw on material presented in my article '[The Twentieth Century:] Germany–Austria–Switzerland', *History of Opera*, ed. Stanley Sadie (London: Macmillan, 1989).

9. Carl Dahlhaus, 'Schreker and Modernism: On the Dramaturgy of *Der ferne Klang*', *Schoenberg and the New Music*, trans. Derrick Puffett and Alfred Clayton (Cambridge: Cambridge University Press, 1987), p. 198.

10. See Strauss's and Hofmannsthal's correspondence about *Der Rosenkavalier*, in which frequent reference to *Die Meistersinger* is made: *The Correspondence between Richard Strauss and Hugo von Hofmannsthal*, trans. Hanns Hammelmann and Ewald Osers (Cambridge: Cambridge University Press, 1980), pp. 26–69.

11. See Carner, op. cit., pp. 6–7.

12. *Gustav Mahler–Richard Strauss: Correspondence 1888–1911*, ed. Herta Blaukopf (London: Faber and Faber, 1984), p. 151.

13. See the letter to Webern cited in Karen Monson, *Alban Berg: a Biography* (London: Macdonald and Jane's, 1980), p. 52.

14. Alban Berg, 'The Musical Impotence of Hans Pfitzner's "New Aesthetic"', trans. in Reich, op. cit., pp. 205–18. Carner suggests that this article may have been one reason why *Wozzeck* was not performed until 1925: see Carner, op. cit., p. 55.

15. Letter of 15 December 1921, *Alban Berg: Letters to his Wife*, p. 295.

16. Perle, op. cit., p. 37.

17. See Carner, op. cit., pp. 51–2. But see also Schoenberg's 1949 essay on Berg, where he writes of *Wozzeck* with warmth and generosity: 'Alban Berg (1)', *Style and Idea: Selected Writings of Arnold Schoenberg*, ed. Leonard Stein, trans. Leo Black (London: Faber and Faber, 1975), p. 474.

18. Berg always had the highest regard for Zemlinsky. He attended as many performances of his music as possible and, around 1920, planned to write a book about him: see Carner, op. cit., p. 59, n. 1, and Rosemary Hilmar, *Alban Berg: Leben und Wirken in Wien bis zu seinen ersten Erfolgen als Komponist* (Vienna: Verlag Hermann Böhlaus Nachf., 1978), p. 154. After Berg's death, Zemlinsky was one of the composers who were considered for the task of completing *Lulu*: see Perle, *The Operas of Alban Berg*, vol. 2: *Lulu* (Berkeley and Los Angeles: University of California Press, 1985), pp. 262ff.

19. Manfred Gurlitt, in his setting of *Wozzeck* (premièred 1928), did not divide the scenes into acts: see Perle, *The Operas of Alban Berg*, vol. 1: *Wozzeck*, p. 36.

20. See Ernst Hilmar, 'Die verschiedenen Entwicklungsstudien in den Kompos-

itionsskizzen', *50 Jahre Wozzeck von Alban Berg*, p. 22.

21. Berg's lecture on *Wozzeck*, quoted in Redlich, op. cit., pp. 90–91. Redlich in fact gives two translations of this passage, one in his version of the lecture as a whole and the other in his main text. I quote the latter.

22. See Ernst Hilmar, *Wozzeck von Alban Berg: Entstehung–erste Folge–Repressionen* (Vienna: Universal Edition, 1975), p. 21 and note.

23. Robin Holloway, *Debussy and Wagner* (London: Eulenburg Edition, 1979), p. 78.

24. Berg's lecture on *Wozzeck*, in Redlich, op. cit., p. 267; translation amended.

25. Ibid., p. 266.

26. See Reich, op. cit., pp. 120–2.

27. See Derrick Puffett, review of Carner, *Alban Berg*, *Tempo*, no. 117 (June 1976), p. 41.

28. See for example Egon Wellesz, *The Origins of Schönberg's Twelve-tone System* (Washington: Library of Congress, 1958), pp. 4–5, cited in Jim Samson, *Music in Transition* (London: J.M. Dent and Sons, 1977), p. 226; Rudolf Stephan, 'Aspekte der *Wozzeck*–Musik', *50 Jahre Wozzeck von Alban Berg*, p. 18. See also n. 30 below.

29. Hans Keller, 'The Eclecticism of *Wozzeck*', *Music Review*, vol. 12 (1951), p. 312.

30. See Rudolf Stephan, 'Zu Franz Schrekers *Vorspiel zu einem Drama*', *Franz Schreker: am Beginn der neuen Musik*, ed. Otto Kolleritsch (Graz: Universal Edition, 1978), pp. 120–21. Schreker's analysis of Act II of *Der ferne Klang* occurs in 'Entstehungsfragen der Oper', *Die Böttcherstrasse*, vol. 2, no. 2 (1930), pp. 15–17, which I have been unable to consult: it is cited in Stephan, 'Aspekte der *Wozzeck*–Musik', p. 20, n. 20.

31. Nicholas Chadwick, 'Franz Schreker's Orchestral Style and its Influence on Alban Berg', *Music Review*, vol. 35 (1974), pp. 29–46. It is difficult to obtain a clear view of Berg's relations with Schreker. Reich maintains that they enjoyed a lifelong friendship (Reich, op. cit., p. 35), but Carner paints a less rosy picture (Carner, op. cit., pp. 29–31, especially 31n.). In 1925 Berg heard *Der ferne Klang* and described it as 'awful' (*Alban Berg: Letters to his Wife*, p. 345).

32. Chadwick, op. cit., p. 33. See also Jürg Stenzl, 'Franz Schreker und Alban Berg: Bemerkungen zu den *Altenberg-Liedern* op. 4', *Franz Schreker: am Beginn der neuen Musik*, pp. 44–58.

33. Jarman, *The Music of Alban Berg*, pp. 54–5.

34. T. W. Adorno thought this passage was a parody of Schreker: *Alban Berg: Der Meister des kleinsten Übergangs* (Vienna: Verlag Elisabeth Lafite, 1968), p. 26.

35. Keller, op. cit., *Music Review*, vol. 13 (1952), p. 133.

36. Quoted in Reich, op. cit., p. 222.

37. Chadwick, op. cit., p. 32.

38. Joseph Kerman, *Opera as Drama* (New York: Vintage Books, 1952), pp. 230–32.

39. Ibid., p. 233.

40. Synopsis from Peter Franklin, *The Idea of Music: Schoenberg and Others* (London: Macmillan, 1985), pp. 146–7.

41. Alma Mahler, *Mein Leben* (Frankfurt: Fischer, 1960), p. 24.

42. Haidy Schreker-Bures, H. H. Stuckenschmidt, and Werner Oehlmann, *Franz Schreker* (Vienna: Verlag Elisabeth Lafite, 1970), p. 72.

43. *Alban Berg: Letters to his Wife*, pp. 329, 332. Berg was writing on the occasion of the first Vienna performance (22 November 1923).

44. Kerman, op. cit., p. 228.

45. Jarman, *The Music of Alban Berg*, p. 231.

46. Ibid.

47. Adorno remarked upon Berg's 'humour noir', Adorno, op. cit., p. 19.

48. Redlich, op. cit., p. 74.
49. See Kim H. Kowalke, *Kurt Weill in Europe* (Ann Arbor: University Microfilms International, 1979), p. 32.
50. See Peter Heyworth, *Otto Klemperer: his Life and Times*, vol. 1 (Cambridge: Cambridge University Press, 1983), Chaps 12–16.
51. See Arnold Schoenberg, 'Krenek's *Sprung über den Schatten*' (1923), *Style and Idea*, pp. 477–81.
52. See Derrick Puffett, 'Schoecks Opern: Ein Beitrag zur Frage der Gattung', *Musiktheater*, ed. Dorothea Baumann (Bonstetten: Theaterkultur Verlag, 1984), pp. 55–6.
53. See Werner Vogel, *Othmar Schoeck in Gespräch* (Zurich: Atlantis Verlag, 1965), p. 76. Berg probably heard a 1934 Vienna performance organized by Krenek (information supplied by Christopher Walton).
54. Rudolph Stephan distinguishes as many as twelve types of vocal writing: 'Zur Sprachmelodie in Alban Bergs *Lulu*-Musik', *Dichtung und Musik: Kaleidoskop ihrer Beziehungen*, ed. Günter Schnitzler (Stuttgart: Cotta, 1979), pp. 246–64.
55. Quoted and trans. in Norman Del Mar, *Richard Strauss: a Critical Commentary on his Life and Works*, vol. 2 (London: Barrie and Jenkins, 1978), p. 261.
56. See for example Jarman, *The Music of Alban Berg*, pp. 187–9, 198–222.
57. Robin Holloway, 'The Complete *Lulu*', *Tempo*, no. 129 (June 1979), p. 37.
58. Jarman, 'Weill and Berg', p. 156. Clive Bennett argues that Berg was also influenced by Max Brand: 'Maschinist Hopkins: A Father for Lulu?', *Musical Times*, vol. 127 (1986), p. 484.
59. Kurt Weill, 'Alban Berg: *Wozzeck*', *Kurt Weill: Ausgewählte Schriften*, ed. David Drew (Frankfurt: Suhrkamp, 1975), pp. 153–4.
60. Another moment of parody comes in bar 760 of Act II, when the Athlete is picturing himself in pink tights. At this moment the orchestra lands on a '6-4' chord reminiscent of the Silver Rose music in *Der Rosenkavalier*.
61. Pierre Boulez, '*Lulu*: the Second Opera', *Orientations* (London: Faber and Faber, 1986), pp. 393–4.
62. David Ewen, *A Journey to Greatness: the Life and Music of George Gershwin* (London: Allen, 1956), p. 120.

BETWEEN INSTINCT AND REFLECTION: BERG, OPERA AND THE VIENNESE DICHOTOMY

CHRISTOPHER HAILEY

There are few cities in which music assumes such central importance in the municipal identity as Vienna. Quite aside from the impressive facts of their music history, the Viennese take pride in the utter assurance of their musical instincts. Their fabled nonchalance, cosy *Gemütlichkeit*, and easy sensuality, matters of course in the conduct of daily life are articles of faith in making music. The lilting rhythms, the uncanny sense for phrasing, the dark mellow sound of the brass and woodwind, the sweet, full tone of the strings, the expressive, plaintive character of the Viennese sound conjured up by a host of familiar adjectives—*süss, einschmeichelnd, innig, fein, weich, warm, gefällig, sinnlich*—these are qualities that create music, elements that make composers but incidental mediators.

Vienna's native culture is insular, the product of a unique constellation of geographic and cultural factors. 'There is different blood in Vienna', wrote Paul Stefan in 1921. 'The South and especially Italy plays its part, the peoples, customs, and lifestyles of the East are mixed in, along the soft lines of the landscape, along the mysterious, primeval current between East and West'.[1] Viennese music veers accordingly between urbane elegance and the spirit of the Austrian hinterlands, between the grace of the waltz, the gaudy splendours of the march, the spritely buoyancy of the operetta, and the homely sentimentality of the Schrammel quartet, the lyric intimacy of a Schubert song, or the cosmic majesty of a Bruckner symphony.

During the course of the 19th century the insularity of Vienna's native culture—as opposed to her court culture—was challenged by those processes that transformed the city from a Mediaeval walled fortress of several hundred thousand to a modern metropolis of nearly two million. During the so-called *Gründerjahre* a generation of industrialists and statesmen, learned professionals, and enlightened aristocrats constructed a solid, pragmatic world upon the broken ideals of 1848. They were joined by a generation of immigrants who came to Vienna from the eastern provinces aspiring to be assimilated into the city's well-ordered, self-assured liberal bourgeois society.

These immigrants were a constant reminder that Vienna was the capital of a multinational state and that her culture was somehow expected to embody the supraconsciousness, the common identity of that polyglot empire. Superimposed, then, upon Vienna's unabashed provincialism was the lingering legacy of the Holy Roman Empire. This is perhaps best illustrated in the ostentation of the *Ringstrasse*, where the mixture of pseudo Gothic, Renaissance, Baroque, and Classical motifs bespeaks the need to legitimize Vienna's sovereign control over its present through self-conscious identification with hallowed traditions of the past. At its worst this impulse degenerated into pompous historicism; at its best there emerged a stylistic synthesis that transcended national and ethnic boundaries.

In music the 'Viennese classics'—above all Beethoven and Brahms—provided just such a formal and syntactical vocabulary for a truly international style.[2] In Vienna, however, where the letter, if not the spirit, of the Classical style came to be jealously guarded by the city's academic institutions, this precious patrimony also represented a weighty burden. It was, in a sense, a legacy imposed from without, a kind of masculine sobriety grafted on to the sensuous spontaneity of Vienna's indigenous musical heritage. It was the difference between Johannes Brahms and Johann Strauss, between the rigours of a sonata and the lyric inspiration of a song. In the early 19th century the contrast between the motivic concentration of Beethoven and the melodic expansiveness of Schubert was an indication of a gulf scarcely present a generation earlier. By the early 20th century the unresolved tension of Vienna's dual inheritance would prove one of the well-springs of the city's musical culture.

It was Gustav Mahler who first brought these dichotomies into sharp focus and made them a central issue for his time. With his famous dictum 'Tradition ist Schlamperei' ('tradition is slovenliness') he attacked the Viennese on a sensitive point, one of the unassailed bastions of local pride: their musical instincts. Mahler demanded disciplined self-reflection of his musicians. But he was seeking not so much the elimination of Viennese traditions as their conscious articulation. Paul Stefan wrote in 1921: 'What it means to experience music, to make music on the grand scale, as well in all details, phrasing, emphasis, metre, rests, tempo, dynamics, rhythm, melodic delivery, and so forth, all this we first learned from him'.[3]

The tension between instinct and reflection also characterizes Mahler's achievement as a composer. With his near exclusive preoccupation with the song and the symphony—forms representing the poles of Vienna's musical culture—he confronts the dichotomy head on. Viennese and Austrian composers from Schubert to Bruckner and Wolf had found it difficult to reconcile these two worlds and their most ambitious instrumental works betray palpable insecurity with the constraints of classical form. Mahler, in his insistent self-reference and audacious eclecticism, sought to make the unconscious conscious by forging a style that flaunted that schism. He was a composer, as Adolf Weissmann wrote, who 'for one last time united Old Vienna and New Vienna, folk music and art music in exemplary fashion'.[4] Not since Mozart's *Magic Flute* had any composer combined such diverse musical realms with such reckless abandon while still claiming the prerogatives of high art.

Mahler's appeal among the Viennese was broad, but the disparate elements of his works, the extremes between philosophical pretension and wry humour, between cultured restraint and rustic sentimentality, could be alienating. 'One is continually enticed to ponder,' wrote Walter Schrenk in 1924, 'the positive and negative aspects of this oeuvre in its strange suspension between naïveté and supreme refinement.'[5] Mahler attempted no reconciliation, achieved no synthesis; he simply laid bare contradictions which for many Viennese composers struck uncomfortably close to home. To the intellectual there were disturbing breaches in musical taste, to the more naïve an unsettling ambiguity of intent. It is well known, for instance, that Arnold Schoenberg's reverence for Mahler vacillated widely; indeed, his determined defence of Mahler against the charges of banality and sentimentality only serves to underline his uneasiness. Franz Schreker, on the other hand, seems to have been less disturbed by Mahler's sentimentality than by his irony, as he once implied in a letter to Paul Bekker:

> I'm not really sure yet what I think. I understand his works and yet I don't feel them. ... Perhaps in Mahler one also finds the naïveté of Schubert and Bruckner (the Austrians), but there is so much else, quite contradictory there too, so that I don't really know what is genuine, what I should believe.[6]

It is revealing that Alban Berg embraced the dichotomous nature of Mahler's music without apparent reservation. True, his formative years coincided exactly with Mahler's tenure at the Court Opera, but his ready acceptance of the premises of Mahler's music had less to do with early exposure than to his own experience of the contradictions of Vienna's musical environment.

In many ways Berg was a typical representative of Vienna's privileged upper middle class. He was an 'insider' in a way that Mahler, Schoenberg, and Schreker could never be. Though, like Schoenberg and Schreker, the son of an immigrant father, Berg's father did not come from one of the Jewish enclaves of the east, but from bourgeois, Catholic Bavaria. Berg enjoyed the advantages of his class, including a *Gymnasium* eduation and leisurely summer vacations on the family estate. Upon graduation (delayed because of having to repeat two classes) he spent two years in a government job, but after his mother inherited a substantial fortune, he was able to live from the part-time duties of managing the family's Viennese property. The Berg of these years was self-indulgent and imbued with neither energy nor ambition. By his carefully mannered bearing and appearance one might have mistaken him for a supercilious aesthete, which, indeed he might have been had it not been for his passion for music.

Berg began composing with very little formal training. He was the quintessential amateur, the dilettante who had grown up in a household where cultivation of the arts belonged to the innocent pastimes of youth. His more-or-less instinctual approach to composition was transformed by his studies with Schoenberg. Berg recalled those studies, which began in the autumn of 1904, as a moment of awakening, the beginning of self-reflection; as he wrote in a letter to Schoenberg of 4 December 1930: 'At that time, before I came to you (at the age of 20), I hadn't bothered with study at all, but simply bungled at "composing" until I found out from you that one can also *learn* something.'[7]

Berg's ready dismissal of his own by no means insignificant beginnings points to an important mechanism in his artistic personality. By the time he came to Schoenberg, Berg's fundamental musical tastes and attitudes had been formed, and yet, because of his scanty formal training, Schoenberg assumed forbidding authority. Moreover, Schoenberg, himself an autodidact and very conscious of having acquired his learning outside of Vienna's official academic institutions, tended to reinforce his authority by an aggressive identification with Classical tradition. As a consequence, all of his students came to feel the weight of Vienna's Classical legacy with particular force. For Berg, Schoenberg and the legacy he represented were, in psychological terms, a kind of super-ego that caused him to submit his strong musical instincts and aesthetic judgments to continual scrutiny and revision.[8] Schoenberg's constraining hand is present everywhere in Berg's works, as are Berg's efforts to maintain a degree of independence within those constraints.

Nowhere is this more readily apparent than in Berg's relationship to opera. Like most of Vienna's youth, Berg had cut his musical teeth at the Court Opera in the inexpensive seats of the fourth gallery, one of the primary institutions of Viennese cultural education. In the fourth gallery Vienna's young learned the repertoire, were initiated into performance traditions, and developed their musical instincts. In 1909 Hermann Menkes captured the essence of the fourth gallery when he wrote:

> a small state in the theatrical empire, a firmly established group within that ill defined mass one calls the public. In Viennese theatre the fourth gallery is the court of first and sometimes even final appeal. Below in the stalls and in the boxes are the representatives of society, the *arrivés*; high above is the future, the essential, the strongest resonance for every artistic act.[9]

The fourth gallery is an evocative metaphor for that unique Viennese continuum linking audience and performers, tradition and its cultivation, heritage and its inheritors.[10] It is above all the perfect expression of the intimate and unfettered relationship between the Viennese and their theatrical passion.

Despite opera's central role in Viennese cultural life, the history of *Viennese* opera is striking in its discontinuity. The comfortable integration of opera and instrumental works in the Classical tradition of the 18th century is notably absent in the Classical legacy of the 19th. Opera occupies a minor position in Beethoven's oeuvre, no place at all in the works of Bruckner and Brahms, and was a source of continuing frustration for Schubert, Wolf, and Mahler. Neither Viennese Classicism nor the native culture provided viable models for indigenous operatic forms and Viennese composers found themselves buffeted by the prevailing tastes of Vienna's fickle audiences. Seeking in vain to find a voice of their own, they found instead a Goldmark.[11]

The situation was quite different a generation later. One has only to think of Franz Schreker, Erich Wolfgang Korngold, Alexander von Zemlinsky, Wilhelm Kienzl, Julius Bittner, Egon Wellesz, Hans Gál, Franz Schmidt, and Ernst Krenek, to realize the extent to which opera was a central preoccupation of early 20th-century Viennese music history. In Austria, as in Germany, the works of Wagner had provided much of the impetus for this renewal of operatic aspiration. But whereas in Germany Wagner's music dramas spawned an endless number of imitators, in Vienna the natural receptivity to French, Italian, and Slavic, as well as German impulses (above all, Richard Strauss), encouraged a synthesis only partially indebted to Wagner.

Most important, Wagner's influence in Vienna was offset by the pervasive presence of the city's Classical tradition, with its implied aesthetic challenge to opera. Writing in 1921, Richard Specht underlined that tension when he observed: 'it is a curious phenomenon that nowhere is the realm of "absolute music" quite as emphatically and wilfully maintained as in Vienna, the home of the richly imaginative, sensuous, colourful theatrical spirit.'[12] Nowhere, certainly, is the confrontation between the naïve joys of the theatre and the rarified abstraction of absolute forms more painful and tortured than in the works of Schoenberg and his circle.

Schoenberg wrote four stage works, and dramatic plans occupied him throughout his life, but he was by nature inherently hostile to the theatrical experience. He once stated as much in a 1912 aphorism, when he said of dramatic music: 'I find it more trouble than it's worth to immerse myself in the inner motivation of people indifferent to me, in order to portray them through their actions.'[13] Schoenberg rightly singles out empathy with contradictory characters, some of whom may be quite different from the author, as one of the prerequisites of the effective dramatist. Certainly neither *Die glückliche Hand* nor *Moses und Aron* contains anything even remotely resembling character development, both being pedestals for the exposition of personal philosophical ruminations.[14] But Schoenberg's antipathy to theatre was based on more than the bother of concerning himself with characters who did not interest him. In a letter to Berg of 5 December 1929 he comes very close to admitting his blatant disregard for the fundamentally collaborative nature of the theatrical experience. Schoenberg concluded of Clemens Krauss, who had not acknowledged receipt of *Von Heute auf Morgen*:

> In other words he doesn't like it: but that's nothing new. That's what's good about it! That is just what he should expect: that is precisely where one must begin! Or doesn't he like the text? Also a mistake; one should have more faith in

me than in oneself: if I liked it, it is good and, most important: the opera is good. Surely it would be a sad state if I couldn't take any text and write the kind of opera in which one sees and hears only what I intend and becomes blind and deaf to all else.

There is a good bit of pique and defensiveness in these words, but they reflect an ingrained attitude in Schoenberg, which could not help influencing his opera aesthetic. Nothing in Schoenberg's operas is supplicative. He places extraordinary demands upon his listeners' ability to follow him along complex lines of intellectual argument. The thought of undermining that argument with extraneous ideas, not to mention concessions to audience appeal, was clearly repugnant to a man who equated artistic integrity with proprietary autonomy and absolute control.

If Schoenberg paid the price for such 'integrity' with four remarkably untheatrical stage works,[15] one can well imagine his ambivalence toward the very *theatricality*—and success—of the operas of his student, Berg. Schoenberg lacked genuine sympathy for Berg's decision to set *Wozzeck* and *Lulu*, both of which aroused in him moral and aesthetic scruples. Beyond that, however, he had misgivings about reconciling the broad strokes of theatrical gesture with the kind of musical precision to which he was devoted. After seeing *Wozzeck* for the first time he wrote a card to Berg that is curiously lukewarm in its praise. He complains about the stark contrasts of the sets and lighting and the theatricality of the performance, which he found imprecise and termed 'an orgy of temperament', but he also delivers a rather revealing criticism of the score by objecting to the fact 'that almost every scene builds to a great orchestral *fff*'.[16] The fact that this is rarely the case in Berg's score merely points up Schoenberg's hypersensitivity to this kind of obvious music-dramatic gesture.

Alban Berg considered himself first and foremost an opera composer, but his relationship to the genre was not unproblematic, and clearly reflects Schoenberg's influence. Adorno relates in his Berg biography that he spent long hours after the *Wozzeck* première comforting Berg over his success. According to Adorno, Berg felt that the approval of an official audience was both incomprehensible and an argument against the work.[17] These misgivings may have been half in jest, but probably only half; they are reminiscent of Schoenberg's sarcastic response to the report of an enthusiastic reception given to a performance of his Wind Quintet: 'Then they didn't understand it.'

Schoenberg's disdain for audiences, apparent in his attitude towards theatre, reveals the operation of the Viennese dichotomy on another level. His Society for Private Musical Performances (1918–22), which admitted only members (and no critics) and strictly prohibited any exhibition of approval or disapproval, introduced a crucial element of self-conscious reflection into the relationship between composer, performer, and listener. On the one hand, the closed membership of the Society and Schoenberg's injunctions against audience response simply represented the desire to avoid the scandals that had marred earlier performances of his own music. On the other hand, by removing unwanted distractions one could concentrate audience attention upon new and unfamiliar works. Painstaking rehearsal, a legacy of the Mahler era, and frequent programme repetitions assured the primacy of the work of art as an object of individual contemplation. Understanding, then, was the criterion of performance success, short of which any audience response, good or bad, was irrelevant.

The frustration that led Schoenberg to such extremes is succinctly stated in a letter to Berg of 6 December 1920 in which he reports on a performance of his String Quartet no. 1 in Holland:

> The whole thing made an excellent impression. It was successful, very successful, in fact; [the success] was based, however, primarily on the 'timbral effects': harmonics, pizzicato, *sul ponticello*, etc., and the Adagios. The audience here seems a long way from grasping the 'symphonic' and melodic qualities. Insofar as it is 'well-disposed', it responds only to 'mood' and 'poetry', while the modern-minded cling to the abstruse and only enjoy it if it remains unclear to them. The usual fate of my music.

To the extent that the underlying musical argument remains hidden, the work remains misunderstood and the response largely invalidated. It is therefore not surprising that Schoenberg and his circle found it more difficult to cope with success than with failure. Failure was a self-fulfilling prophecy, moral vindication over an uncomprehending mob.[18] Success was a tragic misunderstanding for which there was no consolation.[19]

It is not difficult to see how Schoenberg's distrust of positive audience response might give rise, as Adorno implies of Berg, to a distrust of the work of art itself—that is to say, of those elements in a work whose appeal lies outside a composer's autonomous control. This might on the one hand apply to a popular work that a composer would like to repudiate. Berg, for instance, found the success of his music in a 1907 concert of works by Schoenberg's students 'more painful than pleasing', and was frankly embarrassed that what he considered his 'weakest' song, 'Die Nachtigall', garnered the most applause.[20] Schoenberg, on the other hand, was disturbed that the unfamiliar timbral qualities of his String Quartet no. 1 might exert their own independent titillating appeal. In both instances we see a distrust of *effect*, intended or unintended, which for the Schoenberg circle was tantamount to a corruption of *meaning*.[21]

But one suspects that Berg's misgivings about his success with *Wozzeck* reflected less his scepticism regarding the audience's comprehension or even concern about possible implications for the value of his work, than his ambivalence about the medium itself. Opera is by definition a communal art form and audience response an essential ingredient in the equation of theatrical achievement. Hence every stage work is a speculation upon audience response. Berg's success represented an awkward moment of self-revelation, which struck at the very heart of an intense conflict of loyalties. The impulse that made Berg an opera composer—and not, like Schoenberg, a composer who wrote operas—the impulse that led him to create a uniquely synthetic musical language capable of moving an 'official' opera (and concert) audience, stood at odds with some of the fundamental premises of Schoenberg's aesthetic sensibility. It also brought him far closer to a number of Viennese contemporaries outside the so-called 'Second Viennese School' than he or his apologists cared to admit.

The conflict in Berg between his inherent identification with the theatre and the conscious denial of that impulse, between his natural instincts and their revision is perhaps best exemplified in his relationship to Franz Schreker. Berg knew Schreker well, and for a time the two men were quite close. In 1910–11 Berg prepared the piano score of the second and third acts of Schreker's opera *Der ferne Klang*, 'whose absolute success,' Berg wrote in 1928, 'I already predicted—perhaps before anyone else—on the basis of studying this, at that time, completely novel score'.[22]

Der ferne Klang was a work which exercised an enormous influence on Berg's dramatic works. *Wozzeck* and *Lulu* are populated with characters who could be reincarnations, musical and dramatic *Doppelgänger* of characters from Schreker's opera.[23] Further similarities of mood, milieu, atmosphere, musical gesture, and dramaturgic forms are readily apparent and led one early critic to exclaim:

> Stylistically, Alban Berg's *Wozzeck* comes directly from Franz Schreker's *Der ferne Klang*. This work occupies an exceptional place in Schreker's creative output, analogous to *Elektra* among Strauss' works. On a purely intellectual level, it is a stimulus of the highest order for the thinking operatic production of today.[24]

Yet when Berg actually saw *Der ferne Klang* in 1925 in Berlin, his succinct reaction in a letter to his wife was that 'the opera is awful'.[25]

In his Berg biography Adorno points to what he interprets as a Schreker parody in one passage of *Wozzeck*, observing that 'one usually parodies that to which—however ambivalently—one is drawn'.[26] Berg's ambivalence has to do with the immediacy of Schreker's operas—a certain theatricality which accounts for their extraordinary effectiveness in the opera house—as well as with Schreker's seeming lack of restraint in crossing aesthetic boundaries. Berg's attitude is captured in a letter to Schoenberg in which he describes Schreker's dramatic reading of his libretto for *Die Gezeichneten*: 'Not long ago I heard Schreker give a reading of his IIIrd drama, parts of which I liked very much and which is incredibly effective, powerful, and skillfully done—, granted, also a bit kitschy'.[27]

This hasty disclaimer was not just for Schoenberg's benefit, but bound up with complex cross-currents in Berg's own aesthetic make-up. Like Mahler's symphonies, Schreker's operas embrace the awkward discrepancies of Viennese culture. They present a juxtaposition of the petty tawdriness of daily life with the sublime ecstasies of romantic longing, the high tone of drama with the sentimental language of popular culture. Accordingly their musical vocabulary is an arresting and unsettling combination of revolutionary daring and naïveté —sometimes recalling the 'banality' and irony of Mahler's symphonies, at other times the lush style of Vienna's popular lighter music. Unlike Mahler, Schreker does not restrict himself to the ideal, abstract plane of instrumental music, but embraces the earthy, sensual appeal of opera and of theatrical effect. His librettos tap into the eruptive sensuality of Viennese culture and explore what John Barish, in another context, has called the 'anarchy of sexual instincts', which can threaten the class and moral distinctions of a fixed social order.[28] Moreover, Schreker's aesthetic preoccupation with sensory perception, above all with the alluring, shimmering, beguiling world of timbral effects that are conjured up by the very title of his first opera, seems to undermine Classical ideals of formal and thematic coherence. Schreker's art was a source of both fascination and horror to his contemporaries. No other 20th-century operas enjoyed such spectacular success or generated such vehement condemnation. Berg was too much the product of Viennese society, its repressive conventions and its cultivation of appearances, good breeding, and good taste, not to find Schreker's operas disturbing. He himself could never permit himself to breach the 'high tone' of cultural discourse, whose musical limits had been set for him by Mahler and Schoenberg and whose literary arbiter was Karl Kraus. While the subject matter of *Wozzeck* and *Lulu* and Berg's plans to compose *Und Pippa tanzt*[29] demonstrate the intersection of interests with Schreker, Berg was careful to preserve his bearing in navigating such precarious aesthetic shoals. The productions in 1905 of Wedekind's *Erdgeist* and in 1914 of Büchner's *Woyzeck* were cultural 'events', directly associated with a small, progressive audience representing the cream of Vienna's intellectual élite (a significant factor reinforcing Berg's determination to set these plays over objections by Schoenberg and others). The choice of established works of drama served to lift both the librettos and their musical settings out of the sordid domain of operatic theatricality and into the realm of literature and musical drama. Thus Berg's exploration of the squalid circumstances of the life and death of Wozzeck and Lulu, as well as the pervasive flirtation with the theatrical motif in Wedekind's *Erdgeist* cycle—including the character of Lulu herself, whose protean nature is the very soul of theatrical transformation—were like a sanctioned bite of forbidden fruit. While Berg may have been perplexed by the success of *Wozzeck* with a traditional opera audience, he had nonetheless taken every precaution to see that his opera was 'fit for good society', as Schreker's rather more impulsive works were not.

Berg's compositional response to opera reflects the same distancing process, and this is precisely the point at which *Der ferne Klang* exercised its greatest influence. Schreker the dramatist had written his libretto for Schreker the musician. 'I was fascinated by the possibilities inherent in the sharpest contrasts,' he wrote in a 1930 lecture.[30] 'I was challenged by the second act (at that time I was already a respectable artist), by the technical contrapuntal problems of the intermingling of the instrumental and choral ensembles of a large dance establishment'. In that same lecture Schreker advised that one of the most important considerations in writing or adapting a libretto is architectonic, 'shaping the whole to a musical form'. Not only would the Act II bordello scene of *Der ferne Klang* have a decided influence on the tavern scenes of *Wozzeck*, but Schreker's conscious use of forms drawn from absolute music to structure the first and second acts of his opera served as the model for a similar procedure in *Wozzeck*.

Berg's own preoccupation with the technical and formal aspects of his operas, which of course reaches deep into the compositional process itself, reflects something of the same awareness of what was expected of the 'respectable artist'. But the painstaking and self-conscious care with which Berg clothed theatrical gesture in elaborate organizational schemes also reflects, amongst other things, his need to reconcile the lower impulses of the theatre with the requirements of 'high art', the sensual self-indulgence of his Viennese heritage with the discipline of the Classical legacy. There was beneath it all a genuine discomfort with the very irrational qualities in opera which Schreker wholeheartedly embraced.

The level of Berg's achievement can be gauged by the distance between the poles, for Schoenberg had inculcated in Berg a fanaticism for both purely musical autonomy and the conscious interplay of meaning. The value Berg himself placed on these qualities is evident in his essays on and guides to Schoenberg's music; it is also contained in a letter to Schoenberg, in which, in a discussion of the *Gurrelieder*, he wrote that:

> all great works are distinguished from the lesser ones in that they are saturated with music, like full, ripened fruit, ever ready to be savoured in complete freshness. That's my yardstick: for example, I just took a look at Schreker's 5 Songs ... —when I heard them at your place in Ober St. Veit I thought they weren't bad. Today they meant *absolutely nothing* to me! It, *too*, is music, but not music in the above sense. Not only do I feel this in my soul, but I could explain it theoretically as well!![31]

Theoretical rationalization, however, cannot explain away effect, even where one would like to believe that that effect is purchased at the expense of musical substance. Effect and success have their own dynamic, for they involve the creative collaboration of the audience. Schreker, who had a healthy respect for both the audience and success, once addressed the misconceptions and hypocrisy that surrounded the relationship of the contemporary composer to the audience:

> Some people believe that the artist writes a work that they don't understand only in order to—upset them. What a mistake! Years of work—and then—such paltry satisfaction! Others believe that we're not even interested in success. That we feel above it, that controversy is music to our ears. Oh, don't

believe it! We may smile about it—but we suffer.[32]

For Schreker, the Romantic, art meant the communication of experience, and his experience was of such an intensely sensual nature that his quest lay in achieving precision of effect.[33] In this quest the audience was always the final judge:

> But we, who feel and experience music, have within us membranes that either resonate or remain unresponsive—and there you have the secret of effect [*Wirkung*]! The receiver, the listener, is an instrument with its part to play and if it refuses to participate [*Mitwirkung*], you will try in vain to make us believe: This is art, music![34]

Berg, who once wrote of the Act III interlude in *Wozzeck* that it was 'an appeal to the audience as representatives of humanity',[35] laid far more importance upon effect and audience response, upon *Wirkung* and *Mitwirkung*, than he would probably have cared to admit. While he may have distrusted the 'ever-present' immediacy of Schreker, he was also disturbed by the didactic tone in much of Schoenberg's later music, as well as by the self-sufficiency of Webern's perfect, impenetrable miniatures.[36]

Berg recognized that in the theatre *meaning* could prove a detriment to *communication*, undermining the relationship of music to drama—and that of the audience to music. In his essay 'Why is Schoenberg's Music so Difficult to Understand?' Berg draws this implicit conclusion when he writes that music that employs in such profusion the 'possibilities bequeathed from the classical masters', that is so abundant in 'those properties we recognize as virtues in all good music'—that such music, 'precisely because of its excessive richness in all musical disciplines, can only be as difficult to understand as indeed Schoenberg's music is'.[37]

What may be laudable in a string quartet can prove fatal in a stage work, where the demands of intelligibility require clean delineation. It was a source of great pride for Berg that he was so successful in concealing the 'excessive richness' of his first opera and he insisted that

> from the moment when the curtain rises until it descends for the last time, there must not be anyone in the audience who notices anything of these various fugues and inventions, suite movements and sonata movements, variations and passacaglias. Nobody must be filled with anything else except the idea of the opera—which goes far beyond the individual fate of Wozzeck.[38]

Berg once summed up the ideal relationship of music to drama when he asked if it were not enough to make 'beautiful music for good theatre works, or,—better said: to make beautiful music in such a way that—in spite of that—the result is good theatre?'[39] What Berg achieves he achieves in spite of the layered meaning of his music, its density, its autonomy. He maintains a distance that seldom allows dramatic gesture to be overwhelmed by compositional detail. He establishes a communality with his audience without resorting to either dictation or manipulation, speaking to the fourth gallery as one who has been there.

The central importance of opera in early 20th-century Viennese music history lies with the very hybrid nature of the genre which, like Vienna herself, was nestled between the compass points of sensuality and intellectual reflection, sentiment and refinement. Viennese opera was both the product of these contradictory impulses and the principal vehicle for exploring the social, intellectual, and artistic questions they raised. To be sure, the dichotomies present in Viennese culture are evident elsewhere in music history, but seldom has their tension been so productive or been embodied so variously by artists of such stature. If Gustav Mahler brought conscious articulation to the instinctual, then it is one of Alban Berg's supreme accomplishments to have embraced and transmitted the warm ambience of Viennese inheritance without compromising the high art of his inherited legacy, to have found *his* resolution of the Viennese dichotomy by making the conscious unconscious.

Notes

1. Paul Stefan, *Neue Musik und Wien* (Vienna, Leipzig, Zurich: E. P. Tal & Co., 1921), p. 8. Unless otherwise noted, all translations are by the author.
2. In his study, *Alexander Zemlinsky* (Vienna: Verlag Elisabeth Lafite, 1978), p. 11, Horst Weber illustrates how this international style fulfilled a useful cultural-political function in Austria's multinational culture, where nationalistic tendencies (such as those evident in Wagner's works or in the works of such non-German Wagnerians as Smetana) were understandably discouraged.
3. Stefan, op. cit., p. 22.
4. Adolph Weissman, 'Österreichische Musikwoche in Berlin', *Musikblätter des Anbruch*, vol. 5, nos 6–7 (June–July 1923), p. 182
5. Walter Schrenk, *Richard Strauss und die neue Musik* (Berlin: Wegweiser Verlag, 1924), p. 172.
6. Schreker to Bekker, 22 August 1918, Library of Congress.
7. Julianne Brand, Christopher Hailey, and Donald Harris, eds and trans., *The Berg-Schoenberg Correspondence: Selected Letters* (New York: W.W. Norton, 1987, p.407.
8. It is painfully evident from their early correspondence that this psychological mechanism was operative on a personal level as well, for Schoenberg frequently admonished Berg to change in all areas of his life.
9. Hermann Menkes, review of Oskar Rosenfeld, *Die vierte Galerie*, in *Neues Wiener Journal*, vol. 18, no. 6024 (31 July 1910), p. 13.
10. See Christopher Hailey, 'Die vierte Galerie: Voraussetzungen für die Wiener Avantgarde um 1910', *Bericht über den 2. Kongress der Internationalen Schönberg-Gesellschaft*, ed. Rudolf Stephan and Sigrid Wiesmann (Vienna: Verlag Elisabeth Lafite, 1986), pp. 242ff.
11. This is in no way intended as a disparagement of Goldmark's achievements, which are most interesting precisely where they reveal the uneasy synthesis of the diverse elements of his compositional personality.

12. Richard Specht, 'Neue Musik in Wien', *Musikblätter des Anbruch*, vol. 3, nos 13–14 (September 1921), pp. 245–6.

13. Arnold Schoenberg, *Der Ruf* (February 1912).

14. Schoenberg's insistence upon the primacy of his own personality is illustrated in a letter to Berg of 9 August 1930 in which he defends the libretto of *Moses und Aron* against any suspected similarities with Strindberg's *Moses*:

> my main idea, as well as the many, many explicitly stated and symbolically represented subsidiary ideas, all that is such an integral part of my own personality that Strindberg couldn't possibly have presented anything bearing even a superficial similarity. ... Today I scarcely remember what is mine, what is still mine: but one thing you must grant me (I insist on that): everything I have ever written bears a certain intrinsic similarity with myself.

Brand, Hailey, and Harris, op. cit.

15. This is not to dispute the effectiveness of a work like *Moses und Aron* as a musical and philosophical argument, but to state that staging adds only incidentally to its argument and effectiveness; hence its proximity to oratorio, where dramatic effect is conveyed through the expressive and evocative power of theatrically static forces.

16. Schoenberg to Berg, 11 January 1926, concerning a performance of the orginal Berlin production of *Wozzeck* under Erich Kleiber, Brand, Hailey and Harris, op cit .

17. Theodor W. Adorno, *Berg: Der Meister des kleinsten Übergangs* (Vienna: Verlag Elisabeth Lafite, 1968), p. 18.

18. This attitude is illustrated by a letter to Schoenberg of 23 December 1911 in which Berg hoped the negative reviews of the premiere of *Friede auf Erden* might bolster Schoenberg's self-confidence 'by way of *negation*: namely that you perceive the *true and eternal value* of your works by the very distance between their wise message and the stupid, monotonous drivel of the base'. Brand, Hailey, and Harris, op. cit.

19. Berg's relative popularity during his lifetime placed him in a decidedly awkward position, neatly summed up by Adorno when he observed that Schoenberg envied Berg his successes as much as Berg envied Schoenberg his failures. See Adorno, op. cit., p. 36.

20. From a letter to Frida Semler of 18 November 1907, quoted in Willi Reich, *Alban Berg*, trans. Cornelius Cardew (London: Thames and Hudson, 1965), p. 24. Berg went on: 'So you will not be surprised, Miss Frida, that I have no respect for the "crowd" and am happy when I can keep out of their way.'

21. In his famous essay, 'Why is Schoenberg's Music so Difficult to Understand?', Berg asserted that he would answer the question without recourse to 'philosophical or literary' arguments, stating rather,

> I am concerned solely with what happens musically in Schoenberg's works; the compositional mode of expression which, like the language of any work of art (which we have to accept as a premise), must be considered the only one adequate to the object to be represented. To understand this language through and through and grasp it in all its details ... to follow a piece of music as one follows the words of a poem in a language that one has mastered through and through means the same—for one who possesses the gift of thinking musically—as understanding the work itself. (Reich, op. cit., p. 189).

22. Alban Berg, 'Für Franz Schreker', *Musikblätter des Anbruch*, vol. 10, nos 3–4

(March–April 1928), p. 86.

23. Virtually all of Schreker's female protagonists bear detailed comparison with Lulu and Marie, especially Grete in *Der ferne Klang*, the Princess in *Das Spielwerk*, Carlotta in *Die Gezeichneten*, Els in *Der Schatzgräber*, and Lisa in *Christophorus*.

24. Ernst Viebig, 'Alban Bergs *Wozzeck*', *Die Musik*, vol. 15 (1923), pp. 506–11. Nicholas Chadwick's article, 'Franz Schreker's Orchestral Style and its Influence on Alban Berg', *Music Review* vol. 35 (1974), pp. 29–46, offers a good starting point, but in no way exhausts the subject of Schreker's stylistic influence on Berg, especially on the formal and dramaturgic aspects of Berg's stage works.

25. Alban Berg to Helene Berg, 1 December 1925. This observation, which was excised from the German edition, is included in *Alban Berg, Letters to his Wife*, ed., trans., and annot. Bernard Grun (New York: St Martin's Press, 1971), p. 348.

26. Adorno, op. cit., p. 26.

27. Alban Berg to Arnold Schoenberg, 8 May 1912, Brand, Hailey, and Harris, op. cit.

28. John Barish, *The Antitheatrical Prejudice* (Berkeley and Los Angeles: University of California Press, 1981), p. 85. In his thought-provoking study, Barish outlines the recurring arguments of the antitheatrical bias from ancient times to the present. Discussing William Prynne's antitheatrical treatise, *Historiomastix* (1633), Barish points to 'the author's fearful aversion to anything ... that might suggest active or interested sexuality, this being equated with femininity, with weakness, with the yielding of feeling, and consequently with the destruction of all assured props and boundaries.'

29. Schreker also wanted to set Hauptmann's *Und Pippa tanzt*; his second opera, *Das Spielwerk*, is to some degree the result of that preoccupation.

30. Franz Schreker, 'Entstehungsfragen der Oper', *Die Böttcherstrasse*, vol. 2, no. 2 (1930), pp. 15–17.

31. Berg to Schoenberg, 5 June 1912, Brand, Hailey, and Harris, op. cit.

32. From aphorisms first published in *Zwischenakt: Blätter der Nationaltheater* (Munich), vol. 1, no. 3 (February 1919), pp. 3–6.

33. Ernst Decsey once remarked in a review of Schreker's *Der Schatzgräber*:

> At one point in his score he instructs the celesta player: 'Play precisely, don't fake it!' This is characteristic for the precision work of his opera, which is full of intuitive, amorphous timbral experience. And herein lie the hazards of a performance, especially for a repertoire stage. It must wed machine-like precision with the inspired freedom of musical performance. (*Musikblätter des Anbruch*, vol. 4, nos 7–8 (April 1922), p. 119)

34. Franz Schreker, 'Die Oper wie ich sie erstrebe', as quoted in Christopher Hailey, 'Franz Schreker in seinen Schriften', *Österreichische Musikzeitschrift*, vol. 33, no. 3 (March 1978), pp. 119–127.

35. In Berg's 1929 lecture on *Wozzeck*; reprinted in H. F. Redlich, *Alban Berg: The Man and his Music* (London: John Calder, 1957), p. 326.

36. In his discussion of Berg's relationship to Webern and Schoenberg, Adorno (op. cit., pp. 35ff.) makes a similar point and notes, in addition, that Berg found in Schoenberg's early twelve-note works a certain 'lack of expressive content'.

37. Willi Reich, *Alban Berg: mit Bergs eigenen Schriften und Beiträgen von Theodor Wiesengrund-Adorno und Ernst Krenek* (Vienna: Herbert Reichner Verlag, 1937), p. 151.

38. Reich, op. cit., p. 66.

39. Alban Berg, 'Das Opernproblem', republished in Reich, op. cit., p. 174.

THE SKETCHES FOR *LULU*

PATRICIA HALL

In 1959 Helene Berg, Alban Berg's widow, deposited the first group of *Lulu* sketches in the Music Division of the Austrian National Library. The complete collection of sketches became available for study in 1981, beginning a new and promising phase in *Lulu* scholarship.[1] In the following essay I shall describe the nature of these sketches and suggest their value to current and future scholars.

Format of the sketches

'Sketch' is a general term that refers to the working out of a musical idea before it reaches its final form. One can further classify sketches according to their format. Martha Hyde, for instance, divides Schoenberg's sketches into four categories: row charts, row sketches, compositional sketches, and form tables and charts.[2] In describing these categories she writes:

> Row tables include sheets that tabulate all transpositions or inversions of a twelve-tone row (or basic set) for a piece. Row sketches can best be described as partial or incomplete row tables. They usually present two or more forms of the basic set, but not all its transpositions or inversions. Compositional sketches, the third category, represent drafts of specific passages in a piece. Unlike row sketches, they have such identifying features as rhythm, pitch, contour, and register. ... The final category includes tables and charts in which Schoenberg outlines the form of a section or movement. These have diverse formats but share one common feature: unlike other kinds of sketches they do not use musical notation.[3]

These categories are also appropriate for Berg's twelve-note compositions, and I shall refer to them in this essay.

In addition to sketches, the Austrian National Library has a wealth of other autograph material relating to *Lulu*. These include, among other items, Berg's

235

copies of Wedekind's *Die Büchse der Pandora* and *Erdgeist*, the *Particell* and full score, and a booklet Berg used to learn jazz techniques. While these materials are not sketches *per se*, they are, nonetheless, frequently annotated with sketches and other information that give us important insights into the opera. This makes it difficult—perhaps even misleading—to cite an exact number of leaves of 'sketches'; nonetheless, if we exclude this annotated autograph material, Berg's sketches for *Lulu* comprise approximately 700 leaves.[4]

Chronology

An important preliminary task facing *Lulu* scholars is to establish the chronology of the opera, that is, the order in which Berg composed its different parts. Until now our information has been based almost entirely on correspondence—mostly between Berg and Webern or Schoenberg—as Berg reported his slow but steady progress on the opera. These progress reports are not as detailed or frequent as one might hope, but they do provide a general framework for when Berg worked on or completed major sections.

Our quest now is to use this framework, as well as other evidence, to assign dates to individual sketches, and it is a challenging quest indeed. To begin with, very few of the sketches bear dates, and sketches from different periods of composition are often mixed together into a single folder.[5] Furthermore, Berg did not compose the opera entirely consecutively. We know from Berg's correspondence that he composed the Prologue last, but it is also apparent from his sketches that he sometimes skipped among sections within the main body of the opera. For instance, Berg would experiment with large-scale plans for later sections—sometimes even completing important musical themes.[6]

Given these difficulties, then, how should one establish chronology? We do not have one of the important tools of Beethoven scholars, watermarks, but there are at least four other kinds of evidence that appear to be equally reliable. Firstly, Berg had the fortunate habit of drafting letters and other material on his sketches while he composed. A few of these drafts are dated, others are easily datable by their content. Secondly, one can sometimes recognize the year of composition from Berg's style of sketching. Very early sketches (1928–9) are often meticulously labelled with transposition levels, operations (retrograde, inversion, etc.) and occasionally the method by which a row was derived from the Source Row; he seems to have relaxed this style in later years, although on occasions one can still find order numbers in certain passages. Thirdly, if one catalogues the various types of paper for the complete sketches it is sometimes possible to determine the type that Berg used during a particular period. For instance, Berg used twelve-stave paper almost exclusively in his first two years of writing. Fourteen-stave paper is much more frequent beginning in 1930. Fourthly, as with paper types, it is sometimes possible to connect particular writing implements with a period of composition. Figure 1, for instance, an

Figure 1 ÖNB Musiksammlung, F21 Berg 80/VII, fol. 1v

early (and soon abandoned) compositional sketch of the opening of the Prologue, contains several clues that reveal it to be an early sketch: it is on twelve-stave paper; the transposition levels, operations, and method of derivation are labelled;[7] and it even bears the date '6/23/[19]28' in its upper left-hand corner. Furthermore, it is embellished with an olive-green pencil which Berg used only through 1928.[8]

The above dating techniques come under the heading of external evidence, that is, evidence drawn from the outward appearance of a sketch.[9] One can, in addition, use internal evidence gleaned from analysing the sketch's musical content. Besides simply noting the section of the opera being sketched and linking this with the date of a progress report, one can observe the style of twelve-note writing. For instance, letters from Reich to Berg, as well as a letter from Berg to Webern, make it clear that Berg developed a new set of twelve-note rows in 1929 to augment those he had used previously.[10] Thus, if we observe sketches using these new twelve-note rows, we can safely assume that they were completed after 1929.

What I present here are trends, and all trends are laden with exceptions. To date a sketch on a single piece of evidence can easily lead to an error that at this early stage of study could be particularly harmful. Clearly, the most reliable dating will occur when we combine as many pieces of evidence as possible.

What are the benefits of dating individual sketches? It will allow us, first, to link a sketch with a specific event. For instance, in his letters Berg occasionally reports of discoveries or innovations concerning his twelve-note writing that cannot be identified specifically. However, if we know the date of the letter, and if we can establish that date in a sketch whose content links it to the letter, then we may identify a discovery that was inaccessible from a letter alone.[11] Second, chronology allows us to discern the evolution of Berg's writing over an extended period of time. This process is not always clear from the music alone since Berg habitually 'touched up' earlier sections of music and sometimes composed segments of the opera non-consecutively.[12] In fact, Berg's twelve-note style undergoes a gradual and logical transformation, yet this transformation only appears logical after one has sorted out the proper chronology of his autograph manuscripts.

Compositional Process

A second use of the sketches is closely related to chronology: study of Berg's compositional process.[13] Over a long span this tells us how a work came into being; did it flower from a germinal idea? did it evolve slowly, finally assuming its final form, or did Berg have its form in mind from the beginning and mould the composition to fit it?

Berg's sketches for *Lulu* verify an idea suggested in one of his letters to Schoenberg: that he had the large-scale form of the opera planned from the beginning.[14] Among Berg's early sketches there are many that show his attention to the opera's palindromic form. In the middle of Figure 2, for instance, we see one of Berg's many diagrams that indicate the work's symmetrical structure. Near the bottom he writes,'Interludium bis Mitte dann Krebs[.] von hier geht die ganze Oper *zurück.*' ('Interludium up to the middle then retrograde. From here the whole opera goes backwards.') And further, he comments on the form of two scenes that flank the centre of the palindrome: 'II2 gekürzter Krebs von III' ('Act 1, scene 2 shortened retrograde of Act II, scene 1').

After determining the opera's overall structure, Berg then composed sections largely consecutively, working out most of the details of a passage before moving on to the next section. Large-scale ideas, for instance, the major forms that might fit into a later section, or a row form to be used by a later character were experimented with in advance. These plans would later be revised or occasionally abandoned as he arrived at that section and began to realize its details.

On a more local level, study of compositional process reveals how Berg composed specific passages—and here the sketches show in microcosm how Berg worked on the opera as a whole. Berg usually began by arranging the text of a section to adhere to a particular form. For instance, in the form sketch shown in Figure 3, (transcribed and translated in Figure 4) we see him assigning one of four text themes in the conversations between Lulu and Schön (Act I) to each of the four sections of the Sonata. Thus the main theme (column one) represents Dr Schön, which Berg describes as 'his complete personality, multisided, domineering, possessed by deep feeling'. The bridge passage depicts Lulu's current husband, Walter, and the other men in her life. The second subject, (column three) is for Schön's fiancée, 'the Bride'. And finally, Berg entitles the coda, 'the Possession', referring to Lulu's fatal love for Dr Schön.

What is remarkable about the Sonata is that each time the exposition returns as a reprise, Berg retains this pairing between text theme and Sonata theme. Thus, if we look at column three, 'the Bride', we see that the first time the second subject appears Lulu is praising Schön's fiancée. When the second subject returns in the first reprise, however, Schön and Lulu are now arguing over his bride. The final time that the second subject appears, Schön has realized that he can no longer return to his fiancée, and it is here that Lulu dictates 'the letter' in which he ends his engagement. By using this parallel construction between text and musical theme, Berg makes the structure of the Sonata more apparent to the listener.

Another task at this early stage of writing was the working out of themes. For the Sonata, many of these thematic sketches appear in a small, home-made notebook dating from 1930.[15] Figure 5 shows one leaf of this notebook in which Berg sketches out the different sections of the main theme of the Sonata. Typically, sketches from this stage show only the melodic line, or perhaps the melodic line with a simple accompaniment.

Figure 2 ÖNB Musiksammlung, F21 Berg 28/III, fol. 38v

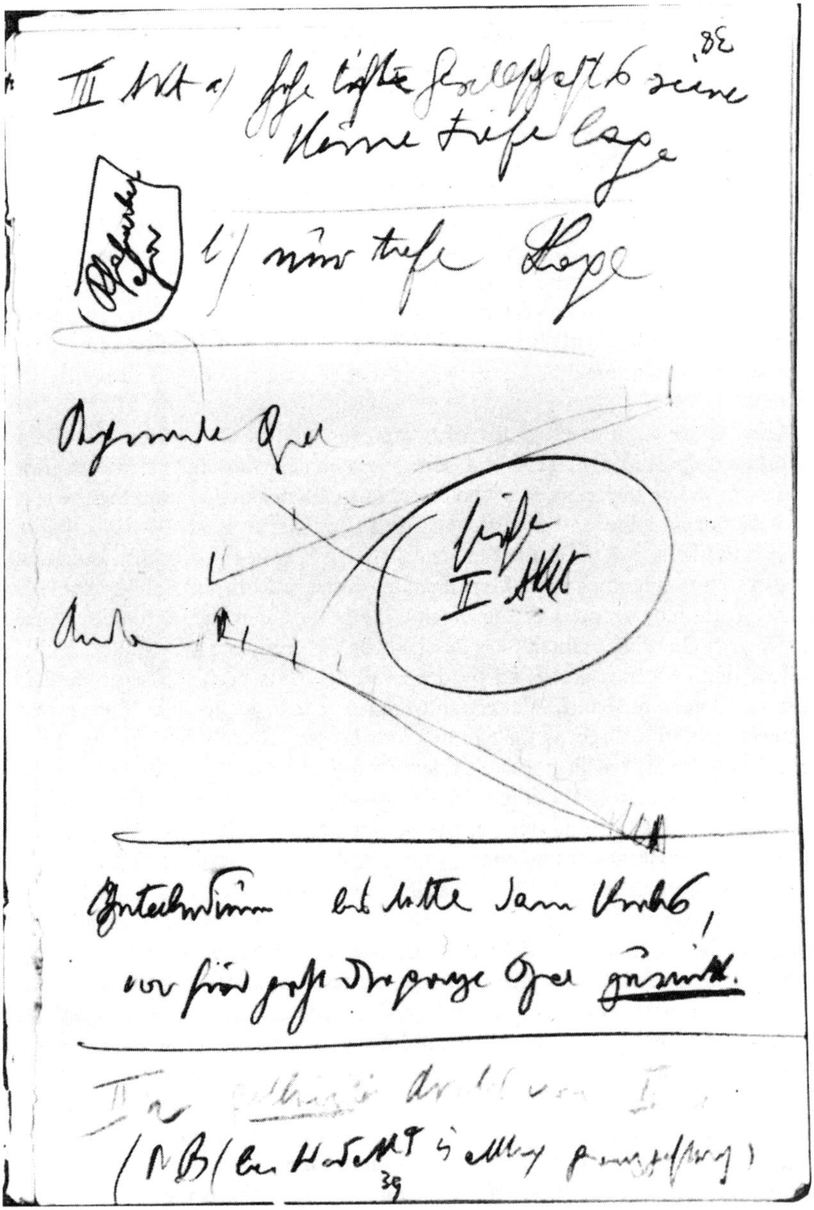

Figure 3 ÖNB Musiksammlung, F21 Berg 28/XXVII, fol. 1v

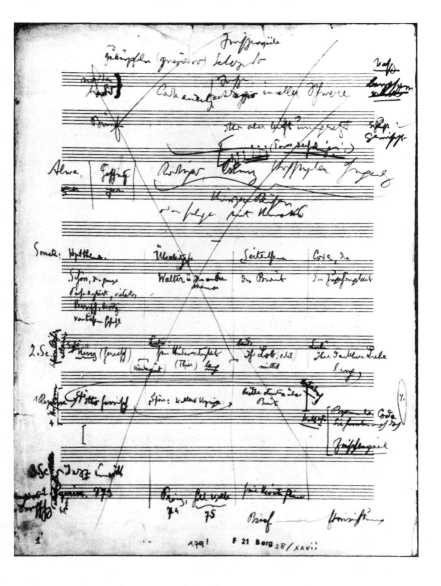

Figure 4

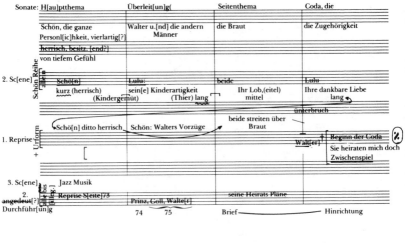

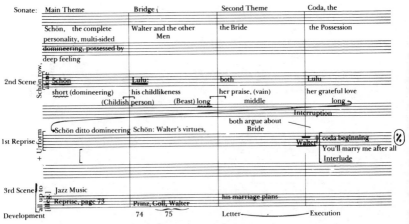

Once the form was prepared and the themes established, Berg turned to the actual working out of a passage. He frequently began by mapping out a passage using a shorthand first described by Ernst Hilmar in Berg's sketches for *Wozzeck*.[16] Figure 6(a) (transcribed in Example 1(a)) shows an early compositional sketch of the opening of the main theme of the Sonata in which Berg utilizes this graphic notation. Typically Berg uses it to indicate the durations of the notes, but not their exact pitches. He used it as shorthand for passages for which he already knew many of the notes (we can see, for instance, the contour of Schön's theme on the second staff) or he used it as a method for

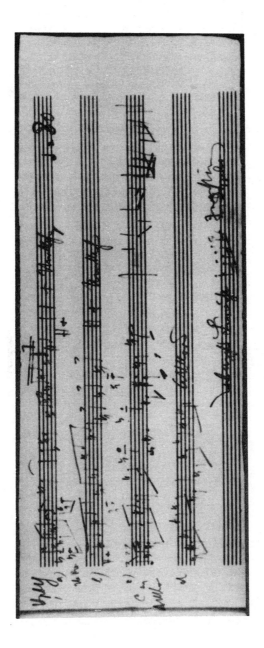

Figure 5 ÖNB Musiksammlung, F21 Berg 80/V, fol. 12

Figure 6 ÖNB Musiksammlung, F21 Berg 28/XXVI, (a) fol. 8, staves 1–4, (b) fol. 13, staves 1–4

(a)

(b)

mapping out the syllabic stress of the vocal line before he added pitches to it. The first staff of the sketch shows the latter technique.

Ex. 1 Transcription of Figure 6

(a)

(b)

In a final stage of composition, Berg would complete the passage by filling in these earlier graphic notes and making the needed additions and revisions. Figure 6(b) (transcribed in Example 1(b)) shows this final stage in a slightly later compositional sketch of the opening Sonata theme. Here Berg has assigned pitches to the earlier graphic notes and completed the accompaniment. Beneath the pitches one can see the rhythmic skeleton of the vocal line; the opening of the main theme, representing Schön, is also present, but transposed to P-8.

Although Berg did not always compose so methodically, his compositional process, as suggested by these few sketches, frequently consisted of four stages: (1) arrangement of text to adhere to a particular form; (2) melodic sketching of themes; (3) partial sketch of a musical passage; and (4) completion of partial sketch. What is remarkable—considering the complexity of the music—is the lack of revision. Apparently, this procedure allowed Berg to progress forward very gradually, although, as Hilmar notes, it is also possible that Berg was simply solving his compositional problems at the piano rather than on paper.[17]

Restoration

Undoubtedly the most valuable use of Berg's autograph material to date is Friedrich Cerha's orchestration of Act III.[18] Through careful study of Berg's sketches, autograph *Particell*, and full score, Cerha restored the opera so closely to Berg's style that George Perle comments, 'one does not have the impression that a hand other than the composer's has had to take over the instrumental realization of the unscored portions of the *Particell*'.[19] The most important sketch materials for Cerha's restoration were instrumentation lists appearing in the margins of the *Particell* next to their corresponding passage. Cerha first compared instrumentation lists with Berg's realized sections in the autograph full score. Finding that Berg had followed these lists exactly, Cerha knew that he could safely use them to orchestrate Berg's unscored sections. This emphasizes a perhaps obvious but nonetheless essential rule for using sketches for restoration: the sketches must represent, as nearly as possible, the composer's final thoughts on how a passage should be realized.

Perle's study of Berg's Film Music represents another careful and precise use of sketches for restoration.[20] Describing this music, Perle notes that:

> The orchestral interlude between the two halves of the opera accompanies a silent film that depicts Lulu's history from the moment of her arrest to the moment of her escape from prison. ... Lulu is arrested, committed for trial, tried and imprisoned, and then—in a sequence that shows visually analogous events in reverse order, accompanied by the retrograde of the music that has accompanied the film to this point—she is removed from her cell because of illness, examined by a medical council, committed to the isolation ward of the hospital, and escapes, disguised as Countess Geschwitz.[21]

Inserted in Berg's *Particell*, Perle found a detailed scenario of the film music that superseded a sketch previously published by Reich. He then compared the scenario with the music in the *Particell* to determine its accuracy and finality. Perle mentions, for instance, that Berg's bar numbers in his scenario were consistently one bar less than in the *Particell*, moreover there were several other minor errors that Berg probably would have corrected later on.[22]

In restorations of this type one does not, of course, always have such complete or finished versions with which to work; for instance, only Alwa's vocal line is present in bars 976–1000 of the Quartet of Act III, scene 2. While, as Perle notes, Cerha's solution of forming the remaining vocal lines from orchestral doublings is 'eminently successful', any sketches of this material, no matter how preliminary, would be of great interest.[23]

Cryptography and dramatic symbolism

Berg had a passion for cryptography that bordered on the obsessive. Nothing seemed to delight him more, for instance, than incorporating his number of fate, 23, into the music of *Lulu*, and the sketches are filled with exuberant annotations. Berg uses 23 and its multiples to signal an important dramatic event (the Medical Specialist falls dead of a stroke 23 bars after appearing on stage); to mark the duration of a section (the opening Recitative of Act I, scene 1, is 46 bars long); and to determine metronome markings (note, for instance the tempi of the bridge passage and second theme of the Sonata, crotchet = 46 and dotted crotchet = 69).

While most of these examples have been noted from the printed score, there are many others that require the aid of sketches. For instance, in one of Berg's sketches in the *Particell* he notes: 'N.B. $23\frac{1}{2} = 11\frac{1}{2}$'. He then derives all the metronome markings for the Sonata from multiples of $11\frac{1}{2}$. Thus, the Coda's metronome marking of 58 is $11\frac{1}{2}$ x 5 rounded up to 58. The main theme is $11\frac{1}{2}$ x 7 rounded down to 80.[24] This suggests such an abstract level of cryptography that one wonders if Berg wanted tempo markings of approximately 58 and 80 and simply found a way to arrive at them using his number.

Also of interest are a few humorous examples of numerology that appear in the sketches but not in the final score. According to a note in the margin of one sketch, when Schön calls the police to report the Painter's suicide, Berg (perhaps jokingly) has Schön direct the police to '23 Malergasse' ('23 Painter Street'). And one can see Berg struggling to make the duration of the 'Lied der Lulu' 46 measures.[25]

A second type of cryptography, Berg's use of initials (his or Hanna Fuchs-Robettin's) is an entirely different matter. Their initials pervade the Lyric Suite, but this is a special work that is dedicated to Hanna; use of her or Berg's initials in other works is far less frequent. Perle calls attention to an annotation in the *Particell* in which Berg comments on the sustained B at the midpoint of the Film Music and his use of B in the last scene of the opera. Perle interprets this as 'confirmation of the private H–F symbolism of the closing bars of the opera'.[26] I have not found references to Hanna in Berg's sketches, however; therefore we can only speculate about Berg's use of initials or other devices to evoke her. Is it chance, for instance, that the coda music of Act I, scene 2, the most passionate music of the opera, with its text, 'If I belong to anyone in this world, I belong to you ...' is ten bars long, Hanna's number?

Berg's absorption with detail extends to another non-musical aspect of the opera: dramatic symbolism. Explaining the importance of drama in *Wozzeck*, Berg writes:

> I had nothing else in mind at the moment when I decided to write an opera, nothing else in mind even as regards the technique of composition, than to render to the theatre what is the theatre's, and that means to shape the music in

such a way that it is aware in every moment of its duty to serve the drama.[27]

As with *Wozzeck*, Berg's use of dramatic symbolism in *Lulu* is the motivating force behind much of the music. It ranges from minute levels (for instance the specific ordering of a row to reflect a line of text) to extended statements (the use of large-scale forms to represent specific characters; the palindromic form of the opera to represent Lulu's ascent and fall).

A characteristic of Berg's dramatic symbolism, whether large-scale or small, is that it is often both subtle and specific. Thus, sketches frequently clarify instances of dramatic symbolism that are, in fact, necessary to our understanding the music. We can note, for instance, that Berg has the same singer play the roles of the Prince, the Manservant, and the Marquis and that they share the same twelve-note row, but until we realize that Berg intended them all to represent slavery (of marriage, the household, and the bordello) then the whole sense of the tripling will remain unclear.[28] We can hear the dramatic changes in orchestration in the interlude in Act III of the opera, and the gradual dissolution of tonality that accompanies it, but until we understand that this 'turned-around Bolero' (as Berg called it), is a metaphor for Lulu's surroundings, from the 'false glitter' of Act III, scene 1, to the poverty of Act III, scene 2, where she experiences 'her deepest humiliation', then we have missed the music's *raison d'être*.[29] When we study Berg's sketches for dramatic symbolism we have the sense that Berg is confiding the essential dramatic secrets of his opera. And indeed, among all his autograph manuscripts, these sketches are often the most fascinating.

Toward a better understanding of Berg's twelve-note technique

A final important use of the sketches is how they clarify aspects of Berg's twelve-note composition. There has already been considerable debate among Beethoven scholars about the usefulness of sketches for analysis. Douglas Johnson, the instigator of this debate, argues that they can show us little that is not already apparent from the finished score.[30] Whatever the merits of this reasoning, with Berg's music, as with much 20th-century music, while everything is there in the printed score, ironically we often fail to discern it. Easily lost in the complexity of Berg's writing, with its multiple layers and extended twelve-note techniques, we can use sketches to fill the mundane but essential function of road map. Thus, the problem is one of perception: properties of Berg's music that do not stand out in the finished score suddenly become obvious when we see them laid out in a sketch.

On the simplest level, Berg's sketches allow us to identify order numbers and row forms that can otherwise be indecipherable. Berg's row technique is so complex that frequently when we analyse passages from *Lulu* we find ourselves in a labyrinth of possible rows and permutations. One can easily spend hours trying to identify row forms and order numbers (often in vain), or one can look instead at a sketch where Berg has conveniently labelled them himself—which he frequently does in the most difficult passages. Example 2, for instance, shows the opening of the Duet between the Painter and Lulu, from Act I, scene 1. Following Lulu's indifferent reaction to the death of her husband, the Medical Specialist, the Painter wonders what sort of person he is dealing with and initiates a question-and-answer session with Lulu, beginning with his query, 'Kannst du die Wahrheit sagen?' ('Can you speak the truth?').

Ex. 2 *Lulu*, Act I, bars 305–8

Ex. 3 *Bild Harmonien*

If we try to analyse this passage without sketches, we shall probably notice—from both the melodic line and the previous few bars—that Berg is using the *Bild Harmonien* (picture chords) (Example 3). The second half of the Painter's vocal line (C–G–E♭–D♭) is more difficult to analyse, however, for it does not form a recognizable segment of any of Berg's twelve-note rows. This, and the even more complex passage in bar 308, might make us suspect that Berg's writing here is what some call 'free'.[31] However, if we look at Berg's compositional sketches for the passage (one of which appears as Figure 7, summarized in Example 4) we see that, on the contrary, Berg derives all the notes from his twelve-note rows. In the sketch Berg identifies twelve-note rows in a variety of ways: he uses brackets to mark off a complete statement of a row; he labels order numbers; he uses Roman numerals to indicate the transpositional level and the letters O and U to indicate *Original* and *Umkehrung* (prime and inversion); and he occasionally identifies the form of the row, that is, how it is derived from the Source Row.

As noted earlier, the first phrase, bars 305–6, begins with the *Bild Harmonien* (P-9). Berg's order numbers in the second half of bar 305 and bar 306 identify our mystery row as the Source Row at I-0 (order numbers 9–12 of the *Bild Harmonien* overlapping with order numbers 1–4 of the Source Row). Berg does not identify the repeating E–F–G figures in bar 306 and the second half of bar 305 because they are repetitions of order numbers 5, 8, 10 of the *Bild Harmonien*. (Note that these figures extend into the statement of Source Row I-0.) Likewise, the unlabelled G–E♭–D♭'s are repetitions of order numbers 3, 6, 9 of Source Row I-0. Both melodic patterns, E–F–G and G–E♭–D♭ originally occur within an ordered statement of their respective rows and are then extracted and stated as independent melodic fragments.[32]

The second phrase, beginning with the Painter's next question, 'Glaubst Du an einem Schöpfer?' ('Do you believe in a Creator?') begins similarly to phrase one with the *Bild Harmonien* (P-0). The three ordered statements of the Source Row that follow (P-2, I-11, and P-10) are spliced into one another to form distinct melodic lines. Thus, the melodic line B♭–B–C♯–D–E♭–C–A (piano) is formed from the segments P-10: 1, P-2: 6, 9, P-10: 2, 3, 4, I-11: 4. The vocal line A♭–B♭–F♯–E–C♯ is formed from P-2: 7, 8, I-11: 3, 5, P-2: 9. Berg reveals this splicing in his sketch by placing the order numbers for each row in separate layers. Note also that Berg is again extracting segments from ordered statements and expressing them as melodic fragments; I refer here to the A♭–B♭–F♯–E in the piano part, bar 308, that derives from the vocal line of that same bar.

Once we have conquered this basic level of analysis, we can ascend to more sophisticated or creative realms. Specifically, we can begin to understand Berg's musical and dramatic motivations for some of the complicated row manipulations we have just observed.[33] For instance, Berg's E–F–G figure that extends into Source Row I-0 (bars 305–6) functions as a bridge to the next phrase, which also begins with E–F–G (see Example 4). Note that Berg expresses these figures using different rows and order numbers: the statements

Ex. 4 Summary transcription of bars 305–8 of Figure 7 with order numbers completed

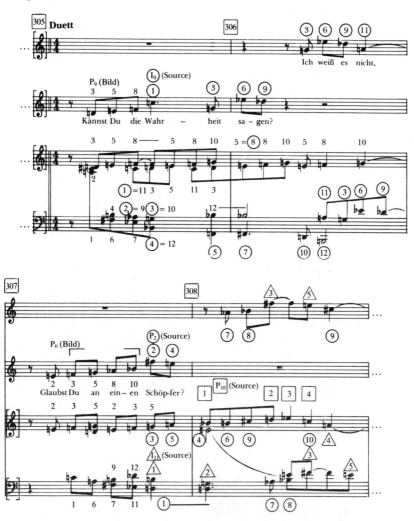

of E–F–G of phrase 1 are formed from order numbers 5, 8, 10 of *Bild Harmonien* P-9 and the E–F–G that opens phrase 2 from order numbers 2, 3, 5 of *Bild Harmonien* P-0. Berg's wish to repeat previous melodic figures while using different rows and order numbers also explains the spliced melodic lines of bar 308. Compare, for instance, the Ab–Bb–F♯–E vocal line of bar 307 (*Bild Harmonien* P-0: 8, 10, Source Row P-2: 2, 4) with the identical G♯–A♯–F♯–E segment of the vocal line in bar 308 (Source Row P-2: 7, 8, I-11: 3, 5). The

Figure 7 ÖNB Musiksammlung, F21 Berg 28/XXIV, fol. 13v, staves 1–8

melodic figure B♭–B–C♯–D is a transposition of the opening melodic line of bar 307, E–F–G–A. By using this technique, Berg achieves the same continuity using contrasting row material as he does by merely repeating a row segment verbatim—as in the first phrase where he takes the latter part of the Painter's vocal line, G–E♭–D♭, and repeats it twice as a melodic fragment.

In this example, Berg's sketches have allowed us to unravel highly complicated aspects of his compositional style that otherwise would most probably remain hidden or ambiguous. Another instance in which sketches prove helpful for analysis is when we are able to decode a passage, but we are unsure how to interpret our results. Here the sketches answer the question: how did Berg intend the passage to function?[34]

The coda of the Sonata furnishes an excellent example of this problem. Analysing it in isolation from the sketches, we note that the passage consists of the Source Row, with the notes of Dr Schön's row separated into the melody (Example 5). One question arises: did Berg intend this to demonstrate musically the derivation of Schön's row from the Source Row?

Ex. 5 *Lulu*, Act I, bars 615–20

Ex. 6 Transcription of Figure 8(a) stave 1, (b) staves 7– 8

Sketches for this passage (one of which appears as Figure 8, transcribed in Example 6) reveal that Berg wrote the coda immediately after discovering a method of deriving Schön's row from the Source Row. Various annotations in these sketches, like his note in the left margin 'with derivation from the Source Row' and his use of order numbers (he notes those of the Source Row while delineating Schön's row with upward stems) make it clear that Berg—perhaps in his own cryptic way—felt that this passage demonstrated the relation between the two rows. We see this same attention to the derivational properties of the rows in a later sketch (Figure 9) in which he labels the unfolding with order numbers from the Source Row and then again with the order numbers for Dr Schön's row. Above the passge he writes: 'Ur (+ Schön-) Reihe' ('Source (+ Schön) Row'). Other sketches in which Berg refers to the Source Row as the 'Lulu row', Berg's title for the coda, 'the Possession', as well as the text that the unfolding sets forth also make it clear, however, that the event is 'in the service of dramatic symbolism'.[35] For, as Lulu says to Schön, 'If I belong to anyone in this world, I belong to you.': the two rows begin to unfold, and Schön's row literally belongs to Lulu's row, the Source Row of the opera.

This example aptly demonstrates the reciprocal nature of sketches and final version. Too often both are treated as discrete entities: we analyse music to learn about the piece, but study sketches to learn how the composer worked. In reality, however, they should form a kind of dialogue: the music should prepare and augment the ideas we see in sketches, and the sketches should provide insights that we may not see or understand in the music.

In both examples the sketches show processes that are present, but nonetheless obscure in the finished score. When we make use of sketches, it is as if we were somehow able to X-ray the music, or peel back its layers to see its inner workings; and through this process we arrive at a more precise view of Berg's twelve-note language.

Figure 8 ÖNB Musiksammlung, F21 Berg 28/X, fol. 1

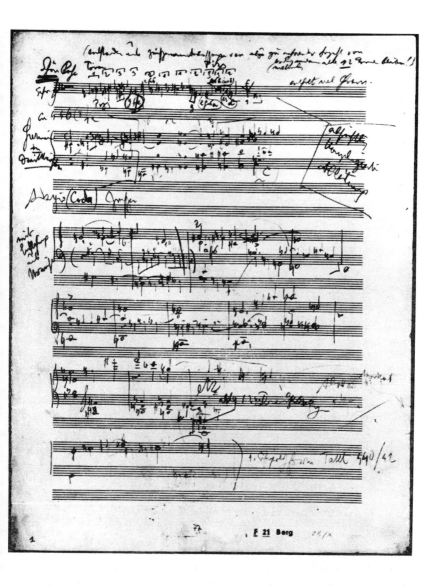

Figure 9 ÖNB Musiksammlung, F21 Berg 28/XXVI, fol. 6

Discussing Cerha's orchestration of Act III of *Lulu*, Perle remarks:

> Our first and most important obligation to Berg's artistic legacy is achieved—
> the rescue, for ourselves and posterity, of his *chef d'oeuvre* and one of the
> supreme masterpieces of its genre in the entire repertory, through its
> restoration, in every most essential respect, to the composer's own
> conception.[36]

Perle stresses the necessity of restoring *Lulu* 'in every most essential respect, to
the composer's own conception'. Yet we owe this same degree of precision and
individuality to analyses and discussions of the opera. Berg's sketches give us
these kinds of valuable insights—insights about his creative procedures, the
evolution of his style, and his hidden extra-musical devices—from the composer
himself. And our knowledge will undoubtedly increase as more letters and
documentary evidence become available.

I should like to thank Joan Smith, Janet Naudé, and particularly my advisor, Martha
Hyde, for their comments and suggestions on earlier drafts of this article. Reinhard
Strohm and Rosemary Hilmar provided invaluable help in deciphering Berg's
handwriting.

Notes

1. Personal communication from Rosemary Hilmar. Although Helene Berg deposited
   the first group of sketches in the ÖNB in 1959 they did not become available for
   study until 1981.
2. Martha Hyde, 'The Format and Function of Schoenberg's Twelve-tone Sketches',
   Journal of the American Musicological Society, vol. 36 (1983), pp. 453–80.
3. Ibid., p. 454.
4. For a more detailed description of Berg's autograph material for *Lulu*, see Rosemary
   Hilmar, *Katalog der Musikhandschriften, Schriften und Studien Alban Bergs im Fond
   Alban Berg und der weiteren handschriftlichen Quellen im Besitz der Österreichischen
   Nationalbibliothek*, Alban Berg Studien, vol. 1 (Vienna: Universal Edition, 1980).
5. Berg's sketches probably arrived at the Austrian National Library in this condition.
6. For instance, Berg completed a draft of the coda for the Sonata immediately upon
   discovering a method to derive Dr Schön's row from the Source Row. There are also
   many sketches that show Berg skipping back and forth between compositional stages
   on a single leaf.
7. Berg's tranposition levels, which appear as Roman numerals in his sketches,
   correspond to those found on the row charts he used during the composition of *Lulu*.
8. Douglass Green discusses this sketch in detail in 'A False Start for *Lulu*: an Early
   Version of the Prologue', *Alban Berg: Analytical and Historical Perspectives*, ed.
   David Gable and Robert Morgan (Oxford University Press, forthcoming).
9. Changes in handwriting and address stamps are other types of external evidence;
   however I have not included them in my discussion. After careful study of Berg's
   handwriting during the seven years he composed *Lulu*, I have not been able to

discern any consistent changes that one could use for dating purposes. And while Berg does occasionally use address stamps I have found them minimally helpful.

10. See Patricia Hall, 'The Progress of a Method: Berg's Tone-rows for *Lulu*', *Musical Quarterly*, vol. 71 (1985), pp. 500–19.

11. Ibid. In this article I link a letter from Berg to Webern to specific *Lulu* sketches in order to identify a discovery concerning Berg's row derivation.

12. Many examples of Berg's 'touching up' become apparent when one studies the autograph sources. I discuss one of these instances in 'The Progress of a Method', pp. 516–18.

13. I make this distinction because often it is not necessary to know the exact dates of sketches in order to discern compositional processes.

14. See Berg's letter to Schoenberg, 7 August 1930 in Hans Ferdinand Redlich, *Alban Berg: the Man and his Music* (London: John Calder, 1957), p. 175.

15. The sketchbook does not actually bear a date; however, the content of the sketchbook does suggest the year 1930.

16. Ernst Hilmar, 'Die verschiedenen Entwicklungsstudien in den Kompositionsskizzen', *50 Jahre Wozzeck von Alban Berg*, ed. Otto Kolleritsch (Graz: Universal Edition, 1978), p. 23.

17. Ibid., p. 24.

18. For a detailed description of his orchestration of Act III see Friedrich Cerha's contribution to this volume and his *Arbeitsbericht zur Herstellung des 3. Akts der Oper 'Lulu' von Alban Berg* (Vienna: Universal Edition, 1979).

19. George Perle, *The Operas of Alban Berg*, vol. 2: *Lulu*, (Berkeley and Los Angeles: University of California Press, 1985), p. 276.

20. Ibid., pp. 149–57.

21. Ibid., pp. 48–9.

22. Ibid., pp. 151, 156.

23. Ibid., p. 277.

24. ÖNB Musiksammlung F 21 Berg PhA 2177 fol. 65.

25. ÖNB Musiksammlung F 21 Berg 28/XXXIV fol. 1^L–2.

26. Perle, op. cit., pp. 156–7.

27. Willi Reich, *Alban Berg*, trans. Cornelius Cardew (London: Thames and Hudson, 1965), p. 64.

28. See the sketch, ÖNB Musiksammlung F 21 Berg 28/VI fol. 11. I discuss this sketch in detail in my article, 'Role and Form in Berg's Sketches for *Lulu*', *Alban Berg: Analytical and Historical Perspectives*.

29. See the sketches, ÖNB Musiksammlung F 21 Berg 28/VIII fol. 3 and 3^l and F 21 Berg 28/III fol. 25^l.

30. Douglas Johnson, 'Beethoven Scholars and Beethoven's Sketches', *Nineteenth Century Music*, vol. 2, no. 1 (1978), pp. 3–17.

31. Berg in reality does not write in a 'free style'; this is an unfortunate euphemism that often conceals confusion about his compositional procedures.

32. Perle discusses this phenomenon, op. cit., pp. 129–30.

33. In the above analysis, I am restricting my commentary to aspects of the music that the sketches clarify. There are, of course, many additional properties worth investigating.

34. And then we must ask ourselves if Berg truly succeeded in his intentions.

35. Mosco Carner, *Alban Berg: The Man and The Work* (London: Gerald Duckworth, 1975), p. 205. Carner uses this phrase to describe the absorption of Schön's row into the Source Row at his death. It is also for reasons of dramatic symbolism that the

unfolding of Schön's row and the Source Row is less convincing in the coda; Berg is constructing a large-scale event, beginning with the unfolding in the opening of the Sonata, that only culminates with Schön's death.

36. Perle, op. cit., p. 294.

SOME FURTHER NOTES ON MY
REALIZATION OF ACT III OF *LULU*

FRIEDRICH CERHA

In the first three years following the appearance of my *Arbeitsbericht* on Act III of *Lulu*[1] I gradually carried out a series of minor improvements to my score. These were done: (1) on the basis of findings obtained from an examination of some material to which I had not previously had access; (2) on the basis of a better reading and clearer insights gained by looking at originals where I had previously only been able to see copies; (3) on technical and practical grounds. All these revisions concern small musical details: their degree of importance is shown by the fact that nobody has registered them at performances except the performers concerned. No major alterations have proved necessary.

As regards the relationship of the *Particell* to the sketches, the following details may be helpful. A comparison between the *Particell* and the sketch material previously available to me led me to conclude (p. 7 of my report) that even a thorough familiarity with the sketches, which clearly represent an earlier stage of composition than the *Particell*, would be unlikely to yield sufficiently precise data for the realization of a definitive full score. This conclusion has indeed been borne out and confirmed by my study of the sketch material in Berg's posthumous papers. It has become increasingly clear that the *Particell* is the final version of a work which was repeatedly revised, reworked and improved. Many traces of this process are visible (as already pointed out in my report): pieces of paper stuck on over the original (e.g. pp. 136 and 137 of the *Particell*), erasures, surviving remnants of discarded earlier versions which are recognizable as such, and certain jottings and corrections which have obviously been added at a later stage.

The sketches contain early versions of some passages which turn out significantly different in the *Particell*; mainly, however, the corrections take the form of refinements and improvements to the setting. An example is the lightening of the texture and the elimination of harshnesses in the harmony in bars 346–8.[2] Many slips concerning pitch in the sketches have already been rectified in the *Particell*. Passages which I pointed out as problematic have had little light shed on them by the sketch material. The basic cell in bar 691 (piano), which is dubious and marked off in brackets in my score, is entirely lacking from the sketches at this point.

The most important corrections, carried out after consultation with the source material, are in the Pantomime and the Quartet.

The sketch for the Pantomime contains specifications of instrumentation at two points: 'Horn offen' ('horn open') at the Banker's thirds in bar 356, and 'Picc.' at the Lulu theme in bar 364. For the Circus music (bars 353ff.) the *Particell* specifies 'Gliss. on the horns to be reinforced by gliss. on the strings'. In between the sketches and the *Particell* Berg obviously changed his mind about the kind of sound he wanted: he would not have given the same instrumental colour to material as different as the Circus music and the Banker's thirds, especially as the one is placed immediately next to the other. This is proved by his note 'new colour' for the Banker's thirds, which appears in the *Particell*. As the *Particell* is clearly definitive, an alteration based on indications in the sketches would not be justifiable here. However, at bar 364 the indication 'Picc.', and a note in which Berg gives each character in the Pantomime an individual rhythmic motive, did seem to authorize a modification (Example 1). These two clues caused me to rethink the sound quality of the whole scene and led to a more systematic organization of it.

Ex. 1

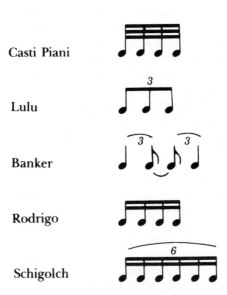

The Lulu motive occurs on various different instruments. Bar 364 of the sketch ('Picc.') gives it to the piccolo, i.e. gives it a flute colouring. As I had used flute colouring for the often independently occurring motive of the last four notes, and as Berg usually gives this motive a colouring of its own, the change in instrumentation in bar 364 entailed another change; I therefore gave the last four notes to the oboe.

The other change in instrumentation was made for motivic reasons. The demisemiquaver figures in bars 353, 362, and 364 are now, like the beginning of the cadenza (bars 470 and 490), given to the solo violin, the instrument which specially characterizes the Procurer and which is given similar figures in the Chorale Variations (e.g. bars 84, 87, 89, 183, 186, 195, 224–7).

If we follow, as I have done, the instrumental specifications for the circus music, quoted above, the cross signs indicating stopped notes, the markings, 'as if from far away' and 'new colour' for the Banker's thirds, and also the hints in the sketches concerning the Lulu theme and the Procurer themes, a sound-picture emerges which may fairly be said to be based on Berg's intentions in all important aspects.

A correction to the musical text occurs at bars 519ff.: one of the sketches has, at the end of the trill on B, the same five-note termination as in the upper voice of the bar before. This shows, significantly, that Berg wanted every trill ending in an identical manner. I have therefore completed the second trill to match the first. (The *Particell* has only the last two notes of the termination of the trill on E and B (bar 519) and similarly with the trill on A in bar 520.) At bar 540 the first note of the termination has also been supplemented in a similar way.

Further corrections arose from a study of the sources of the text. While I was working on the realization of Act III I had a typescript of the text before me, which was remarkable for its coyness as regards the 'Jewish element'. Generally speaking it corresponded otherwise with the *Particell* text, but it showed traces of editorial intervention such as a tautening and abbreviation of the texts of the Ensemble, the removing of stage directions, etc. This points to the typescript's having been made during the years after Berg's death. Perle suggests that it goes back to Erwin Stein, but this is doubtful. Given the political situation of the mid-1930s, Stein must certainly have found Berg's characterization of certain 'Jewish' features embarrassing, especially with publication in view, but he was far too scrupulous and had far too clear a conception of his role as faithful servant of the composer to have intervened to such an extent on his own initiative. All he did was to omit from the piano reduction the stage direction 'mauschelnd' ('in a Yiddish accent', with overtones of cheating) (bar 597) and the Banker's repeated 'Gott der Gerechte' ('God of the Righteous') (bars 253ff.), retaining instrumental notes of the same pitch and rhythm. The originator of the typescript is more likely to have been someone on the editorial staff of Universal Edition, though they have long since lost track of it.

The difficulties Berg encountered in the ensembles are the result of the fact that he could not find sufficient textual material in Wedekind. The only solutions were to repeat sections of Wedekind's text, continue and paraphrase them, or invent new ones. Berg only used extensive repetitions where he wished the text to be totally incomprehensible (as in the first 'Rhubarb' ensemble, as he called it, bars 26ff.), or where he wanted an effect like a caricature, as in the operetta-like 'Alle Welt gewinnt' ('Everybody wins') (bars 245ff.) in Ensemble II, and 'Alle Welt verliert' ('Everybody loses') (bars 614ff.) in Ensemble III.

Wherever Berg did not complete the ensemble I found myself faced with similar textual difficulties. Only in 1981 did I gain access to his papers, and there, as Perle had led me to expect, I found documents relating to the wording of the texts. The most important were a copy of *Die Büchse der Pandora* (Pandora's Box) (R. H. 394)[3] which had served as the basis for the libretto of the opera, and a continuous libretto (R. H. 381). R. H. 394 contains a quantity of comments, remarks and crossings-out, together with all kinds of jottings including some concerning the formal structure, rhythmic system, etc. R. H. 381 was typed by Berg himself and corrected by hand. Now I was in a position to verify to what extent I had dealt with the textual problems in accordance with Berg's own intentions. For the continuation of Ensemble II, Berg had given precise instructions (compare my report, pp. 11–12). The passages of text added by me for Geschwitz (bars 284–294) could obviously not be in the original libretto because the need for their insertion only emerged during the course of composition. In the printed edition of *Die Büchse der Pandora* the passage of text used by me for the insertion is not only not deleted, the closing passage 'welcher Kreaturen Sklavin du bist' ('of what creatures you are the slave') is even underlined—a thing that Berg only did where he considered the passage particularly important. This seems to vindicate my decision to include this piece of text rather than simply repeating the text of bars 262–75. Berg's work contains plenty of examples of the tautening and rearrangement of text to suit the exigencies of the music.

In Ensemble III, in which some of the voice parts are incomplete (see my report, p. 13), the continuation of the Banker's text (bars 646ff.) 'Morgen früh hab' ich das Vergnügen, den Kampf um meine Existenz zum sechsund-dreissigsten Male aufzunehmen.' ('Tomorrow morning I shall have the pleasure of taking up the fight for my existence for the 36th time.') is not deleted in R. H. 394; Berg must have intended at some stage to set it. A textual repetition here would certainly have been inappropriate in view of the fact that the passage would be the continuation of one of the dominant vocal parts, in a setting, moreover, where the words would be more likely to come across than in the Ensemble II passage discussed above. A perusal of the printed edition at this point confirmed to me that I had made the right decision in inserting the text quoted.

The papers proved to be particularly rewarding as regards the Quartet in Act III, scene 2. R. H. 394 contains two variants, one clearly crossed out in pencil, the other emphasized by blue pencil brackets in the right-hand margin, which actually overlap the expunged text. This would seem to indicate that some of the crossed-out material was to be reinstated, so presumably the brackets were added later. This theory is based on the fact that the pencilled markings were obviously part of a process of 'marking-up', whereas the blue pencil was used in matters of detail and emphasis and to bracket together interrelated or connected material etc. Berg's typescript contains a third, precisely worked-out variant: the text of Alwa's aria as it is to be found in the *Particell* is followed by a note which reads: 'Simultaneously with this aria of Alwa the following conversation takes place, forming a vocal quartet', and which introduces texts that Berg intended for Lulu, Geschwitz and Schigolch in the Quartet. Unfortunately this variant does not entirely solve the textual problems raised by the Quartet.

Awareness of these texts made a revision of the Quartet necessary and this in turn entailed musical amendments. The new version was written in the late autumn of 1981. Berg's typescript formed the basis and point of departure for my work. As a result the textual allusion I had originally planned for Lulu to make to her scene with Schön had to be abandoned; she would have said 'Ich war ihm nichts als Weib und wieder Weib. Er liebte mich, aber er kannte mich nicht.' ('I was just a woman to him, just a woman. He loved me, but he did not know me.') (compare Berg Act I, scene 2, bars 558ff.; Wedekind's *Erdgeist* (Earth Spirit) Act II, scene 3). It should be noted that in Berg's typescript Schigolch's words 'Sie kann mit Selbstbewusstsein sagen: Das war ich mal!' ('She can say with proud composure: That's what I was like!') are given to Lulu ('I can say ...'), which does not make much psychological sense, since in this situation, where she is brought face to face with the image of her own youth, Lulu is hardly likely to develop a sense of pride and composure. The words conflict with her previous exclamation 'Mein Bild! Mir aus den Augen! Werft es zum Fenster hinaus!' ('My portrait! Out of my sight! Throw it out of the window!') and her subsequent 'Ich bring mich um.' ('I'll kill myself.'). (Here it should be noted that the first person singular has again been substituted for Wedekind's second person plural: 'Ihr bringt mich um.' ('You're killing me.') and 'Ich halt's hier nicht mehr aus.' ('I can't stand it here any longer.').) I have used Berg's text in the new version because it is at least more authentic than the one I had chosen. Nevertheless it is really too short for the Quartet to develop to the intended length. This may be a reason why he postponed his completion of the ensemble. There are indications that he was thinking of adding to the text in the typescript: at bars 1000–1002 the parts for Lulu and Geschwitz are written in. In the *Particell* at this point Lulu's part includes the words 'ob ihr recht habt' ('if you are right'). The text of bar 1000 has been rubbed out; only faint traces remain. The words 'ob ihr recht habt' can only be the ending of Wedekind's line, 'Ich werde ja sehen, ob du recht hast.' ('Well, I'll see if you're right.'; the 'you' is singular in the Wedekind play, plural in the *Particell*), which was a response to Schigolch's previous words, of which I have selected the first sentence: 'Unten im Laternenschimmer nimmt sie es (sie's) noch mit einem Dutzend Strassengespenstern auf.' ('Down there in the lamplight she's still a match for a dozen of the girls that haunt the streets.'). In R. H. 394 this sentence is underlined, which means that Berg considered it important. The use of the plural ('ihr') is hard to explain. The only other character involved, Geschwitz, does not share Schigolch's view because she is opposed right up to the end, as part of her own outlook on life, to Lulu's activities as a prostitute. I have therefore replaced the plural by Wedekind's original singular 'du'. In Berg's typescript Schigolch has the somewhat colourless line 'Ja, man macht sich keinen Begriff von unserer Jugendzeit.' ('They've got no idea of what things were like when we were young.'); for musical reasons I have replaced this by Wedekind's 'Wem sie heute in die Hände gerät, der macht sich keinen Begriff mehr von unserer Jugendzeit.' ('Whoever's hands she falls into now, will have no idea of what things were like when we were young.'). In the edition of the play Berg used, this sentence is crossed out in pencil but is included within one of the blue brackets in the right-hand margin, which indicates that it might have been reinstated at a later stage. Though absent in the typescript, textual requirements also made it necessary to retain Geschwitz's line 'Ich hörte nur zuweilen abfällige Bemerkungen von euch, dass er in seinem Verfolgungswahn den Hals sich abgeschnitten habe.' ('Now and then I've heard you sneer that, in his persecution mania, he cut his own throat.'). (Wedekind's actual wording had to be slightly modified to fit the music.) In Berg's copy of the play this sentence is also crossed out in pencil but a blue bracket in the margin again suggests that he had second thoughts.

Turning to the Act III finale, the sketches contain a detail which may be of some interest in practical performance. In Wedekind's play Geschwitz utters the word 'Verflucht!' ('Damn!') as she dies, and this has also tended to be the case in performances of the opera ever since the première. It is true that in one of the sketches of the Finale the syllable 'ver-' is written under the C, though there is only a blank under the B. In the *Particell*, however—and we have repeatedly shown it to be the final version —there is no text at all at this point. To have Geschwitz say 'Verflucht!' at the end must therefore be contrary to Berg's intentions.

Taken as a whole, the sketches reflect the considerable discrepancy between Berg's first ideas and the finished score. Amongst other things they show how he distributed the various characters amongst a mere handful of performers and drew the musical consequences. The performance of multiple roles by one singer produces in the final version a psychological depth and subtlety which is given expression in the complex and many-layered web of musical allusion. By comparison the perfunctory nature of the characters' relationship to each other in one of the early sketches comes as something of a suprise:

Wardrobe mistress (I, 3)		
Schoolboy (II, 1 & 2)	Breeches	Contralto
Groom	part	
Medical Specialist (I, 1)	Silent	Character
Last Visitor (Jack) (III, 2)	role	baritone

Painter (I, 1 & 2) 3rd Visitor (Dr Hilti) (III, 2)	Lyric tenor
Dr Schön, newspaper editor (I; II, 1) 2nd Visitor (Negro) (III, 2)	Heroic baritone with touch of lyric
Singer of Prologue (I) Athlete (Rodrigo) (II; III, 1) 1st Visitor (Herr Hunidei)	Heroic bass
Prince (I, 3) Manservant (II, 1) Procurer (III, 1)	Tenor buffo
Theatre Director (I, 3) Police Commissioner (II, 1) Banker (III, 1)	Bass buffo

Broadly speaking, the casting of one singer in several roles results in some degree of detachment, yet Berg uses his limited material to create a wide variety of retrospective cross-references on various musical and compositional levels, with the result that an extremely sophisticated complex of associations is brought into play.

George Perle has drawn attention to the fact that even Berg's final list of Dramatis Personae does not quite accord with the actual score, since it makes no mention of the doubling of the Medical Specialist and the Banker which occurs in his final version. (Compare the Act I Melodrama, bars 196ff., with the Act III Pantomime, bars 356, 359, 361, 363, and Ensemble III, bars 652–8.)

[translated by Celia Skrine]

Notes

1. Friedrich Cerha, *Arbeitsbericht zur Herstellung des 3. Akts der Oper 'Lulu' von Alban Berg* (Vienna: Universal Edition, 1979).
2. All bar references are to the orchestrated score of Act III and the piano reduction.
3. Rosemary Hilmar, *Katalog der Musikhandschriften, Schriften und Studien Alban Bergs im Fond Alban Berg und der weiteren handschriftlichen Quellen im Besitz der Österreichischen Nationalbibliothek*, Alban Berg Studien, vol. 1 (Vienna: Universal Edition, 1980).

THE FIRST FOUR NOTES OF *LULU*

GEORGE PERLE

For me, the first and most striking fact about the four-note figure that opens the opera *Lulu* (Example 1) is the important role that the same figure plays in certain works by Béla Bartók.

Ex. 1 *Lulu*, Act I, bars 1–2

It is a notoriously difficult problem to find an acceptable definition of 'atonality', or even an acceptable term for it. Schoenberg thought we should call it, whatever 'it' may be, 'pantonality', Sessions preferred the thoroughly non-committal 'post-tonal music', and Babbitt has suggested 'contextual composition', to which the objection has been raised that all music is 'contextual'. Clearly, however, some music is much more 'contextual' than other music. When we are talking about tonal music we can take two pieces that are as far apart in time and style as the second English Suite of Bach and the Prelude to *Tristan und Isolde* and say of both that they are in the key of A minor. Can we characterize in comparably explicit, relevant, and general terms two atonal pieces, even two atonal pieces by the same composer? The term 'reflexive reference' has been suggested by a literary critic to describe a similar situation in modern poetry:

> Instead of the instinctive and immediate reference of words and word-groups to the objects or events they symbolize, and the construction of meaning from the sequence of these references, modern poetry asks its readers to suspend the process of individual reference temporarily until the entire pattern of internal

references can be apprehended as a unity. This explanation, of course, is the extreme statement of an ideal condition rather than of an actually existing state of affairs, but the conception of poetic form that runs through Mallarmé to Pound and Eliot, and which has left its traces on a whole generation of modern poets, can be formulated only in terms of the principle of reflexive reference.[1]

I have never really been satisfied with my attempt to define 'atonality' on the first page of my book *Serial Composition and Atonality*:

> The composer working within the diatonic tonal system may take for granted the existence of specific properties of that system: a seven-tone scale, triadic harmonic structure, a key center, and so forth. The atonal composer, however, can take for granted nothing except the existence of a given limiting sound world, the semitonal scale. Aside from this assumption, it is impossible to state the fundamental conditions of atonality *in general*, except in a negative way, merely stipulating the absence of a priori functional connections among the twelve notes of the semitonal scale.[2]

Compare the signal in the trombones that calls us to attention at the beginning of *Lulu* and the prolonged statement of exactly the same figure at the same transpositional level with which Bartók's Fifth Quartet commences. The structural implications of what I call 'Basic Cell I' in my book on *Lulu*[3] are the same for Bartók as for Berg, so this, at least, must be an exception to the principle of 'reflexive reference', or, if we prefer, 'contextuality'.

In 1955 I published an article entitled 'Symmetrical Formations in the String Quartets of Béla Bartók',[4] in which, for the first time, I discussed what, for convenience, I shall continue to refer to as 'Basic Cell I', regardless of whether it appears in the music of Berg or Bartók. After some introductory remarks on certain precedents in the music of Debussy and Musorgsky, I quoted Example 2 from the finale of the Fifth Quartet. I pointed out that the arrival of this

Ex. 2 Bartók, Fifth Quartet, V, bars 188–95

progression at its destination, G/F♯, is postponed, and that a continuation beyond this point would unfold the same six dyads in the opposite direction, or, equivalently, at the tritone (Example 3 (a)). Thus this postponed destination is an axis of symmetry of the progression, and at the tritone we have a corresponding axis. Every symmetrical progression converges in this way upon a dual axis of symmetry. That dual axis may be 'odd' (a semitonal dyad and its tritone, as in Example 3 (a)) or 'even' (a unison and its tritone, as in Example 3 (b)).

Ex. 3

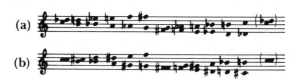

Immediately following the last bar of Example 2, Bartók completes the progression, 'but not in the form which a mechanistic continuation ... would necessitate, and it is immediately followed by a reiteration of the first axis, so that the four notes are isolated from the complex which they had generated' (Example 4). This conjunction of the four axial notes of the progression gives us Basic Cell I. I continue as follows in my article:

> These notes immediately assume a new function by establishing the tonal orientation and the germinal intervallic relations of an important new theme [Example 5]. The subsequent entry of the lower strings in strict canonic imitation of the upper strings at the octave below reaffirms the tonality, and a reiteration of the original axis-tones alone at the conclusion of the whole section [Example 6] differentiates that section from what precedes and follows it and articulates its formal function within the movement as a whole.

Ex. 4 Bartók, Fifth Quartet, V, bars 196–201

Note my assignment of the term 'tonality' to the structural functions that Bartók derives from Basic Cell I. Though we are still far from implying, in employing this word in this context, a system of precompositionally definable relationships of the scope and comprehensiveness implied when we speak of two different pieces as being in the key of A minor, we have taken a step in that direction, a step away from 'reflexive reference' and 'atonality'. My 1955 article also discusses at some length the important role that Basic Cell I plays as both a melodic and harmonic structure in the Second Quartet, but curiously enough, I neglected to identify it as the same, perhaps because it does not seem to function in this work as a statement of the axial notes of complete symmetrical progressions.

Ex. 5 Bartók, Fifth Quartet, V, bars 202–6

Ex. 6 Bartók, Fifth Quartet, V, bars 346–53

The concluding pages of my article dealt with the first movement of the Fourth Quartet. I showed how 'in the course of the first six bars two symmetrical four-note chords are evolved, which thereafter function as primary focal points and generators of subsequent musical events', how these two cells are 'invariably employed in some kind of conjunction', and how this progression (Example 7) pervades the movement. I went on to point out that whereas each of these cells is symmetrical in itself, the two together result in a non-symmetrical progression, since their respective axes of symmetry are different. A collection is symmetrical if it can be partitioned into dyads that share a common axis of symmetry. That axis will be either a semitonal dyad or a unison. For cell x it is the former, and for cell y the latter (Example 8). The two cannot be components of the same symmetrical progression, regardless of their respective transpositional levels, since cell x is based on an odd axis of symmetry and cell y on an even one. However, the progression itself may be literally inverted, so that it 'becomes a necessary component of a larger symmetrical relationship', and this is exactly what Bartók does near the conclusion (bars 152–6) of the first movement of the Fourth Quartet, where cells x and y are each inverted around the same axis of symmetry (Example 8). We shall see that this

Ex. 7

Ex. 8

Ex. 9

extension of the concept of symmetry to embrace non-symmetrical formations has vast implications for the question that concerns us here—the extent to which valid and general pre-compositional structural relations can be asserted in 'post-tonal' or 'atonal' music—implications that are not yet realized in the work of either Bartók or Berg.

A most important supplement to my remarks on the Fourth Quartet was published by Leo Treitler in 1959.[5] Mr Treitler showed that 'a third group emerges from melodic material in the second subject of Movement I, beginning at m. 15', and that this cell, *z*, which is nothing less than our Basic Cell I again, functions at two different pitch levels a minor third apart, a relationship which derives from the fact that it is a symmetrical structure that may be interpreted as converging upon either of two different axes separated by that interval (and, as we have seen above, their tritone transpositions) (Example 10). It is through cell *z* and the symmetrical relations that it shares with cell *x* that the primary transpositional relations of the first movement are established. Though cell *x* is most characteristically represented at the transposition shown in Example 7, in its initial statements in bars 1 and 3 it occurs at the minor third above and below respectively, and in the inverted statement of the *x–y* progression it again occurs at the minor third below. Basic Cell I functions as a pivotal connection between these primary pitch levels of the principal subject of the movement (Example 11). In my article I pointed out that the symmetrical progression from the finale of the Fifth Quartet illustrated in Example 2 is transposed at the minor third in an expanded and embellished version near the end of the movement (bars 763ff.). The new dual axis of symmetry is D♯/E and A/B♭, which brings us back to the 'tonality' of the opening bars of the first movement. Here too we can undoubtedly refer the transpositional relation to the important role assigned to Basic Cell I.

Ex. 10

Ex. 11

The property of Basic Cell I to which we can attribute its pivotal function is its divisibility into two tritones, a property that it shares with two other tetrachordal collections, structurally equivalent to the chords traditionally known as the 'French sixth' and the 'diminished seventh'. Berg's String Quartet op. 3, composed in 1910, 18 years before Bartók wrote his Fourth Quartet (which appears to be the earliest work in which he employed this device), presents an isolated early instance of such a reinterpretation as a means of establishing a new transpositional level. Symmetrical progressions play a prominent role in the opening bars of the second movement of this work, with the unison E as principal axis. At the conclusion of the exposition (bars 68ff.) a 'French sixth' chord that may be interpreted as symmetrical to either E or G converges upon the ostinato G that initiates the development section (Example 12).

Ex. 12

In my first article on *Lulu*, published in 1959,[6] I differentiated between the two types of twelve-note set-structure in the opera—tropes and series. A series characterizes the dodecaphonic collection by defining the order of pitch classes; a trope characterizes it by partitioning the collection into unordered segments of independent pitch-class content. The three principal tropes of the opera (Example 13), and particularly Basic Cell I as a motive in itself, 'represent the staged world of Lulu's drama in a general sense, not specific characters or events of the drama'. My book on *Lulu* refers to 'inherent structural properties [which] make Basic Cell I particularly suitable for the signal role assigned to it by Berg. ... Whatever permutation we may choose will partition itself into two identical, or complementary intervals [Example 14].'[7] This property is one that Basic Cell I shares only with the other two tetrachordal collections that may be partitioned into two tritones, the 'French sixth' and the 'diminished seventh' chords.

Ex. 13

Successive transpositions of Basic Cell I have certain inherent characteristics:

> The symmetrical tetrachord which was labelled 'cell z' in our discussion of the first movement of Bartók's Fourth Quartet ... plays an important structural role as the chief non-reflexive component of the fourth of Webern's Five Movements for String Quartet, Opus 5. It appears at four transpositional levels which intersect through common dyads to form the series of tritones illustrated in [Example 15]. Exactly the same relation between successive transpositions of the same cell [Example 16] plays an important role in the second movement of Bartók's Second Quartet. The movement opens with a signal figure that outlines the principal pitch level of the cell. Overlapping statements lead to a continually reiterated d, the latter being part of an incomplete statement (a–eb– d) whose close is found in a melodic figure outlined by the tritone d–g♯. The two compositions are as unlike one another stylistically as they could possibly be, but the immediate harmonic meaning of the overlapping statements of the cell is exactly the same in both.
>
> The structural function of cell z is inherent. The interval couple of two tritones eliminates tritone transpositions as independent forms, since the tritone is its own [tritone] transposition. Any given transposition of the cell will intersect with any other transposition through a shared tritone, or not at all. Successive intersecting transpositions will generate a progression that may be interpreted as unfolding along a [perfect fifth] cycle, as in [Example 15], or a [minor second] cycle, as in [Example 17]. Successive transpositions by [major thirds] generate [Trope I] and are equivalent to successive transpositions by

[major seconds]. Successive transpositions by [minor thirds] are symmetrically related, sharing either of two axes of symmetry ... as explained in our earlier discussion of Bartók's Fourth Quartet. ... Whatever we choose to do with cell z, its structural implications are impossible to evade.[8]

The self-invertible and self-transposable segmental content of Trope I generates only two non-equivalent forms, instead of the 24 invertibly related forms of tropes that are not similarly characterized by their segmental content.

Ex. 14 *Lulu*, (a) Act II, bars 568–91, (b) Act II, bars 600–602, (c) Act III, bars 179–80

Ex. 15

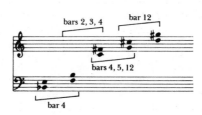

Ex. 16

Ex. 17

Since Trope II consists of all three transpositions of the diminished seventh chord, it generates only a single set form. Trope III, which consists of two symmetrically related minor-third transpositions of Basic Cell I and the residue of the dodecaphonic collection, the diminished seventh chord, will generate three non-equivalent set forms. It is precisely the highly invariant character of the three tropes that gives them 'their signal and salient character and distinguish[es] them from all the other twelve-tone sets of the opera':

> The Prologue opens with Trope I followed by Trope II, and concludes with the reversed sequence of the same tropes; Lulu's *Todesschrei* in the Finale of Act III is marked by Trope I, stated as a simultaneity; Tropes II and III accompany the discovery of the Painter's corpse. ... In the Film Music, Trope III represents the closing of the door of the prison cell upon Lulu after her conviction for the murder of Dr. Schön (mm. 680–682), her imprisonment (m. 687), and the opening of the door of her cell (mm. 692–694) for her removal to the hospital and her subsequent escape. The climax of the duet between Lulu and the Marquis in Act III, Scene 1, is marked by Trope I, representing the dramatic keynote of the scene—Lulu's refusal to accept the role of a professional prostitute.[9]

Trope III is of special interest because of its surprising connection with Skryabin. All of Skryabin's 'atonal' compositions are based on an 'octatonic' scale of alternating tones and semitones, and on certain variant forms of this scale.[10] The same scale plays a very significant role in the pre-serial compositions of Stravinsky, who inherited it from his teacher, Rimsky-Korsakov.[11] For all three composers, it seems reasonable to explain this scale as combining the pitch-class content of any two of the three diminished seventh chords. Treitler refers to Bartók's occasional use of the same scale and describes it as consisting of 'overlapping' statements of symmetrically related transpositions of cell z.[12] In the sketches for the projected *Acte préalable* on which Skryabin was working at the end of his life there is a detail that suggests he was moving toward the concept of a pre-compositional structure embracing all twelve pitch classes, a vertically notated twelve-note trope that is exactly analogous to Trope III of *Lulu* (Example 18).

Ex. 18

Douglas Jarman, in his 1970 article, 'Dr. Schön's Five-Strophe Aria: Some Notes on Tonality and Pitch Association in Berg's *Lulu*',[13] was the first to discuss Berg's extensive exploitation of large-scale symmetrical formations in *Lulu*. In Schoenberg's twelve-note system the concept of inversional equivalence on which these are premised is as axiomatic as the traditional concept of transpositional equivalence. In Dr Schön's Aria we find a pervasive and generalized exploitation of this concept that goes far beyond anything in the twelve-note works of Schoenberg or Webern. Schoenberg consistently pairs the prime set and the inversion in a fixed transpositional relation, so that a given transposition of the one necessitates the parallel and equal transposition of the other. With every transposition the axis of symmetry changes. The opposite principle is represented in several of Webern's works: each transposition of one form of the set is paired with an equal transposition in the opposite direction of the inversionally related form, so that the same axis of symmetry is maintained. Thus, for example, in the second movement of the Piano Variations set forms are always respectively transposed so as to maintain the following complementary relations:

$$
\begin{array}{ccccccc}
A & B\flat & B & C & C\sharp & D & E\flat \\
A & A\flat & G & F\sharp & F & E & E\flat
\end{array}
$$

In Dr Schön's Aria the same principle is extended to include various note rows, and non-serial elements as well. One has the sense that Berg is looking to symmetry as a structural principle that may be applied with the same pervasiveness and exclusivity as triadic structure in tonal music. Basic Cell I plays a special role in this context. The primary collection of complementary relations is as follows:

$$
\begin{array}{cccccc}
F & F\sharp & G & G\sharp & A & B\flat \\
E & E\flat & D & C\sharp & C & B
\end{array}
$$

Since Basic Cell I can be analysed in two different ways as a symmetrical structure, it can be represented as a component of this collection at two different pitch levels (Example 19).

Ex. 19 *Lulu*, (a) Act II, bar 387, (b) Act II, bar 407

A striking metaphor is derived from these fixed symmetrical relations at Dr Schön's response to Lulu's suggestion that they might get divorced (bars 472f.). The 'Jetzt kommt die Hinrichtung' ('Now comes the execution') leitmotif returns, at its original transpositional level, as the setting of 'Ich mich scheiden lassen!' ('I—divorce you!). Since the first four notes of this motive can be partitioned into two dyadic components of the same symmetrical collection, they may be inverted with no change of pitch-class content. Both forms of the motive are stated concurrently (Example 20) as a metaphor of the text that follows as Dr Schön continues: 'Lässt man sich scheiden, wenn die Menschen ineinander hineingewachsen und der halbe Mensch mitgeht?' ('Does one divorce, when two people have grown into each other and half of one goes along?')

Ex. 20 *Lulu*, Act II, bars 473–4

I concluded my 1955 article with a question: 'Can symmetrical formations generate a total musical structure, as triadic relations have done traditionally?' I was not ready to answer this question at the time, but it is now well past a half-century since *Lulu* and the Fourth and Fifth Quartets of Bartók were composed. My own views of the implications of these works for musical composition today are set forth in my book *Twelve-Tone Tonality*. I shall limit myself here to some suggestions as to how these implications directly impinge on elements in the music of Bartók and Berg.

I start with the assumption that intervals can be identical in two different ways. One of these is familiar to everyone. C–E, D–F♯, E♭–G are different instances of the same interval. We call this 'interval-4' because that is the *difference* in semitones between the two notes.

I have been discussing another kind of identity. C–E belongs to a family of symmetrically related dyads, as follows:

D	D♯	**E**	F	F♯	G	G♯
D	C♯	**C**	B	A♯	A	G♯

These dyads are identical as *sums*. Taking C as 0, C♯ is 1, D is 2, etc. Just as we previously had a constant difference of 4, so we now have a constant sum of 4. From this point of view D–F♯ and E♭–G are not the same as C–E. D–F♯ is a member of the sum-8 family of dyads, and E♭–G is a member of the sum-10 family. The sums fall into two categories—even and odd. Here, for example, are the sum-3 and the sum-9 series of dyads:

	Sum-3							Sum-9					
(C♯)	D	D♯	E	F	F♯	G	(G♯)	(E)	F	F♯	G	A♭	A	B♭	(B)
(D)	C♯	C	B	B♭	A	G♯	(G)	(F)	E	E♭	D	D♭	C	B	(B♭)

In the Bartók Fourth Quartet we saw a non-symmetrical progression of two tetrachords, each symmetrical in itself, interpreted as a component of a larger symmetrical structure. At one point in *Lulu* we have non-symmetrical chords, i.e., chords that cannot be partitioned into dyads that share the same axis of symmetry, in a symmetrical progression—a progression that maintains the *same* pair of *different* axes for each chord (Example 21(a)). Such a progression may always be interpreted in terms of an alternative pair of axes, and this alternative interpretation permits an extension of the progression to include a new chord that cannot be interpreted in terms of the former pair of axes (Example 21(b)).

Ex. 21

The aggregate tetrachordal sum, modulo 12, for such alternative interpretations will always be the same of course—10 in the present instance. An interval-3 transposition of a tetrachordal collection[14] will maintain the same aggregate sum, since 4 × 3 = 12. Through alternative reinterpretations it is always possible to modulate to a minor-third transposition of the original progression without recourse to Basic Cell I or either of the analogous tritone-based chords. Thus, for instance, Example 21 can be extended into an alternative interpretation that gives us dyads of sums 9 and 1, through which it may be restated at the minor third above or below (Example 22).

Symmetrical equivalence plays such a clearly referential role in Examples 21 and 22 as to suggest the possibility that such things as octave displacements, passing and neighbour notes, and suspensions can be defined in respect to it, just as these are defined in respect to the triad and scale-degree tendencies in the diatonic tonal system. Surely the figuration I have added in Example 23 to the citation from *Lulu* in no way disrupts the harmonic sense of the passage.

We can find an example of octave displacement in a symmetrical progression in the opening bars of Berg's String Quartet (Example 24). The sum-1 symmetrical relations are literally represented in the fourth bar, with Ab moving to G and E♯ to F♯. This sum-1 progression actually commences in the second bar, with the sum-1 dyad, F–Ab, presented at a pitch level that has two

Ex. 22

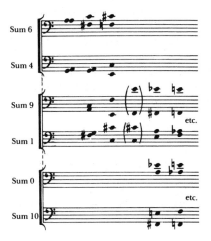

Ex. 23

functions in relation to the last note of the head-motive: (1) F establishes an octave ambitus with the first note of the head-motive that is symmetrically partitioned by the tritones, F–B, B–F; (2) Ab symmetrically partitions the second tritone into two minor thirds, in contrast to the symmetrical whole-tone partitioning, F–Eb–Db–(C)–B, of the first tritone. The initial sum-1 dyad, however, is displaced relative to the sum-1 dyad, G–F♯, in the following bar. The gap between the two sum-1 dyads is filled in symmetrically, the Ab moving through G to F♯ and the F through C to G. Such 'cyclic passing notes' are characteristic of Berg.

Ex. 24 String Quartet, I, bars 1–4

The example I have just cited from Berg goes back to a work that was composed more than three-quarters of a century ago. I will take the liberty of citing a more recent example, my own *Windows of Order* for string quartet (Example 25). The boxed passage shows a progression of three tetrachords of

Ex. 25 Perle, *Windows of Order*, bars 102–5

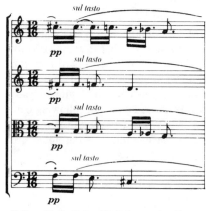

sum-couple 0, 9. In Example 26 the progression is reduced to its basic form through the elimination of octave displacements and figuration (suspensions and passing notes). In Example 26(a) I show the primary symmetrical relations, with all the voices moving equally in parallel or contrary motion. In Example 26(b) I show the actual voice-leading of the two top parts and how these become the inner voices through a three-octave displacement of the F♯ in the bass, which moves to the highest part and thus opens space between the first two chords. That space is filled, in Bergian fashion, by cyclic passing notes. In Example 26(c) I show how the three chords also represent a secondary sum-couple, 1 and 8. Through this secondary sum-couple another tetrachord, of primary sum-couple 10, 11, which also happens to be available in the context of this episode, momentarily becomes part of the progression. Example 26(d) shows the final stage of the analytical process, with dissonant suspensions that seem to me as clear in character and function as such things are in traditional tonal music.

Inversional symmetry, derived by the unfolding of pitch classes through a shared sum, is one of the two kinds of symmetry that one can have in a musical language based on a twelve-note scale. The other kind is derived by the unfolding of pitch classes through a single interval, i.e., an interval cycle.

Ex. 26

* consonant double suspension
† dissonant suspensions

Where that interval is other than 1 (or 11) or 5 (or 7) the pitch classes are distributed into partitions. Thus we have two different whole-tone (interval-2) cycles, three different diminished seventh chords (interval-3 cycles), four different augmented triads (interval-4 cycles), and six different tritones (interval-6 cycles). (It is also ultimately necessary, for the coherence of the system, and in fact it has important practical consequences, to say that we have twelve interval-0 cycles.) Both kinds of symmetry are a natural consequence of the replacement of a diatonic scale of unequal intervals between scale degrees by a semitonal scale of a single recurring interval. Diatonic scales can be differentiated as to pitch-class content and mode, but there is only one semitonal scale (as to pitch-class content) and one semitonal mode (as to interval structure).

I have arbitrarily laid out the above collections of symmetrically related dyads as interval-1 cycles, which seems a reasonable choice where cyclic relations are not defined. The opening bars of Bartók's Fourth Quartet are obviously based on the sum-9 collection, and the opening bars (following the introduction) of Berg's Lyric Suite are also obviously based on the sum-9 collection, but in the latter case these dyads are laid out in the following twelve-note row:

$$\text{F E} \quad \text{C A} \quad \text{G D} \quad \text{A}\flat \text{ D}\flat \quad \text{E}\flat \text{ G}\flat \quad \text{B}\flat \text{ C}\flat$$

The inversion of this, beginning on E, gives us the same dyads:

$$\text{E F} \quad \text{A C} \quad \text{D G} \quad \text{D}\flat \text{ A}\flat \quad \text{G}\flat \text{ E}\flat \quad \text{C}\flat \text{ B}\flat$$

(Tritone transpositions will give us the same dyads, in retrograde order.) But instead of this Berg uses the inversion beginning on B or F. Now if one will compare this to the prime set beginning on F it will be seen that this duplicates another dyadic segmentation:

(F)   E C   A G   D A♭   D♭ E♭ G♭ B♭ C♭ F
(B)   C E   G A   D A♭   E♭ D♭ B♭ G♭ F B

Berg employs this segmentation of the series at the beginning of the recapitulation (compare bars 2–11 and 45–7). This alternative segmentation unfolds sum-4 dyads except at the midpoint, where we have a sum-10 tritone.

Successive statements of the row will present what Babbitt calls a 'secondary twelve-tone set':

F E C A G D   A♭ D♭   E♭ G♭   B♭ C♭   F E   C A   G D   A♭ D♭   E♭ G♭   B♭ C♭

This brings us to what I call the 'cyclic set'. The alternate notes of the cyclic set unfold the same interval cycle in opposite directions. The series which we have just derived through a cyclical permutation of Berg's series, for example, may be seen as a horizontal unfolding of paired interval-7 (or interval-5) cycles moving in opposite directions:

Ab	Eb	Bb	F	C	G	D	A	E	B	F♯	C♯	(G♯ ...
C♯	F♯	B	E	A	D	G	C	F	Bb	Eb	Ab	(Db ...

This gives us the same collection of sum-9 dyads that was laid out above in an interval-1 (or interval-11 cycle). What the cycle is called depends on whether one subtracts the left element from the right or vice versa. The former gives us a P-7 cycle for the top line and the latter an I-7 cycle for the bottom line. Or, if one chooses to define the cyclic interval as 5, the subtraction of the right element from the left gives us I-5 for the top line and the left from the right gives us P-5 for the bottom line.

The above paired P-7/I-7 cycles may be read in two ways. If the P-7 cycle supplies the left note of each sum-9 dyad we derive a series whose alternative segmentation unfolds the sum-4 dyads (as in the principal series of the Lyric Suite). If the I-7 cycle supplies the left note of each sum-9 dyad we derive a 'cognate' inverted series whose alternative segmentation unfolds the sum-2 dyads. The two cognate series are:

Sums 9/4:	Ab	Db	Eb	Gb	Bb	Cb	F	E	C	A	G	D
Sums 9/2:	Db	Ab	Gb	Eb	Cb	Bb	E	F	A	C	D	G

For the cognate inverted series that Berg employs the I-7 cycle must be shifted one degree to the right relative to the P-7 cycle:

Ab	Eb	Bb	F	C	G	D	A	E	B	F♯	C♯	(G♯ ...
G♯	C♯	F♯	B	E	A	D	G	C	F	Bb	Eb	(Ab ...

Here are Berg's two sets, cyclically permuted to start with their second hexachord:

Sums 9/4:	Ab)	Ab	Db	Eb	Gb	Bb	Cb	F	E	C	A	G	D	(D
Sums 11/4:	Ab)	Ab	Eb	Db	Bb	Gb	F	B	C	E	G	A	D	(D

Cyclic sets may be generated by any pair of inversionally related cycles. From the sum-9 pair of semitonal cycles that show the symmetrical relations on which the opening bars of Bartók's Fourth Quartet are based we derive the following inversionally related cognate sets:

Sums 8/9:	E)	E	F	Eb	F♯	D	G	Db	Ab	C	A	B	Bb	(Bb
Sums 10/9:	F)	F	E	F♯	Eb	G	D	Ab	Db	A	C	Bb	B	(B

I referred earlier to an 'expanded and embellished' symmetrical progression whose dual axis of symmetry is D#/E and A/B♭ near the conclusion of the Fifth Quartet (bars 763ff.). Until bar 778 (Example 27) one can regard either of the following cyclic sets as a representation of this progression:

Sums 6/7:   D#)D# E   D   F   C# F# C   G   B   G# B♭ A (A
Sums 8/7:   E) E   E♭ F   D   F# C# G   C   G# B   A   B♭ (B♭

Ex. 27 Bartók, Fifth Quartet, V, bars 763–87

In bar 778 G♯ ascends to A without a corresponding descent of B to B♭. The new sum-8 axis of symmetry, B♭–B♭/E–E, is confirmed, after a dramatic pause, in bars 781ff., and establishes the second of these cognate-related sets as the basis of this passage, and, indeed, of the remainder of the movement. The priority of the sums-7/8 set is already implied in the scale figures of the first ten bars. These are inversionally complementary transpositions of a non-symmetrical scale, composed of two, tritone-related, Ionian tetrachords, and simultaneously stated in its ascending and descending versions. Each of the five paired statements of this scale unfolds the same series of dyadic sums: 7 8 8 7 7 8 8 7. Earlier I had described our choice of the interval-1 cycle as an 'arbitrary' one in laying out the symmetrical relations where the cyclic interval is not defined. At the conclusion of the Fifth Quartet, however, as in the first movement of the Lyric Suite, the cyclic interval that generates these relations is implied by the compositional context.

The following cyclic set is based on interval 2:

Sums 7/9: E♭ E F D G C A B♭ B A♭ C♯ F♯ (D♯

Where its axes of symmetry are even, two partitions are required to generate all twelve notes for an interval-2 cyclic set:

Sums 8/10: E) E F♯ D A♭ C B♭ (B♭ ... ‖ E♭ F) F E♭ G D♭ A B (B...

Two or more partitions will be required for each of the remaining types of cyclic set.

Through their shared sums, all the transpositions of the inversionally related sets of any given cyclic interval form a closed system, analogous to the transpositions of the diatonic scale through the circle of fifths. Here are the respective closed systems for the cyclic set of interval 7 from which we derive the series of the first movement of the Lyric Suite and for the cyclic set of interval 1 from which we derive the symmetrical relations in the finale of Bartók's Fifth Quartet:

Sums 4/9:	D	D	G	A	C	E	F	B	B♭	G♭	E♭	D♭	A♭	A♭
Sums 2/9:	G	G	D	C	A	F	E	B♭	B	E♭	G♭	A♭	D♭	D♭
Sums 2/7:	G	G	C	D	F	A	B♭	E	E♭	B	A♭	G♭	D♭	D♭
Sums 0/7:	C	C	G	F	D	B♭	A	E♭	E	A♭	B	C♯	F♯	F♯
Sums 0/5:	C	C	F	G	B♭	D	E♭	A	G♯	E	C♯	B	F♯	F♯
Sums 10/5:	F	F	C	B♭	G	E♭	D	G♯	A	C♯	E	F♯	B	B
Sums 10/3:	F	F	B♭	C	E♭	G	A♭	D	C♯	A	F♯	E	B	B
Sums 8/3:	B♭	B♭	F	E♭	C	A♭	G	C♯	D	F♯	A	B	E	E
Sums 8/1:	B♭	B♭	E♭	F	A♭	C	C♯	G	F♯	D	B	A	E	E
Sums 6/1:	E♭	E♭	B♭	A♭	F	D♭	C	F♯	G	B	D	E	A	A
Sums 6/11:	E♭	E♭	A♭	B♭	D♭	F	F♯	C	B	G	E	D	A	A
Sums 4/11:	A♭	A♭	E♭	D♭	B♭	G♭	F	B	C	E	G	A	D	D

Sums 6/7:	D♯	D♯	E	D	F	C♯	F♯	C	G	B	G♯	B♭	A	A
Sums 8/7:	E	E	E♭	F	D	F♯	C♯	G	C	G♯	B	A	B♭	B♭
Sums 8/9:	E	E	F	E♭	F♯	D	G	C♯	G♯	C	A	B	B♭	B♭
Sums 10/9:	F	F	E	F♯	E♭	G	D	G♯	C♯	A	C	B♭	B	B
Sums 10/11:	F	F	F♯	E	G	E♭	A♭	D	A	C♯	B♭	C	B	B
Sums 0/11:	F♯	F♯	F	G	E	A♭	E♭	A	D	B♭	C♯	B	C	C
Sums 0/1:	F♯	F♯	G	F	G♯	E	A	E♭	B♭	D	B	C♯	C	C
Sums 2/1:	G	G	F♯	G♯	F	A	E	B♭	E♭	B	D	C	C♯	C♯
Sums 2/3:	G	G	G♯	F♯	A	F	B♭	E	B	E♭	C	D	C♯	C♯
Sums 4/3:	A♭	A♭	G	A	F♯	B♭	F	B	E	C	E♭	C♯	D	D
Sums 4/5:	A♭	A♭	A	G	B♭	F♯	B	F	C	E	C♯	E♭	D	D
Sums 6/5:	A	A	A♭	B♭	G	B	F♯	C	F	C♯	E	D	E♭	E♭

What conclusions are we to draw from the extensive and remarkable connections, commencing with the first four notes of *Lulu* and the opening bars of the Fifth Quartet, that we find in the work of these two, seemingly very different, composers?

Notes

1. Joseph Frank, 'Spatial Form in Modern Literature', *Criticism: the Foundations of Literary Judgment*, ed. Mark Schorer et al (New York: Harcourt Brace and World, 1958), p. 383.
2. George Perle, *Serial Composition and Atonality* (Berkeley and Los Angeles: University of California Press, 5th edn, 1981).
3. George Perle, *The Operas of Alban Berg,*, vol. 2: *Lulu* (Berkeley and Los Angeles: University of California Press, 1985).
4. George Perle, 'Symmetrical Formations in the String Quartets of Béla Bartók', *Music Review*, vol. 16 (1955), pp. 300–312.
5. Leo Treitler, 'Harmonic Procedures in the Fourth Quartet of Béla Bartók', *Journal of Music Theory*, vol. 3 (1959), pp. 292–7.
6. George Perle, 'The Music of *Lulu*: a New Analysis', *Journal of the American Musicological Society*, vol. 12 (1959), pp. 185–200.
7. Perle, *The Operas of Alban Berg*, vol. 2: *Lulu*, p. 88.
8. George Perle, *Twelve-Tone Tonality* (Berkeley and Los Angeles: University of California Press, 1977), pp. 166–7.
9. Perle, *The Operas of Alban Berg*, vol. 2: *Lulu*, p. 90.
10. See George Perle, 'Scriabin's Self-Analyses', *Music Analysis*, vol. 3 (1984), pp. 101–22.
11. Arthur Berger was the first to draw attention to the relevance of the octatonic scale to Stravinsky's music and the first to call that scale by this name: 'Problems of Pitch Organization in Stravinsky', *Perspectives of New Music*, vol. 2, no. 1 (fall-winter 1963), pp. 11–42. Pieter C. van den Toorn, *The Music of Igor Stravinsky* (New Haven: Yale University Press, 1983) is an exhaustive study of octatonicism in Stravinsky. For the Russian sources of the octatonic scale see Richard Taruskin,

'Chernomor to Kashchei: Harmonic Sorcery; or, Stravinsky's "Angle"', *Journal of the American Musicological Society*, vol. 38 (1985), pp. 72–142.

12. For the role of the octatonic scale and of symmetry in general in the music of Bartók, see Elliott Antokoletz, *The Music of Béla Bartók* (Berkeley and Los Angeles: University of California Press, 1984).

13. Douglas Jarman, 'Dr. Schön's Five-Strophe Aria: Some Notes on Tonality and Pitch Association in Berg's *Lulu*', *Perspectives of New Music*, vol. 8, no. 2 (spring-summer 1970), pp. 23–48. In 'Alban Berg: the Origins of a Method', *Music Analysis*, vol. 6 (1987), pp. 273–88, Jarman shows how Berg exploits Basic Cell I in association with symmetrical formations as early as the Altenberg Songs.

14. In the present context, of course, a 'tetrachord' may include more than one instance of the same pitch class. A 'tetrachordal collection' of two sum-0 dyads, for instance, may consist of four instances of pitch class C.

LIST OF COMPOSITIONS

Juvenilia and student works

The large collection of Berg's juvenilia and student works may be divided into four categories:

(1) Songs

There exist in manuscript 86 songs dating from the period c1900–1908, just over half of which have been published. Eight of these songs were published during Berg's lifetime, the Seven Early Songs (1905–8) and the first version of *Schliesse mir die Augen beide* (1907); another song, *An Leukon* (1908), was published in Willi Reich, *Alban Berg* (Zurich: Atlantis Verlag, 1963); more recently 46 songs have been published as two volumes of *Jugendlieder*.

(2) Choruses and canons

16 canons for accompanied and unaccompanied voices; two-part canon for clarinet and horn with piano accompaniment (1907); four-part chorus.

(3) Works for string quartet and quintet

Miscellaneous fugues, dances, variations, and other movements. The collection includes one complete four-movement string quartet and a double fugue for string quintet and piano (1907).

(4) Works for piano

Miscellaneous scherzos, variations, etc. for piano or piano duet; the drafts of five (mainly unfinished) piano sonatas. Of these works only the Twelve Variations on an Original Theme (1908) have been published.

All of the unpublished works should appear in the near future as part of the forthcoming Alban Berg *Gesamtausgabe*.

Published works

Jugendlieder, vol. 1(1901–4), 23 selected songs for voice and piano
Schliesse mir die Augen beide [I], for voice and piano (1907)
Jugendlieder, vol. 2 (1904–8), 23 selected songs for voice and piano
Seven Early Songs, for voice and piano (1905–8); orchestral arrangement (1928)
Am Leukon, for voice and piano (1908)
Twelve Variations on an Original Theme, for piano (1908)
Sonata op. 1, for piano (1907–8)
Four Songs op. 2, for voice and piano (1909–10)
String Quartet op. 3 (1910)
Five Orchestral Songs on Picture-Postcard Texts of Peter Altenberg op. 4, for voice and orchestra (1912)
Four Pieces op. 5, for clarinet and piano (1913)
Three Orchestral Pieces op. 6 (1914–15)
Wozzeck op. 7, opera in three acts after Georg Büchner (1917–22)
Three Fragments from *Wozzeck*, for soprano and orchestra (1924)
Chamber Concerto, for piano, violin, and 13 wind instruments (1923–5)
Adagio, for violin, clarinet, and piano (1925) [arrangement of second movement of Chamber Concerto]
Schliesse mir die Augen beide [II], for voice and piano (1925)
Lyric Suite, for string quartet (1925–6)
Der Wein, concert aria for soprano and orchestra (1929)
Four-part Canon 'Alban Berg an das Frankfurter Opernhaus', for chorus (1930)
Lulu, opera in three acts after Frank Wedekind (1929–35)
Five Symphonic Pieces from *Lulu* [*Lulu* Suite], for soprano and orchestra (1935)
Concerto for violin and orchestra (1935)

NOTES ON THE CONTRIBUTORS

Bruce Archibald is Professor of Music Theory at the College of Music, Temple University, Philadelphia. A composer and pianist, he studied with John Kirkpatrick. His PhD dissertation for Harvard concerned the harmony of the early works of Berg.

Friedrich Cerha is a distinguished composer and conductor whose works have been widely performed throughout Europe. He was co-founder of the Die Reihe Ensemble. His definitive realization of the unorchestrated portion of Act III of *Lulu*, which made possible the first complete performances of Berg's masterpiece, has met with universal acclaim.

Brenda Dalen is visting assistant Professor of Musicology at the University of Alberta, Edmonton, Canada. She is an editor of the *International Alban Berg Society Newsletter* and a doctoral candidate at Yale University, where she is currently completing her dissertation 'A Study of Berg's *Chamber Concerto* Based on the Source Documents'.

Mark DeVoto, Professor of Music at Tufts University, is editing Berg's Altenberg Songs for the forthcoming *Alban Berg Gesamtausgabe*. He is a member of the Board of Directors of the International Alban Berg Society and was the first editor of the Society's *Newsletter*. A student of Walter Piston at Harvard, DeVoto has recently revised and edited the new fifth edition of Piston's *Harmony*.

Martin Esslin has been Professor of Drama at Stanford University since 1977 when he left the BBC after a long and distinguished career that culminated in a 14-year period as Head of Drama, BBC Radio. His many publications include books on Brecht, Beckett, Pinter, the Theatre of the Absurd, and German Drama. He was awarded the OBE in 1978.

Christopher Hailey is Assistant Professor of Music at Occidental College, Los Angeles. Co-editor and translator of the Berg–Schoenberg Correspondence, and editor of the Song volume of the *Alban Berg Gesamtausgabe*, he has also edited the correspondence between Franz Schreker and Paul Bekker and is author of a forthcoming biography of Franz Schreker.

Patricia Hall is an Acting Assistant Professor at the University of California at Santa Barbara. In 1983 she was awarded a Fulbright Fellowship to Vienna to study Berg's sketches for *Lulu* and has published several articles and reviews on the topic.

Douglas Jarman is Principal Lecturer in Academic Studies at the Royal Northern College of Music, Manchester. A member of the Board of Directors of the International Alban Berg Society and editor of the forthcoming Concerto volume of the Alban Berg *Gesamtausgabe*, he is author of *The Music of Alban Berg, Kurt Weill; an Illustrated Biography*, and a forthcoming monograph on *Wozzeck*.

Stephen Kett, Management Consultant for Bain & Co., received his AM from Harvard University and is working on a thesis on Berg's Four Songs op. 2. During the 1985 centennial year he was co-director of the Harvard University Symposium on Berg's early music. He has for a long time been responsible for the bibliographical material in the Newsletter of the International Berg Society.

George Perle is a distinguished composer and a leading authority on the music of Alban Berg. A member of the American Academy and Institute of Arts and Letters and of the National Academy of Arts and Sciences, Professor Perle has recently been awarded the Kinkeldey Award of the American Musicological Society, the Pulitzer Prize for his Fourth Wind Quintet, and a MacArthur Fellowship. His most recent book, *The Listening Composer*, is shortly to be published by the University of California Press.

Derrick Puffett is a Lecturer in Music at Cambridge University. He is editor of *Music Analysis* and of two forthcoming Cambridge Opera Handbooks on Richard Strauss's *Salome* and *Elektra*.

Joan Allen Smith is author of *Schoenberg and His Circle* and editor of the *Newsletter of the International Alban Berg Society*. A violin student of Rudolf Kolisch, she received her PhD in music theory from Princeton and currently teaches at the University of California, Santa Barbara.

Michael Taylor is lecturer in Music at Trinity College, Dublin and was a member of the Arts Council of Ireland 1984–8.

INDEX

Adler, Oskar, 182
Adorno, Theodor, 146, 182, 191-2, 226-8, 233
Akademischer Verband für Literatur und Musik, 49
Albert, Eugen d'
  Tiefland, 202
Altenberg, Peter [Richard Engländer), 7-9, 19, 26, 29, 48, 182
Askenase, Stefan, 16, 22, 24, 30
Ayrey, Craig, 81

Babbitt, Milton, 269, 284
Bach, Johann Sebastian, 67, 200, 269
  Es ist genug, 185, 189
Balàzs, Béla, 11
Balzac, Honoré de
  Seraphita, 111
Barish, John, 229
Bartók, Béla, 11, 269, 289
  Bluebeard's Castle, 214
  String Quartet no. 2, 271, 275
  String Quartet no. 4, 272, 274-6, 279-80, 284-5
  String Quartet no. 5, **270-72**, 273, 279, **286**, 287-8
Baudelaire, Charles, 9, 22, 63, 189

Beethoven, Ludwig van, 1, 22, 63, 67, 84, 96, 222, 224, 236, 248
  Symphony no. 9, 129
Bekker, Paul, 223
Berg, Alban,
  Altenberg Songs op. 4, 47-52, **53**, 54, **55-7**, 58, **59**, 60, **61-2**, 63, 68, 106, 108, 112, 121, 124, 139
  An Leukon, 37
  Chamber Concerto, 22, 68, 96, 141, **142**, 143-7, **148-9**, 150-51, **152-3**, 154-61, **162**, 163-4, **165**, 166, **167-73**, 174-80, 181, 185, 188
  Double Fugue, for string quartet and piano, 96
  Four Pieces op. 5, for clarinet and piano, 51, 91, 106-8, **109-10**, 111-12, 139
  Four Songs op. 2, 37, 43-4, **45-6**, 47, 67-71, **72-3**, 74, **75-80**, 81-2, **83**, 84, **85**, 86-7, 96, 111
  Jugendlieder, 37-40, **41**, 70-72
  Lulu, 15, 20, 29, 63-4, 68, 84, 119, 139, 147, 150, 186, 189, 191-2, 200-201, 208, 212-16, 226, 228-9, 235-44, **245**, 246-8, **249**, 250, **251**, 252, **253-4**, 255-9, 261-7, **269**, 270-75, **276**, 277-8,

278-9, 280-89
Lulu Suite, 150, 177
Lyric Suite, 63-4, 105, 147, 150,
　177, 181, 185-6, 189, 191, 205,
　247, 284-5, 287
Piano Sonata op. 1, 36, 43-4, 47,
　68, 71, 91-2, **93-5**, 96, 119
Piano Variations, 36, 91, **92**, 96,
　119
Schliesse mir die Augen beide
　(1907), 37
Schliesse mir die Augen beide
　(1925), 63
Seven Early Songs, 37, 39, **40**, 41,
　42-3, 96, 176
String Quartet op. 3, 37, 43, 47-8,
　68, 71, 91, 96, **97-100**, 101, **102**,
　103, **104-5**, 108, 110-11, 274,
　281, **282**
Three Orchestral Pieces op. 6, 51,
　63, 91, 104, 110-12, **113-15**,
　116-17, **118**, 119-120, 123-5,
　126-33, 134, **135-7**, 138-39
Violin Concerto, 8, 84, 181-94
Der Wein, 9, 63-4, 147, 150, 186
Wozzeck op. 7, 11, 16, 18, 24, 26,
　28, 37, 59-61, 63, 67, 104,
　119-21, 147, 168-71, 189-91,
　197, **198-9**, 200-203, 205-7,
　208-9, 210-12, 214-18, 226,
　228-31, 242, 247-8.
Analytical Guide to *Gurrelieder*,
　48, 50
'Open Letter', 141-2, 171, 174-5,
　181
Letters to His Wife, 17, 25-6, 106
'The Problem of Opera', 200
'Why is Schoenberg's Music so
　Difficult to Understand?', 231,
　233
Berg, Charly [brother], 22-3, 96
Berg, Conrad [father], 1, 22-3, 223
Berg, Erich Alban [nephew], 19,
　27-8, 70

Berg, Helene [née Nahowski], 2,
　7-8, 13, 16-20, 22, 25-9, 31, 37-8,
　48, 96, 105, 110, 158, 182, 190,
　192, 194, 211, 228, 235, 257
Berg, Herman [brother], 22
Berg, Johanna [mother], 1, 23, 28,
　223
Berg, Smaragda [sister], 8, 16, 22,
　96
Berghof, 17-18, 22
Berlin, 11, 47, 106, 183, 212
Bittner, Julius, 225
Blavatsky, Helena, 181-2
Blond, Kasper, 28
Boruttau, Alfred, 50
Boulez, Pierre, 206, 216
Brahms, Johannes, 22, 64, 67-8, 84,
　91, 96, 222, 224
Brecht, Bertolt, 12, 213
Brno *see* Brünn
Broch, Herman, 9
　Der Tod des Vergil, 9
Bruckner, Anton, 1, 39, 221-4
Brünn [Brno], 11
Büchner, Georg, 5, 206
　Woyzeck, 5, 212, 229
Budapest, 11
Buschbeck, Erhard, 51
Busoni, Ferruccio, 212
　Arlecchino, 212
　Turandot, 212

Carner, Mosco, 188, 191
Cerha, Friedrich, 246, 257-8
Cervantes, Miguel de, 22
Chadwick, Nicholas, 38, 207-8,
　210
Chopin, Fryderyk, 40
Cracow, 11

Dahlhaus, Carl, 200, 202
Debussy, Claude, 204, 270
　Feux d'artifice, 65
　Pelléas et Melisande, 167, 206

Préludes, 65
DeFotis, William, 108
DeVoto, Mark, 70, 86
Dollfuss, Engelbert, 11
Donat, Misha, 146-7
Dvořák, Antonin, 11

Eichendorff, Joseph, 213
Einstein, Albert, 182, 184
Engelhart, Josef, 69-70
Engländer, Richard, *see* Altenberg, Peter

Fackel, Die, 4, 6,
Fischer-Dieskau, Dietrich, 38
Fliess, Wilhelm, 6, 183-4, 193
  Vom Leben und Tod, 183-4, 193
Foerster, Josef Bohuslav, 53
Freud, Sigmund, 5, 6, 22, 184
Freund, Marya, 50
Friedell, Egon, 9
  Cultural History of Modern Times, 9
Fuchs-Robettin, Hanna, 9, 27, 105, 147, 181, 185-6, 189-92, 247

Gál, Erna, 16
Gál, Hans, 225
Galimir, Felix, 25
George, Stefan, 8-9
Gershwin, George, 216
Gerstl, Richard, 8, 166, 168, 171, 179-80
Gleim, Johann Ludwig, 37
Gluck, Christoph Willibald, 200
Goethe, Johann Wolfgang von
  Faust, 206
Goldmark, Karl, 225, 232
  'Rustic Wedding' Symphony, 38
Greissle, Felix, 158, 178
Grillparzer, Franz, 22
Gropius, Manon, 8, 184-91
Gropius, Walter, 8, 184

Hailey, Christopher, 38
Hamsun, Knut, 22
Hauptmann, Gerhart, 5
  Und Pippa tanzt, 229
Hebbel, Friedrich, 43, 69-70, 76
  Dem Schmerz sein Recht, 69
Hegel, Georg Wilhelm Friedrich, 22
Heidelberg, 110
Herlinger, Růžena, 63
Hilmar, Ernst, 242, 246
Hilmar, Rosemary, 38, 70
Hindemith, Paul, 204, 212
  Cardillac, 212
  Die Harmonie der Welt, 212
  Hin und zurück, 212
  Mathis der Maler, 212
  Neues vom Tage, 212
Hitler, Adolf, 2, 11
Hofmannsthal, Hugo von, 8-9, 203, 213
Hohenberg, Paul, 37
Holloway, Robin, 206, 215
Hugo, Victor, 204
Humperdinck, Engelbert, 202
Hyde, Martha, 235

Ibsen, Henrik, 5-6, 22
  Peer Gynt, 206

Janáček, Leoš, 11, 212
Jarman, Douglas, 107, 147, 201, 211-12, 215, 277
Johnson, Douglas, 248

Kafka, Franz, 11, 21
Kaiser, Georg, 213
Kammerer, Paul, 182-4
  Das Gesetz der Serie, 182-3
Keller, Gottfried, 21
Keller, Hans, 207, 210
Kemperling, 87
Kerman, Joseph, 210-11
Kienzl, Wilhelm, 225
Kierkegaard, Søren, 22

Klein, Fritz Heinrich, 150-51
Kleist, Heinrich von, 213
Klemperer, Otto, 212
Klimt, Gustav, 8
Knaus, Herwig, 188
Kodály, Zoltán, 11
Kokoschka, Oskar, 8
Kolisch, Gertrud, *see* Schoenberg, Gertrud
Kolisch, Rudolf, 145, 171, 175, 180, 191
Korngold, Erich Wolfgang, 202-4, 212, 225
    Der Ring des Polykrates, 204
    Die tote Stadt, 204
    Violanta, 204
Krasner, Louis, 182, 194
Kraus, Karl, 3-12, 19-22, 25, 29, 182, 229
Krauss, Clemens, 225
Krenek, Ernst, 8, 19, 212-13, 219, 225
    Jonny spielt auf, 213
    Karl V, 213
    Leben des Orest, 213
    Der Sprung über den Schatten, 212

Laulitsch, Anna, 18
Lehár, Franz, 208
Lehner, Eugen, 16
Liszt, Franz
    First Mephisto Waltz, 40
Loos, Adolf, 8, 21-2, 29
Loos, Lina, 8

Maeterlinck, Maurice
    Pelléas et Melisande, 166-7
Mahler, Alma, 8-9, 28, 52, 182, 184, 192, 211
Mahler, Gustav, 2-3, 8, 13, 19, 22, 24-5, 29, 38, 52, 64, 68, 106, 119, 176, 201, 204, 208, 222-3, 225, 227-9, 232
    Kindertotenlieder, 51

Lieder eines fahrenden Gesellen, 38
Das Lied von der Erde, 48
'Revelge', 189
Symphony no. 6, 118-19
Symphony no. 9. 110-11, **112-13**
Mann, Thomas
    Doktor Faustus, 182
Mannheim, 110
Menkes, Hermann, 224
Mérimée, Prosper, 213
Meyerbeer, Giacomo, 204
Milhaud, Darius, 22
Molnár, Ferenc, 11
Mombert, Alfred, 43, 69, 71, 74, 78, 80, 83-4
    Der Glühende, 44, 69
Morgenstern, Soma, 13-31
Mozart, Wolfgang Amadeus, 1, 63-4, 67
    The Magic Flute, 181, 223
Munich, 11
Musil, Robert, 21
Musorgsky, 270
Mussolini, Benito, 11-12

Nahowski, Helene, *see* Berg, Helene
Nehar, Caspar, 213
Newes, Tilly, 5
Nietzsche, Friedrich, 202

Perle, George, 54, 85, 101, 119, 185, 191, 197, 205-6, 246-7, 263-4, 267
    Windows of Order, **282**
    Serial Composition and Atonality, 270
    Twelve-Tone Tonality, 279
Pfitzner, Hans, 203-4, 212
    Der arme Heinrich, 202
    Palestrina, 204
Pisk, Paul, 145
Poe, Edgar Allen, 22
Polgar, Alfred, 14
Polnauer, Josef, 145, 175-6
Poulenc, Francis, 22

Prague, 11
Puccini, Giacomo, 204-5

Ravel, Maurice, 210
    Gaspard de la nuit, 44
    L'Heure espagnole, 214
    La valse, 119
Redlich, Hans, 37, 106, 146, 150,
    167, 191
Reich, Willi, 35, 37, 106, 110, 185,
    188, 207, 238, 246
Reinhardt, Max, 11
Réti, Rudolph, 145
Rilke, Rainer Maria, 11
Rimsky-Korsakov, Nikolay, 277
Rittner, Thaddeus, 11
Rosegger, Peter, 21-2
Roth, Joseph, 14, 21
Rufer, Josef, 105

Salten, Felix, 9
    Josefine Mutzenbacher, 9
Salzburg, 105
Scheuchl, Albine, 190
Scheuchl, Marie, 189-91
Schiele, Egon, 8
Schmalfeldt, Janet, 200
Schmidt, Franz, 204, 210, 225
    Fredigundis, 204
    Notre Dame, 204
Schnitzler, Arthur, 5-6
    Liebelei, 5-6
    Reigen, 5-6
Schoek, Othmar, 213
    Notturno, 213
    Penthesilea, 213
    Venus, 213
    Von Fischer un syner Fru, 214
Schoenberg, Arnold, 8, 11-12, 15,
    19, 21-5, 27, 29-30, 35-9, 43-4,
    46-51, 56, 58, 64, 67, 70, 73-4, 80,
    84, 87, 91-3, 96, 101, 106-11,
    141-46, 150-75, 178-80, 182-3,
    201, 203-5, 208, 212-15, 223-34,

238, 269, 277-8
    Brettl-Lieder, 38
    Das Buch der hängenden Gärten, 82
    Chamber Symphony no. 1, 36, 44,
        50, 91-2, **93**, 94, 120, 207, 210
    Erwartung, 36, 44, 201, 203-5,
        208, 210
    Friede auf Erden, 233
    Die glückliche Hand, 36, 58, 203,
        205, 225,
    Gurrelieder, 36, 47-50, 54, 58, 92,
        204, 230
    Moses und Aron, 67, 213, 225, 233
    Pelleas und Melisande, 36, 92, **167**,
        171, 180
    Pierrot lunaire, 36, 47, 106
    Six Little Piano Pieces op. 19,
        106-7
    String Quartet no. 1, 36
    String Quartet no. 2, 44, 96, 178
    Von Heute auf Morgen, 67, 213,
        225
    Wind Quintet, 226
    Harmonielehre, 36, 47, 80, 92, 108
Schoenberg, Gertrud [née Kolisch],
    171, 180
Schoenberg, Mathilde [née von
    Zemlinsky], 158-71, 178-80
Schopenhauer, Arthur, 22
Schreker, Franz, 50, 202-4, 207-8,
    212, 218, 223, 225, 228-31, 234
    Christophorus, 204
    Die ferne Klang, 47, 204, 207-8,
        210, 215, 218, 228-30
    Five Songs, 230
    Die Gezeichneten, 204, 210-11, 228
    Der Schatzgräber, 204, 234
Schrenk, Walter, 223
Schubert, Franz, 1, 22, 38, 64, 200,
    221-3, 225
Schumann, Robert, 22, 38, 91
Schuschnigg, Kurt von, 11
Seabury, Frida Selma, 37
Seidlhofer, Bruno, 17-18

Shakespeare, William, 22, 206
Shostakovich, Dmitri, 66
Simon, Eric, 189
Skryabin, Alexander, 277
Smetana, Bedřich, 11, 232
Society for Private Musical
    Performances, *see* Verein für
    musikalische Privat-
    auffürungen
Specht, Richard, 145, 225
Stefan, Paul, 221-2
Stein, Erwin, 18, 145, 175, 263
Steiner, Rudolph, 22
Steuermann, Eduard, 145, 175
Stifter, Adalbert, 21
Storm, Theodor, 37, 63
Strauss, Johann, 222
Strauss, Richard, 11, 22, 200-205,
    207-10, 212-13, 215, 225
    Alpensinfonie, 22
    Arabella, 213
    Ariadne auf Naxos, 214
    Elektra, 200-201, 203, 208, 214,
        217, 228
    Feuersnot, 202
    Die Frau ohne Schatten, 207, 210
    Guntram, 202, 214
    Ein Heldenleben, 202
    Intermezzo, 213-14
    Der Rosenkavalier, 203, 208, 219
    Salome, 58, 200-202, 210, 214,
        217
    Die schweigsame Frau, 213
Stravinsky, Igor, 116, 119, 212-13,
    277, 288
    The Firebird, 58
    Histoire du soldat, 212-13
    Oedipus Rex, 213
    The Rite of Spring, 47, 51
Strindberg, Johan August, 5-6, 22
    Moses, 233

Tausig, Carl
    Das Geisterschiff, 65

Trahütten, 158, 160
Traunkirchen, 158
Treitler, Leo, 273, 277

Verdi, Giuseppe
    Rigoletto, 202
Verein für musikalische
    Privataufführungen, 16, 108, 110,
    145, 175, 226
Vienna, 1-12, 15, 47, 49-50, 108,
    160-61, 183, 221-234

Wagner, Richard, 22, 39, 67-8, 84,
    93, 119, 200-202, 204-5, 207, 210,
    212, 225, 232
    Götterdämmerung, 44, 200, 203,
        206, 208
    Lohengrin, 202
    Die Meistersinger, 202
    Parsifal, 39, 200-202
    Das Rheingold, 206
    Der Ring des Nibelungen, 202
    Tannhäuser, 50, 202
    Tristan und Isolde, 36, 69, 120,
        202, 210, 269
Walter, Bruno, 48
Watkins, Glen, 189
Watznauer, Hermann, 22-3, 31, 37,
    39
Webern, Anton, 10, 23-4, 35, 46-7,
    49, 51-2, 67, 87, 106-7, 124,
    141-2, 145, 158, 160, 166, 174-5,
    231, 234, 236-8, 278
    Five Movements op. 5, 275
    Four Pieces op. 7, 106
    Piano Variations op. 27, 278
    Six Bagatelles op. 9, 106
    Six Pieces op. 6, 50-51, 96
    Three Little Pieces op. 11, 106
Wedekind, Frank, 4-7, 11, 189, 203,
    263, 266
    Die Büchse der Pandora, 4, 7, 236,
        264
    Der Erdgeist, 7, 229, 236, 265

Weill, Kurt, 204, 212-13, 215
  *Austieg und Fall der Stadt
  Mahagonny*, 213-15
  Die Bürgschaft, 213
  Die Dreigroschenoper, 213, 215
  Der Protagonist, 213
  Der Silbersee, 213
  Der Zar lässt sich photographieren,
    213
Weimar, 212
Weininger, Otto, 6-7, 22
  Geschlecht und Charakter, 6
Weissmann, Adolf, 223
Wellesz, Egon, 145, 225
Werfel, Franz, 8-9, 11-12, 22, 27
Wilde, Oscar
  The Birthday of the Infanta, 203
  Salome, 203
Wolf, Eugene, 150
Wolf, Hugo, 39, 41, 201, 222, 225
  Der Corregidor, 202

Zemlinsky, Alexander von, 22,
  50-51, 166, 201-2, 205, 212, 217,
  225
  Eine florentinische Tragödie, 205
  Kleider machen Leute, 205
  Der Kreiderkreis, 212
  Lyric Symphony, 189, 205
  Sarema, 205
  Der Zwerg, 205, 210-11
Zemlinsky, Mathilde von, *see*
  Schoenberg, Mathilde
Zweig, Stefan, 182